Scientific Realism

'Stathis Psillos has written the definitive treatment of scientific realism. He ranges widely, from the founding fathers of modern philosophy of science, through detailed studies of crucial scientific episodes, to the intricacies of current debate. Yet he is entirely sure-footed throughout, telling us exactly what we need to know at each stage, with ease and elegance. This authoritative study will become an essential resource for students and experts alike.'

David Papineau, King's College, London

Philosophical issues in science
Edited by W. H. Newton-Smith
Balliol College, Oxford

Scientific Realism
How science tracks truth

Stathis Psillos

London and New York

First published 1999
by Routledge
2 Park Square, Milton Park, Abingdon, Oxon, OX14 4RN

Simultaneously published in the USA and Canada
by Routledge
270 Madison Ave, New York NY 10016

Routledge is an imprint of the Taylor & Francis Group

Transferred to Digital Printing 2005

Typeset in Times by Florence Production Ltd, Stoodleigh, Devon

British Library Cataloguing in Publication Data
A catalogue record for this book is available from the British Library

Library of Congress Cataloging in Publication Data
Psillos, Stathis, 1965–
    Scientific realism: how science tracks truth/Stathis Psillos.
        p. cm.
    Includes bibliographical references and index.
    1. Realism.   2. Science–Philosophy.   I. Title.
    Q175.32.R42P75 1999   99-29721
    501–dc21   CIP

ISBN 0-415-20818-1 (hbk)
ISBN 0-415-20819-X (pbk)

For my parents Maria and Demetris,
without whom not,
and for Athena

Contents

x *Contents*

Illustrations

Figures

Tables

Preface

The present book would not have been written, had I not been fortunate enough to spend almost a decade in London, and to study philosophy and work in one of the most vibrant of philosophical environments. Britain was a second home for me and the departments of philosophy at King's College London and the London School of Economics were as hospitable and friendly as could be. This book started its life as a PhD thesis under the supervision of David Papineau. David has been a real teacher and friend. I owe him much more than he can imagine. It was his ideas, encouragement, inspiration and support that guided me throughout the past years. An examiner of my thesis, subsequent colleague, and friend John Worrall has also been an enormous source of help, support and intellectual stimulation. I had the benefit to work with two realists who have very different broad philosophical views. I hope the book at hand does not disappoint them, although neither of them will agree with all that is said in it, and neither of them should be held responsible for any errors, possible misconceptions and infelicities that appear in it. My colleagues at the London School of Economics – Nancy Cartwright, Colin Howson, Thomas Uebel and Craig Callender – created a wonderful intellectual environment for me to work. I spent a lot of time with the last three discussing my work and general philosophy while drinking real ale at The Beaver's, the LSE pub – a memory of which I am very fond. I learned a lot about Carnap and logical positivism from Thomas, Bayesianism and probability theory from Colin, modern physics from Craig, and models and causation from Nancy. I wish I had the time and energy to discuss Cartwright's views on realism in this book. This lack might be the greatest shortcoming of my book. But this task has to wait for another time. Peter Lipton deserves special thanks too for lots of discussions of, and comments on, my work and for his heartening encouragement to put together and publish the present book. I also wish to acknowledge with thanks the generous help of Bill Newton-Smith, who, in addition to John Worrall, examined my PhD thesis, made lots of useful comments on it, and accepted this book for his series.

Many colleagues and friends have commented on different parts of the book – especially the papers that form the backbone of the book – though none of them has seen the final outcome. My deepest thanks go to: Robert Almeder, Samet Bagce, Otavio Bueno, Marco DelSeta, Chris Daly, William Demopoulos, Igor Douven, Robert Fox, Steven French, Jonardon Ganeri, Kostas Gavroglu, Donald Gillies, Adam Grobler, Robin Hendry, Keith Hossack, James Ladyman, Jeff Ketland, D. H. Mellor, Andrew Powell, Towfic Shomar, Scott Sturgeon, John Watkins and Elie Zahar; to several anonymous readers for professional journals; to an anonymous reader of the book who made challenging suggestions as to how the book might be improved; to my students at the London School of Economics – who heard most of the book in lectures and criticised it relentlessly in classes and seminars; to several philosophical audiences in departmental seminars and conferences; and to any others whose help I have inadvertently failed to acknowledge. A few face-to-face or mail-mediated encounters with Arthur Fine, Michael Friedman, Cliff Hooker, Theo Kuipers, Andre Kukla, Larry Laudan, Ernan McMullin, Alan Musgrave, Illka Niiniluoto, Bas van Fraassen and Timothy Williamson have helped me a lot to articulate and clarify my ideas. They all deserve special thanks. I wish to thank especially Richard Boyd for a wonderfully encouraging and inspiring eponymous referee report which gave me the confidence to carry on with my naturalistic defence of realism. In the very final stages of preparing the book for publication I was very fortunate to have Ron Price as my copy editor. Our extensive electronic correspondence helped immensely to make the book more readable, both in style and content. Many thanks are also due to Adrian Driscoll, Anna Gerber and Anne Owen of Routledge.

The Greek State Scholarships' Foundation and the British Academy have honoured me with a doctoral scholarship and a postdoctoral research fellowship, respectively. To both I express my gratitude.

All material from the Carnap Archive is quoted by permission of the University of Pittsburgh. All rights reserved. The material from the Feigl Archive is reproduced with the permission of the Minnesota Centre for the Philosophy of Science. All rights reserved. Many thanks to the Archives' Curators for their permission and especially to Brigitte Ulhemann, Curator of the Philosophical Archives of the University of Konstanz for her generous help while I was working through the archival material of Carnap and Feigl.

Last, but not least, a personal note: I wish to thank Aspassia Daskalopulu for being there for me for many years and for all the help and devotion I received while I was working on my PhD, without which this book would never have been contemplated. My partner Athena Xenikou deserves enormous thanks for her encouragement, patience and love, without which this book could not have been completed. The final touches were put to the book while I was doing my compulsory military service, in the Hellenic Navy, and without Athena's support and unconditional love I would not have got through. My parents, siblings and their kids have always been a tremendous source of support and happiness. I am eternally grateful to them.

A substantial portion of the book derives from papers that have already appeared, although most of them were further revised before becoming part of the book. Here is a list of these papers.

- Chapter 5 is a based on 'Scientific Realism and the "Pessimistic Induction"', *Philosophy of Science* 63(3) (1996): S306–S314. Reprinted by permission of the University of Chicago Press. © 1996 Philosophy of Science Association. All Rights Reserved.
- The first half of Chapter 6 is a shortened and slightly revised version of 'A Philosophical Study of the Transition from the Caloric Theory of Heat to Thermodynamics: Resisting the Pessimistic Meta-Induction', *Studies in History and Philosophy of Science* 25 (1994): 159–190. Reprinted by permission of Elsevier Science.
- The second part of Chapter 6 is based on 'The Cognitive Interplay between Theories and Models: The Case of 19th Century Optics', in W. E. Herfel, W. Krajewski, I. Niiniluoto and R. Wojcicki (eds) *Theories and Models in Scientific Processes: Poznan Studies in the Philosophy of the Sciences and the Humanities* 44 (1995): 105–133. Reprinted by permission of Rodopi Publishers.
- Chapter 7 is a shortened and improved version of 'Is Structural Realism the Best of Both Worlds?', *Dialectica* 49(1) (1995): 15–46. Reprinted by permission of the editors.
- Chapter 8 is based on 'Naturalism Without Truth?', *Studies in History and Philosophy of Science* 28(4) (1997) 699–713. Reprinted with permission from Elsevier Science.
- Extensive parts of Chapter 9 derive from: 'Agnostic Empiricism vs Scientific Realism: Belief in Truth Matters', *International Studies in the Philosophy of Science* 13(3) (1999). Appearing by permission of the Editor. 'On van Fraassen's Critique of Abductive Reasoning', *The Philosophical Quarterly* 46(182) (1996): 31–47 and 'How Not to Defend Constructive Empiricism – A Rejoinder', *The Philosophical Quarterly* 47(188) (1997): 369–372. Reprinted by permission of Blackwell Publishers.
- Parts of Chapter 11 are based on my Review of *Realism Rescued* by J. Aronson, R. Harré and E. C. Way; *International Studies in the Philosophy of Science* 9(2) (1995): 179–183 and on 'Kitcher on Reference', *International Studies in the Philosophy of Science* 11(3) (1997): 259–272. Reprinted by permission of the Editor, *International Studies in the Philosophy of Science*.

S.P.
Athens, Greece
December 1998

Introduction

Modern science has transformed the way we think of the world. Nature is no longer taken to be as our senses indicate it to be. Entities and mechanisms invisible to the naked eye, such as electromagnetic waves, electrons, protons, neutrinos and DNA molecules – to mention but a few – are said to populate the world and to cause the observable phenomena. Why, however, should we take scientific theories to be true, or nearly true? Why should we believe that all these entities posited by our best theories are real? Why not take such theories to be mere instruments for the systematisation and prediction of observable phenomena, without attributing reality to the invisible entities they posit? Or, why not just suspend our judgement as to the truth of the assertions that theories make about invisible entities and believe only that theories are empirically adequate, i.e. that whatever they say about the observable phenomena – and only this – is true?

The philosophical debate over scientific realism revolves mostly around the foregoing questions. This book is an attempt to defend scientific realism: the view that mature and genuinely successful scientific theories should be accepted as nearly true. I have always thought scientific realism to be an intuitively compelling philosophical position. But my systematic engagement with philosophy convinced me that my own intuitions need both clarification and underpinning by argument, and also that they are not shared by everybody. Some of the arguments against scientific realism appear to be so powerful that, if sound, they undercut even its intuitive plausibility. I was therefore persuaded that scientific realism needs a thorough explication and a systematic defence. Hence, the need to write this book, which aims to reassert the intuitively compelling status of scientific realism by showing how it can survive the most systematic criticisms that have been thrown against it.

In the first few lines of the Preface to the first edition of *The Critique of Pure Reason*, Immanuel Kant called philosophy (to be sure, he referred to metaphysics) 'the battle-field' of endless controversies. I very much share this image. In the case of scientific realism, there are a number of such related controversies. One is whether science can possibly describe a mind-independent world. The main question here is whether it makes sense to say that there is a mind-independent world which science aims to describe and explain. Another is whether science can go beyond whatever can be observed by the naked eye and reveal truths about unobservable causes of the phenomena. A third is how exactly scientific theories should be understood: should they be taken as attempts to reveal truths about the unobservable entities that populate the world, or should they be taken to be no more than sophisticated instruments for the systematisation and classification of observable phenomena? A fourth is whether one needs to accept the truth of scientific theories in order to account for the success of science and for salient features of its practice. The contrast here is with an attitude which says that one may treat scientific theories as attempts to describe the structure of the unobservable world but still remain agnostic as to whether the descriptions offered by those theories are true. This is not an exhaustive list of the 'controversies'. And the attentive reader will surely notice that the list contains overlaps; or, better, that these controversies are related to each other. In taking my place on the 'battle-field', I aspire to show how these controversies, properly analysed and explicated, can be resolved in favour of scientific realism. The reader will judge whether and to what extent my aspiration will be fulfilled. Scientific realism does not come out of these controversies unwounded. Nor should it fail to learn from its opponents' arguments. But if my strategy in the book is successful, then scientific realism is still 'the best game in town'.

The debate about scientific realism has a history. The philosophical positions implicated in it have evolved and changed, just as the items of the philosophical agenda have shifted. Whereas, for instance, in the first few decades of the century, the philosophical argument was cast in linguistic terms – can theoretical discourse be at all meaningful? or, can theoretical terms denote anything? – in the last few decades, the argument has shifted to epistemic issues: can theories reveal truths about unobservable reality? or, should we believe that current theories are true, or nearly true? Here, again, the questions turn out to be interconnected, and the shifted philosophical positions turn out to be adaptations of old positions to new data and circumstances.

This book explores the historical development of the scientific realism debate in the twentieth century. It will search for the philosophical origins of current arguments to positions advocated by eminent scientists and philosophers in the early part of the century when a massive revolution in physics occurred. It will show, for instance, that a good deal of the current debate is a continuation and a reframing of the debate between Ernst Mach, Pierre Duhem, Henri Poincaré and others at the turn of the century, when atomism was gaining ground and a hope that science can go beyond appearances started to glimmer. It will also track the development of the empiricist alternatives to scientific realism, from the early attempt of Rudolf Carnap to show that talk of theoretical entities can be fully reduced to talk about observable entities, to his mature attempt to show that empiricists can happily remain neutral in the realism–instrumentalism debate, and to Herbert Feigl's espousal of 'empirical realism'.

But the main focus of the book is on the current debates over realism. Its bulk is devoted to a defence of realism against Larry Laudan's argument from the pessimistic induction, the argument from the under-determination of theories by evidence, and to a critique of Bas van Fraassen's promising alternative: constructive empiricism.

When it comes to broader epistemological issues, the book has an agenda to push. It presupposes a broad externalist–naturalistic perspective and suggests that the realist cause is best defended from this perspective. I learned this lesson from the two philosophers I admire most: David Papineau and Richard Boyd. Going for realism is going for a *philosophical package* which includes a naturalised approach to human knowledge and a belief that the world has an objective natural-kind structure.

What exactly, then, is scientific realism? I take it to incorporate three theses (or stances), which can be differentiated as *metaphysical, semantic* and *epistemic*. Each of these three stances is meant to warn off a particular non-realist view of scientific theories, or, to express them in terms of what they each propose:

1   The metaphysical stance asserts that the world has a definite and mind-independent natural-kind structure.
2   The semantic stance takes scientific theories at face-value, seeing them as truth-conditioned descriptions of their intended domain, both observable and unobservable. Hence, they are capable of being true or false. Theoretical assertions are not reducible to claims about the behaviour of observables, nor are they merely instrumental devices for establishing connections between observables. The theoretical terms featuring in theories have putative factual reference. So, if scientific theories are true, the unobservable entities they posit populate the world.
3   The epistemic stance regards mature and predictively successful scientific theories as well-confirmed and approximately true of the world. So, the entities posited by them, or, at any rate, entities very similar to those posited, do inhabit the world.

The *first* thesis is a basic philosophical presupposition of scientific realism. It is meant to make scientific realism distinct from all those anti-realist accounts of science, be they traditional idealist and phenomenalist, or the more modern verificationist accounts of Michael Dummett and the later Hilary Putnam, which reduce the content of the world to whatever gets licensed by a set of epistemic practices and conditions. In particular the metaphysical stance implies that if the unobservable natural kinds posited by theories exist at all, they exist independently of humans' ability to know, verify, recognise, that they do. Instead of projecting a structure onto the world, scientific theories, and scientific theorising in general, discover and map out an already structured and mind-independent world. My defence of (Chapter 3) realism against Carnap's irenic position shows that this metaphysical thesis is prerequisite to any meaningful defence of scientific realism.[1]

The *second* thesis, which is the essence of *semantic realism*, differentiates scientific realism from *eliminative instrumentalist* and *reductive empiricist accounts* (which are analysed in Chapters 1 and 2). Briefly put, eliminative instrumentalism is the position that the 'cash value' of scientific theories is fully captured by what theories say about the observable world. This position typically treats theoretical claims as syntactic-mathematical constructs which lack truth-conditions and, hence, any assertoric content. I take eliminative instrumentalism to be a species of what I call 'syntactic instrumentalism'. I distinguish it from another species of syntactic instrumentalism – *non-eliminative* instrumentalism (a kind of which can be associated with the anti-explanationist stance of Pierre Duhem). This is the view that one *need not* assume there to be an unobservable reality behind the phenomena, nor that science aims to describe it, in order to do science and to do it successfully. Reductive empiricist accounts, on the other hand, treat theoretical discourse as disguised talk about observables and their actual (and possible) behaviour. Reductive empiricism is consistent with the claim that theoretical assertions have truth-values, but it understands their truth-conditions *reductively*: they are fully translatable into an observational vocabulary. Insofar as reductive empiricists are committed to the existence of observable entities, and provided that a certain theoretical statement is fully translated into a statement couched solely in an observational vocabulary, they allow 'theoretical' assertions to have truth-values. But they would not thereby be committed to the existence of unobservable entities. Opposing these two positions, scientific realism is an 'ontologically inflationary' view. Understood realistically, the theory admits of a literal interpretation – an interpretation in which the world is (or, at least, can be) populated by a host of unobservable entities and processes.

The *third* thesis of scientific realism, which might be called 'epistemic optimism', is meant to distinguish it from *agnostic* or *sceptical* versions of empiricism. The thrust of this realist thesis is that science can and does attain theoretical truth no less than it can and does attain observational truth, where by 'theoretical truth' we understand the truth of what scientific theories say about unobservable entities and processes, and by 'observational truth' we understand the truth of what theories say about observable entities. It should be taken to be implicit in the realist thesis that the ampliative-abductive methods employed by scientists to arrive at their theoretical beliefs are reliable: they tend to generate approximately true beliefs and theories. For, it should be noted, agnostic empiricists do *not* deny that science can hit upon theoretical truth. This might well happen, if only by accident. What they *do* deny is that we can ever be in a position to legitimately claim that science has achieved theoretical truth. Hence, the 'epistemic optimism' of scientific realism intends to stress that it is *reasonable*, at least occasionally, to believe that science has achieved theoretical truth. In other words, the third realist thesis implies that there is some kind of *justification* for the belief that theoretical assertions are true (or nearly true), where this justification comes primarily from the ampliative-abductive methods employed by scientists. What should also be noted is that agnostic empiricism comes in two varieties: *naive* and *sophisticated*. The naive variety stresses that the *only* rational option is suspension of judgement as to the truth of theoretical assertions. The sophisticated variety, associated with van Fraassen's approach, is that being agnostic is *no less* rational than being scientific realist. I take van Fraassen's main position to be the following. Even if it were shown that theoretical truth is attainable in a non-accidental way, realism would not be rationally compelling. For there is an alternative *empiricist* image of science in which the search for theoretical truth, and the belief in the truth of theories, drop out of the picture *without any loss* for the practice of science. Van Fraassen's constructive empiricism, is then, the view that in our philosophical reflection on science we do not have to interpret science as an activity which involves search for, and acceptance of, theoretical truth in order to account for science's salient features and its empirical success. Opposing this view, realists argue that an attitude towards science which involves less than aiming at theoretical truth and acceptance of the truth of theories would leave us, in some concrete respect that empiricists should recognise, *worse off* than would the recommended realist attitude. The details of all this are discussed in Chapter 9.

Having mapped out the basic scientific realist theses and the main rival positions, a note on terminology is in order. 'Realism' and 'anti-realism' mean different things to different people, so it is important to clarify my usage of these terms. Many philosophers, especially in the USA, call any rival of scientific realism 'anti-realism'. I do not follow this usage. For the purposes of this book, I take 'realism' to refer to *scientific* realism. But I reserve the term 'anti-realism' for the philosophical position associated with Michael Dummett and his followers, while I employ more specific terms to refer to other rivals of scientific realism. For there is, I think, a broader understanding of the realism debate, one that I endorse, which associates realism with the view that *truth* is a non-epistemic concept. This implies two things: first, that assertions have truth-makers; and second, that these truth-makers hinge ultimately upon what the world is like. A non-epistemic account of the concept of truth is motivated to provide the best way to capture the intuition that scientific discourse is about a 'mind-independent' world, that is a world whose structure and content are logically and conceptually independent of the epistemic standards science uses to appraise theories. The rival anti-realist view takes the concept of truth to be essentially epistemically constrained: the truth of an assertion is conceptually linked with the possibility of recognising this truth. On typical anti-realist accounts, if an assertion cannot be known to be true, or if it cannot be recognised as true, then it cannot possibly be true. Truth is conceived as 'warranted assertibility', 'ideal justification' and other cognate notions. Hence, on these accounts, there cannot possibly be a divergence between what is true of the world and what can be warrantedly asserted of it.

All this is explained in Chapter 10. What I want to stress now is the following. Anti-realists no longer insist on ontological economy, or on the possibility of reducing theoretical to observational discourse, or on the elimination of theoretical discourse. In fact, they would agree that, for instance, electrons exist.[2] Does that make them scientific realists? I do not think so, since scientific realists endorse a non-epistemic account of truth.[3] Despite their many differences with the early empiricists, modern anti-realists do share with them the view that existential claims should be tied to some possibility or other of verification, a thesis which scientific realists deny. To be sure, the strict notion of verification is replaced by weaker notions such as 'warranted assertibility'. But the point remains that for modern anti-realists it does not make sense to assert the existence (or reality) of an entity unless we understand this assertion to mean that . . . , where the ellipsis is replaced by a suitable epistemic/conceptual condition. Putnam's favourite replacement of the ellipsis would be 'it is (ideally) rationally acceptable that, say, electrons exist', whereas Dummett's line would relate to warranted assertibility. Since, however, it is typical of scientific realists to argue that the content of the world can in principle exceed what human beings (even ideal observers) can access epistemically, none of these modern anti-realists is a scientific realist.

The main argument for the epistemic optimism associated with scientific realism is known as 'The no miracle argument' because it is based on Putnam's slogan: 'Scientific realism is the only philosophy of science that does not make the success of science a miracle.' Modern defenders of scientific realism have based their defence on the idea that the impressive predictive and explanatory successes of scientific theories would remain unaccounted for, unless we accept that the entities, processes and causal mechanisms they posit to operate behind the phenomena are real. They dismiss instrumentalist accounts of scientific theories by noting that they leave the success of science unexplained. If theories are merely 'black boxes' whose only virtue is that they offer the most economical classification of the observable phenomena, then there is no reason to expect that they are capable of being, as the French philosopher and scientist Pierre Duhem put it, 'prophets for us'. To counter that these 'black boxes' are empirically adequate, i.e. that they save all phenomena, would not be much of an improvement on the instrumentalist position. For what needs explanation is precisely the fact that scientific theories save the phenomena. To say that they do is merely to assert what needs to be explained.

One line of criticism is that empirical success is too easy to get: just 'write into' the theory the right observational consequences. Then, the theory will not fail to predict them. So, the realist argument needs regimentation: there is a kind of prediction which can only support a realist understanding of the theory which entails it – the prediction of *novel* phenomena. For the best, if not the only, explanation of why the theory predicts the existence of a novel phenomenon is to say that the theoretical mechanisms posited to bring about the phenomenon are real. A 'novel' prediction is sometimes taken to be a 'temporally novel' prediction, that is a phenomenon whose presence is ascertained only after a theory suggests its existence. This, however, cannot be the whole story since theories also get support from their ability to explain already known phenomena. So realists need to adopt a conception of 'novelty' which goes beyond the 'temporal view'. Following John Worrall and John Earman, Chapter 5 defends a 'novelty in use' view of predictions: the prediction of an already known phenomenon can be use-novel with respect to some theory provided that information about this phenomenon was not used in the construction of the theory.[4]

But the realist explanation of the success of science faces more, and perhaps deeper, philosophical challenges. The first is that the central realist argument – the 'no miracle argument' – is viciously circular and question-begging. For, it is maintained, it aims to defend the rationality and reliability of inference to the best explanation (or abduction), where the very argument itself is an instance of the inferential rule it tries to defend. The second challenge comes, allegedly, from the history of science itself. It is argued that the history of science is the graveyard of aborted 'best theoretical explanations' of phenomena. Hence, it is claimed, the realist optimism that our current best explanations of phenomena are approximately true flies in the face of the history of science and, therefore, has very little credibility. This is the essence of the argument from 'the pessimistic induction'. The third challenge springs from the observation that more than one theory can, and often do, entail the very same body of evidence. So, the claim is, since evidence underdetermines theory, it cannot possibly guide rational theory choice. The conclusion drawn is that faced with a choice among two or more theories which entail the same evidence, the best we can do is suspend our judgement as to which of them is true, and possibly make our choice on pragmatic grounds.

All these challenges are discussed in detail in Chapters 4–8. If successful, my rebuttal of these arguments against realism will show that there is still room for warranted epistemic optimism. Not only can there be rational choice between theories which entail the same body of observational consequences, but most importantly realism can survive the deep historical challenge. A detailed study of past mature and genuinely successful theories suggests that not only were they not plain wrong and so abandoned, but that those theoretical constituents which enjoyed empirical support and contributed to their success were carried over to the successor theories. There is therefore a very substantial theoretical continuity in theory change in science. Realists should ground their epistemic optimism on the fact that newer theories incorporate many theoretical constituents of their superseded predecessors, and especially on those constituents which have led to empirical successes. Yet, realism gets stronger by learning from its opponents' arguments. So, it should be acknowledged that the whole truth, and nothing but the truth, cannot be had in science; but this does not mean that scientific theories have not latched upon important truths, or near truths, about the unobservable structure of the world. The substantial continuity in theory change suggests that a rather stable network of theoretical principles and explanatory hypotheses has survived revolutionary changes to become part and parcel of our evolving scientific image of the world.

Although I have already hinted at the content of the subsequent chapters, a brief and ordered summary of what is on the menu should be helpful. Chapter 1 explains the failures of reductive empiricism and defends semantic realism. Chapter 2 reveals the limitations of eliminative instrumentalism and discusses in some detail Duhem's attempt to establish a middle ground in the realism–instrumentalism debate. Chapter 3 takes a systematic look at the later Carnap's re-invention of the Ramsey-sentence approach to theories and at his attempt to base on it the thesis that empiricism can stay neutral in the realism–instrumentalism debate. It ends by showing the limitations of a purely structuralist understanding of scientific theories. Chapter 4 articulates and explains the 'no miracle argument' in favour of scientific realism, defending it against the charge of vicious circularity, and suggesting that this defence should be seen as part of a thorough externalist–naturalistic epistemological perspective. Chapter 5 concentrates on the pessimistic induction and puts forward a way – the *divide et impera* move – in which realists can diffuse this argument. Chapter 6 illustrates and strengthens the realist defence against the pessimistic induction by considering the two mature and genuinely successful theories alleged to have been characteristically false: the caloric theory of heat and nineteenth-century optical theories. Chapter 7 examines Worrall's attempt to reconcile the 'no miracle argument' and the 'pessimistic induction' by defending *structural realism*: the thesis that there is a significant continuity in theory change at the formal–mathematical level – a continuity which Worrall, following Poincaré, takes to suggest that empirically successful theories have 'latched on to' the structure of the world. Chapter 8 focuses on the argument from the underdetermination of theories by evidence and argues that it fails to show that there is no room for rational theory choice in science. It also discusses Larry Laudan's recent attempt to defend *normative naturalism* and the argument that truth is a 'utopian aim' which cannot be taken to be the cognitive aim of science. Against Laudan, it is argued that truth is a basic cognitive good which is not inherently beyond our reach. Chapter 9 turns to consider naive agnostic empiricism and van Fraassen's sophisticated alternative, motivating the view that constructive empiricism fails to be as rational an account of science as is scientific realism. Chapter 10 starts with a detailed examination of Arthur Fine's 'Natural ontological attitude' and finishes by arguing that 'entity realism' is an unstable philosophical intermediary; in between, it defends a substantive 'correspondence' account of truth. Chapter 11 looks at the notion of 'truth-likeness' and motivates an 'intuitive approach' which does not run together the need for conceptual clarity and the need for formalisation. Chapter 12 outlines a hybrid theory of reference for theoretical terms – which, following David Lewis, I call 'causal–descriptive'.

As always, the reader will be the judge of whether the book's aspirations are realistic. For my part, what I want to stress is that this book would not have been written had not the debate on scientific realism been so rich and so full of important arguments and incisive contributors. Even though the tone of the book is critical, perhaps occasionally polemical, I have learned as much from the opponents of scientific realism, especially van Fraassen and Laudan, as I have from its defenders. If this book furthers this debate, it will be by taking up and trying to meet the challenge of defending realism on as many fronts as possible and showing that there are cogent realist answers to the most powerful of rival arguments.

A brief word on the citation of primary sources in the text is called for. I have given, wherever possible, the year of original publication for works by, mainly, eighteenth- and nineteenth-century scientists; the page numbers which accompany those dates are, however, invariably the pagination of the latest revision or edition of the work in question. Readers will find the year of the edition to which page numbers refer given as the final item in the bibliographical entry for the work concerned.

Part I

Empiricism and the realist turn

1 Empiricism and theoretical discourse

Scientific theories posit a number of unobservable entities and employ theoretical terms – e.g. 'electron', 'proton', 'electromagnetic field', 'DNA molecules', etc. (henceforth, *t*-terms). How is this theoretical discourse, the discourse involving *t*-terms, to be understood? There are two broad philosophical traditions – an empiricist and a realist tradition – each with an answer to this question. Broadly speaking, the empiricist tradition aims to show that theoretical discourse may be so construed that it does not commit to the existence of unobservable entities. The realist tradition, on the other hand, aims to show that a full and just explication of theoretical discourse in science requires commitment to the existence of unobservable entities. The dialectic of the debate between the two traditions which will be explored throughout Part I will show how forceful the realist position is.

The empiricist tradition is actually multi-faceted. *Concept empiricists* have always tied meaningful discourse to the possibility of some sort or another of experiential verification. According to the verification criterion of meaning, assertions are meaningful if and only if they can be verified. Some empiricists suggest that observational terms, such as 'is red', 'is square', 'is heavier than', get their meaning directly from experience: the conditions under which assertions involving them are verified coincide with the conditions under which they are true. But when it comes to *t*-terms things are different. Assertions involving them cannot be verified. This seems to create a problem. Are theoretical terms meaningless? Are theoretical assertions (henceforth, *t*-assertions), then, not genuine assertions?

Reductive empiricists argue that they need not be. But, they note, insofar as *t*-assertions have meaning, it is because they are really assertions about observable entities (henceforth, *o*-entities): they are just disguised talk about *o*-entities.[1] How can that be? Reductive empiricists think that semantics might be able to cover for metaphysics. An assertion which *prima facie* commits one to some undesirable entity, e.g. a *t*-entity, need not be so committing. For the truth-conditions of such an assertion might be specifiable in a language which commits one only to one's preferred ontology, in this case *o*-entities. If so, what would make a *t*-assertion truth-valued would be a truth-condition couched in observational language. (Let us call it an *o*-condition.) *O*-conditions are, for reductive empiricists, verification conditions. So, *t*-assertions might be provided with verification conditions, hence become meaningful and, if these conditions obtain, even true. Such has been the big promise of the project of *translatability*: provide verification conditions for *t*-assertions without inflating one's ontology beyond *o*-entities and logico-mathematical entities.

Failures of verificationism

The early Rudolf Carnap has been probably the only philosopher to take seriously the challenge of examining whether theoretical terms and predicates can be *explicitly defined* by virtue of observational terms and predicates. The failure of this project, as we are about to see in some detail, shows the implausibility of reductive empiricism: the meaning of theoretical terms cannot be completely defined by virtue of the meaning of observational terms.

An explicit verbal definition of *a* (the *definiendum*) in terms of *b* and *c* (the *definiens*) has the following two virtues. First, the meaning of *a* is fully specified by the meaning of *b* and *c*; hence, if the definiens are meaningful so is the definiendum. Second, given *a*'s explicit definition, *a* can be systematically replaced, without loss, by its definiens in any (extensional) context. It then becomes obviously appealing to an empiricist to attempt to show that *t*-terms can be explicitly defined in a vocabulary which involves only observational, and hence antecedently meaningful, terms. An explicit definition of the *t*-term Q has the following form:

$$\forall x \, (Qx \leftrightarrow (Sx \rightarrow Ox)). \tag{D}$$

(D) states that the theoretical term Q applies to an object (or a set of space–time points) x if and only if, when x satisfies the *test conditions S*, x shows the *observable response O*. So, for instance, an explicit definition of the theoretical term 'temperature' would be like this. An object a has temperature of c degrees centigrade if and only if the following condition is satisfied: if a is put in contact with a thermometer, then the thermometer shows c degrees on its scale. The conditional $(S \rightarrow O)$ is what Carnap once called a 'scientific indicator'. Scientific indicators express observable states of affairs which are used as the definiens in the introduction of a term. Early on, Carnap asserted that 'in principle there are indicators for all scientific states of affairs' (1928: §49).[2] This already presupposes a commitment to the verification criterion of meaning. Carnap's thought is that all theoretical terms introduced in the language of science should be meaningful, their meaningfulness being guaranteed by the availability, in principle, of scientific indicators appropriate to the definition of each and every legitimate theoretical term. But such an assertion is nothing but a hypothesis, the credibility of which depends on the verification criterion of meaning.

Without the latter, there is no ground to require each and every *t*-term to be definable by scientific indicators. Instead, as we shall see in detail momentarily, empiricists can leave happily with the idea that *t*-terms are meaningful, even though they are not explicitly definable.

An unwelcome consequence of the process of explicit definitions is that if theoretical concepts are defined operationally, then we end up with a multiplicity of concepts, defined by virtue of some specific experimental set-up. So, instead of a single concept of temperature, we would end up with a great number of such concepts, depending on whether temperature is measured by an air thermometer, or by an alcohol thermometer, or by a mercury thermometer, or what have you. On an operational understanding of theoretical concepts, there is no reason to think that all these concepts correspond to the same physical magnitude since, on this account, what makes a concept what it is is an operational procedure. Different operational procedures define different concepts. After all, how can one establish purely operationally that all these definitions pick out the same physical magnitude, unless one is already committed to the view that *there is* such a common physical magnitude? Some radical operationalists (e.g. Bridgman 1927) chose to live with this consequence: there is not just one magnitude of, say, *temperature*, and merely different ways to measure it or to apply it to experiential situations. On Bridgman's view, there is a multiplicity of different magnitudes which we wrongly characterise by a single concept: *temperature*. This move, however, is in conflict with sound scientific practice. It does much more justice to such practice to accept that what all these operations have in common is that they measure one and the same physical theoretical magnitude (cf. Hempel 1965). It then follows that this single magnitude is irreducible to any of those operational procedures. Nor is it reducible to a disjunction of known experimental procedures, since we should allow that hitherto unknown procedures may be devised which can be used to measure this very magnitude.

Suppose, however, that the foregoing problem is set aside. Still, if the conditional ($S \to O$) featuring in the explicit definition is understood as material implication, then one can easily see that ($S \to O$) is true even if the test conditions S do not occur. So, explicit definitions turn out to be empty. Their intended connection with antecedently ascertainable test conditions is undercut. For instance, suppose that we never put the object a in contact with a thermometer. Since the antecedent S of ($S \to O$) is false, the conditional is true. It then follows from the explicit definition of 'temperature' that the concept '*temperature* of c degrees centigrade' applies to a (whatever the numerical value c may be). In order to avoid this problem, the conditional ($S \to O$) must be understood not as material implication but rather as strict implication, i.e. as asserting that the conditional is true only if the antecedent obtains. But, even so, there is another serious problem. The suggested reading of ($S \to O$) as strict implication makes it inevitable that attribution of physical magnitudes is meaningful only when the test conditions S obtain. Yet, in scientific practice, an object is not supposed to have a property only when the test conditions S actually occur. For instance, bodies are taken to have masses, charges, temperatures and the like, even when these magnitudes are not being measured.

In order to avoid this conflict with sound scientific practice, the conditional $(S \rightarrow O)$ must be understood counter-factually, or subjunctively. Then the explicit definition of Q is understood as saying that the object a has the property Q if and only if, were a to be subjected to test conditions S, then a would manifest the characteristic response O. Theoretical terms should then have to be understood to be on a par with *dispositional* terms.

However, the introduction of dispositional terms, such as 'is soluble', 'is fragile' and the like, faces another bunch of problems. Their essence is that a counter-factual introduction of dispositional terms requires a prior understanding of the 'logic' of counter-factual conditionals, in particular of what exactly makes a counter-factual conditional true. Now that all theoretical terms have to be understood to be ultimately on a par with dispositional terms, the problem in hand intensifies. A natural way to deal with this problem is to appeal to nomological statements in order to subsume subjunctives such as 'if a were submerged in water, a would dissolve' under the jurisdiction of general laws such as 'For all x, if x is put in water, then x dissolves' and of certain initial conditions. Such a move would provide *prima facie* truth-conditions to counter-factual conditionals and a basis for introducing dispositional terms in general (cf. Goodman 1946). It is well known that this account of counter-factuals faces some interesting problems of its own (see Horwich 1987). But, for the issue of the explicit definability of t-terms, what it is relevant to stress is that nomological statements express laws of nature. Not only are laws of nature *not* observable, but also nomological statements are *not* explicitly definable in terms of observables (at least for non-molecular languages). Nor can the meaning of nomological statements consist in their conditions of verification, precisely because they typically range over an infinite domain. So, insofar as the project is to define t-terms in a vocabulary that involves observable terms and predicates, the counter-factual reading of explicit definitions cannot get off the ground.

Even if all of the foregoing problems concerning explicit definition were tractable, it is not at all certain that all of the theoretical terms which scientists consider perfectly meaningful can be given explicit definition. Terms such as 'magnetic field vector', 'world-line', 'gravitational potential', 'intelligence', etc. cannot be defined effectively in terms of (D), even were (D) to be unproblematic.

The futility of the project of explicit definition was asserted by Carnap as early as 1936, in his magnificent 'Testability and Meaning'. This failure marks the end of strict reductive empiricism. If theoretical terms are not explicitly definable, then they cannot be dispensed with by semantic means. Well, one may say, so much the worse for them, since they thereby end up meaningless. Not quite so, however. Suppose one were to accept the view that theoretical terms end up meaningless because assertions involving them cannot be fully translated into assertions involving observational terms and predicates, which, one might think, can be fully verified. The problem with this supposition is that, strictly speaking, even assertions involving only observational terms and predicates cannot be verified. Hence, if verification is a guide to meaningfulness, then neither *t*-terms nor *o*-terms end up meaningful. This is the real problem with the verification theory of meaning: that even singular statements about observables are not, strictly speaking, verifiable.

When it comes to nomological statements, radical empiricists can happily accept that they are, strictly speaking, meaningless because they are unverifiable. They might choose to retreat to the inference-ticket account of law-like statements: strictly speaking, law-like statements are meaningless, but they provide the major premiss in arguments whose minor premiss and conclusion are verifiable. So, for instance, 'All Ravens are Black' might end up being meaningless, but we can use it as a *rule of inference* to infer that '*a* is Black' from '*a* is a Raven'. Moritz Schlick toyed with this idea for quite some time.[3] But even were one willing to adopt this view, verificationism still would not be home and dry. As noted above, even singular statements about observables are not, strictly speaking, verifiable. Take the statement 'A black raven sits in the garden'. No amount of evidence will logically entail that statement. (Just consider a case of hallucination.) In other words, all evidence is perfectly consistent with the negation of the statement. Verification can never be conclusive. Hence if meaning(fulness) rests on verification conditions, then all *o*-assertions might well end up being meaningless too, undermining the very foundations of reductive empiricism. Carnap (1936, 1937) recognised this problem early on, and abandoned verification in favour of confirmation.

Liberalisation

What follows from the analysis thus far is that the empiricists' criterion of meaning should be weakened. This, as we are about to see, has significant implications for the empiricists' attitude to theoretical discourse.

Having abandoned the idea of explicit definability, Carnap does not thereby abandon the empiricist demand that theoretical terms be introduced by reference to observables. What changes is his position on the possibility of eliminating theoretical discourse, not his view that it is necessary to specify, *as far as possible,* the meaning of theoretical terms by reference to overt and intersubjectively specifiable observable conditions. He still insists that, *qua* empiricist, one should require that descriptive predicates and synthetic statements should not be admitted in the language of science unless they have some connection with possible observations. But a viable connection must be furnished by something other than explicit definability. So, Carnap opts for a weaker account of reduction. As he puts it: 'Reducibility can be asserted, but not unrestricted possibility of elimination and re-translation' (1936: 464).

A *t*-term Q is now introduced by means of the following *reductive pair*:

$$\forall x \, (S_1 x \rightarrow (O_1 x \rightarrow Qx))$$

$$\forall x \, (S_2 x \rightarrow (O_2 x \rightarrow \neg Qx)) \quad \text{(RP)}$$

in which S_1, S_2 describe experimental (test-)conditions and O_1, O_2 describe characteristic responses, (possible experimental results). In the case that $S_1 \equiv S_2 \, (\equiv S)$ and $O_1 \equiv \neg O_2 \, (\equiv O)$, the reductive pair (RP) assumes the form of the *bilateral reductive sentence*

$$(x) \, (Sx \rightarrow (Qx \leftrightarrow Ox)). \quad \text{(RS)}$$

Suppose that we want to introduce the term 'temperature of c degrees centigrade' by means of a reductive sentence. This will be: if the test conditions S obtain (i.e. if we put object a in contact with a thermometer), then a has temperature of c degrees centigrade if and only if the characteristic response O obtains (i.e. if the thermometer shows c degrees centigrade). It should be clear that the reductive introduction of theoretical terms by means of (RS) does *not* face the problems of explicit definition. If an object a is not under the test conditions S, then, treated as material implication, the sentence $(Sa \rightarrow (Qa \leftrightarrow Oa))$ becomes true, but this implies nothing as to whether the object under consideration has or has not the property Q. However, the reductive sentence (RS) does not define the predicate Q. For although (RS) provides a necessary and a sufficient condition for Q, these two conditions do not coincide – it is easy to see that $(S \rightarrow (Q \leftrightarrow O)$ is analysed as follows: $(S\&O) \rightarrow Q$ and $(S\&\neg O) \rightarrow \neg Q$. So, the concept Q definitely applies to all things which are $S\&O$, and definitely does not apply to all things that are $\neg(S\&\neg O)$. But since $\neg(S\&\neg O)$ is different from $S\&O$, the foregoing procedure does not specify *all and only* those things to which the concept Q applies.

Thus, the meaning of Q is *not* completely specified by virtue of observable predicates. At best, the reductive sentence gives 'a conditional definition' of Q (Carnap 1936: 443). Accordingly, it can give only partial empirical significance to a theoretical term. A theoretical term can be associated with a whole set of reductive sentences which specify, in part, empirical situations to which the term applies (ibid.: §9). But no amount of reductive sentences is enough to explicitly define, and hence render eliminable, a theoretical term. Feigl has rightly called Carnap's project a generalised case of 'if–thenism'. For, it amounts to the introduction of theoretical terms (e.g. 'magnetic field') by means of a set of 'if ... then' statements which specify observational conditions for their applicability. The end result however is that theoretical terms are shown to exhibit an 'openness of content' such that no chain of reductive sentences will render them fully interpretable in an observational language, and hence eliminable (see Hempel 1963: 689).

The shift from explicit definitions to reductive sentences marks also a shift from verification to confirmation. *T*-discourse is rendered meaningful because it is confirmable. And it is confirmable because reductive sentences specify the conditions for the application of *t*-terms in certain observable situations. *T*-assertions entail several observational predictions. Insofar as the latter can be confirmed, so can the former. What reductive sentences do is show how the confirmation of a theoretical assertion (e.g. that an electric current flows in a wire) can be reduced to the confirmation of several observational predictions (e.g. that a magnetic needle will move). Observational predictions are no longer required to be verifiable: it is enough that they are confirmable. Carnap is now fully aware that all that can be hoped for is a high degree of confirmation. In practice, a high degree of confirmation can be reached by means of few observations. But even when it comes to observational predictions, it is theoretically possible that their testing can go on for ever and that further evidence might show them wrong.

All this implies that *t*-assertions and *o*-assertions are different only in degree. It is not the case that the latter are confirmable whereas the former are not. Their only difference is that the latter are *more easily* confirmable than the former. This difference in degree, and not in quality, is reflected in Carnap's characterisation of what it is for a term or predicate to be observable. Contrary to the conventional wisdom which has Carnap committed to a sharp dichotomy between observational terms and *t*-terms, Carnap makes the following rather astonishing point:

> There is no sharp line between the observable and non-observable predicates because a person will be more or less able to decide a sentence quickly, i.e. he will be inclined after a certain period to accept the sentence. For the sake of simplicity we will here draw a sharp distinction between observable and non-observable predicates. But thus drawing an arbitrary line between observable and non-observable predicates in a field of continuous degrees of observability we partly determine in advance the possible answers to questions such as whether or not a certain predicate is observable by a given person.
>
> (1936: 455)

For Carnap, a predicate, *P*, of a given language is an *observational* predicate if a person can, under suitable circumstances, decide with the aid of 'few observations' whether or not an object belongs to the extension of this predicate. In other words, (monadic) predicate *P* is observational if for a given object, *a*, few observations can lead to a high degree confirmation of either '*Pa*' or '$\neg Pa$' (cf. 1936: 445–446). Analogously, a theoretical predicate is one which does not satisfy the foregoing condition. But the only privilege that observational predicates enjoy over non-observational ones is that, in the case of the former, a community (or an organism) can reach a high degree of confirmation for sentences which involve them in relatively quick time and with the aid of 'few observations'.

An interesting question that crops up here is why Carnap makes the distinction at all, if it is one merely of degree. Briefly put, the answer is that Carnap wants to show how intersubjective confirmation of theories is possible. It is possible because there can be a set of easily and uncontroversially confirmable assertions – those that are taken to involve observational predicates. The latter cannot be fully circumscribed in terms of whether or not they stand for observable entities. Observability is a vague notion, and there is no natural way to say which things should count as observable and which not. Rather, the observational predicates are precisely those that can be confirmed easily, and to a high degree, whether or not the confirmation procedure involves elementary instruments or only naked-eye observations. In a piece which follows his 'Testability and Meaning' (1936), Carnap draws the distinction on the basis of the degree of abstractness of a term. The more elementary terms are those that are applicable in concrete cases 'on the basis of observations in a more direct way than others'; the more abstract are the terms whose application rests 'on a more complex procedure, which, however, also finally rests on observations' (1939: 61). Here again, Carnap refrains from offering any precise definition of 'degree of abstractness'. Instead, he rests his case with only a few examples. In any case, although the circumscription of the set of observable predicates is malleable and changeable, it can still play its intended role: to provide a relatively uncontroversial basis for the confirmation of theories. As Carnap states: 'if confirmation is to be feasible at all, this process of referring back to other predicates must terminate at some point' (1936: 456). The terminal point is *not* the point of absolute observability, since there is no such thing, but the set of predicates which can be easily and uncontroversially confirmed.

Indispensability arguments

The recognition of a confirmational parity between observational and theoretical discourse is a turning-point in the empiricist programme. It coincides with the admission that *t*-discourse is indispensable. This last admission is the natural consequence of the fact that *t*-discourse *cannot* be fully eliminated in favour of *o*-discourse. Recognising all this, Carnap put forward the following explicit indispensability argument:

1   Without using theoretical terms it 'is not possible to arrive ... at a powerful and efficacious system of laws' (1939: 64). That is, without appealing to theoretical entities, it is impossible to formulate laws applying to a wide range of phenomena. (Carnap is careful to add that

'this is an empirical fact, not a logical necessity'.) Laws which involve only observational terms cannot be comprehensive and exact: they always encounter exceptions and have to be modified or narrowed down. On the other hand, laws that involve theoretical terms manage to encompass and unify a wide range of phenomena. In a single phrase, Carnap's first premiss is: No theoretical terms, no comprehensive laws.

2   Scientific theories do formulate comprehensive laws with the help of theoretical terms.

Therefore, theoretical terms are indispensable.

We can now tie together the two threads of the liberalised (post-verificationist) empiricist programme: the recognition of a confirmational parity between observational and theoretical discourse and the admission that *t*-discourse is irreducible, and indispensable. They each give rise to the question: Is a full commitment to unobservable entities alongside the observable ones now inevitable? It certainly appears that, on the post-verificationist new empiricist approach, a full explication of *t*-discourse requires commitment to irreducible *t*-entities, pretty much as *o*-discourse requires commitments to irreducible *o*-entities. At least, there is no longer an obvious argument that while *o*-discourse is ontologically committing *t*-discourse is not.

In their attempts to deal with the issue just discussed, empiricists have divided into three groups: those who move over to *semantic realism*; those who turn to *instrumentalism*; and those who aim to set up a *neutral*, or irenic, position. Semantic realists are those who, following Feigl (1950), argue that a full and just explication of *t*-discourse requires that *t*-terms have factual reference to unobservable entities. Instrumentalists are those who, following the early Ernst Nagel, argue that an instrumentalist stance towards theories can dispense with commitments to *t*-entities, while acknowledging that theories are neither translatable into, nor reducible to, classes of observational statements. Those who try to remain neutral, like the early Carl Hempel and the Carnap of the 1950s, want to render the new liberalised empiricism neutral in the realism–instrumentalism debate.

In what follows, I discuss these positions in detail, beginning, in the next section, with semantic realism. Then, I examine a quick reaction to semantic realism due to Hempel. In Chapter 2, I turn attention to instrumentalism. Chapter 3 discusses in some detail Carnap's attempt to establish the position that empiricism can remain neutral in the realism–instrumentalism debate.

Semantic realism

Semantic realism takes both *o*-assertions and *t*-assertions at 'face value', meaning that both *o*-assertions and *t*-assertions are not reduced to assertions couched in another vocabulary. So, the *o*-assertion 'The cat is on the mat' is true if and only if the cat is on the mat, and the *t*-assertion 'For every quark there is a corresponding lepton' is true if and only if for every quark there is a corresponding lepton. Does that sound trivial? It is clearly not trivial if we bear in mind what the issue is: specifying the truth-conditions of an assertion. This task has to be distinguished from the different task of specifying the conditions under which an assertion may be accepted as true; that is, specifying what the evidence should be for the truth of an asser-tion.

As Herbert Feigl (1950: 48) noted (and he was among the first, if not the first, to make this point), the empiricist programme had long been a hostage to verificationism. Verificationism runs together two separate issues: the 'epistemic reduction' of an assertion – also known as 'the evidential basis' for the truth of the assertion – and 'the semantical relation of desig-nation (i.e. reference)'. That is, verificationism conflates the issue of what *constitutes evidence for the truth* of an assertion with the issue of *what would make this assertion true*. If evidential basis and truth-conditions are separated, then reductivism loses its bite. Both *o*-assertions and *t*-assertions are true if and only if their truth-conditions obtain. One might well acknow-ledge a difference with respect to their testability. This difference might be reflected in the degree of confirmation enjoyed by each assertion. But this difference ought to have *no* semantic import. Both kinds of asser-tion should be treated as semantically on a par, that is as being truth-conditioned. This requires simply that theoretical terms as well as (and no less than) observational terms have putative factual reference. Theoretical terms refer putatively to unobservable entities, while observational terms refer putatively to observable ones. So, semantic realism asserts that there should not be double semantic standards, one for *o*-assertions and another for *t*-assertions. If *t*-assertions cannot be given truth-conditions in an ontology that dispenses with *t*-entities, then a full explication of *t*-discourse requires merely commitment to irreducible *t*-entities, pretty much as *o*-discourse requires commitment to *o*-entities.

It is important to stress that semantic realism is an anti-reductive posi-tion. Truth-conditions are treated compositionally: the truth-conditions of an assertion obtain when the referred-to entities stand in the referred-to rela-tions. So, for instance, the truth-conditions of the assertion '*Neutrinos have no mass*' obtain when (and insofar as) neutrinos are indeed massless. But, on top of that, the referred-to entities and the referred-to relations are *not* to be reconstructed on a reductive basis: when *t*-assertions are at issue they should be taken to be about unobservable entities, their properties and relations. What is more, I think semantic realism can adequately capture the realist intuition that the entities posited by scientific theories are mind-independent. Let us now see how and why.

When realists talk of mind-independent entities, their position would be miscontrued if understood as merely covering themselves against the possibility that those entities turn out to be mental entities or to be constituted by mental entities (such as ideas, sense-data and the like). This would be enough to warn off extreme forms of idealism and phenomenalism, but it would make reductive empiricism *compatible* with realism. As I have already noted, reductive empiricists might well admit theoretical entities, and they may also consider them as non-mental entities. But if they admit them at all, they do so because and insofar as they link the claim that they exist to the possibility of fully reducing assertions about them to assertions about observables. When reductive empiricists took theoretical discourse to be disguised talk about observable entities and their actual and possible behaviour, the implication was that theoretical entities might be thereby legitimised: they can be admitted in an empiricist ontology, but not as irreducible entities. Rather, they can be innocuously admitted in their ontology precisely because, in the end, the so-called theoretical entities (or, better, theoretical concepts) are *nothing but* shorthands for complicated relations between observable phenomena. Definitions legitimise: given that one defines 'bachelor' to mean 'unmarried man', if one admits unmarried men in one's ontology, then one can also admit bachelors at no extra cost. Similarly, if one were to define 'electron' by reference to observable entities (e.g. tracks in cloud chambers), then if one was ready to admit these observable entities in one's ontology, one would be ready also to admit electrons, at no extra cost. So, reductive empiricists can live happily with the idea that the theoretical entities posited by scientific theories exist, as well as with the idea that they are not mental entities. Where they differ from realists is in thinking that what legitimises these existential claims is that theoretical terms are fully reducible to (combinations of) observational ones.

There is a sense, however, in which reductive empiricists render the existence of theoretical entities mind-dependent, although the entities themselves, insofar as they are admitted to exist, are not mental. To see this, let us first note that what makes the reduction of theoretical discourse desirable for empiricists is not just ontological economy: it is also the fact that the reductive basis, the set of observable entities, is taken to be *epistemically privileged*. If the entities of the reductive basis stand in a special epistemic relation to us, if for instance we can verify assertions about them, or if we can be in a position to rationally accept assertions about them, then insofar as other entities are reducible to those of the reductive basis, we can stand in exactly the same epistemic relation to these other entities. Assertions about them would be true just in case, and because, the special epistemic relation was instantiated. So, for instance, if we were in position to readily accept claims about tracks in cloud chambers, and if talk about electrons was reducible to talk about (among other things) tracks in cloud chambers, then we could readily accept claims about electrons. The result of all this is that theoretical entities end up being mind-dependent in a different – and broader – sense: their existence is tied to the possibility of verifying, or rationally accepting, assertions about them. In particular, the claim that such entities exist falls short of legitimacy unless a certain epistemic relation with such entities is instantiated. On the present view, the content of the world (i.e. what entities there are in it) is determined fully by what can be known, verified and the like.

What makes realism about theoretical entities distinctive – and distinct from reductive empiricism – is precisely the *denial* of such a link between what there is and the instantiation of a suitable epistemic relation between us humans and whatever entities are taken to exist. In particular, realists would argue, if the entities posited by scientific theories exist, they do so independently of us humans being able to assert, rationally accept, verify and the like, that they do. In order to capture this claim, 'mind-independence' should be understood in a broader way. To say of a non-mental entity which features in one's ontology that it is *mind-independent* is to say that assertions about this entity are true because and insofar as their truth-conditions obtain, and not because and insofar as such assertions can be verified, rationally accepted, believed and cognate epistemic notions. In other words, what makes such assertions true is that they capture correctly facts about independently existing entities and their behaviour. In order to distinguish them from truth-conditions, let us call the conditions under which an assertion stands verified, is rationally acceptable and the like, verification conditions. The realist claim, then, is that truth-conditions should be taken to be distinct from verification conditions. What makes an assertion about theoretical entities true, if it is true, is not any kind of evidence we might have for its truth, though such evidence is important in its own way to justify our belief in its truth. Rather, what makes such an assertion true is that it is indeed the case that the referred-to entities stand in the referred-to relations.

It is precisely this distinction between truth-conditions and verification conditions that semantic realism intends to make the cornerstone of a realist understanding of theoretical discourse. It thereby severs the verificationist link between verification conditions and truth-conditions, and captures the realist intuition that theoretical entities are mind-independent.

It should be stressed, however, that by divorcing truth-conditions from verification conditions, semantic realism does *not* entail the unknowability of unobservable entities, or their epistemic inaccessibility and the like. It merely explains the sense in which science (or any other activity for that matter) describes a world (or a domain) in which it is in principle possible that the content is in excess of what can be known. The suggestions that *t*-terms have factual reference, and that the truth-conditions of *t*-assertions should not be conflated with their verification conditions, aim precisely to show that there is (or that there *can* be) more in the world than whatever falls within the reach of the physically possible observational evidence.

To sum up then, semantic realists treat *t*-discourse as having truth-conditions which are irreducible in that the referred-to entities themselves are irreducible and the truth-conditions of an assertion as a whole are not reducible to evidence – or verification conditions.

Hempel's half-way house

Is semantic realism forced upon empiricists? The early Hempel (1950) tried to show that it is not. He does admit that *t*-assertions have 'excess content', i.e. that their content cannot be exhausted by any set of *o*-assertions. In fact, Hempel adopts semantic holism and asserts that *t*-terms have 'excess content' precisely because their meaning is reflected in the totality of their logical relationships (both those of strict entailment and of confirmation) to all other statements of the language. And he adopts the view that *t*-assertions indispensably contribute to the experiential output of the theory. Yet, for him, all this does not commit the theory-user to the claim that the excess content of the theories is accounted for by having *t*-terms designating unobservable entities. He suggests a half-way house position: it is not necessary to accept that *t*-terms designate unobservable entities, yet there can still be a sense in which unobservable entities may be accepted as real. For Hempel, accepting a well-confirmed and coherent theoretical system constitutes grounds for affirming the reality of certain unobservable entities. He says:

> This interpretation of 'surplus meaning' [i.e. the holistic interpretation] of a hypothesis seems to me to be in agreement with scientific usage; it calls attention to the systematic interconnection between the hypotheses on the one hand and other theoretical statements as well as observation sentences on the other; and it is precisely this logical coherence, in combination with the empirical confirmation, of a given theoretical system which to the scientists constitutes grounds for affirming the 'actual existence' or 'reality' of whatever hypothetical entities the system assumes.
>
> (1950: 172)

It should be clear, however, that building Hempel's half-way house cannot be a satisfactory resolution of the issue of whether a full explication of *t*-discourse requires commitment to irreducible *t*-entities. In addition to what I have said in defence of semantic realism, let me note the following objection to Hempel's early position. Liberalised empiricism allows that theories be confirmable. Yet, if theoretical statements are not truth-conditioned, how can they possibly be confirmed or disconfirmed by evidence? To say that a *t*-assertion is confirmed by the evidence is to say that the evidence makes it likely to be true, or – if one adopts an incremental account of confirmation – that, after the evidence is accepted, the hypothesis is more likely to be true than it was before. Similarly, to say that a *t*-assertion is disconfirmed by the evidence is to say that the evidence is inconsistent with the conditions under which the *t*-assertion is true. If *t*-assertions require truth-conditions, and if the latter are no longer definable in terms of observables, then they should involve reference to unobservable entities. The truth-conditions of *t*-assertions may well fall outside the scope of direct experience. But since *t*-assertions no less than *o*-assertions can enjoy confirmation by evidence, it should be clear that there can be evidence that the truth-conditions of *t*-assertions obtain.

This, though, is not the end of the story for semantic realism. For empiricists can still try to find a suitable interpretation of *t*-discourse such that it does not commit the theory-user to factual reference to unobservable entities. This is what the mature Carnap tried to do, as we shall see in Chapter 3. But, we need first to discuss instrumentalism.

2 Theories as instruments?

After admitting that theoretical discourse has 'excess content', empiricism seems to be forced into the following position: a full explication of theoretical discourse requires commitment to irreducible unobservable entities, pretty much as observational discourse requires commitment to irreducible observable entities. One way in which it is possible to deny this conclusion is by adopting a radical view which I call *syntactic instrumentalism*.

As Nagel (1950) suggests, an instrumentalist stance towards theories can dispense with commitments to *t*-entities, while acknowledging that theories are neither translatable into nor equivalent to classes of observation statements. In light of this, theories may well be said to have 'excess content'. But theoretical statements are not assertions, strictly speaking. They should be considered as merely syntactic constructs for the organisation of experience, for connecting empirical laws and observations that would otherwise be taken to be irrelevant to one another, and for guiding further experimental investigation. Theories may employ whatever symbolic means is available to organise experience, but they do not represent anything 'deeper' than experience.

Syntactic instrumentalism comes in two variant forms: eliminative and non-eliminative. The *non-eliminative* variant (a kind of which can be associated with Duhem) is that one *need not* assume that there is an unobservable reality behind the phenomena, nor that science aims to describe it, in order to do science and to do it successfully. I discuss this position later in the chapter. For the time being, I will concentrate on the eliminative versions.

Eliminative instrumentalism takes a stronger view: theories should not aim to represent anything 'deeper' than experience, because, ultimately, there is nothing deeper than experience to represent. However, it will typically resist the project of translating away *t*-discourse. Instead, it treats *t*-discourse simply as symbol manipulation, without proper theoretical content. How then do eliminativists react to the positing by scientific theories of a number of unobservable entities and processes and their employment of *t*-terms to refer putatively to them? If scientific theories have only instrumental value, what is being gained by engaging in theoretical discourse?

Eliminativists face a quandary. They need either to account for the role of theoretical discourse in science without being committed to any existential implications about unobservables, or to show that this discourse is ultimately dispensable, and hence non-committal. The next two sections show how eliminative instrumentalists have dealt with this quandary. We shall begin with Ernst Mach's attempt to show that the aim of science is 'economy of thought'. Then we shall move on to see how Craigian instrumentalism tries to eliminate theoretical discourse altogether.

Machian themes

Under the motto 'science is economy of thought', Ernst Mach suggested that the aim of science is to *classify* appearances in a concise and systematic way; or, as he puts it, 'to replace, or save, experiences, by the reproduction and anticipation of facts in thought' (1893: 577). Under Mach's nominalism, all that exist are particular matters of facts, what, in order to use a neutral word, he calls the *elements* (cf. 1910: 208–209). The so-called 'laws of nature' are merely convenient devices for the systematisation and co-ordination of such facts. Take, for instance, the case of light-refraction. Mach thinks that there are only particular light-rays being refracted at particular angles. When scientists 'pack' all this information into a *single expression*, the law of refraction $\sin a/\sin b = n$, (where a is the angle of incidence, b is the angle of refraction and n is the refractive index), they merely provide themselves with a convenient way to memorise (and recall) all these facts. 'In nature', says Mach, 'there is no law of refraction, only different cases of refraction' (1893: 582). The so-called law of refraction is only 'a concise compendious rule, devised by us for the mental reconstruction of fact'. The case of unobservable entities is similar to that of laws. An appeal to unobservable entities, e.g. to atomic structures, can be accepted, if at all, only as a means to achieve an economical classification/systematisation of the 'laws' of the phenomena. As he puts it, the atomic hypothesis should only be seen as a 'mathematical model for facilitating mental reproduction of the facts' (ibid.: 589). Even so, however, Mach suggests that unobservable entities (and theoretical concepts) should be admitted only as 'provisional helps'. Ultimately, one should try to attain 'more satisfactory substitute(s)'. These are what Mach calls 'direct descriptions of a widely extended domain of facts' (1910: 248). Helpful though theoretical concepts may be as a guide in research, they should be used only as the scaffold-ing for the construction of *direct descriptions*. The latter are, basically, phenomenological descriptions of the facts, descriptions 'which contain nothing that is unessential and restrict [themselves] to the abstract apprehension of facts' (1910: 248). What Mach takes 'unessential' to mean should be quite clear: it includes all theoretical-explanatory hypotheses, such as the atomic hypothesis, which purport to explain the law-like behaviour of the phenomena.

Mach's insight is that a consistent instrumentalist should aim to show how theoretical discourse is eliminable and dispensable. For, if, in doing science, we cannot dispense with theoretical terms and theoretical entities and structures, then it seems totally unsatisfactory to argue that they are only 'provisional helps'. If they are only provisional helps then it should be possible, at least in principle, to find more satisfactory helps which are clearly not theoretical. To put the same point in a different way, it is not enough to say that *t*-terms are merely meaningless syntactic constructs which help with the organisation of experience. For this flies in the face of the fact that *t*-terms are treated as meaningful by their users. To say to someone who is apparently engaged in assertoric discourse that all he is doing is manipulating symbols is not likely to meet with a favourable response; unless, of course, one also shows *either* how this apparently meaningful discourse is dispensable *or* how symbol-manipulation does acquire some content, the latter being parasitic on the content of *o*-discourse. The latter has led to reductive versions of empiricism, whose failures were discussed in Chapter 1. The former was in Mach's time merely a promissory note, but one which gained support when Craig's theorem was proven. This issue is discussed in the next section. For the moment, let us focus on the following question.

Why is recourse to unobservables so unappealing to Mach? What is noteworthy is that Mach wants to distance himself from the naive *idealist* view that something exists if and only if it can be directly perceived. He correctly perceives that this principle is too restrictive for science. Here is one of his examples. Take a long elastic rod and attach it to a vice. One can strike the rod and observe its vibrations. Suppose now that one cuts and shortens the rod and strikes it again. No vibrations are observed. Or if something like vibrations are observed, they are very hazy. Should one infer from this that the vibrations ceased altogether? One should not. Mach suggests that if one retains the concept of vibration, that is, if one supposes that the vibrations are still there although they are not observable, one can anticipate and detect several effects which should be attributed to the presence of vibrations, e.g. certain tactile impressions if the rod is touched (1893: 587). Admitting the existence of non-visible vibrations is, then, still 'serviceable and economical'. It helps to systematise, organise and anticipate the phenomena. Supposing some things to exist even if they are invisible 'makes experience intelligible to us; it supplements and supplants experience' (ibid.). So Mach seems to suggest, after all, that positing entities or processes which are not directly visible is legitimate, but only insofar they play an 'economical' role.

One would expect this reason to be as good as any for being committed to the existence of an entity. One might call this reason 'economical', but that does not really matter. If positing a certain entity makes experience intelligible, and if experience cannot be made intelligible otherwise, then we have reason enough to accept that this entity exists. After all, is not the rendering intelligible of experience the main reason for positing material objects (as distinct from collections of sense data)? And if Mach is right that invisibility is *not* a good enough reason to refrain from positing the existence of an entity which is otherwise 'serviceable and economical', then what stops us from believing in the existence of, say, atoms?

What, then, is so different in the case of atoms? They are invisible, to be sure, but do they not play an equally economical role in science? If one is ready to accept invisible vibrations, why not accept invisible atoms, too? Mach counters this reasoning by observing that, unlike vibrations, atoms cannot possibly be perceived by the senses. Moreover, when scientists posit atoms, they have to drastically modify their experience. Mach accounts for this difference using what he called the 'principle of continuity', according to which:

> Once we have reached a theory that applies in a particular case, we proceed gradually to modify in thought the conditions of such case, as far as it is at all possible, and endeavour in so doing to adhere throughout as closely as we can to the conception originally reached.
>
> (1893: 168)

This sounds obscure, but the idea is simple: when we cut the rod, we did not have to modify the original concept of vibration in order to apply it to the case of the shortened rod; we said merely that the *vibrations* were then invisible. Although we could not observe vibrations, we could still anticipate and detect their effects in experience. But, Mach adds, the case of atoms is different. When we move from chemical, electrical and optical phenomena to the existence of atoms which supposedly cause them, we invest atoms 'with properties that absolutely contradict the attributes hitherto observed in bodies'. The concept of atom is radically different from the concepts occurring in the description of the phenomena which it is supposed to explain. The properties of atoms are formed in a way discontinuous with the properties observed in the phenomena. In positing atoms, the principle of continuity is violated. For Mach this means that 'the mental artifice atom' is suspect: something, perhaps, to be used provisionally, but to be disposed of ultimately.

Mach is certainly right to note that there are big differences between atoms and the macroscopic things which are supposedly made of atoms. But is there no continuity at all? The fact of the matter is that atoms and other macroscopic entities have a number of properties in common with observable entities, and they also obey similar laws. Following an example given by Max Planck (1909), the atomic weight of a hydrogen atom is a well-defined and well-calculated property. We might not have used scales to measure it, but neither did we put the moon on scales when we calculated its weight and said that we were very confident about it. The visibility of moon and the invisibility of atoms are irrelevant here. We can use the same methods which calculate the weight of moon to calculate the weight (or volume) of invisible planets, as was Neptune before it was observed by telescope.

Be that as it may, the strength of the principle of continuity lies elsewhere: it disallows causal gaps, and hence demands the restoration of causal continuity between phenomena. Positing invisible vibrations is legitimate because it restores the *causal continuity* of the phenomena when the vibrations of the rod are visible and when no vibrations are visible. It is because we can detect several of the effects of the vibrations that we say, according to the principle of continuity, that vibrations are still present, though invisible. But if it is causal continuity that does all the work, then there seems to be no reason to stop at vibrations and not extend the argument to atoms. For atoms, too, are posited to establish causal continuity between phenomena and physical magnitudes, e.g. between the temperature of a gas and its pressure. What makes invisible entities 'serviceable' is that their positing restores causal continuity between ontologically disconnecting phenomena, and this is what really counts.

The principle of continuity notwithstanding to the contrary, Mach's resistance to atomism was dealt a rather serious – if not a fatal – blow by atomic science itself. In his renowned book *Les Atomes*, the French physicist Jean Perrin (1870–1942) summarised his experimental work and the evidence for the reality of molecules and atoms. He cited thirteen distinct ways by which to calculate the precise value of Avogadro's number, that is the number of molecules contained in a mole of a gas. This spectacular development suggested an almost irresistible argument in favour of the reality of atoms and which found expression in the late conversion of Henri Poincaré to atomism: we can calculate how many they are, therefore they exist; or, to put it in a more slogan-like form: *we can count them, therefore they exist.* Here is a long and beautiful passage from Poincaré:

> The brilliant determinations of the number of atoms computed by Mr Perrin have completed the triumph of atomicism. What makes it all the more convincing are the multiple correspondences between results obtained by totally different processes. Not too long ago, we would have considered ourselves fortunate if the numbers thus derived had contained the same number of digits. We would not even have required that the first significant figure be the same; this first figure is now determined; and what is remarkable is that the most diverse properties of the atom have been considered. In the processes derived from the Brownian movement or in those in which the law of radiation is invoked, not the atoms have been counted directly, but the degrees of freedom. In the one in which we use the blue of the sky, the mechanical properties of the atoms no longer come into play; they are considered as causes of optical discontinuity. Finally, when radium is used, it is the emissions of projectiles that are counted. We have arrived at such a

point that, if there had been any discordances, we would not have been puzzled as to how to explain them; but fortunately there have not been any. The atom of the chemist is now a reality . . .

(1913 [1963]: 91)

The point Poincaré made should be well-noted. Although atoms are invisible, we can (and have) amass(ed) much indirect evidence for their existence. In particular, all the different ways to calculate the number of atoms in a certain volume, and that there is a fixed number of atoms, make it highly plausible that these microscopic entities are real. Unless we accept their reality, we can hardly explain the observable phenomena. Nor can we explain that we can calculate with such a great precision how many atoms there are in a certain volume. In other words, it would be a great coincidence if atoms did not exist and yet all experimental findings were exactly those predicted by atomic theory. The very fact that the atomic hypothesis finds empirical support in the many and distinct domains in which atoms supposedly operate causally to generate certain observable phenomena gives good reason to accept that atoms are real. So, eliminative instrumentalism flies in the face of the fact that certain properties of atoms, including how many of those there are in a certain volume, can be fully determined by sound experimental practice.[1]

Whatever happened to the theoretician's dilemma?

The failures of Machian instrumentalism suggest that if instrumentalism is to be viable it has to show that, appearances to the contrary, theoretical discourse *is* dispensable. Craig's theorem comes to the rescue exactly at this point. It suggests that instrumentalists need no longer worry about reducibility, nor about the grave consequences of treating *t*-discourse as non-assertoric. Instead, they can forget altogether about the semantics of *t*-discourse, since *t*-assertions are deemed to be fully eliminable. So, Craig's theorem appears to give a great boost to eliminative instrumentalism. Its advocates need no longer commit themselves to the thesis that there is nothing beyond the realm of appearances for scientific theories to represent. That is, the advocates of eliminative instrumentalism need no longer adopt a Machian line. Instead, all they need to point out is that, whether or not there is anything beyond appearances, if people want to restrict the scope of scientific theories to observable phenomena, Craig's theorem suggests that they can happily do so, since the theoretical part of theories is fully eliminable. Hence, the theoretical part of theories is not even a candidate for representing anything. Given all this, it is vital for realists to rebut the use of Craig's theorem in defence of instrumentalism. To this task we now turn.

In his PhD thesis in 1951, William Craig constructed a general method according to which given any first-order theory *T* and given any effectively specified sub-vocabulary O of T, one can construct another theory T' whose theorems are exactly those theorems of T which contain no constants other than those in the sub-vocabulary, O. Hempel was the first to recognise the broader significance of this theorem: for any scientific theory T, T is replaceable by another (axiomatisable) theory, Craig(T), consisting of all and only the theorems of T which are formulated in terms of the observational vocabulary, V_O.

Craig requires that two conditions be satisfied:

1   The non-logical vocabulary of the original theory T is effectively partitioned into two mutually exclusive and exhaustive classes, one containing all and only theoretical terms, the other containing all and only observational ones. Let V_T ($= T_1, T_2, \ldots, T_n$) be the theoretical vocabulary and V_O ($= O_1, O_2, \ldots, O_n$) be the observational one.
2   The theory T is axiomatisable, and the class of proofs in T (the class of applications of a rule of inference with respect to the axioms of the theory and whatever has been previously inferred from them) is effectively defined.

Then Craig shows how to construct these axioms of the new theory Craig(T). There will be an infinite set of axioms (no matter how simple is the set of axioms of the original theory T), but there is an effective procedure which specifies them. Craig(T), which replaces the original theory T, is 'functionally equivalent' to T, in that all observational consequences of T also follow from Craig(T): the latter established all those deductive connections between observation sentences that T established. So, for any V_O sentence O_0, if T implies O_0 then Craig(T) implies O_0 (see Hempel 1958: 75–76 and 1963: 699).[2]

The significance of Craig's theorem for the instrumentalism project should be obvious. Instrumentalists argue that theoretical commitments in science are dispensable. Craig's theorem offers a boost to instrumentalism, by proving that theoretical terms can be eliminated *en bloc*, without loss in the deductive connections between observables established by the theory. Hempel (1958: 49–50) presented the significance of Craig's theorem in the form of a *dilemma for the theoretician*: If the theoretical terms and the general principles of a theory do not serve their purpose of a deductive systematisation of the empirical consequences of a theory, then they are surely unnecessary. But, given Craig's theorem, even if they serve their purpose, 'they can be dispensed with since any chain of laws and interpretative statements establishing such a connection should then be replaceable by a law which directly links observational antecedents to observational consequents'. Theoretical terms and principles of a theory either serve their purpose or they do not. Hence, the theoretical terms and principles of any theory are dispensable.

Unnatural splits in the language of science

The fact of the matter, however, is that Craig's theorem is not so damaging. For a start, since Craig's theorem requires a separation of the language of a theory in two vocabularies, its worth is no more than the claim that we can divide the language of science into a theoretical and an observational vocabulary. But there is no principled way to draw a line between theoretical and observational terms.

The revolt against logical empiricism in the early 1960s took as one of its most important tasks that of uprooting the alleged dichotomy between theoretical and observational terms. One main objection has been that although there are differences between observable and unobservable entities, they are so diffuse and context-dependent, that it is impossible to create a principled and absolute distinction between terms which refer only to unobservable entities and terms which refer only to observable ones. Take for instance the term 'electron'. The term is theoretical when it is used in connection with the detection of particles in a cloud-chamber. But it becomes observational when it is used in connection with modern accelerators detecting the generation of other elementary particles. Based on such considerations, and lots of examples, Peter Achinstein (1965) and others (see e.g. Feyerabend 1958, 1965 and Hesse 1970a) suggested that, depending on the context, the set of theoretical terms is circumscribed differently. Given that some (probably most) terms which are classified as 'theoretical' in context C_1 may be classified as 'observational' in context C_2 (and conversely), it follows that there is no principled way to draw such a distinction; that is, one cannot separate out two classes of terms, one comprising all and only observational predicates, the other comprising all and only non-observational ones.

Putnam pushed this line to its extremes by arguing that 'if an "observation term" is a term which can, in principle, only be used to refer to observable things, then there are no observation terms' (1962: 218). The point here is not that there are no observational terms. Rather it is a *reductio ad absurdum* of the thesis that there is a clear-cut dichotomy between *o*-terms and *t*-terms. Since any observational term could be used in application to some unobservable without changing its meaning, the so-called 'observational terms' can refer to unobservable entities. Putnam's example is Newton's reference to red corpuscles to explain red light. But other examples can be easily thought of. Conversely, many theoretical terms can be seen as referring to observational states of affairs (e.g. when one says that the guy who stuck his finger in the mains was electrocuted.)

So, the point I want to endorse is *not* that there are no observational terms and predicates. Rather, the point is that any distinction between observational and theoretical terms is based largely on pragmatic considerations, and therefore has neither semantic nor epistemic significance. In a given context, or with respect to a given class of theories, one can distinguish between terms that are 'observational' (in the sense that the presence or absence of the entities they refer to can be easily agreed on, relying mostly on unaided senses, elementary instruments and commonly accepted background theories) and terms that are 'theoretical' (in the sense that the entities they refer to can be detected only indirectly, or inferred). But such a distinction is neither absolute nor sharp. Its only purpose is to facilitate confirmation. This rough pragmatic distinction of degree is all we need in order to confirm scientific theories. For scientific theories can be seen as still entailing predictions couched in a common 'observational' language (in the above broader and relativised sense), although the boundaries of this language shift, and some of the terms of this language would count as theoretical in a different context.

If the distinction between observational and theoretical terms is not absolute but context-dependent, then the application of Craig's theorem becomes context-dependent, and so loses most of its force. Some terms might end up being eliminable in some contexts where they are considered 'theoretical', but the very same terms are not eliminable in contexts where they are considered 'observational'. Naturally, one might argue that Craig's theorem is intended to apply to a 'total science', where all terms are partitioned into two subsets – those that count as theoretical in all contexts, and the rest (cf. Hooker 1968). Leaving aside the stretch of the imagination that is necessary to envisage a total science with a full partition of its vocabulary into two sets, the *logical* point is well-taken. Craig's theorem guarantees that if we deem a class of terms 'unwanted', then it can be dispensed with. Although from a logical point of view theoretical terms can be dispensed with, there are two good reasons – the second being the more forceful – why scientific theories would as a result be worse off, in respects which even instrumentalists would acknowledge.

Diachronic gains and inductive support

If theories are replaced by their Craig-transforms, then they will lose several of their salient features – simplicity and predictive fertility, in particular. If the Craig(T) replaces a theory T, then the comparative simplicity of a theoretical system will be lost. Craig(T) will always have an infinite number of axioms, no matter how few, simple and elegant were the axioms of the original theory. If one replaces T with Craig(T), then scientific theories may lose in predictive fertility. Suppose we have two theories, T_1 and T_2 which have the same observational and theoretical vocabularies and which are consistent (individually and jointly). Suppose also that we conjoin T_1 and T_2 to form the theory T_1 & T_2. Generally, T_1 & T_2 will entail some extra observational consequences that neither T_1 alone nor T_2 alone entail. If we had replaced T_1 by Craig(T_1) and T_2 by Craig(T_2), and then had formed the conjunction Craig(T_1) & Craig(T_2), we might have failed to generate these extra observational consequences. For, generally, the set of observational consequences of Craig(T_1) & Craig(T_2) is a proper subset of the observational consequences of T_1 & T_2. The point then is that the original theory T has *a potential over time* over Craig(T): the theoretical terms of T may help the generation of new observational predictions which cannot be generated by means of Craig(T) alone.[3]

The above argument, however, is not the end of the story. The stubborn Craigian might well stick to his guns and argue that, despite its awkwardness, a total-science Craig-transform shows that *t*-terms are dispensable. That is, however, too quick. If we look carefully at Craig's theorem, it becomes apparent that although it does force us to abandon something, it offers us a choice. As Hempel ingeniously has put it (long before his 'The Theoretician's Dilemma'): 'There is also a theorem of Craig proved in an unpublished doctoral thesis which is damaging to the idea that a theory is necessary at all *or* to the idea that explanation is deduction' (Carnap Archive, University of Pittsburgh. All rights reserved. Doc. 090–62–06, p. 4). So one should *either* accept that theoretical terms are dispensable as far the deductive systematisation of observable phenomena are concerned *or* that theories do not merely establish deductive connections but also inductive ones. Instead of scrapping *t*-terms, we have the option to expand their role so that they establish *inductive connections* among observables. Then *t*-terms are no longer dispensable: Craig(T) is no longer functionally equivalent with T.

Hempel (1958, 1963) offers a few examples to illustrate how theories can establish inductive transitions between observables. The basic idea is this. Most scientific theories are such that theoretical hypotheses entail several observational consequences but are not themselves entailed by them. So, for instance, a hypothesis H (or a cluster thereof) entails observational consequences $O_1, O_2, \ldots, O_n$. When these obtain, although we cannot deductively infer H, we can inductively conclude that H holds. Suppose, further, that H together with other theoretical hypotheses entail an extra testable prediction O_{n+1}. This new prediction could not have been issued by the observational consequences $O_1, O_2, \ldots, O_n$ on their own. Instead, its derivation rests essentially on accepting the inductively inferred theoretical hypothesis H. So, H is indispensable in establishing this inductive connection between $O_1, O_2, \ldots, O_n$ and O_{n+1} in that Craig(H) could not possibly establish such connection.[4]

On the basis mainly of the last point, Hempel himself dismissed the paradox of theorising by saying that it 'starts with a false premise' (1958: 87). Theories are *not* just a deductive systematisation of data. There is no compelling reason to interpret them in this way, without their irredeemable loss of some of the very fruitfulness which ought to be appealing even to instrumentalists.

Instrumentalism and probability statements

I will not resist the temptation to offer another argument which, if plausible, affects all kinds of syntactic instrumentalism, insofar as they treat theories as uninterpreted (or semi-interpreted) *syntactic structures*.

Syntactic instrumentalists argue that, apart from having interpreted observational consequences, all that is necessary for the analysis and use of a theory is to grasp its syntactic structure. A theory is not even a truth-valued construction or, better, makes no truth-valued claims for things other than observables. If this were accepted as an adequate account of scientific theories, then theories would be impotent to assign probabilities to particular observable phenomena and predictions. Nor would one be able to interpret certain experimental procedures that brought out particular predictions. Since we can do both of the above, the syntactic instrumentalist construal must be wrong. Let me explain.

The atomic theory, taken literally, assigns a certain probability that slamming together two rocks of the radioactive material U_{235} will result in a nuclear explosion. The assignment of probability depends on a theory-driven difference between the presence of a sub-critical mass and of a critical mass, as well as on a similar theory-driven difference between an ordinary rock and a rock of uranium. Suppose, however, that instead of trying to understand the theory, we treated the atomic theory as a mere syntactic calculus, where theoretical terms are merely abstract parameters in a largely uninterpreted logico-mathematical structure which 'surfaces' with some observational terms and predicates. Since 'rock' and 'explosion' will be among these terms and predicates, the instrumentalist version of the atomic theory will also predict that an explosion may happen from time to time when two rocks are slammed together. However, not only this fact would remain without theoretical interpretation. More importantly, without a literal understanding of the theory which generates this prediction, there would be no basis whatever to specify how likely it is that a *particular* slamming of two rocks (O_1) will lead to an explosion (O_2). Without the identification of the two rocks as *uranium* rocks whose mass is *above critical*, etc. (call this description T), $prob(O_2/O_1)$ is indeterminate. But clearly, once we take T into account, then $prob(O_2/O_1 \& T)$ becomes determinate and readily available.[5]

So, uninterpreted calculi, even if they systematise known observable phenomena under a syntactic framework, cannot guide certain future expectations that arise from within interpreted theories. As it stands, the above argument would not necessarily commit us to believe the theory, as opposed to treating it as meaningful but remaining agnostic of its truth. But it would commit us to view the theory as more than a syntactic structure that classifies appearances.

The main point established thus far is that theoretical talk has always 'excess content' over talk about *o*-entities: there is no way to reduce *t*-assertions about material objects to *o*-assertions. Hence, there is no way in which an ontology restricted to *o*-entities can provide truth-conditions for *t*-assertions. If, on top of that, one accepts the arguments against eliminative instrumentalism, the only option it seems available is to accept semantic realism. This is the option that many enlightened empiricists have chosen to take. What resistance to this option persists among empiricists stems from awareness of an alternative: there seems to be another way to avoid the commitment to realism. This is the line that Duhemian instrumentalists take. In a nutshell, the claim is that *t*-discourse avoids commitments to unobservable entities in a different way: on the basis of the alleged dispensability of theoretical explanations offered by scientific theories. Duhemian instrumentalists resist realism by taking a different view on the aim of science. On their view, theories should not be taken as aiming to explain the phenomena, as realists would have it. The next section discusses in some detail this Duhemian line. One thread of this line, but with many interesting variations, reappears in the discussion of van Fraassen's 'constructive empiricism' in Chapter 9 (see pp. 185–186).

Duhem I: anti-explanationist instrumentalism

Before, but also after, Perrin's work on atoms, the existence of atoms (as well as of other unobservable entities) was grounded mainly in their *explanatory value* of the atomic hypothesis, which explains a range of phenomena, from the chemical combinations of elements through the kinetic theory of gases to Brownian motion. Earlier, we saw even Poincaré being moved by such a consideration. An interesting brand of instrumentalism arises from the denial of the claim that scientific theories should aim to explain the phenomena. This is the position advocated by Duhem. Duhem was a very profound thinker and it is impossible to do justice to his complex ideas in a few pages. In the sequel, I shall look only at his position in the realism versus instrumentalism debate.[6]

Duhem's position is anticipated in the famous unsigned Preface to Copernicus' *On the Revolutions of the Celestial Spheres* (1543). The author of the Preface – Andreas Osiander – stated:

> [The] astronomer's job consists of the following: to gather together the history of the celestial movements by means of painstakingly and skilfully made observations, and then – since he cannot by any line of reasoning reach the true causes of these movements – to think up or construct whatever hypotheses he pleases such that, on their assumption, the self-same movements, past and future both, can be calculated by means of the principles of geometry. .... It is not necessary that these hypotheses be true. They need not even be likely. This one thing suffices, that the calculation to which they lead agree with the result of observation.
>
> (Quoted in Duhem 1908: 66)

Although Osiander here talks only about astronomy, his is one of the most accurate statements of the Duhemian instrumentalist conception of scientific theories. Theories aim only to *save the phenomena* – to offer a (mostly mathematical) framework in which the phenomena can be embedded. On the contrary, the *realist* conception of scientific theories – which was defended by Copernicus himself – is, as Duhem has put it for the case of astronomy, as follows: 'a fully satisfactory astronomy can only be constructed on the basis of hypotheses that are true, that conform to the nature of things' (1908: 62).

Duhem starts with the assumption that explanation is a concern not of science but rather of metaphysics. An explanation of a set of phenomena aims at 'strip[ping] reality from the appearances covering it like a veil, in order to see the bare reality itself' (1906: 7). But for Duhem the very idea of looking behind the 'veil of appearances' belongs to the realm of metaphysics. Science is concerned only with experience, and as such it 'is not an explanation. It is a system of *mathematical propositions deduced from a small number of principles, which aim to represent as simply and as completely and as exactly as possible a set of experimental laws*' (ibid.: 19). So physics does not aim to explain the phenomena, nor to describe the reality 'beneath' them. It aims only to embed descriptions of the phenomena in a mathematical framework. To be sure, the phenomena should not be embedded in just any mathematical framework, but in that which provides the most comprehensive classification.

This last move allows Duhem to disentangle observational ties between theories. For, at any given time there may be more than one mathematical system in which a certain set of phenomena can be embedded. Which one should scientists choose? A case in point is the dispute between the geocentric Ptolemaic planetary system and the heliocentric Copernican one. Both systems can accommodate the apparent motions of the planets, although they do so by means of different sets of hypotheses. If all that matters is the classification of the relevant phenomena, and since the Ptolemaic system achieves this feat, why should an instrumentalist recommend the adoption of the Copernican system? From a realist point of view the answer is obvious: the Ptolemaic system is false, whereas the Copernican system is approximately true. Duhem does want to recommend acceptance of the Copernican system. But if truth does not matter, on what grounds can he do this?

His suggestion is that that system of hypotheses be accepted which offers the most comprehensive classification of all phenomena 'by *one and the same* set of postulates' (1908: 116). In the case at hand, this is Newton's system, which unites and saves *all* phenomena, be they kinematic or dynamic, in our vicinity and in the remotest corners of the universe. It is because Copernicus' theory can be embedded in this system but Ptolemy's can not, that Duhem recommends acceptance of Copernicus' theory and claims that the 'falsity [of Ptolemy's theory] must be acknowledged' (ibid.: 109–110).

However, Duhem stresses, only claims about empirical facts can be properly judged in respect of their truth or falsity. As he puts it: 'We can say of propositions which claim to assert empirical facts, and only of these, that they are *true* or *false*' (1906: 333). Theoretical hypotheses lack truth-value. He notes: 'As for the propositions introduced by a theory, they are neither *true* nor *false*; they are only *convenient* or *inconvenient*' (ibid.: 334). And, elsewhere, he comments: 'hypotheses [are] not judgements about the nature of things, only premises intended to provide consequences conforming to experimental laws' (ibid.: 39). Hence, in Duhem's view, all that can be asserted of scientific theories is that they either square with the phenomena or they do not. If they do, they are deemed empirically adequate. If they do not, they are empirically inadequate (ibid.: 21).

Is not Duhem's anti-explanationist stance itself based on a certain metaphysics? One may justifiably think that Duhem's position inflates both the role and the limits of experience: there is a 'veil to perception' which limits what can be known, and what can be epistemically accessed; science cannot 'pierce through' this veil to unveil a hidden unobservable reality. Perhaps, one may think, Duhem suggests that there is nothing beyond appearance for science to attend to. But is this not just empiricist metaphysics? And, if so, does not his explicit disavowal of metaphysics make him inconsistent?

To answer affirmatively would be wrong, however. For, this is not Duhem's position. He wants to suggest that physics can be developed without first having to answer these two questions: Does there exist a material reality distinct from sensible appearances? And if there does, what is the nature of this reality? (see 1906: 10). Duhem does not assert that these questions are unanswerable. Rather, he suggests that one can refrain from answering them, that is, one can remain *agnostic* as to their answers. More specifically, he wants to motivate the view that physics need not answer these questions in order to proceed successfully. This is what Duhem means when he talks about the 'autonomy' of physics: a science which does not need to be committed to explanations of the phenomena and to entities going beyond the observable phenomena (see 1906: 19–21).

If scientific theories are properly analysed and reconstructed, Duhem suggests, no commitment to explanations and hypotheses about the causes of the phenomena, e.g. atomism, is needed (ibid.: 304–305).[7] But, unlike Mach, Duhem does not take seriously the project of eliminating theoretical discourse in terms of *direct descriptions* couched in an observational vocabulary. In fact, he does not think that one can usefully talk of such a separate vocabulary. Duhem is well-known for his thesis that all observation is theory-laden. As he puts it: 'An experiment in physics is not simply an observation of a phenomenon. It is, besides, the theoretical interpretation of this phenomenon' (1906: 144). Suppose that someone enters a laboratory and sees a physicist observing the motion of the pointer of an ammeter attached to a wire. He can report an observed fact: that the pointer moves in a certain way. But that is not what the physicist would report. She would say that she measures the intensity of the electric current flowing through the wire. The physicist would report what she observes by saying: 'An electric current of such and such an intensity flows through the wire'. Observation in science is not just the act of reporting a phenomenon (whatever that means!). It is the *interpretation* of a phenomenon in the light of some theory and other background knowledge. In fact, strictly speaking, a phenomenon is an already interpreted regularity (or event).

What this suggests is that there might be a tension in Duhem's position. On the one hand, theories are not truth-valued constructions, but rather convenient systems in which (description of) the phenomena are embedded. On the other hand, the phenomena can be made sense of only if they are interpreted from within some theory, and hence only if they find their place within that theory. Without an understanding of these theories, as Duhem notes, we cannot 'understand the meaning [the physicist] gives to his own statements' (1906: 159). But how can we consider a theory to be understood if it is taken to be merely a mathematical system for the classification of the phenomena? If, in other words, it is not taken to be at least, truth-conditioned?

I will not pursue this issue in any detail here, since it is not central to the argument of this chapter. But the following is worth speculating about. Duhem might be usefully thought of as a *fictionalist* with regard to theoretical discourse. The language of science is so theory-infected that it would be impossible to understand what scientists do without understanding this language. But for Duhem, I claim, understanding the language of theories is just to take them as telling theoretical stories about useful fictions. The interpretation of the phenomena is then just a matter of incorporating their description within the fictitious story told by the theory. So, when one interprets the motion of the pointer of the ammeter as 'electric current flows through the wire', one is not committed to the truth of a certain theoretical story, nor to the truth of the particular theoretical description. One simply tries to understand what the physicist is talking about by accepting a fictitious story and by extending *that* story so that the motion of the pointer finds its place in it. Be that as it may, the problem is that theoretical discourse cannot be eliminated since the language of science, including experimental science, is infected by it. One may choose to treat this discourse as being about useful fictions, but there is an unsatisfactory ring in this move. Where do we draw the line between entities which we consider real and those which we consider fictitious?

I want to suggest that Duhem offers a quite sophisticated argument to the effect that although theoretical discourse is indispensable when it comes to the interpretation of the phenomena, there is still a sense in which it is superfluous. Duhem argues that the theoretical/explanatory hypotheses of scientific theories are gratuitous: the history of science shows that it is these hypotheses that are abandoned when theories change. So, Duhem offers an *historical–epistemic argument* against theoretical claims: that although they can be usefully employed in interpreting the phenomena, the explanations they offer do not become part of the accepted body of scientific knowledge. Rather, they are all subsequently quelled.

In order to support this argument, Duhem suggests that theories are divided into two parts: a *representative* (or classificatory) part, which classifies a set of experimental laws; and an *explanatory* part, which 'takes hold of the reality underlying the phenomena'. The representative part of a theory is said to comprise the empirical laws as well as the mathematical formalism which is used to represent, systematise and correlate these laws. The explanatory part is said to relate to the construction of explanatory hypotheses about the unobservable causes of the phenomena. Duhem then makes the rather bold claim that the explanatory part of a theory is *parasitic* on the representative. In support of this view, he turns to the history of science, especially the history of optical theories and of mechanics. He argues that when a theory, *T*, is abandoned because it fails to cover new experimental facts and laws, its representative part is *retained*, partially or fully, in the successor theory, *T'*, while the attempted explanations offered by *T* get abandoned ('constant breaking-out of explanations which arise to be quelled' [1906: 33]). This is the kernel of an important argument against scientific realism, the so-called *pessimistic induction*. In effect, Duhem's point is that the history of science is the graveyard of attempted explanations of natural phenomena. So, one can have little warranted optimism about current explanations of the phenomena. For all we know, they too have arisen only to be subsequently quelled. A full discussion of this argument has to wait until Chapter 5. Here, I address only Duhem's division of theories into two parts.

Duhem is well aware that, with very few exceptions, the representative and explanatory parts of a scientific theory are fully interwoven in actual theories. How then can we distinguish between the parts that count as representative and those that are merely explanatory? His basic thought seems to be that the representative part is the *mathematical formalism* in which the phenomena are encoded, while the explanatory part comprises all hypotheses concerning the *causes* of the phenomena. Take, for instance, Newton's law of universal gravitation. Duhem suggests that it typically belongs to the representative part of Newton's theory, since it 'condenses' the laws of all celestial phenomena. But any attempt to characterise the cause of gravitational attraction belongs to the realm of explanation (or of *metaphysics*, as Duhem would put it), and as such it should not be the concern of physicists (1906: 47).

Is Duhem perhaps too quick here? I think that the representative–explanatory distinction is suspect. Consider the question: why is Newton's law merely representative and not explanatory? Newton's law *does* explain the phenomena of planetary motion by positing an attractive force between the sun and the orbiting planets. In doing so, it does posit a theoretical entity

– gravitational force. It also mathematically represents this force by stating the basic equation it obeys, and by showing how the laws of planetary motion follow from it. It is true that Newton's law does not in itself explain the provenance of gravitational attraction; it just posits it. But this, surely, does not make Newton's law merely representative. The source of gravitational attraction might itself need explanation, but this does not entail that positing such a force is not explanatory of Kepler's lower-level laws. More generally, one might say that scientific explanations (i.e. theoretical hypotheses) are representative in that they too are cast in mathematical form and, normally, entail predictions which can be tested. And, conversely, mathematical equations which express laws of nature are explanatory in that they can be used as premises for the derivation of other low-level laws. Duhem might have thought that all explanations worthy of the name are couched in explicitly causal terms. But, at least, according to a central philosophical account of explanation (see Friedman 1974; Kitcher 1981), the explanation of a phenomenon, or a law, amounts to showing how it can be subsumed under more comprehensive and fundamental laws. Kepler's laws are *explained* by showing that they follow from Newton's laws, together with certain initial conditions. This pattern is explanatory simply because it promotes understanding of low-level laws. The planets obey Kepler's laws because their behaviour is, *ultimately*, determined by Newton's laws.

The other thing worth noting is that although there should be no doubt that there is retention at the level of mathematical formalism (equations) when theories change, it is not the case that whatever non-empirical retention occurs is at the level of mathematical equations. This issue will crop up again in relation to Worrall's structural realism in Chapter 7. It suffices at this point to observe that when science moves from one theory to another, there is rarely a wholesale replacement of the old theory by the new one. There is retention at the level of empirical laws, at the level of mathematical equations (formalism) as well as at the level of the theoretical properties attributed to the causal agents posited to account for the observable phenomena. The entities posited by the old theory in order to explain the phenomena and those posited by the new one will differ in many respects, but be similar in others. They will nonetheless play the same causal role *vis-à-vis* a set of phenomena, and they will do so by virtue of the fact that they are posited to have some basic properties in common, properties which are taken to be (causally) responsible for the generation of the phenomena. Given that there is some substantive continuity at the theoretical level regarding the properties with which these entities are endowed, we can say that there is *explanatory continuity* between the entities/mechanisms posited by the new theory and those of the superseded one. This continuity is present not only at the level of the phenomena to be explained but at the level of *what is doing the explaining*. The line of thought sketched here is developed in detail in Chapter 5, where realism is defended against the 'pessimistic induction'.

Duhem II: the critique of instrumentalism

Having shown how Duhemian instrumentalism is supposed to work, we must also note that Duhem himself offers three important arguments *against* an instrumentalist understanding of theories.

The theoretician's practice

The first of Duhem's arguments is that instrumentalism contradicts the scientific intuition that theories are not merely means of cataloguing information amassed through experiments. Rather, they aim to promote understanding of the world. Suppose that a physicist follows an instrumentalist's advice that scientific theories are to be understood as mere systematisations of empirical laws. Duhem says that such a physicist would

> at once recognise that all his most powerful and deepest aspirations have been disappointed by the despairing results of his analysis. [For he] cannot make up his mind to see in physical theory merely a set of practical procedures and a *rack filled with tools*. . . . [H]e cannot believe that it merely classifies information accumulated by empirical science without transforming in any way the nature of these facts or without impressing on them a character which experiment alone would not have engraved on it. If there were in physical theory only what his own criticism made him discover in it, he would stop devoting his time and efforts to a work of such a meagre importance.
>
> (1906: 334)

This argument does not aim to bring out the psychological discomfort of the author of an instrumental theory who would feel that the product of his painstaking reconstruction has very little, if any, cognitive value. Rather, it suggests that it is against scientists' pre-philosophical intuitions that the aim of a theory is not to improve our understanding of the world but rather to classify information amassed through experiments in a convenient mathematical framework. Since there is nothing wrong with these intuitions, what needs to be abandoned is *not* these intuitions, but the philosophical theory which contradicts them.

Novel predictions

The revised aim of science is the subject of Duhem's two other arguments. If theories are understood as mere classifications of already known experimental laws, the second argument says, then it is difficult to explain how and why the theory manages to predict *novel* effects. If a theory were just a 'rack filled with tools', it would be hard to understand how it can be 'a prophet for us' (1906: 27). Duhem is justifiably struck by the ability of some scientific theories to predict hitherto unforeseen phenomena; e.g. the prediction of Fresnel's theory of diffraction, that if the light from a source is intercepted by an opaque disk a bright spot will appear at the centre of the shadow of the disk. This 'clairvoyance' of scientific theories would be unnatural to expect – it would be a 'marvellous feat of chance' – if 'the theory was a purely artificial system' which 'fails to hint at any reflection of the real relations among the invisible realities' (ibid.: 28). But this same 'clairvoyance' would be perfectly natural if the principles of the theory 'express profound and real relations among things'. These relations, one can easily imagine, will hold across the domain of the applicability of the theory, and they might reveal novel, hitherto unsuspected, phenomena. Given that theories have been successful prophets for us, if we had to bet on theories being either artificial systems or *'natural classifications'*, we would find it natural to bet on the latter. For Duhem,

> the highest bet of our holding a classification as a natural one is to ask it to indicate in advance things which the future alone will reveal. And when the experiment is made and confirms the predictions obtained from our theory, we feel strengthened in our conviction that the relations established by our reason among abstract notions truly correspond to relations among things.
>
> (1906: 28)[8]

Duhem's point is that the fact that some theories generate *novel* predictions cannot be accounted for on a purely instrumentalist understanding of scientific theories. For how can one expect that an arbitrary (artificial) classification of a set of known experimental laws – i.e. a classification based only on considerations of convenience – will possibly be able to reveal unforeseen phenomena in the world? This might happen by chance. But persistent novel and successful predictions cannot be seriously attributed to mere chance, any more than persistently successful forecasts of the shown face of a tossed coin can be attributed to pure chance. Barring persistent coincidences, an adequate account of the ability of a theory to generate novel predictions can rest only on the claim that the theory has somehow 'latched onto' the world, that its principles and hypotheses correctly describe the mechanisms or processes which generate these phenomena. If, for instance, there were no light-waves of the kind described in Fresnel's theory, and if the behaviour of these waves were unlike that described in this theory, how could Fresnel's theory reveal unforeseen phenomena? Would that not be a fluke? Duhem's conclusion was that theories which generate novel predictions should be understood as *natural classifications* and that the aim of science should be precisely the construction of natural classifications of the phenomena.

The link between successful novel predictions and a theory's tending to be a natural classification is central to Duhem's thought. It is not enough to require a theory to accommodate known facts. What really matters for the assessment of the theory is whether it yields novel predictions which are subsequently confirmed. Any such novel predictive success makes more plausible the thought that the theory tends to be a natural classification. Here is another relevant comment of Duhem, this time concerning the discovery of the planet Neptune:

> If [the theorist] wishes to prove that the principle he has adopted is truly a principle of natural classification of celestial motions, he must show that the observed perturbations are in agreement with those which had been calculated in advance; he has to show how from the course of Uranus he can deduce the existence and position of a new planet, and find Neptune in an assigned direction at the end of his telescope.
>
> (1906: 195)

Searching for unity

Before we try to understand what Duhem means by 'natural classification', let us consider Duhem's third argument against instrumentalism and in favour of natural classifications. It is motivated by the following question: If theories are mere instruments for the classification/systematisation of experimental laws, why should scientists try to unify them in one grand theoretical scheme and offer a coherent overall system within which all phenomena can be embedded?

On the instrumentalist account, one could do equally well with a piece-meal approach. One can have a cluster of different, even contradictory, systems of classification each being suitable for some purposes, or some domain, or some aspects of it, or a single phenomenon, or what have you. Insofar as instrumentalists avoid mixing up different accounts, they can live happily with an array of mutually inconsistent theories. In his instrumentalist moments (e.g. 1908), Duhem seems content with the thought that instrumentalists should take the aim of a unified theoretical system as primitive: good and desirable in its own right, without further justification. In his more realist moments, Duhem argues that if science aims at a natural classification, then unification is the most natural thing to look for. A natural classification cannot possibly be 'an incoherent collection of incompatible theories' (1893: 67), even though each and every theory may save some phenomena. Whatever else it is, nature cannot be such that it allows contradictions to be true of it.

Unification is then seen as a way to remove inconsistencies and to approach what Duhem calls the 'perfect theory'. On a realist account of science, of two contradictory models or theories only the one is true. Hence, if we aim at truth, we must remove contradictions. This happens *either* by rejecting all but one of a set of mutually inconsistent theories *or* by trying to devise a framework which synthesises or unifies apparently contradictory theories, by removing the cause of the conflict. This is the case with the unification of electricity and magnetism with the 'wave' theory of light phenomena. The electromagnetic theory of light became possible when an important incompatibility was removed from the theories of electric and magnetic phenomena and the theories of light. Before Faraday and Maxwell electric and magnetic phenomena were taken to be based on action-at-a-distance, whereas light phenomena were known to be based on framework in which light propagates with finite velocity. The Faraday–Maxwell medium-based laws of the electromagnetic field yielded the notion that electromagnetic action takes time to propagate, and the possibility of showing that light-waves are electromagnetic waves was thereby opened.

Duhem III: between realism and instrumentalism

Duhem's arguments point to the claim that theories should aim to be natural classifications. But what exactly is a natural classification? This is best understood in connection with what Duhem calls the perfect theory. Such a theory 'would be the complete and adequate metaphysical explanation of material things' (1893: 68). The perfect theory would classify experimental laws in a natural way: 'an order which would be the very expression of the metaphysical relations that the essences that cause the laws have among themselves. A perfect theory would give us, in the true sense of the world, a natural classification of laws' (ibid.) Although Duhem talks of meta-physical relations between essences, what he is really referring to are relations between unobservable entities. Remember that for him the atomic hypothesis (as well as any other hypothesis which refers to unobserv-able entities) is a 'metaphysical' hypothesis. 'Metaphysical' for Duhem simply means falling outside the strict scope of experimental verification and observation.

So a perfect theory is a true theory, and a natural classification is what issues from a true theory. There is no reason to suppose that we shall ever attain such a perfect theory. But aiming at it is important in its own right: to the extent that we progress in our endeavour, we improve our under-standing of the world. Duhem's second and third arguments – the arguments from novel predictions and from unity – intend to show that this endeavour can make progress. Or, better, that in light of the confirmed predictions yielded by theories, and in light of the successful unification of distinct theoretical schemes, we can reasonably expect science to track the natural classification of the phenomena. The more predictively successful a theory is, and the more it participates in a unified scheme of things, the more it tends towards a natural classification, i.e. the more likely it is that the world is as the theory says it is. What these arguments offer, then, is a way to increase the likelihood that the relations stated in the theory 'are true relations, showing the connections that really exist among essences' (1893: 68).

Is Duhem's position realist? It is difficult to say, really.[9] On the one hand, Duhem resisted to the very end, refusing to subscribe to atomism and other theories which posited unobservable entities. On the other hand, however, his adherence to natural classifications may be plausibly seen as a realist-enough position, given that Duhem understands 'natural classification' as revealing real relations among *unobservable entities*. But it can be argued that Duhem's realism reaches up only to the structural level, so to speak. A natural classification is such that it gets right the *relations* among unobservable entities, but not necessarily the unobservable entities themselves. This line of thought can be developed into a *prima facie* sustainable realist position, that of so-called *structural realism*. This is the view advocated by Worrall, who traces it back to Duhem and Poincaré. I discuss this position in detail in Chapter 7 (see pp. 147–151).

What is worth stressing here is that Duhem's arguments against instrumentalism are very strong. They suggest that a straightforward instrumentalist understanding of theories leaves too many features of science and scientific theories unexplained. Not only does it leave unexplained the fact that, intuitively, science aims at an understanding of the world; more importantly, it leaves unexplained the fact that scientific theories tend to yield novel predictions as well as that they tend to become part of a unified theoretical scheme of the world. One can plausibly argue that there is a link between improving our understanding of the world and devising a unified theoretical scheme of which apparently disparate scientific theories become part. Hence, one may suggest that there is an intimate link between Duhem's first and third arguments against instrumentalism in that the search for theoretical unification captures and formulates properly the intuition that science aims at a better understanding of the world. I think that, by arguing against instrumentalism, Duhem reaches a position which undermines what he had initially set out to show – that science can proceed without answering the questions: Does there exist a material reality distinct from sensible appearances? And, if so what is the nature of this reality? To be sure, Duhem's arguments do not entail that science has to answer these questions. But they do suggest that our understanding of science, its aim and its structure, would be incomplete and impaired if we did not try to answer these questions, and if, in trying to answer them, we did not rely on the conclusions drawn from an attempt to explain the novel predictive success and the practice of science. Whatever else they do, Duhem's arguments show that the novel predictive success of science is accounted for only on the assumption that science has somehow 'latched onto' an unobservable reality; they show, too, that a realist understanding of theories and the search for unification go hand-in-hand.

There is an important caveat to what I have just said: Duhem presented all of the foregoing arguments as falling totally outside the 'method of physical sciences' (1906: 27, 334–335). This is crucial. When Duhem talks about natural classifications, he is always careful to say that we shall never be in a position to assert conclusively that a theory offers a natural classification. Witness the following:

> but the more complete [the theory] becomes, the more we apprehend that the logical order in which the theory orders experimental laws is the reflection of an ontological order, the more we suspect that the relations it establishes among the data of observation correspond to real relations among things, and the more we feel that theory tends to be natural classification.
>
> (1906: 26–27)

Duhem is very careful in the words he uses: we *apprehend*, we *suspect*, we *feel*. Duhem's point is not just that our judgements about natural classifications are fallible. Rather – and this is the crucial issue – he intends to argue that the claim that theories tend to be natural classifications, plausible though it may sound, cannot be justified (or issued) by scientific method itself.

In response to this, two points are worth making. First, one can indeed conceive of Duhem's arguments in favour of natural classification as *philosophical* arguments. As such, they may fall outside the scope of scientific method. Even so, they are not without rational force. They are arguments based on judgements of plausibility, and plausibility is certainly a reason to prefer one position over another. We return to this issue in Chapter 4 (pp. 72–77), where we shall see that Smart and Maxwell have made a variant of Duhem's argument from novel predictions into a central part of their own defence of realism. Second, I think the real issue between a non-instrumentalist reading of Duhem and the modern scientific realists concerns the credentials of Duhem's second argument against instrumentalism (or, *for* a kind of realism). This is an *explanatory* argument. It argues that if instrumentalism does offer an explanation at all, it is a very poor explanation of a salient feature of scientific theories. As we shall see in detail in Chapter 4, modern realists accept and defend Duhem's argument on the basis that scientists offer explanatory arguments of this form all the time. In fact, scientists employ such explanatory arguments in order to decide which to accept from among a set of rival theories. So, *contrary* to Duhem, realists argue that it is part and parcel of science and its method to rely on ampliative arguments and explanatory considerations in order to form and defend rational belief. This is exactly where the modern defence of scientific realism rests: that the kinds of argument offered by Duhem against instrumentalism can be integral to a defence of scientific realism which utilises precisely those resources and methods that scientists use to evaluate, adopt and defend their theories. This is the main theme of Chapter 4.

We are now ready to tie up a loose end. Having examined instrumentalism in some detail, we may now turn to Carnap's attempts to show that instrumentalism *can be* compatible with some form of realism.

3 Carnap's neutralism

The position of Rudolf Carnap in the scientific realism debate has not yet been fully examined and appreciated. The present chapter will aim to do just this. For the Carnap of the 1950s and early 1960s tried hard to show that there was space for an *irenic* position in the realism debate, a position which could render realist and instrumentalist understandings of scientific theories compatible. In his attempt to develop such a position Carnap took a *structuralist turn*. He re-invented what came to be called the Ramsey-sentence approach to theories, an approach which was first enunciated by the Cambridge philosopher Frank Plumpton Ramsey in the late 1920s, but had not been fully appreciated until Carnap made it popular. As I show in some detail in this chapter, Carnap thought that the Ramsey-sentence approach can form the basis of a position which takes on board the instrumentalist reluctance to accept that theoretical discourse commits to unobservable entities, while it also accommodates the realist view that theories explain and predict observable phenomena by reference to unobservable entities. On the face of it, the very possibility of such a compromise does not seem to make sense. We shall, however, see that Carnap built a *prima facie* case for such a compromise. Yet, the resulting position brings together a weak form of realism, according to which only structural claims about unobservable entities can be known and asserted, and an atypical form of instrumentalism, which does not deny that unobservable entities exist. Having explained Carnap's position in some detail, we shall see that it it open to a damning objection, which was first raised in 1928 by the Cambridge mathematician M. H. A. Newman against Bertrand Russell's own structuralism. The essence of the objection is that the structuralist claim that only the structure of the unobservable world can be known is either false or else trivial. The message of this chapter is that any meaningful defence of realism presupposes the view that the world is already 'carved up' in natural kinds, i.e. that it already possess a natural-kind structure.

The two-language model

In the work of the mature Carnap, the idea that theoretical discourse has 'excess' or 'surplus' meaning is reflected in his representation of a scientific theory, whose *locus classicus* is Carnap's 'The Methodological Character of Theoretical Concepts' (1956) – henceforth MCTC. There, Carnap advances a general logico-linguistic framework L in which scientific theories can be developed. The total language of science is divided into two sub-languages: an observational language, L_O, which is completely interpreted, and a theoretical language, L_T, the descriptive vocabulary of which, V_T, consists of theoretical terms. L_O is such that the values of its variables are concrete observable things (what he called the 'requirement of nominalism') and their domain is finite (what he called the 'requirement of finitism').

The theoretical sub-language L_T is much richer: it contains a type-theoretic logic with an infinite sequence of domains $D^0, D^1, D^2, \ldots$, where D^n is the domain of the nth level.[1] Each variable and each constant belong to a definite level. D^0 comprises the infinite sequence $O^0, O^0, O^0, \ldots$, which can be thought of as the domain of natural numbers. Then the domain of each D^{n+1} is the domain of all subclasses of D^n. L_T contains the whole of classical mathematics, i.e. expressions and variables for all objects that appear in classical mathematics.

This strong language has a certain theoretical advantage which Carnap is keen to exploit: all physical concepts occurring in theories can be shown to be represented by elements of D. L_T can accommodate a space–time coordinate system such that each space–time point is assigned a 4-tuple of numbers. Physical magnitudes are introduced as functions from space–time points (quadruples of numbers) to numerical values (numbers). Physical objects (e.g. a particle) are conceived of as four-dimensional regions inside of which certain physical magnitudes have a certain distribution.

Within L, a scientific theory is characterised as a set T of theoretical axioms (the so-called theoretical- or T-postulates) and a set C of correspondence rules (or C-postulates) which are mixed sentences connecting the theoretical vocabulary V_T with the observational vocabulary V_O. So, a theory is the set of all logical consequences of the conjunction of T- and C-postulates. The set of T-postulates and the V_T-terms get some partial interpretation by means of the C-postulates.

In this setting, theories have 'excess content' precisely because they make full use of irreducible (and ineliminable) theoretical terms and theoretical postulates. The latter, together with C-postulates, play a dual role: on the one hand, they contribute to the meaning of the T-terms of the language; but, on the other hand, they contribute to the empirical content of the theory and assert factual relations (e.g. they state basic laws of nature).

Metaphysical versus empirical realism

When Carnap enters the debate on the existential implications of scientific theories, his main position is close to Hempel's half-way house (see pp. 15–16): good old empiricism might be in danger, if it accepts that theoretical entities are real in the sense of having independent existence. Is this not just another metaphysical claim? What I try to show in this chapter is that Carnap's own aim is to defend a sort of *genuine neutralism* with respect to the question of the existential implications of scientific theories: no ontological commitments to unobservable entities are dictated by scientific theories, but scientific theories are not merely instruments for 'prediction and control' either. Can this neutral stance be achieved, while verificationism is abandoned and the 'excess content' of theories is asserted? Although I shall answer this question in the negative, it is instructive to see exactly how Carnap strove to achieve this aim.

As is well known, Carnap wanted to dismiss ontological questions, at least if understood in the traditional metaphysical sense: 'The usual ontological questions about the "reality" (in an alleged metaphysical sense) of numbers, classes, space–time points, bodies, minds, etc. are pseudo questions without cognitive content' (1956: 44–45). However, he does accept that 'there is a good sense of the word "real", viz. that used in everyday language and in science'. He suggests that there are two different kinds of existential question, and two senses of 'real' ('although', he noted, 'in actual practice there is no sharp line between them'). Within L_O, to claim that a certain observable event is real is tantamount to claiming that a sentence of L_O describing this event is true.

When it comes to L_T, Carnap points out that the situation is more complicated. Questions concerning the reality of a *specific event* described in theoretical terms (e.g. questions about the reality of a particular configuration of electrons moving in a specified way) are treated like those in L_O: 'to accept a statement of reality of this kind [i.e. the reality of an event described in theoretical terms] is the same as to accept the sentence of L_T describing the event' (1956: 45). However, questions concerning the reality of a system of entities in general, e.g. of electrons in general, or of the electromagnetic field in general, are 'ambiguous'. But, Carnap adds, we can give them a genuinely scientific significance

> if we agree to understand the acceptance of the reality, say, of the electromagnetic field in the classical sense as the acceptance of a language L_T and in it a term, say 'E', and a set of postulates T which include the classical laws of the electromagnetic field (say, the Maxwell equations) as postulates for 'E'. For an observer to 'accept' the postulates of T means here not simply to take T as an uninterpreted calculus, but to use T together with specified rules of correspondence C for guiding his expectations by deriving predictions about future observable events from observed events with the help of T and C.
>
> (1956: 45)

Carnap refrains from saying anything about the issue of the factual reference of theoretical terms, although he acknowledges that *t*-terms have excess meaning, and that they contribute to the experiential output of the theory. He also distances himself from the strict instrumentalist view of theories which, as we saw in Chapter 2, takes the theoretical 'superstructure' to be a merely *syntactic construct*. Yet, he seems keen to endorse double existential standards: assertions about observable events as well as assertions about particular theoretical entities are truth-valued; and, if true, they issue in certain existential commitments. But, he claims, assertions concerning the reality of a system of entities as a whole are of a different kind: they should be understood as questions concerning the acceptance of a certain logico-linguistic framework.

The reader will note that Carnap's 'double existential standards' concerning theoretical entities resonates with his external–internal questions distinction as this was laid out in his 'Empiricism, Semantics and Ontology' (1950 [1956]), henceforth ESO. In this piece, Carnap attempts to disperse the view that talking about and quantifying over certain entities implies a metaphysical commitment to them, a commitment to their *independent* existence. His suggestion is that questions of the existence of a certain kind of entity can be understood in two different ways: either as *external* or as *internal* questions. External questions are meant to be metaphysical in nature: they concern the existence or reality of 'the system of entities as a whole' (ESO: 206). Answering questions such as 'Are there entities of such and such nature (e.g. numbers, properties, classes, etc.)?' is taken to presuppose that the existence of such entities can be asserted or denied independently of a certain discourse. *Qua* external, such questions require that one must first establish the existence of such entities before one starts talking about them. For Carnap, all this is fundamentally wrong. No metaphysical insight into their nature is needed for the introduction of a new kind of entity. Instead, he argues, all that is needed is the adoption/construction of a certain linguistic framework the linguistic resources of which make it possible to talk about such entities. Once such a framework is adopted, questions about the existence, or reality, of the relevant entities lose any apparent metaphysical significance. They become *internal*: it follows from the very adoption of the framework that one is committed to the existence of such entities. Hence, asserting their existence becomes analytic. On this way of looking at things, what remains of the external questions relates to a certain *practical decision* to adopt that linguistic framework. No facts about the world, Carnap says, will ever force us to adopt a particular framework – least of all the alleged independent existence, or reality, of the talked-about entities. Only pragmatic considerations are relevant: the efficiency, fruitfulness and simplicity of each proposed linguistic framework. Take, for instance, questions of the existence of space–time points. Carnap notes that, seen as external questions, they are either metaphysical pseudo-questions ('Are there (really) space–time points?') or else practical questions concerning the adoption of some framework for the development of scientific theories such that its variables range over space–time points. Once, however, this framework is adopted, it becomes an analytic truth that there are space–time points (ESO: 212–213).

What exactly does it mean to introduce a new framework, or, as Carnap puts it, a system of entities? He specifies two conditions:

1   the introduction of a new general term T (e.g. 'number', 'property', 'proposition', etc.) for the new kind of entity, so that one can make statements of the form 'ϕ is T';
2   the introduction of a new type of variable that ranges over the new entities, so that one can make statements of the sort '$\forall \phi$ if ϕ is so-and so, then ... ' (see ESO: 213–214).

After the new general term and the new type of variable have been introduced in the framework, we can ask internal questions about these entities, which admit of either analytic or synthetic answers.

Given this analysis, it is therefore tempting to argue that when it comes to the question of the *reality of theoretical entities* Carnap just re-iterates and applies the distinction between external and internal questions. Seen as an external/metaphysical issue, the existence or reality of theoretical unobservable entities is a pseudo-issue. Seen as an internal issue, it follows analytically from the adoption of a framework whose variables quantify over theoretical entities. The existence of theoretical entities as a *whole* (e.g. electrons) is a framework principle, while the existence of *particular* entities (e.g. of a certain configuration of electrons) is an empirical issue which is being raised and investigated after the electron-framework has been accepted.

In order to avoid unnecessary complications, I refrain from discussing the fact–framework distinction. I am happy just to grant, for the sake of the argument, that an appeal to this distinction frees Carnap from metaphysical commitments.[2] (But a few brief comments are in order in connection with Feigl's use of this distinction, see pp. 45–46). What I want to show is that even if this distinction were granted, Carnap's neutralism would still face a problem. For suppose we do dismiss as a pseudo-issue the allegedly metaphysical aspect of the existence of theoretical entities: still, it would seem, Carnap's empiricism should be happy with internal existential claims concerning physical unobservable entities. This is certainly a claim that instrumentalists would not accept. Hence, the alleged neutrality of Carnap's empiricism is betrayed. In sum, why is Carnap's position not what realists have always argued for?

To highlight this query we need to focus on a different, but related, distinction that Carnap drew: the distinction between *metaphysical* and *empirical realism*. As Parrini (1994: 262) notes, in Carnap's early writings this distinction is depicted as follows. Claims about metaphysical reality pertain to traditional metaphysical questions of existence as conducted, say, between realists, idealists and phenomenalists: do material objects exist in a mind-independent way, or not? However, one can dismiss such questions or issues and still wonder about the *empirical reality* of an object: is it real, or is it an illusion, a dream, a legend, etc.? The metaphysical–empirical distinction re-appears briefly in Carnap's later writings, too. This time, however, Carnap's usage is motivated by Feigl's pleas for the adoption of empirical realism. Feigl says:

> The term 'real' is employed in a clear sense and usually with good reason in daily life and science to designate that which is located in space–time and which is a link in the chains of causal relations. It is thus contrasted with the illusory, the fictitious and the purely conceptual. The reality, in this sense, of rocks and trees, of stars and atoms, of radiations and forces, of human minds and social groups, of historical events and economic processes, is capable of empirical test.
>
> (1943 [1949]: 16)

For Feigl, empiricism should extend to empirical realism. And this carries with it commitments to the empirical reality of middle-sized material objects as well as to scientific unobservables.

Feigl's 'semantic realism' – explained in Chapter 1 – was proposed as 'a corrected form and refinement of the empirical realism held by some logical positivists or empiricists' (Feigl 1950: 50). For him the semantic notion of reference captures the, as it were, residue of valid claims about independent existence: to say that electrons exist is to say that the term 'electron' has factual reference, that there are things in the world which are the referents of the term 'electron'. Unobservable entities are no less real than observable entities, given that, as Feigl put it, 'they are on a par within the nomological framework' of modern science (ibid.). Having thus explicated what it is for an entity to be real, whether or not it should be considered to be real depends on whether or not this entity is an indispensable and irreducible element of the well-confirmed nomological framework of science.[3]

Feigl's metaphysical–empirical distinction seems to bear some resemblance to Carnap's external–internal distinction. In fact, in ESO Carnap refers the reader to Feigl (1950) 'for a closely related point of view on these questions [how do we adopt a framework?]' (1950 [1956]: 214). And, conversely, in his own defence of semantic realism, Feigl refers the reader to Carnap (1946 [1949]: 345), where Carnap says: 'I am using here the customary realistic language as it is used in everyday life and in science; this use does not imply acceptance of realism as a metaphysical thesis but only what Feigl calls "empirical realism".' More generally, Feigl, too, claims that the adoption of the empirical realist 'frame' is not itself subject to empirical confirmation. Rather, he takes it to suggest itself as a basic convention. He notes that his choice of this framework rests, ultimately, on a pragmatic decision to adopt the realistic framework as a basis for the explanation of the phenomena: this framework is chosen because it is methodologically fruitful (cf. Feigl 1950: 57).

How threatening to the cogency of the realist position is Feigl's claim that the choice of the framework of empirical realism is ultimately conventional? Conventions do involve decisions, but these decisions are not necessarily arbitrary. If it makes sense at all to say that we can *choose* a language, the language choice is always relative to an aim. Languages are set up and chosen, if at all, in order to communicate, convey certain information, or capture certain facts. Now, relative to the aim for which we want the language, not *all* language-choices are equally good. Suppose that we face a choice between a linguistic framework which admits theoretical concepts and one that does not. Suppose, for instance, that we face a choice between a realistic language, (one that admits of theoretical terms which purport to refer to unobservable entities) and a language in which theories are formulated without theoretical terms (e.g. a language in which Craig-theorem-style theories are formulated; see pp. 22–23). The choice between the two frameworks is far from arbitrary and conventional. Relative to the aim of explaining observable phenomena, the choice is decisive: only a realistic framework has the resources to adequately explain the phenomena. One may, however, object that even if this argument is right the choice of the aim is still a matter of decision. In particular, the point may be that adopting the explanation of the observable phenomena as an aim is *itself* a conventional matter. To this I reply by noting the suggestion made by Grover Maxwell (1962) that, when it comes to the adoption of a linguistic framework suitable for developing scientific theories, a *condition of adequacy* is that it should allow for the development of explanations of the phenomena. For otherwise the framework is too narrow. It may well be able to capture known observable phenomena and regularities, but it will typically be unable to capture hitherto unforeseen observable phenomena and regularities. In particular, it will typically leave out those novel empirical predictions which can be established only after theoretical explanations of the phenomena have been formulated; that is, those regularities whose existence in nature can be ascertained only after a theoretical hypothesis has predicted them. Now, if the explanation of observable phenomena *requires* theoretical concepts and commitments to theoretical entities, then, as again Maxwell (1962: 136) suggests, we need nothing else before we claim that 'the facts about the ("theoretical") entities that we invoke in our explanations comprise an indispensable realm of the totality of "facts about the world"'. There is nothing conventional in this claim. The burden of proof is clearly on the non-realists: they must produce a framework which fulfils the condition of adequacy but does not quantify over such entities. And given that no such framework has been produced, the adoption of a realist framework seems well-motivated and inevitable. In fact, as we have already seen in Chapter 1, it was the failure to devise a framework that dispensed with theoretical terms which, in the first place, led to the process of the liberalisation of empiricism.

So, whatever else it does, empirical realism does imply strong enough realist commitments: understood from the empirical realist point of view, scientific theories imply commitments to unobservable entities no less than to observable ones. Besides, unobservable entities are said to exist independently of our capacity to gather direct evidence for their existence. Hence, their independent existence can be asserted, albeit the claim is empirical (in Feigl's sense) rather than metaphysical. And, for Feigl at least, not only is this a realist enough position, but it is the way empiricism should go.

Early structuralism

Although Carnap paid lip-service to empirical realism, he did take his neutralist stance very seriously. To this end, he aimed to offer an empiricist account of scientific theories which did not imply commitments to physical unobservable entities. In order to support this claim, I now discuss briefly the way Carnap tackles the 'problem of the admissibility of theoretical entities' in his MCTC (1956: 43–47).

Recall (p. 41) that the logico-linguistic framework L has two types of variable. Those of L_O range over observable events. But the variables of L_T are taken to range over the domain D, the domain of classical mathematics. So, the variables of L_T are taken to range over *mathematical entities*.

Carnap notes that this remark about variables ranging over natural numbers, classes of them, etc., 'should not be taken literally' but as a 'didactic help' (1956: 45–46). But in the end, all this does not matter much to him. For, the important feature of the denumerable domain D^0 of the language L_T is that it has a 'particular kind of structure, viz. a sequence with an initial but no terminal member' (1956: 46). This structure is isomorphic to the structure of natural numbers. Hence, the variables of L_T range over the elements of a certain structure which is isomorphic to the structure of natural numbers. The natural numbers can, then, conveniently be taken to be the domain of quantification of the variables of L_T. What really matters, however, is the *structure* of the domain of the theory, not its elements. As he puts it: 'the structure can be uniquely specified but the elements of the structure cannot. Not because we are ignorant of their nature; rather because there is no question of their nature' (ibid.).

I take this to be a rather bold, if still vague, subscription to structuralism: what matters for the functioning of theories is the specification of the structure of the domain of L_T and, therefore, of the theory TC which is couched in terms of L_T. Since classical mathematics is adequate for the representation of any physical concept, a theory TC is presented as exemplifying a certain logico-mathematical structure which gets connected to the observable world via C-postulates. Once we get clear about the structure of the domain of the theory, the remaining questions about the kinds of entities designated by the theoretical expressions of TC lose their significance: we may take them to be mathematical entities (ultimately, natural numbers, classes of them, etc.) 'as long us we are not misled by these formulations into asking metaphysical pseudo questions' (Carnap 1956: 46).

So, Carnap's early structuralism emerges as an extension of his empiricism and seems to underscore his neutralism. Theoretical concepts are accommodated within the language of science. Their 'excess content' is guaranteed by the fact that they are not reducible to observational concepts. But the appeal to structuralism seems to free Carnap from any explicitly realist account of the existential implications of scientific theories. More importantly, it seems to free him from any *internal* commitments to physical unobservable entities as the referents of theoretical terms. For it implies that what really matters is the logico-mathematical structure of the domain of the theory and not what the nodes in this structure may be.

Carnap meets Ramsey

Here starts a fascinating episode in the history of logical empiricism. In an attempt to develop his structuralism and defend his neutralism, Carnap re-invents the Ramsey-sentence approach, what he called the *existentialised form of theories*. But it was Hempel who pointed out to Carnap that all this had already been put forward by Frank Ramsey.

Hempel published his 'The Theoretician's Dilemma' (henceforth TD) in 1958. As was noted in Chapter 2 (pp. 25–26), one of the main themes of this piece is the philosophical significance of Craig's theorem. But its real novelty lies in its account of the Ramsey-sentence. To the best of my knowledge, Hempel was the first among the community of the logical empiricists to recognise and discuss the philosophical and methodological significance of the Ramsey-sentence. My suspicion is that Hempel became acquainted with Ramsey's seminal piece 'Theories' (1929) after reading Braithwaite's book *Scientific Explanation*. This was first published in 1953 – although its content is based on the Tarner Lectures which Braithwaite delivered in Cambridge in 1946. Chapter 3, 'The Status of the Theoretical Terms of a Science', contains a thorough discussion of Ramsey's paper 'Theories'.

When Hempel's TD appeared in print, Carnap was working on his reply to Hempel's contribution to the volume *The Philosophy of Rudolf Carnap*, edited by Paul Arthur Schilpp. Hempel sent this piece to Carnap in July 1954, but as yet, it contained no reference to Ramsey's ideas. In the meantime, however, in June 1956 to be exact, Carnap received the manuscript of Hempel's TD. By an amazing coincidence, Carnap immediately savoured sections 6 and 7 of TD, which discussed Carnap's MCTC and related directly to the issues raised in Hempel's 1963 contribution to Schilpp's volume. Being too busy, Carnap left the rest of Hempel's piece for later. Yet it was not until the end of section 9 that Hempel introduced and discussed, for the first time in this kind of literature, the Ramsey-sentence approach, and coined the term 'Ramsey-sentence'. Carnap had to wander for roughly two more years before he happened to read section 9 and, all of a sudden, found what he thought was the ultimate solution to a number of problems that had bothered him for some time, including the much-wanted and elusive explication of analyticity in a theoretical language and the explication of the early structuralism of MCTC. It is no surprise, then, that Carnap was so delighted and thankful when, in February 1958, he wrote to Hempel:

February 12, 1958

Dear Lante:

In the last week I have thought much about you, your ideas, and writings, because I was working at the Reply to your essay for the Schilpp volume. On the basis of your article 'Dilemma' I reworked a good deal of it and some new ideas came in. I think this article of yours is a very valuable work which helps greatly in clarifying the whole problem situation. Originally I read only §§ 6 and 7 because you had commented that they refer to my article on theoretical concepts. Unfortunately I postponed reading the remainder (and thus the last two sections) because I was too busy with other replies for the Schilpp volume.

The case of the Ramsey-sentence is a very instructive example [of] how easily one deceives oneself with respect to the originality of ideas. At Feigl's Conference here in 1955 [the Los Angeles Conference], where Pap, Bohnert and others were present, I represented the existentialized form of a theory as an original recent idea of my own. Sometime after the Conference Bohnert said that he had now remembered having found this idea some years ago and having explained it to me in a letter to Chicago. Although I could not find that letter in the files, I had no doubt that Bohnert was correct, so I ceded the priority to him. He thought more about it and became more and more enthusiastic about this form and he even gave up his old thesis project (on dispositions) and developed new ideas [on] how to use the existentialized form of the theory in order to clarify a lot of methodological problems in science; this he intended to work out as his thesis. Then, I believe it was last summer, when I read the rest of your 'Dilemma', I was struck by your reference to Ramsey. I looked it up at the place you referred to in Ramsey's book, and there it was, neatly underlined by myself. Thus there was no doubt that I had read it before in Ramsey's book. I guess that was in the Vienna time or the Prague time (do you remember whether we talked about it in Prague?). At any rate, I had completely forgotten both the idea and its origin. Now I am glad that your article saved me from claiming this idea as my own, and it would have been very bad for Bohnert if he had claimed it as his own in a thesis, and then the people in Philadelphia might have found that it is in Ramsey's book. . . . When I began some weeks ago to rework the Reply to your essay for the Schilpp volume, for the first time I put together in my mind on the one hand the Ramsey idea and on the other my proposal (which I had almost forgotten in the meantime) of splitting up a set of reduction sentences into an analytic and a synthetic component, which you explained in your Schilpp paper. Then it suddenly occurred to me that this old idea of mine could be generalised by taking the Ramsey sentence instead of what I called the representative sentence of the set of reduction sentences. In this way I found the solution for the problem of dividing postulates into meaning-postulates and synthetic P-postulates, and this serves then easily for an explanation of analyticity for sentences with theoretical terms.

(Carnap Archive 102–13–53)

What is the 'existentialized form of a theory' to which Carnap refers? In the protocol of the Los Angeles Conference, Carnap is reported to have extended Craig's results to 'type theory, (involving introducing theoretical terms as auxiliary constants standing for existentially generalised functional variables in 'long' sentences containing only observational terms as true constants)' (Feigl Archive 04–172–02: 14). He is also reported to have shown that '[a]n observational theory can be formed which will have the same deductive observational content as any given theory using non-observational terms. (Namely, by existentially generalising non-observation terms)' (ibid.: 19). There should be no doubt that, inspired by the Craig result, Carnap re-invented the Ramsey-sentence approach. But in writing his MCTC he made no use of it. The nearest we get to this existentialised form is Carnap's early structuralism. Although Carnap must have read Ramsey's paper 'Theories', the only reference to Ramsey's work that he makes prior to 1958 is about Ramsey's views on the foundations of mathematics.

The first public announcement of Carnap's new views was his paper 'Beobachtungssprache und Theoretische Sprache' ('Observation Language and Theoretical Language') which was published in German in *Dialectica* in 1958 and reprinted in a *festschrift* to Paul Bernays in 1959. This piece was not translated into English until 1975. Carnap was so thrilled with his new views that he published them in at least three more places, delivered lectures on them and conference addresses. All these were conducted in the same period, from 1958 to 1961, although some appeared as late as 1966. Let me give a brief account of their provenance. Carnap's reply to Hempel's piece in the Schilpp volume was finished in 1958 but did not appear until 1963. Then, in the academic year 1958–59, Carnap gave a lecture course entitled 'Philosophical Foundations of Physics' in which, in Lecture 14 delivered on 6 January 1959, he presented his new views. This lecture course was the basis of his book *The Philosophical Foundations of Physics* which appeared in 1966, although the chapter on the Ramsey-sentence was written in 1961 and finalised in 1964. In December 1959, there was his (still unpublished) address 'Theoretical Concepts in Science', delivered at a symposium in Santa Barbara, on 'Carnap's Views on Theoretical Concepts in Science'.[4] Then, in May 1960, Carnap finished his piece 'On the Use of Hilbert's

ε-operator in Scientific Theories', which appeared in 1961 in a *festschrift* to A. A. Fraenkel.

Not all of these publications say exactly the same thing. In fact, their slight and more important differences alike reflect Carnap's attempt to understand and appreciate the full philosophical significance of the Ramsey-sentence approach and of the use to which it can be put. What is worth stressing is that Carnap thought he had found in the Ramsey-sentence approach a way to tackle all the major methodological problems that had bothered him for so many years: an explication of analyticity for theoretical language, a defence of some form of meaning atomism[5] and a defence of his own neutralist empiricism.

The remainder of this chapter focuses on this third issue.

Structuralism existentialised

In order to get the Ramsey-sentence $^R(TC)$ of a theory TC we replace all theoretical constants with distinct variables $\{u_i\}$, and then we bind these variables by placing an equal number of existential quantifiers $\exists u_i$ in front of the resulting formula. So, suppose that the theory TC is represented as $TC(t_1, \ldots, t_n; o_1, \ldots, o_m)$, where TC is a purely logical $m+n$-predicate. The Ramsey-sentence $^R(TC)$ of TC is: $\exists u_1 \exists u_2 \ldots \exists u_n TC(u_1, \ldots, u_n; o_1, \ldots, o_m)$. For simplicity let us say that the T-terms of TC form the n-tuple $t = <t_1, \ldots, t_n>$, and the o-terms of TC form the m-tuple $o = <o_1, \ldots, o_m>$. Then, $^R(TC)$ takes the more convenient form: $\exists u\, TC(u,o)$.

One can show that a sentence S couched in observational vocabulary follows from the theory if and only if it follows also from the Ramsey-sentence of the theory. Ramsey did not prove this, but Carnap did.[6] But exactly *what* does the Ramsey-sentence say? Ramsey himself says very little by way of explication (see Ramsey 1929). He starts by noting that theories are used to express judgements, i.e. to make truth-valued assertions. But he adds that the latter pertain only to the 'laws and consequences' of the theory, 'the theory being simply a language in which they are clothed, and which we can use without working out the laws and consequences' (1929: 120). And, finally, he points out: 'The best way to write our theory seems to be this $(\exists \alpha, \beta, \gamma)$: dictionary $\cdot$ [and] axioms' (ibid.), where α, β, γ stand for the propositional functions of theoretical language (Ramsey's 'secondary system') (1929: 103).

I think Ramsey's insight is the following. From an empiricist perspective what really matters is the empirical content of the theory. Yet, in presenting a theory, one typically uses theoretical terms and predicates. But one need not treat them as names. This is not required for the legitimate use of the theory. One can simply treat the propositional functions (i.e. theoretical terms and predicates) of the 'secondary system' as *genuine variables* which are, however, bound by existential quantifiers so that the resulting construction is a sentence – as opposed to an open formula. Being a sentence, the resulting construction is truth-valuable. Hence, it can be used to express a judgement. However, the Ramsey-sentence $\exists u\ TC(u,o)$ of the theory implies more than the empirical content of the original theory: it implies that not all statements of the form 'u stands in relation TC to o' are false, and hence it implies that TC is realised. In other words, it implies that there are classes (and classes of classes) which realise the Ramsey-sentence. But the Ramsey-sentence does not commit one to the existence of some *particular* set of such entities. On Ramsey's view, the cognitive (i.e. truth-valuable) content of the theory is captured by its empirical content together with the abstract claim of realisation.

So, Ramsey suggests that the use to which empiricists put a theory can be well-captured by the weaker formulation $\exists u\ TC(u,o)$, instead of the stronger formulation $TC(t,o)$. To be sure, the weaker formulation goes beyond strict empiricism. But the entities which realise the Ramsey-sentence are to be taken purely existentially. What exactly these entities are is a separate issue – one that, Ramsey suggests, we do not have to deal with in order to use the theory and to understand what it says about the observable world. As he puts it: 'We can say, therefore, that the incompleteness of the "propositions" of the secondary system affects our *disputes* but not our *reasoning*' (1929: 121). The point here is that although two parties may disagree over what exactly realises the Ramsey-sentence, they can both use the very same Ramsey-sentence to derive observational consequences. Ramsey is quite clear in taking the second-order variables purely extensionally. He stresses: 'Here it is evident that α, β, γ are to be taken purely extensionally. Their extensions may be filled with intensions or not, but this is irrelevant to what can be deduced in the primary system' (ibid.: 120).

Braithwaite – who publicised Ramsey's views – takes it that Ramsey's way to deal with theoretical discourse is a compromise between the realist claim that theories are true – that, say, electrons exist – and those empiricists who, although they do *not deny* that theoretical entities are real, are reluctant to affirm that the theoretical terms featuring in the deductive system of contemporary physics have factual reference (Braithwaite 1953: 80–81). According to Braithwaite (1953: 79), the Ramsey way of explaining the status of a theoretical concept, in this instance 'electron', goes as follows:

> There is a property E (called 'being an electron') which is such that certain higher-level propositions about this property are true, and from these higher-level propositions there follow certain lowest-level propositions which are empirically testable. Nothing is asserted about the 'nature' of this property E; all that is asserted is that the property E exists, i.e. that there instances of E, namely electrons.

Braithwaite says of theoretical concepts that they should be introduced by the locution: 'There exist properties X, Y, Z, which are such that, etc.' This simply means, first, that even when we take the theory to be a deductive system, the theory can still be taken to imply the existence of properties which realise the theory, without, however, specifying anything about these properties other than that they exist; and, second, that we can write down an existential statement in order to make the relevant commitments explicit. Where the original theory (deductive system) uses the term 'electron', Braithwaite says that the theory asserts that there exists a class of entities such that ... observable phenomena ..., a class which is referred to in the theory by the term 'electron'. Theoretical concepts are not thereby dispensed with; they are just being talked about in a more indefinite way, i.e. by using existentially bound variables instead of names.[7]

I doubt, however, that Braithwaite's interpretation of Ramsey is the compromise between realism and empiricism that it was advertised to be. An empiricist who does not deny the existence of theoretical entities, but who is also unwilling to accept that theories imply existential commitments to physical unobservable entities, would not be moved by Braithwaite's account. For the latter presupposes that, apart from the individuals of the domain of the theory, there are also theoretical properties. This is already beyond a strict empiricist understanding of scientific theories, where theoretical terms are not taken to designate theoretical entities. The only apparent difference between a fully interpreted realist account of a theory and the Braithwaite line is that, instead of naming the properties that satisfy the theory, Braithwaite merely asserts that there exist such theoretical properties. Empiricists need not deny that, but they simply have to refrain from affirming it in order to disagree with realists.

What Carnap offers, by way of interpretation of Ramsey-sentences, is a rather radical reading which aims to serve his neutralism. Carnap does not want to make the Ramsey-sentence approach too close to realism. So, he takes it that theoretical terms are replaced by genuine variables which range over *whatever n-tuples of entities* may realise the Ramsey-sentence of the theory. Following Ramsey, he adopts an extensional understanding of the range of the variables which does not have them extending over classes of theoretical entities (nor, in particular, of theoretical properties). Where the Ramsey-sentence says that there are non-empty classes of entities which are related to observable entities by the relations given in the original theory, Carnap suggests that we are at liberty to think of these classes as classes of 'mathematical objects'.

After the development of the Ramsey-sentence approach in his *Dialectica* paper, Carnap still stresses that the theoretical language L_T does not demand quantification over physical theoretical entities. *T*-terms can be thought of as designating *mathematical entities*, which, however, are physically characterised 'so that they have the relations to the observable processes established by the *C*-postulates while simultaneously satisfying the conditions given in the *T*-postulates' (1958: 81).

By way of example, Carnap notes that the constant 'n_p', defined as 'the cardinal number of planets', although descriptive, designates a natural number which belongs to the domain D^0. The number n_p is identical with the number 9, yet the identity statement '$n_p = 9$' is *synthetic*: the world contributes in deciding whether it is true. Carnap does not assert the truism that descriptive constants can refer to mathematical objects. His point is that since to any (type of) descriptive theoretical constant of L_T there corresponds an extensionally identical (type of) mathematical function, one can take the mathematical entities designated by these functions to be the extensions of the descriptive constants (cf. Carnap Archive: Philosophical Foundations of Physics, Lecture 14: 42).

To be sure, in more realistic cases we do not know what the extension of a descriptive constant is. For instance, take 'E' to be a descriptive functor standing for the electric field vector. The statement $E(x_1, x_2, x_3, t) = (u_1, u_2, u_3)$ asserts that the value of the electric field at point (x_1, x_2, x_3) at time t is a triple of real numbers, which are the values of the components of the electric field vector at that space–time point. We have no clue as to what the extension of this function is, as this would require us knowing the actual distribution of the electric field throughout space and time. What we normally do is find the values of this function for particular set-ups or regions, e.g. the distribution of the field in a certain conductor. In any case, Carnap suggests, we do know that 'E' is of a certain *logical type*: it is a function from quadruples of reals to triples of reals. Therefore, we know that *there is* a mathematical function f which is extensionally identical with E, i.e. E and f have the same value for any argument: for any x_1, x_2, x_3, t, $E(x_1, x_2, x_3, t) = f(x_1, x_2, x_3, t)$. This is an identity statement, like the statement '$n_p = 9$'. Both statements, '$E = f$' and '$n_p = 9$', express an extensional identity between a descriptive constant and a mathematical one, and both are synthetic, too (Carnap Archive: Philosophical Foundations of Physics, lecture 11: 40–41). So although the Ramsey-sentence has 'excess content', the existentially quantified variables do not range over theoretical entities but rather over mathematical entities. This 'excess content' characterises physical mathematical entities. Does this move secure Carnap's neutralism?

Not surprisingly, Feigl thought that with this move Carnap advances some sort of 'syntactical positivism'.[8] In a letter of 21 July 1958 (Carnap Archive 102–07–06) to Carnap, Feigl exclaimed: '[We] are taken aback by your "syntactical positivism", i.e. mathematical interpretation of theoretical concepts in empirical sciences. We shall attempt more "realistic" interpretation, – if this be metaphysics, make the least of it!'

In his reply of 4 August 1958 (Carnap Archive) Carnap admits that the formulations in the *Dialectica* paper 'are really too short to give a clear picture of my view' and, for further clarification, he refers Feigl to his (Carnap's) reply to Hempel – 'Hempel on Scientific Theories' – in the Schilpp volume. Yet, his reply to Hempel, which was finished after the *Dialectica* paper in February 1958, is no more illuminating: 'the Ramsey-sentence does indeed refer to theoretical entities by the use of abstract variables'. But he immediately adds that 'these entities are not unobservable physical objects like atoms, electrons, etc., but rather (at least in the form of the theoretical language which I have chosen in [MCTC] §vii] purely logico-mathematical entities, e.g. natural numbers, classes of such, classes of classes, etc.' (1963: 963). On this reading, the Ramsey-sentence says that 'the observable events in the world are such that there are numbers, classes of such, etc., which are correlated with the events in a prescribed way and which have among themselves certain relations; and this assertion is clearly a factual statement about the world' (ibid.). But, surely we cannot take literally this idea that mathematical entities are correlated with observable phenomena? What, then, does Carnap mean?

The distinctive feature of the Ramsey-sentence of a theory is that it preserves the structure (or form) of the original theory. So, it seems right to interpret Carnap as suggesting the following: when one accepts $^R(TC)$, one is *not* committed to the existence of physical theoretical entities. All one is committed to is

- the observable consequences of the original theory TC;
- a certain logico-mathematical structure in which (a description of) the observable phenomena are embedded; and
- certain abstract existential claims to the effect that there are (non-empty classes of) entities which realise the structure.

Since in L_T to each physical concept there is an extensionally identical mathematical concept, the entities which realise the Ramsey-sentence, if true, can be taken to be sequences of mathematical entities.

Still, Carnap has not moved far enough from instrumentalism, or from what Feigl called 'syntactical positivism'. For, in essence, theories are still taken to be nothing but mathematical models in which observable phenomena are embedded. So, in his attempt to keep his distance from scientific realism, Carnap seems to betray his neutralism, once more. As one might expect, Carnap was unhappy with the idea of 'syntactical positivism'. 'There is no "positivism" here', he says in his letter to Feigl (4 August 1958). And he explains:

[T]he entities to which the variables in the Ramsey-sentence refer are characterised not purely logically, but in a descriptive way; and this is the essential point. These entities are identical with mathematical entities only in the customary extensional way of speaking; see my example in square brackets on p.10.[9] In an intensional language (in my own thinking I use mostly one of this kind) there is an important difference between the intension 9 and the intension n_p. The former is L-determinate .... the latter is not. Thus, if by 'logical' or 'mathematical' we mean 'L-determinate', then the entities to which the variables in the Ramsey-sentence refer are not logical. I hope this will relieve your uneasiness.

(Carnap Archive 102–07–05)

Carnap's reply to Feigl can be clarified by looking at his notion of *L*-determinateness. This is introduced in his *Meaning and Necessity* (1947 [1956]: 72–73) and aims to capture the difference between descriptive and logical designators. A designator is *L*-determinate in a language *L* if and only if the semantical rules of *L* alone, without additional factual knowledge, determine its extension. So, '9' is *L*-determinate, its extension being the class of all classes which are isomorphic to 9. But n_p: 'the cardinal number of planets' is *L*-indeterminate because finding its extension requires factual information. '$N_p = 9$' is a true identity statement. It is, however, synthetic, and hence contingently true. The extension of n_p is determined by the way the world is, although, as it happens, it is identical with the extension of the *L*-determinate designator '9'. In other words, although it is true that '$n_p = 9$', n_p is not *necessarily* equal to 9. Hence, there is a sense in which n_p and 9 are different: they have different intensions. But this sense cannot be captured in an extensional language such as L_T. In an extensional language, '$n_p = 9$' expresses an identity: 'n_p' and '9' are just two expressions for the same class (of classes) of objects, a class which is designated on the one hand by a descriptive constant and on the other by a logical one.[10]

Insofar as we stick to an extensional language, it is tempting for an empiricist to take the second-order variables of the Ramsey-sentence to range over mathematical entities. These variables, extensionally understood, range over classes, classes of classes, etc. What are these classes of? A natural thought is that they are classes of space–time points. But 'space–time point' is itself a theoretical term. Hence it, too, has to be eliminated (in favour of quadruples of numbers, in Carnap's case). But even if one resolved that the variables range over classes of space–time points, etc., one would still miss something. Suppose we replaced the term 'mass' by an existentially quantified variable. From an extensional point of view, the Ramsey-sentence would assert the existence of a mathematical entity: a *function* from classes of space–time points to numbers. The extensional language L_T simply does not have the resources to capture the difference between the theoretical concept *mass* and the relevant extensionally identical mathematical function.

Seen from an intensional perspective, however, the Ramsey-sentence approach looks different: although to each *t*-term there corresponds an extensionally identical mathematical designator, the *intensions* of the *t*-terms are physical concepts, not mathematical entities. So the intensions of *t*-terms are different from the intensions of logico-mathematical terms. Once we switch to an intensional language, the problems of the choice of the variables and their range get resolved. In Carnap's own method of extension and intension (cf. 1947 [1956]), variables are allowed two interpretations, taking intensional values as well as extensional values (e.g. properties as well as classes, or individual concepts as well as individuals). Carnap's method allows the use of the same variables to quantify over theoretical entities (properties – the intensions of *t*-terms) as well as over mathematical entities (the extensions of *t*-terms). So, the value-intensions of the variables will be theoretical entities, although their value-extensions may well be mathematical entities. We should not, however, fail to notice that this appeal to intensions breaks Carnap's desired neutrality once more. If an intensional language is admitted, he cannot escape existential commitments to unobservable entities (properties).

It might seem that the claim that the extensions of descriptive terms are mathematical entities is a mere artefact of Carnap's system without any independent motivation. Yet there is a deep reason why Carnap insists on the extensional identity between theoretical and mathematical concepts. One of Carnap's major concerns is to show that his framework for the analysis of the language of theories can be adaptive enough to include new theoretical concepts that the physicist of the future might think up. Carnap is quite explicit about this problem in his *Dialectica* paper. He says:

> How should we construct a general conceptual scheme in which not only the object of an already given scheme of physics may fit, but also others, perhaps forces, particles, or special objects of an entirely new kind of which we presently have no conception but which a physicist might introduce tomorrow?
>
> (1958: 80)

Carnap's insistence on the extensional identity aims to address precisely this problem. When new physical concepts are introduced, the proposed framework can easily accommodate them because it can always provide the relevant extensionally identical mathematical functions. No matter what the features of a new physical magnitude may be, its logical type will be identical with a certain mathematical function, which can be expressed in the extensional language L_T. So when new entities are introduced, there is no need to radically change the linguistic framework in which scientific theories are developed.

Carnap's motivation is to introduce a framework rich enough to accommodate theories in the process of growth, and to provide means to compare scientific theories. For even when theories employ different concepts, they can still be compared from an extensional point of view, by finding the mathematical functions that correspond to these concepts and by examining whether these are extensionally identical, i.e. whether they have the same values for all points on which they are defined. In other words, Carnap's main motivation is the construction of a stable logico-linguistic environment for the development of scientific theories. In his letter to Feigl, Carnap makes this explicit:

> My emphasis on the kind of variables had only the purpose to indicate that the logical types of the required variables are not of any strange new kind, but just of the kind we are familiar with in mathematics, say

in a simple type hierarchy, beginning not with objects, but with natural numbers, as in my language II in Logical Syntax [*The Logical Syntax of Language* (1937a)].

(Carnap Archive 102–07–05)

Similarly, in his lecture course *The Philosophical Foundations of Physics* he stresses:

Thereby, I believe, we have entirely got rid of the problem how we can foresee the strange entities which physicists might introduce in the future. If you think of the theoretical entities as things of some kind which nobody has ever seen, like electrons or so, then you will think that we cannot foresee what strange kinds of things physicists will conjure up – we might not even be able to imagine them today. But if we assume that every physical theoretical term that will be introduced belongs to a certain type, then that type can be provided for. I think, even the system outlined above, containing all finite types, will presumably be sufficient for all concepts of physics for quite some time.

(Carnap Archive 111–23–01)[11]

Neutralism

It seems as though Carnap's neutralism is difficult to maintain: every attempt to restore an empiricist equidistance between scientific realism and instrumentalism makes him fall towards one of these positions. Carnap has to take sides, doesn't he?

Well, there is still an option available to him: to say that the two positions are, after all, *not* in conflict. This much he says explicitly in the hardback edition of *The Philosophical Foundations of Physics*:

It is obvious that there is a difference between the meanings of the instrumentalist and the realist ways of speaking. My own view, which I shall not elaborate here is that the conflict between the two approaches [realism and instrumentalism] is essentially linguistic. It is a question of which way of speaking is to be preferred under given circumstances. To say that a theory is a reliable instrument – that is, that the predictions of observable events that it yields will be confirmed – is essentially the same as saying that the theory is true and that the theoretical, unobservable entities it speaks about exist. Thus, there is no incompatibility between the thesis of the instrumentalist and that of the realist. At least so long as the former avoids such negative assertions as, '. . . but the theory does not consist of sentences which are either true or false, and the atoms, electrons and the like do not really exist'.

(1966: 256)[12]

Let me call the thesis expressed in this quotation the *strong compatibility thesis*. This claim has justifiably raised many a philosopher's eyebrow (see e.g. Creath 1985; Salmon 1994a). For if instrumentalists give up their instrumentalist convictions, then the two rival positions become automatically compatible. Would Carnap try to make this trivial point? And even if he would, would he not thereby give the game away to scientific realism? The two positions are then compatible, but because instrumentalism is no longer instrumentalism.

We need to go slowly here. Carnap struggles a lot with the formulation of his position and makes several corrections to the manuscript of Chapter 26 of the book (Carnap Archive 111–23–04). In this chapter, Carnap discusses the Ramsey-sentence approach in great detail. His final word on this is:

> To ask whether there really *are* electrons is the same – from the Ramsey point of view – as asking whether quantum physics is true. The answer is that, to the extent that quantum physics has been confirmed by tests, it is justifiable to say that there are instances of certain kinds of events that, in the language of the theory, are called 'electrons'.
>
> (1966: 255)

This is a view that many scientific realists might be happy with because it asserts certain existential commitments. But Carnap takes this position *not* to be a realist one – in fact, Carnap goes on to add 'this point of view is sometimes called the "instrumentalist" view of theories'.

If all there was to instrumentalism had been captured by the 'Ramsey way', then Carnap would be right in saying that realism and instrumentalism are compatible. In the original manuscript of Chapter 26, following the claim that the conflict between realism and instrumentalism is 'essentially linguistic', Carnap explains this compatibility very clearly: 'Any object – from electron to galaxy – can be talked about in the Ramsey sentence, or in the traditional descriptive [realist] language of science. The point I wish to emphasise is that, so far as the powers of a theory to explain and predict are concerned, the two language forms are equivalent' (Carnap Archive 111–23–04). Let me call the thesis expressed in this passage the *weak compatibility thesis*.

Oddly enough, Carnap decides to withdraw this passage which asserts the (weak) compatibility of realism with the 'Ramsey way' and to replace it by the passage that asserts the (strong) compatibility of realism with instrumentalism in general. It is not surprising then that having asserted the strong compatibility thesis, he immediately weakened it by adding the qualification: realism and instrumentalism are compatible so long as instrumentalism 'avoids such negative assertions as, ". . . but the theory does not consist of sentences which are either true or false, and the atoms, electrons and the like do not really exist"'. What Carnap has in mind is the 'Ramsey way'. What he wants to stress is that instrumentalism and realism are compatible insofar as the instrumentalist is not a typical instrumentalist but rather an advocate of the 'Ramsey way'.

It is most unfortunate that Carnap crossed off the weak compatibility thesis. For it is this thesis that underscores his neutralism. Empiricists are concerned with the power of the theory to explain and predict, and so far as this power is concerned realism and the 'Ramsey way' fare the same. To be sure, realists typically assert more than do the Ramsey-sentence proponents: realists use t-terms, they endow them with surplus meaning, and they take these terms to refer to unobservable entities. On the other hand, the Ramsey-sentence dispenses with t-terms. But it does not thereby reduce the 'excess' content of theories. Theories still imply existential commitments to things other than observables. The Ramsey-sentence may not assert that *electrons* exist, as opposed to whatever else, if true, might realise the Ramsey-sentence; but it does assert that there are entities which realise the theory.

Besides, as Carnap (1958) observes, a scientific theory TC is logically equivalent to the following conjunction: $^R(TC)$ & $(^R(TC) \rightarrow (TC))$. The conditional $(^R(TC) \rightarrow (TC))$ says that if there are entities that satisfy the Ramsey-sentence of the theory, then the n-tuple of t-terms of the theory should be taken to designate such entities. Carnap notes that this conditional has no factual content and takes it to be a meaning postulate.[13] On this reconstruction of scientific theories, the difference between the Ramsey-sentence proponents and scientific realists is that the former stick to $^R(TC)$, while the latter also accept the meaning postulate $(^R(TC) \rightarrow (TC))$. This is an analytic statement, and hence has no extra empirical content over $^R(TC)$. It appears, then, that in asserting the existence of, say, electrons, realists take no extra empirical risks over that of the proponents of the 'Ramsey way'. Nor can they, on empirical grounds, persuade the proponents of the 'Ramsey way' to accept the existence of, say, *electrons*. All they can hope for is to convince them to talk about the entities that realise $^R(TC)$, as electrons, etc. The proponents of the Ramsey-sentence approach, on the other hand, could accept that if theories are true, then there are electrons. In doing so, Carnap thinks, they would have to accept a meaning postulate, but they would not go beyond the limits of empirical enquiry.

So, Carnap's empiricism seems able to remain neutral. Within the limits of empirical adjudication, scientific realism and the 'Ramsey way' are deemed equivalent. And that is so without compromising the theory's power to explain and predict. What is, however, important to stress is that the 'Ramsey way' should *not* be equated with an instrumentalist understanding of theories. This is precisely because a typical instrumentalist would deny that theoretical entities exist, while $^R(TC)$ does not: it just offers an extensional treatment of theoretical discourse. All this means that Carnap's neutrality needs some qualification. His liberalised empiricism is not neutral in the debate between realism and instrumentalism. It is neutral *vis-à-vis* a realist or a Ramsey-sentence understanding of scientific theories.[14]

No wonder, then, that Carnap's original strong compatibility thesis, too, is eventually withdrawn when the paperback edition of *The Philosophical Foundations of Physics* appears in 1974. Salmon (1994a) has documented that this change was brought about by Maxwell's insistence that the Ramsey-sentence approach should not be equated with instrumentalism. In fact, as we shall see in the next section, Maxwell thought that the 'Ramsey way' is best understood as *structural realism*. Commenting on Carnap's use of the Ramsey-sentence, Maxwell wrote to Carnap: 'I disagree that thinking theoretical entities "in the Ramsey way" should be associated with instrumentalism' (Maxwell to Carnap, 24 June 1966; Carnap Archive 027–33–29). Interestingly enough, Carnap wrote back on 9 December 1967 saying:

> You are quite right in the one critical remark you make, that the Ramsey way should not be associated with instrumentalism. In an earlier version of the manuscript I had distinguished three instead of two views on the question of the reality of entities, by splitting off instrumentalism into two forms, a negativistic one and a neutral one which I identified with the Ramsey way. Then a reader of the manuscript pointed out that the distinctions were not in agreement with the customary terminology; in particular that the term 'instrumentalism' is always used in the negativistic sense. Then I made a radical change, distinguishing only two points of view. This I did in great haste and so I mixed things up. For a future edition of the book I have decided on a reformulation which you see on the enclosed sheet.
>
> (Carnap Archive 027–33–28)

Empiricism and realism-without-the-tears?

How good is Carnap's final position? *Prima facie*, it seems that Carnap has managed to effect his desired compromise between his liberalised empiricism and some form of realism. For, Carnap thinks, all we need to do in order to achieve this reconciliation is adopt a *meaning postulate* $(\exists u \, TC(u,o) \rightarrow (TC(t,o)))$ for an n-tuple of t-terms and an m-tuple of already interpreted o-terms, which says: *if* the world is so constructed that there are classes of entities which satisfy $^R(TC)$, then the t-terms are to be understood in such a way that they designate these classes. By advocating a Ramsey-sentence approach to scientific theories, Carnap goes beyond strict empiricism, since the Ramsey-sentence approach entails a commitment to entities which realise the Ramsey-sentence. But this is not a fully realist position either, since asserting *what* these entities are is no longer a substantive issue, but instead it reduces to adopting a meaning postulate.

Carnap's attempted reconciliation is too quick and does not work. The point I want to motivate is that there is a big asymmetry between an *interpreted scientific theory* and its *Ramsey-sentence*. Whether an interpreted theory is true or false is an empirical matter. In particular, it is possible that a theory can be empirically adequate and yet false. However, if the Ramsey-sentence of a theory is empirically adequate at all, it is *guaranteed* to be true; i.e. *without further constraints*, it is guaranteed that *there is* an interpretation of the second-order variables which makes the Ramsey-sentence true. So those who, like Carnap, take the Ramsey-sentence of a theory to express whatever can be legitimately captured by a scientific theory fail to do justice to the fact that scientific theories make substantive claims about the world.

What realists should stress is that it is an open question whether the antecedent of the conditional $(\exists u \; TC(u,o) \rightarrow TC(t,o))$, i.e. 'that the world is so constructed that there are classes of entities which satisfy $^{R}(TC)$', is true or false. Consequently, they should stress that it should be an open issue whether or not the t-terms designate anything: the n-tuple of t-terms of the theory does designate something if the Ramsey-sentence is true, but it does *not* designate anything if the Ramsey-sentence is false, i.e. if the world is *not* so constructed that there are classes of entities which satisfy TC. By stressing all this, realists do justice to our pre-philosophical intuition that theories make substantive claims about the world which are true, if at all, empirically and not a priori. This is precisely where Carnap's approach goes wrong. It makes any empirically adequate theory come out true of the world. Let me sketch why this is so.

Unless certain restrictions are imposed on the range of the second-order variables of the Ramsey-sentence, and given that the Ramsey-sentence is *empirically adequate*, then it is *always true* (i.e. it cannot possibly be false) that there are classes, and classes of classes, etc., which satisfy the Ramsey-sentence of the theory. For if the domain of the theory is seen merely as a set of objects which possesses no natural structure, then this domain can be so 'carved up' that the Ramsey-sentence is true of it, and never false of it. Hence, provided that the Ramsey-sentence is empirically adequate, the antecedent of the conditional $(\exists u \; TC(u,o) \rightarrow TC(t,o))$, viz. the claim that 'the world is so constructed that there are classes of entities which satisfy TC', is *always* true. No empirical investigation is required for finding out whether it is true. Notice now that given that the Ramsey-sentence $\exists u \; TC(u,o)$ is always true, and that $(\exists u \; TC(u,o) \rightarrow TC(t,o))$, one can infer that the theory $TC(t,o)$ is also true. What this means is that provided that the Ramsey-sentence is empirically adequate, we can rely just on a priori reasoning in order to discover what entities realise the theory, i.e. what unobservable entities populate the world. No empirical investigation is necessary. In the end, if no constraints are imposed on the range of the variables of the Ramsey-sentence, it is *a trivial and a priori true assertion* that there are electrons, etc. And this is clearly absurd. For, to say the least, it appears obvious that the theory $TC(t,o)$ *could* be false, even though it is empirically adequate. It is false just in case the unobservable entities it posits are not part of the furniture of the world. Hence, if the theory can be false, it is a substantive claim that it is true, if it is true. And no substantive claim can be arrived at by a priori reasoning. Carnap's argument makes the truth of a theory $TC(t,o)$ trivial, since it allows of no possibility of the theory $TC(t,o)$ being false, given that its Ramsey-sentence is empirically adequate.

The objection I have just raised against Carnap is an instance of a bigger problem that has been recently brought into focus by Demopoulos and Friedman (1985), although its original author is the mathematician M. H. A. Newman who raised it (1928) against Russell's structuralism as expressed in *The Analysis of Matter* (1927).

In this work Russell suggested that when it comes to knowledge of the unobservable world, only its structure – the totality of its formal, logico-mathematical, properties – can be known. All first-order properties of the unobservable entities – what Russell called 'qualities' – are inherently unknown. What is so special about the logico-mathematical structure of the world, Russell thought, was that it could be legitimately *inferred* from the structure of the observable world. So, Russell's structuralism appears to be an attempt to reconcile empiricism and realism. His position is empiricist enough because it does not go beyond whatever can be known on the basis of experience, or be inferred from it. But it is also realist, because it posits more than the observable phenomena. Russell admits the existence of an unobservable world, and, on top of that, he asserts that its structure can be known. Having dissociated the Ramsey-sentence approach from instrumentalism, Maxwell suggested that the Russellian position can indeed be seen as a form of realism. This kind of realism, he thought, can be fully captured by the Ramsey-sentence approach to scientific theories. Given that the Ramsey-sentence of the theory preserves the structure of the original theory, Maxwell suggests that the 'Ramsey way' is best understood as 'structural realism'. As such, it suggests both that scientific theories issue in existential commitments to unobservable entities and that all non-observational knowledge of unobservables is *structural*, i.e. it is knowledge not of their *first*-order (or intrinsic) properties but rather of their *higher*-order (or structural) properties (see Maxwell 1970; 1970a). In Maxwell's words: 'our knowledge of the theoretical is limited to its purely structural characteristics and . . . we are ignorant concerning its intrinsic nature' (1970a: 188).

What Maxwell did not see was that there is a damaging objection to the Russellian programme, and had been pointed out by the mathematician Newman (1928). His claim was that the main thesis of Ramsey-style structural realism is either *trivial* or *incoherent*. What follows shows just this.

Triviality

As Newman (1928: 144) notes, it is meaningless to talk of the structure of a set of individuals unless some relations are specified: a class of objects with no relations defined on them has no structure. What relation (or set thereof) structures the domain of unobservable objects? One would expect knowing what exactly this relation is to be imperative for empirical science.

For empirical science deals with concrete objects and concrete relations among them. The structuralists want to get by with a *much weaker* position. They want to assert only that there is such a relation *TC* – where *TC* is expressed by a purely formal logico-mathematical predicate – and that all that is known of it is the structure *W* it generates. In particular, they want to avoid saying what *exactly* this relation is. Note, however, that from an extensional point of view, the structure *W* generated by this relation is nothing but a set of ordered tuples of the individuals of this domain. Suppose, as the structuralists would have it, that we posit the existence of a set of theoretical entities. This is already a step beyond strict empiricism.

But the structuralists want to go even further. They want to say that of *this* set something else is known, viz. its structure *W*. Can this set fail to possess the required structure *W*? The answer is negative. For, in fact, the domain – considered as a set – possesses *all* structures which are consistent with the number of its elements. Intuitively, the idea is that the elements of this domain can be arranged in ordered tuples so that the domain exhibits structure *W*. If all we aim to show is that there is *some* relation which generates structure *W*, there is nothing to stop us from arranging the elements of the domain in tuples such that they correspond to the required structure *W*. More formally, all one needs to note is the following theorem from second-order logic: that every set *A* determines a full structure, i.e. one which contains all subsets of *A*, and hence every relation-in-extension on *A*.[15] Since all relations-in-extension are contained in the posited domain of unobservable entities (considered as a set), it follows that one can never fail to generate the required structure *W* on this domain. So, the claim that *there is* a relation (or a network thereof) such that the structure of the unobservable world is *W* says very little. In fact, all it says is that the posited domain of unobservable objects must have a certain cardinality. Everything else, in particular the assertion that there is a relation-in-extension *TC* such that the structure of the unobservable world is *W*, follows trivially from the cardinality claim as a matter of logic. Newman summed up the argument as follows: 'Hence the doctrine that *only* structure is known involves the doctrine that *nothing* can be known that is not logically deducible from the mere fact of existence, except ('theoretically') the number of constituting objects' (Newman 1928: 144).[16]

We should be careful to distinguish between two distinct problems which the Ramsey-sentence approach faces. The first is the problem of *multiple realisation*. This is the outcome of the fact that structure determines its domain only up to isomorphism. Hence, many (qualitatively) different domains may realise the same structure. But multiple realisation is not an insurmountable problem, insofar as the structure is not treated purely formally, because one can distinguish between important and unimportant interpretations of the domain, as Russell himself was aware (cf. 1927: 5). The second problem, which is the Newman challenge, may be called the problem of *trivial realisation*. It is this: the thesis that there is a relation such that it generates a structure W on a domain of unobservable entities is a trivial claim which follows logically from the fact that there are enough individuals in the domain.

Newman's challenge remains even after the intended interpretation of the domain of discourse has been fixed (e.g. numbers, or space–time points). Put simply, the problem is that of specifying the nature of the relation to which we refer when we say that there are entities which stand in TC to o. What *exactly* is the relation we refer to when we say that there are entities that stand in TC to o? Even if we specify the domain of discourse, not only is the relation TC undetermined but its existence is a truth of logic.

The problem raised by Newman is particularly acute for Carnap's own understanding of the Ramsey-sentence. As we have seen (p. 41), Carnap suggests that all the theory needs to assert is that there are mathematical entities which stand in a certain relation to the observable phenomena, where this relation is expressed by a purely logico-mathematical predicate TC. Since, however, the domain of discourse of L_T is the power set of D^0, (i.e. of the set of natural numbers), it is going to contain any and every relation on D^0 (understood extensionally). Hence, it can possess any and every structure whatsoever, and in particular the desired structure imposed by TC, whatever that may be. No empirical investigation is necessary to find out whether $\exists u\ TC(u,o)$ is true. The very fact that the domain of discourse is rich enough guarantees that $\exists u\ TC(u,o)$ is true, i.e. that there are classes (and classes of classes, etc.) of numbers which stand in relation TC to o, provided of course that $\exists u\ TC(u,o)$ is consistent with the observable facts. Carnap seems to be willing to bite the bullet and impose no restrictions on the range of the variables of the Ramsey-sentence. But, as we have seen (pp. 62–63), he thereby renders all theoretical assertions made by an empirically adequate scientific theory trivial and a priori true.

Incoherence

Can the advocates of the 'Ramsey way' avoid triviality by saying more about the nature of the required relations? Could they not apply some notion of 'importance' to relations? The issue here is the following: can the structuralists avoid the Newman charge of triviality *without* abandoning their structuralist outlook? Not really. The whole point is precisely that the notion of 'important relation' cannot admit of a purely structuralist understanding. Newman sees this point very clearly. The problem is precisely to distinguish 'between the systems of relations that hold among the members of a given aggregate. . . . In the present case we should have to compare the importance of relations of which nothing is known save their incidence (the same for all of them) in a certain aggregate' (1928: 147). And he adds: 'For this comparison [between structurally identical relations] there is no possible criterion, so that "importance" would have to be reckoned among the prime unanalyzable qualities of the constituents of the world, which is,

I think, absurd' (ibid.). In order to pick as important one among the many relations which generate the same structure on a domain, we have to go beyond structure and talk about *what* these relations are, and *why* some of them are more important than others.

One thing should be clear. If triviality is to be avoided, then *some* restrictions should be imposed on the relations defined on a given domain: not all subsets of the power set of the domain of discourse should be taken into account. Some of them must be excluded. Instead of a 'full structure', the domain should already possess a more restricted, but more definite, structure. In other words, the domain should already be structured by a *definite* relation. The natural suggestion here is that among all those relations-in-extension which generate the same structure, only those which express *real* relations should be considered. But, as I have already noted, specifying which relations are real requires knowing something *beyond* structure, viz. which extensions are 'natural', i.e. which subsets of the power set of the domain of discourse correspond to natural properties and relations. Having specified these *natural* relations, one may abstract away their content and study their structure. But if one begins with the structure, then one is in no position to tell *which* of the relations one studies and *whether* or not they are natural.

So, the Ramsey-style structural realists are caught in a dilemma. Either they should choose to avoid addressing the issue of which structures are specified by theories and their Ramsey-sentences, thereby making the claim that theories are true empty and a priori true. Or they should have to appeal to *non-structural* considerations in order to say which structures are important, thereby undermining the distinction between knowledge of structure and knowledge of nature upon which they base their epistemology and their understanding of theories. To put the point in a different way: *either* structural realists do not restrict the range of the variables of the Ramsey-sentence *or* they do. If they do not, then the claim that theories are true, given that they are empirically adequate, becomes an a priori and trivial truth. If, on the other hand, they do opt for a restriction of the range of the variables – so that, for instance, they range over natural classes (kinds, properties) – then in order for them to distinguish between natural and non-natural classes they have to admit that some non-structural knowledge is possible, viz. that some classes are natural, while others are not. And the only way to do that is to rely on interpreted scientific theories and to take them as their guides as to the properties and relations which are the natural constituents of the world.

It might appear that the observable phenomena constrain the interpretation of the range of the second-order variables of the Ramsey-sentence in such a way that it is no longer trivial to assert that there are classes (and classes of classes, etc.) which stand in the relation TC to the observable phenomena o. But this is not so, as the following example will illustrate. Take a simple theory which consists of the following:

$$\forall x\,(Px \rightarrow Fx), \quad \forall x\,(Fx \rightarrow O_1x) \quad \text{and} \quad \forall x\,(Px \rightarrow O_2x),$$

where P and F are theoretical predicates and O_1 and O_2 are observational ones, and the first-order variables range over space–time points. The Ramsey-sentence of this theory is

$$\exists \phi\,\exists \psi\,[\forall x\,(\phi x \rightarrow \psi x)\;\&\;(\psi x \rightarrow O_1x)\;\&\;(\phi x \rightarrow O_2x)]\,.$$

Can this sentence be false? An extensional account of this sentence is given in Figure 3.1.

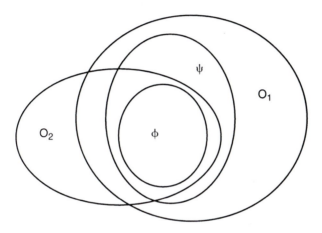

Figure 3.1 Trivial realisation

The assertion that *there are* classes ϕ and ψ such that the class ϕ is subclass of ψ and that they both stand in certain subclass relations to classes corresponding to observable properties is trivially satisfied. (I have just 'drawn' such classes, but that there are such classes is obvious.) If the assertion that *there are* classes ϕ and ψ says anything, all that it says is that the classes ϕ and ψ are non-empty. Note that the problem is not that of multiple realisation. It is Newman's problem of *trivial realisation*.

Resolution

Where does all this leave us? As is well known, David Lewis (1970) employed exactly the Carnap device in order to show how reference can be made to theoretical entities. For him, however, *t*-terms refer only if there is a *unique* realisation of *TC* – only if there are no multiple classes of entities which stand in *TC* to *o*. If there is more than one such class, then the *t*-terms should be considered denotationless. Talking of 'unique realisation' is somewhat ambiguous. It might be taken to exclude *multiple realisations* in the sense of excluding different domains of objects realising the same structure. But, requiring uniqueness of this sort would do nothing to avoid the Newman problem. So, I take it that, in the present context, requiring uniqueness amounts to requiring *that there is a unique relation-in-extension TC* which structures the specific domain such that the entities of this domain stand in *TC* to *o*. Requiring *this* kind of uniqueness is nothing other than requiring that the domain is already carved up in natural kinds, and that there are natural relations holding among them. It is only then that fiddling with extensions so that the required structure is generated will not do, because it will not necessarily respect the objective natural-kind structure of the domain. Lewis does not, as far as I can tell, make this clear in his 1970 paper. But all of his relevant subsequent work on natural kinds (see especially Lewis 1984) makes it clear that this is what he is now arguing for.

My conclusion, then, is that any meaningful defence of the structuralistic approach to realism should at least presuppose realism about natural kinds. In other words, it should imply commitment to the claim that the domain whose structure is being investigated is *already and independently structured*, so that not all relations-in-extension are present in it. If the domain is already 'carved up' in natural kinds, then it is a far from trivial exercise to find a network of relations which generate a certain formal structure. The existence of such a network no longer depends merely on the cardinality of the domain. What is now also required is getting the extensions right, i.e. identifying those and *only those* extensions which mark off the boundaries of – and relations among – natural kinds. This gives us an, as it were, *external standard* with which to compare the 'carvings' of the domain. Perhaps, only one carving will be able to respect the natural-kind structure of the domain. Or else it may be the case that there is more than one carving which respect the natural-kind structure of the domain. Should this happen, there will be some indeterminacy in the extensions of the relations. But the point is that, instead of being a matter of logic, this issue becomes an open empirical problem.[17]

There is a possible comment on my conclusion. The thesis that the world possesses a unique natural-kind structure is surely compatible with the claim that, without also specifying *what exactly* these natural kinds are, of this structure the only thing that *can* be asserted is that it exists. So it seems that structuralists do not, after all, have to go all the way up to realism. They can avoid the Newman problem by adhering to the view that there are natural kinds (or, if you like, relations-in-intension), but by ensuring that of *these* kinds nothing is asserted other than that they are *natural*.

This may well be a plausible position to take. But note two things. First, the position at hand is no longer purely structuralist. Second, once it is accepted that the world has a unique natural-kind structure, it is only *reasonable* not to be content with a Ramsey-sentence approach to scientific theories. For when it comes to the defence of the thesis that science captures the structure of a world already carved up in natural kinds, it is best not to treat theories as abstract structures, but instead to appeal to the success of *interpreted* scientific theories in order to argue that the kinds posited by them populate the world. By so doing, not only is it easy to deflect the charge of trivial realisation – for it is by no means a trivial assertion that there are electrons, protons, etc. – but, more importantly, we can now deflect the charge that nothing can distinguish between natural kinds and 'artificial' or 'gerrymandered' classes. What affords this distinction is what Lewis (1984) has called the 'inegalitarianism' of physics: those kinds are natural which are being posited and talked about by our best scientific theories.

Let me conclude this long chapter with two points. First, Carnap's best case for his own empiricism was put forward in his endorsement of the Ramsey-sentence approach. This seemed to safeguard his own neutralism – but at the price of collapsing his empiricism to structural realism. The latter can be seen as an informative realist position only if, ultimately, it abandons the thesis that only the structure of the unobservable world can be known. Second, where scientific realists differ from Ramsey-style structural realists is in their acceptance of the metaphysical theses that there are natural kinds, and that a certain natural domain has a unique structure of natural kinds. With all this in mind, let us now move on to characterise and defend scientific realism.

4 In defence of scientific realism

Thus far, I have offered arguments against reductive empiricism, several versions of instrumentalism, either of the eliminative variety or of the Duhemian (non-eliminative) variety. We have seen that the so-called 'Ramsey way' does not offer a stable and satisfactory compromise between realism and instrumentalism. So, the only alternative is to adopt a realist attitude towards the unobservable entities posited by our best theories. If *semantic realism* is adopted, then we have a straightforward answer to the question: what is the world like, according to a given scientific theory? (Or, similarly, what is the world like, if a certain scientific theory is true?) The answer is none other than that the world is the way the scientific theory – literally understood – describes it to be.

This answer seems to have certain implications for epistemological questions. Bluntly put, once semantic realism is adopted, the issue of warranted belief in the existence of unobservable entities seems to take care of itself: insofar as scientific theories are well confirmed, it is rational to believe in the existence of the entities they posit. For, what other than our best theories should we look to in order to decide what it is reasonable to believe about the world? If our best science is not our best guide to our ontological commitments, then nothing is.

The *realist turn* in the philosophy of science since the early 1960s has aimed to remove the last scruples one might have against the confirmability and the actual confirmation of scientific theories. What realists have offered is a battery of arguments which aim to defend a scientific realist attitude towards our best scientific theories, while blocking their opponents' counter-arguments purporting to show that scientific theories cannot be accepted as approximately true. So, the realist turn has aimed to secure the epistemic optimism associated with scientific realism – a view which was explained in the Introduction to this book. In this chapter, I try to show that this attitude of epistemic optimism is well-motivated and warranted.

A central argument in defence of scientific realism is the famous 'no miracle argument' (henceforth NMA) which aims to show that our best scientific theories can be reasonably believed to be approximately true. NMA has found its 'textbook' formulation in these words of Hilary Putnam:

The positive argument for realism is that it is the only philosophy that does not make the success of science a miracle. That terms in mature scientific theories typically refer (this formulation is due to Richard Boyd), that the theories accepted in a mature science are typically approximately true, that the same terms can refer to the same even when they occurs in different theories – these statements are viewed not as necessary truths but as part of the only scientific explanation of the success of science, and hence as part of any adequate description of science and its relations to its objects.

(1975: 73)

So, NMA aims to defend the realist claim that successful scientific theories should be accepted as true (or, better, near true) descriptions of the world, in both its observable and its unobservable aspects. In particular, the realist claim is that accepting that successful scientific theories describe truly (or, near truly) the unobservable world *best explains* why these theories are empirically successful. That is, it best explains why the observable phenomena are as they are predicted to be by those theories.

As stated by Putnam, NMA is intended to be an instance of inference to the best explanation (henceforth IBE, or abduction). What needs to be explained, the explanandum, is the overall empirical success of science. NMA intends to conclude that the main theses associated with scientific realism, especially the thesis that successful theories are approximately true, offer the best explanation of the explanandum. Hence, they must be accepted precisely on this ground. This IBE-based reading of NMA underwrites the current defence of realism as developed by Richard Boyd and elaborated by me in the present chapter. Hence, I shall call this argument the Putnam–Boyd argument. It has, however, been repeatedly claimed that the Putnam–Boyd argument is viciously circular and begs the question against the critics of realism. For, it is noted, although the critics of realism deny (or simply doubt) that IBE is a reliable inferential method, NMA presupposes its reliability. As Fine (1991: 82) has put it, an IBE-based defence of realism lacks any argumentative force since it employs 'the very type of argument whose cogency is the question under discussion'. Dispersing the charge of vicious circularity and question-beggingness should be a central task in my own defence of realism. But before that, some detailed discussion is required in respect of the structure of the main realist argument. In particular, in the subsequent sections I try to disentangle several versions of NMA. The next two sections motivate and articulate carefully what I take to be the most forceful version of NMA, showing that it can offer a good defence of realism, provided that it is seen as part-and-parcel of a thorough externalist and naturalistic realist epistemological package.

Cosmic coincidences and the success of science

What appear to be variants of NMA had been put forward long before Putnam's slogan appeared by J. J. C. Smart and Grover Maxwell. Smart argued against instrumentalists that they 'must believe in *cosmic coincidence*' (1963: 39). To be sure, he referred to 'phenomenalism about theoretical entities', but took this to be eliminative instrumentalism, i.e. the view that 'statements about electrons, etc., are only of instrumental value: they simply enable us to predict phenomena on the level of galvanometers and cloud chambers' (ibid.).

We have already seen (Chapter 2) that eliminative instrumentalism takes scientific theories to be merely syntactic/mathematical constructs for the organisation of experimental and empirical facts, and for grouping together empirical laws and observations which would otherwise be taken to be irrelevant to one another. On this view, theoretical claims are not even truth-conditioned, i.e. capable of being true or false; nor do theories imply existential commitments to unobservables. The emergence of Craig's theorem coincided with the culmination of this view. For, as we have seen (pp. 22–23), it offers the instrumentalist a systematic way to eliminate theoretical terms.

On the eliminative instrumentalist account, a vast number of ontologically disconnected observable phenomena are 'connected' only by virtue of a purely instrumental theory: they just *happen* to be, and just *happen* to be related to one another in such a way that a Craig-style theory is true. If so, what other than a gigantic coincidence makes a Craigian theory true? Accepting the vast number of purely instrumental connections implied by the Craig-style theory exceeds the limits of tolerance, especially when there is a handy account that does away with all this happenstance. But look at scientific realism, says Smart. It leaves no space for coincidence on a cosmic scale: it is because theories are true and because the unobservable entities they posit exist that the phenomena are, and are related to one another, the way they are. Here is the contrast in Smart's own words:

> Is it not odd that the phenomena of the world should be such as to make a purely instrumental theory true? On the other hand, if we interpret a theory in the realist way, then we have no need for such a cosmic coincidence: it is not surprising that galvanometers and cloud chambers behave in the sort of way they do, for if there are really electrons, etc., this is just what we should expect.
>
> (1963: 39)

One may take Smart's argument to be a version of the 'no miracle' argument put forward by Putnam. At first glance, it seems that we are indeed dealing with one and the same argument. The only difference seems to be lexical: Smart bars cosmic coincidences, while Putnam bars miracles. Smart himself, after all, has also talked about a 'cosmic miracle' (1979: 364). Both arguments, it seems, rely on what they take to be the best explanation of why the observable phenomena are as they are predicted by scientific theories. As a rough approximation, this might be alright. However, if we look carefully at the details of the two arguments, it is pertinent to distinguish Smart's version from the Putnam–Boyd version of the NMA.

Smart's argument is not meant to be an inference to the best explanation. It is more of a general philosophical argument, what is sometimes called a plausibility argument (cf. Smart 1963: 8–12). For Smart, the argument for realism is largely a priori. He takes it that part, at least, of the distinctively philosophical method is to clarify conceptual disputes, i.e. disputes which are not amenable to empirical tests. On this view, the philosopher's job is to offer arguments in favour of each side of the dispute. Consistency is not at stake here, because every position can be made into a consistent one, given enough ingenuity. Rather, the philosopher should aim to examine the plausibility or arbitrariness of each position, especially in those grand disputes that 'affect our overall world view' (Smart 1963: 8). The realist–instrumentalist controversy is conceived by Smart to be such a grand conceptual dispute about the interpretation of scientific theories. Accordingly, Smart's 'no cosmic coincidence' argument relies on primarily intuitive judgements as to what is plausible and what requires explanation. It claims that it is intuitively more plausible to accept realism over instrumentalism because realism leaves less things unexplained and coincidental than does instrumentalism. Its argumentative force, if any, is that anyone with an open mind and good sense could and would find the conclusion of the argument intuitively plausible, persuasive and rational to accept – though not logically compelling: not because one would recognise the argument as an instance of a trusted inferential scheme, but because of intuitive considerations about what is more and what is less plausible.

An analogous argument for realism was offered Maxwell (1962a). To the best of my knowledge, he was the first to appeal explicitly to the success of scientific theories in order to to defend realism. The overall empirical success of science, says Maxwell, is a fact that calls for an explanation. The instrumentalist claim that theories are 'black boxes', which when fed with true observational premises yield true observational conclusions, would offer no explanation whatsoever of the fact that these 'black boxes' are so successful. In light of this, he claims: 'The only reasonable explanation for the success of theories of which I am aware is that well-confirmed theories are conjunctions of well-confirmed, genuine statements and that the entities to which they refer in all probability exist' (1962a: 18). As he has pointed out elsewhere, the difference between realist and instrumentalist accounts of science is that

> as our theoretical knowledge increases in scope and power, the competitors of realism become more and more convoluted and ad hoc and

explain less than realism. For one thing, they do not explain why the theories which they maintain are mere cognitively meaningless instruments are so successful, how it is that they can make such powerful, successful predictions. Realism explains this very simply by pointing out that the predictions are consequences of the true (or close true) propositions that comprise the theories.

(Maxwell 1970: 12)

Maxwell's argument differs from Smart's in an interesting way. It includes an attempt to ground the plausibility judgements that are required for the defence of realism and to show that such judgements are not, after all, distinctively philosophical. In a certain sense, Maxwell's argument is the 'bridge' between Smart's a priori argument and the subsequent Putnam–Boyd *naturalistic* version. Maxwell suggests that considerations of simplicity, comprehensiveness and lack of ad hocness are virtues that make judgements displaying them more plausible than judgements lacking them. What is more, Maxwell (1970) gives a Bayesian twist to his argument for realism. He emphasises that on standard probabilistic accounts of confirmation, if two or more mutually inconsistent hypotheses entail the same piece of evidence, the only way in which the evidence can be made to support one hypothesis more than the other(s) is via some kind of initial plausibility ranking of the competing hypotheses. This ranking is then reflected in the prior probabilities ascribed to the competing hypotheses. His argument for realism capitalises precisely on this well-worn fact. Suppose, he says, that both realism (R) and instrumentalism (I) *entail* that scientific theories are successful (S). Then, the likelihoods of realism and instrumentalism are both equal to unity; i.e.:

$$prob(S/R) = prob(S/I) = 1.$$

By Bayes' theorem, the posterior probability of realism is

$$prob(R/S) = prob(R)/prob(S)$$

and the posterior of instrumentalism is

$$prob(I/S) = prob(I)/prob(S),$$

where　$prob(R)$ is the prior probability of realism,
　　　　$prob(I)$ is the prior of instrumentalism and
　　　　$prob(S)$ is the probability of the 'evidence', i.e. of the success of science.

Given that $prob(S)$ is the same for both realism and instrumentalism, any difference in the degree of confirmation of R and I should reflect a difference in their respective priors. Based on the thought that the realist explanation of the success of science is simpler, more comprehensive and less ad hoc than any instrumentalist attempt at such an explanation, Maxwell (1970: 17–18) argues that the *prior probability* of realism should be much greater than the prior of instrumentalism: i.e. *prob(R)>>prob(I)*. Hence, the incremental confirmation of Realism is much greater than that of Instrumentalism.

I think Maxwell's point is two-fold. On the one hand, relying on prior probabilities is a routine aspect of all human judgement. It is also evident in scientific practice itself: not all theoretical hypotheses which entail the same evidence are ranked as equally plausible by scientists. In fact, the very virtues of simplicity, comprehensiveness and lack of ad hocness are those used by scientists to rank competing scientific hypotheses. On the other hand, philosophical problems, such as the realist–instrumentalist dispute are not much more difficult than – nor qualitatively different from – ordinary scientific problems, where no evidence can distinguish between two competing hypotheses. So, they call for the same treatment as ordinary scientific problems. As Maxwell puts it: 'My reasons for accepting realism are of the same kind as those for accepting any scientific theory over others which also explain current evidence' (ibid.).[1]

All this is a bit quick, the reader might think. Prior probabilities might indeed be indispensable in ampliative reasoning. But on what basis, the reader may ask, do we say that realism's prior probability is greater than that of (eliminative) instrumentalism? Since the conclusion of the argument depends crucially on assigning different priors to realism and instrumentalism, this conclusion would have been otherwise had we adopted an initial ordering which favoured instrumentalism over realism. How, then, can this ordering be decided? In particular, is this ordering supposed to be objective or subjective? If the former, then we need some further argument as to why realism is *objectively* more probable than instrumentalism. If the latter, what do subjective degrees of belief, or subjective estimates of prior probability, have to do with the alleged superiority of realism?

What it is correct to stress, I think, is that when it comes to the realism–instrumentalism debate an assignment of higher prior probability to realism can be rational – and hence objective – in these two senses. First, judgements of initial plausibility can be the subject and outcome of rational deliberation. One way, for instance, to argue for the greater initially plausibility of realism is to point out that realism derives much of its plausibility from a judgement which all parties in the realism debate would find rational – the very judgement which underlies the positing of middle-sized material objects. Against eliminative instrumentalism, realists rightly stress a certain analogy – and continuity – between positing middle-sized material objects to account for the orderly and coherent streams of sensory experience and positing scientific unobservables to account for the observable phenomena. If common sense has been the only thing required for the former, then so much the better for the latter. In denying the existence of unobservable entities, eliminative instrumentalists have to adopt 'double existential standards'. But as we have seen (pp. 18–22), there are no good arguments to support such double standards.

Second, judgements of initial plausibility can be rational and objective because they rely on sound expectations. Why is it initially more plausible to interpret scientific theories realistically? Because on an instrumentalist construal – such as mere 'black boxes', syntactic calculi and the like – *there is no reason to expect that theories are capable of being empirically successful*. To be sure, 'black boxes' and the like are constructed so that they systematise known observable regularities. But it does not follow from this that black boxes have the capacity to predict either hitherto unknown regularities or hitherto unforeseen connections between known regularities. Nor can such a thing be expected on any rational ground. However, if the theory is understood realistically, then novel predictions about the phenomena occasion *no surprise*. Realistically understood, theories entail too many novel claims, most of them about unobservables (e.g. that there are electrons, that light bends near massive bodies). It comes as no surprise that some of the novel theoretical facts a theory predicts may be such that they give rise to novel observable phenomena, or that they may reveal hitherto unforeseen connections between known phenomena. For instance, James Clerk Maxwell's theoretical identification of light with an electromagnetic wave predicted a hitherto unknown connection between the laws of light-propagation and the propagation of electric waves. At any rate, it would be very surprising if the causal powers of the entities posited by scientific theories were exhausted in the generation of the already-known empirical phenomena that led to the introduction of the theory. So, on a realist understanding of theories, novel predictions and genuine empirical success are to be expected (given, of course, that the world co-operates).

The fact of the matter is that such judgements as those above have been strong enough to mitigate the force of standard instrumentalist accounts. As we saw in Chapter 2, similar plausibility judgements have been put forward by 'textbook instrumentalists' like Pierre Duhem and Henri Poincaré. Both have argued that novel predictive success – a feature that has not been stressed sufficiently well by Maxwell – is at odds with an eliminative instrumentalist construal of scientific theories as 'racks filled with tools' (Duhem 1906: 334) or as 'simple practical recipes' (Poincaré 1902: 174). This is not surprising: on an instrumentalist account, novel predictive success is, if anything, an accidental feature of theories. Maxwell's argument makes good on precisely this state of affairs. It suggests that scientific realism is the only alternative that overcomes the problem which makes instrumentalism implausible – how novel successful predictions are possible. What, I think, it adds to this suggestion is the following. Once theories are treated as semantic realism suggests, then their novel empirical success can accrue only to the theory's confirmation: the more unlikely the prediction, the greater the incremental confirmation of the theory which makes it available.

There is no reason to doubt that Smart's and Maxwell's arguments undermine drastically the rationale of eliminative instrumentalism. But they are ineffective against sophisticated empiricist positions *à la* van Fraassen (1980; 1989). For a long time eliminative instrumentalism was the dominant alternative to a realist understanding of scientific theories. Smart and Maxwell (and, for that matter, Feigl too) aimed to kill two birds with one stone. Their central point was that the success of scientific theories lent credence to the two theses:

- that scientific theories should be interpreted realistically; and
- that, so interpreted, these theories are well confirmed because they entail well-confirmed predictions.

So, their arguments operate on the assumption that an argument for the realist interpretation of scientific theories can be, *ipso facto*, an argument for *believing* in the existence of the entities they posit. Given what has been said in Chapters 1 and 2 about the fate of reductive empiricism and eliminative instrumentalism, this is a reasonable assumption. Once it is accepted that theories should be interpreted realistically, the only remaining issue is whether these theories are well confirmed. If one and the same argument can establish both, then so much the better for realism.

However, the empiricist position advocated by van Fraassen accepts a realist interpretation of the semantics of scientific theories but challenges the *rationality of belief* in unobservable entities the existence of which these theories, if true, imply. Hence, in a certain sense, van Fraassen's position starts precisely where Smart's and Maxwell's arguments stop: that eliminative and reductive accounts of theoretical commitment in science are wrong-headed and discredited. As we shall see in detail in Chapter 9, one of van Fraassen's central points against scientific realism is that abductive–explanatory reasoning, by means of which theoretical beliefs are formed, cannot be shown to be truth-conducive, and therefore that belief in the approximate truth of particular theories is not rationally compelling. In other words, he questions the reliability of the methods scientists employ to arrive at their theoretical beliefs. On van Fraassen's view, the collapse of eliminative instrumentalism does not make realism the only rational option. An agnostic variety of empiricism is not, *ipso facto*, ruled out: one can always remain *agnostic* as to the truth-value of the particular theoretical descriptions of the world offered by a theory.

Boyd's important contribution to the debates over scientific realism, to which I now turn, is precisely that he has employed and strengthened the 'no miracle' argument in an attempt to defend the reliability and rationality of ampliative–abductive reasoning in science.

The explanationist defence of realism

Boyd's 'explanationist defence of realism' (henceforth EDR) is a programme for the development and defence of a *realist epistemology of science*. Boyd suggests that this epistemology should be thoroughly naturalistic. On the one hand, it should rest on the claim that it is a radically contingent fact about the world that scientific theories can and do deliver theoretical truth. On the other hand, in its attempt to investigate the epistemic credentials of science, and in particular to answer the question why scientific methodology is instrumentally reliable, a realist epistemology of science should employ no methods other than those used by scientists themselves. Boyd's defence of realism is *explanationist* because it is based on the claim that the realist thesis that scientific theories are approximately true is the best explanation of their empirical success. Boyd's naturalism makes his use of the NMA distinctively different from Smart's and (to a lesser extent) from Maxwell's: there is no distinctive philosophical method which is either prior to scientific method or can be used to resolve first-order scientific disputes. In this section I focus on the place of the 'no miracle' argument in EDR.

Boyd[2] has set out to show that the best explanation of the instrumental and predictive success of mature scientific theories is that these theories are approximately true, at least in those respects relevant to their instrumental success. I shall reconstruct the main argument as follows:

That the methods by which scientists derive and test theoretical predictions are theory-laden is undisputed. Scientists use accepted background theories in order to form their expectations, to choose the relevant methods for theory-testing, to devise experimental set-ups, to calibrate instruments, to assess the experimental evidence, to choose among competing theories, to assess newly suggested hypotheses, etc. All aspects of scientific methodology are deeply theory-informed and theory-laden. In essence, scientific methodology is almost linearly dependent on accepted background theories: it is these theories that make scientists adopt, advance or modify their methods of interaction with the world and the procedures they use in order to make measurements and test theories.

These theory-laden methods lead to correct predictions and experimental success.

How are we to explain this?

The best explanation of the instrumental reliability of scientific methodology is that: the theoretical statements which assert the specific causal connections or mechanisms by virtue of which scientific methods yield successful predictions are approximately true.

NMA is a philosophical argument which aims to defend the reliability of scientific methodology in producing approximately true theories and hypotheses. Its strength, however, rests on a more concrete type of explanatory reasoning which occurs all the time in science. It can be stated as follows. Suppose that a background theory T asserts that method M is reliable for the generation of effect X in virtue of the fact that M employs causal processes $C_1, \ldots, C_n$ which, according to T, bring about X. Suppose, also, that we follow T and other established auxiliary theories to shield the experimental set-up from factors which, if present, would interfere with some or all of the causal processes $C_1, \ldots, C_n$, thereby preventing the occurrence of effect X. Suppose, finally, that one follows M and X obtains. What else can better explain the fact that the expected (or predicted) effect X was brought about than that the theory T – which asserted the causal connections between $C_1, \ldots, C_n$ and X – has got these causal connections right, or nearly right? If this reasoning to the best explanation is cogent, then it is reasonable to accept T as approximately true, at least in those respects relevant to the theory-led prediction of X. To be more precise, more is needed for the acceptance of T as relevantly approximately true. For instance, T is to be contrasted with available alternative hypotheses, and should emerge as *the* best explanation. T should also offer a 'good enough' explanation in its own right, e.g. an explanation which can adequately account for all salient features of the experimental facts.[3] But such considerations are part and parcel of these more concrete applications of explanatory reasoning in science. And although we may not always be in position to choose a hypothesis as clearly the best explanation, that does not entail that we never are.

The relation between this more concrete type of explanatory reasoning in science and the NMA should be clear: successful instances of such reasoning provide the basis (and the initial *rationale*) for this more general abductive argument. However, NMA is not just a generalisation over scientists' abductive inferences. Although itself an *instance* of the method that scientists employ, NMA aims at a broader target: to defend the thesis that Inference to the Best Explanation, or abduction (that is, a *type* of inferential method), is reliable. The (first-order) instances of explanatory reasoning involve the claim that it is reasonable to accept that *particular* theories are relevantly approximately true. NMA is, then, based on these instances to defend the more general claim that science *can* deliver *theoretical truth*. NMA is a kind of *meta*-abduction. The explanandum of NMA is a general feature of scientific methodology – its reliability for yielding correct predictions. NMA asserts that the best explanation of why scientific methodology has the contingent feature of yielding correct predictions is that the theories which are implicated in this methodology are relevantly approximately true.

So, what makes NMA distinctive as an argument for realism is that it defends the achievability of theoretical truth. But how exactly does this argument defend IBE and hence how exactly does NMA become the pivot for a realist epistemology of science? As I have noted, it suggests that the best explanation of the instrumental reliability of scientific methodology is that background theories are relevantly approximately true. These background scientific theories have themselves been typically arrived at by abductive reasoning. Hence, it is reasonable to believe that abductive reasoning is reliable: it tends to generate approximately true theories. This conclusion is not meant to state an a priori truth. The reliability of abductive reasoning is an empirical claim, and if true is contingently so.

Having said this, let me stress that NMA should be suitably qualified. There is enough historical evidence to persuade any *bona fide* realist, first, that scientific theories have encountered many failures as well as successes and, second, that some past theories which once were empirically successful and were accepted as 'best explanations' of the evidence were subsequently abandoned as inadequate and false. In light of this, the realist argument should be qualified in two respects:

1   The realist argument should acknowledge the existence of failures. Their actuality does not impair scientific methodology. Nor does it sever the explanatory link between approximate truth and empirical success – especially novel empirical success. Clearly, the fact that I have occasionally failed to find my lost keys does not entail that a thorough search of the places where they could have been left is not a reliable method for finding lost keys. In any case, realists should concentrate on *particular* theory-led successes – and there are very many of those – and argue that it is *these* successes that require explanation. It is, after all, a salient feature of scientific methodology that it does lead to empirical successes. Things could be otherwise, and scientific theories might have been *total* failures. So, to ask how it is possible at all that scientific theories yield correct predictions, especially novel ones, and to offer explanations of this contingent feature of scientific methodology are essential for understanding science. (The notion of novelty in prediction, to which realists should appeal, is analysed in Chapter 5.)

2   The realist argument should become more local in scope. Accordingly, the main realist point should be the following: although most realists would acknowledge that there is an explanatory connection between a theory's empirical success and its being, in some respects, right about the unobservable world, it is far too optimistic – if at all defensible – to claim that *everything* the theory asserts about the world is thereby vindicated.

So, realists should *refine* the explanatory connection between empirical and predictive success, on the one hand, and truth-likeness, on the other. They should assert that these successes are best explained by the fact that the theories which enjoyed them have *truth-like theoretical constituents* (i.e.

truth-like descriptions of causal mechanisms, entities and laws). The theoretical constituents whose truth-likeness can best explain empirical successes
are precisely those which are essentially and ineliminably involved in the
generation of the predictions and the design of the methodology which
brought these predictions about. From the fact that not every theoretical
constituent of a successful theory does and should get credit from the
successes of the theory it certainly does *not* follow that none do (or should)
get some credit. If, on top of that, it is shown that, far from being abandoned, the theoretical constituents of past theories which did essentially
contribute to their successes were retained in subsequent theories of the
same domain, then the realist case is as strong as it can be. In Chapter 5
this point is explained in detail, since the argument just expressed captures
in a nutshell the way in which I try to block the argument from the
'pessimistic induction'.

From this point onwards I assume that the above considerations constitute the intended reading of NMA. EDR has caused a heated discussion
among philosophers of science (cf. Laudan 1984; McMullin 1987 and 1991;
Musgrave 1988; Newton-Smith 1987; Lipton 1991). As already noted, the
main line of criticism is that EDR is viciously circular. Since it employs
IBE, critics suggest that it therefore presupposes what needs to be shown
– that IBE is a reliable inferential method. Arthur Fine (1986; 1986a; 1991)
has summarised and defended this line in the most forceful way. He points
out that the realist is 'not free to assume the validity of a principle whose
validity is itself under debate' (1986a: 161). As he has put it elsewhere, an
IBE-based defence of realism lacks any argumentative force since it employs
'the very type of argument whose cogency is the question under discussion' (1991: 82). Fine concludes that 'there is, in general, no rational defence
of realism' (1986a: 163). But Fine has also put forward two more objections. Let us suppose, he says, for the sake of the argument, that abduction
is reliable. It would not be wise for realists to use an abductive argument
in their defence of realism, since they must demand more stringent methods
of proof of their philosophical doctrines (cf. Fine 1986: 114). At any rate,
he notes, there are better instrumentalist explanations of the success of
science (Fine 1986a: 154).

In what follows I explore some new and systematic ways in which realists can attempt to block the foregoing objections.

EDR and circularity

To call an argument viciously circular is to level an epistemic charge which
indicates that the argument in question cannot, and perhaps should not, be
persuasive since it in some way assumes, or postulates, that which needs
to be independently shown. A typically circular argument is one in which
the conclusion is either identical to or a mere paraphrase of one of its
premisses. Note, however, that the mere fact that a premiss is identical to

the conclusion is not sufficient ground for attributing *vicious* circularity. To show that an argument is *viciously* circular one should not just look at the sentences employed in the argument, but also take account of what the argument presumes to show by its use of the specific sentences. So, for instance, if we look only at the sentence-structure involved in it, the argument-type '*a* & *b*, therefore *b* & *a*' is circular. But it is *not* viciously circular since, I take it, it purports to show only the commutativity of logical conjunction. Similarly, the argument-type '*p*, therefore *p*' should not be deemed viciously circular if it is meant to show that every sentence is a logical consequence of itself. But it would be viciously circular were it meant to show that *p* is true. For then it would pretend to *prove* that *p* is true where it just *assumes* that *p* is true.

What is necessary in order for an argument to be correctly judged *viciously* circular is that the argument should purport to offer reasons for accepting a certain sentence (the conclusion), where (one of) the reasons cited is that sentence itself. Following Braithwaite (1953), one may call viciously circular arguments 'premiss-circular'. In the latter, one claims to offer an argument for the truth of α, but explicitly *presupposes* α in one's premisses. Such an argument has no probative force for anyone who does not already accept that α is true.[4]

In his attempt to defend an inductive vindication of inductive learning from experience, Braithwaite (1953: 274–278) also noted that there is a type of circular argument which is not premiss-circular. On the surface level, the argument is as non-circular as anything can be. It begins with the premisses $P_1, \ldots, P_n$, and then, by employing an inference rule R, it draws a certain conclusion Q. However, Q has a certain logical property: it asserts or implies something about the rule of inference R *used* in the argument, in particular that R is reliable. Braithwaite called this argument-type 'rule-circular'. In general, rule-circular arguments are such that the argument itself is an instance of, or involves essentially an application of, the rule of inference vindicated by the conclusion.

Braithwaite took it that rule-circularity was not vicious. I think this is correct. There are a few relevant differences between premiss-circularity and rule-circularity. The conclusion of a rule-circular argument is *not* one of the premisses. Nor is the argument such that one of the *reasons* offered for the truth of the conclusion is the conclusion itself. Hence, to say the least, rule-circular arguments are not *obviously* viciously circular. The case of rule-circular arguments has been defended, in connection with induction, by Braithwaite (1953), van Cleve (1984) and Papineau (1993). But, first appearances aside, there is a *residual* suspicion that rule-circular arguments are vicious. Before I try to disperse this doubt, I want to show that NMA is, if anything, a rule-circular argument.

As we saw in the last section, the premisses of NMA assert the theory-ladenness of scientific methodology and its widely accepted instrumental and predictive success. Then, by means of a meta-IBE, the argument concludes that the background theories are approximately true. Since these approximately true theories have been typically arrived at by *first-order* IBEs, this information together with the conclusion of the meta-IBE entail that IBE is reliable. So, the truth of the conclusion of NMA is (part of) a sufficient condition for accepting that IBE is reliable. NMA is clearly *not* premiss-circular. The conclusion of the meta-IBE (that theories are approximately true) is not among the premisses of the argument. In fact, no assumption about the approximate truth of theories is made within the premisses, either explicitly or implicitly. Besides, there is no a priori guarantee, as clearly there would have been if this argument were premiss-circular, that the conclusion of NMA will necessarily be that theories are (approximately) true. The conclusion is true, if at all, on the basis that it is the best explanation of the premisses, but it might not have been the best explanation. As we shall see, this point is implicitly conceded by the critics of NMA, since they take pains to argue that there are better explanations of the success of science. By arguing that the conclusion of NMA need not be the intended realist conclusion, they acknowledge implicitly that NMA is not premiss-circular.

Let us now examine in some detail whether rule-circularity is, nonetheless, vicious. How could it be? The thought here might be that in a rule-circular argument one has to assume the reliability of the rule invoked in the argument. But if this assumption is based on the prior acceptance of the conclusion of the rule-circular argument, then the proponents of a rule-circular argument apparently traffic in a vicious circle. For they would have to prove the conclusion *before* they accepted the rule used to derive it. But they could not prove the conclusion unless they *first* accepted the reliability of the rule.

I want to reply to this objection by denying that any assumptions about the reliability of a rule are present, either explicitly or implicitly, when an instance of this rule is used. Nor should the reliability of the rule be established *before* one is able to use it in a justifiable way. This is controversial. But here I am in good company. Externalists in epistemology have argued for this extensively (see Goldman 1986). The point is the following. When an instance of a rule is offered as the link between a set of (true) premisses and a conclusion, what matters for the correctness of the conclusion is whether or not the rule *is* reliable that is, whether or not the contingent assumptions which are required to be in place in order for the rule to be reliable *are* in fact in place. If the rule of inference *is* reliable (this being an objective property of the rule) then, given true premisses, the conclusion will also be true (or, better, likely to be true – if the rule is ampliative).[5] Any assumptions that need to be made *about* the reliability of the rule of inference, be they implicit or explicit, do not matter for the correctness of the conclusion. Hence, their defence is not necessary for the *correctness* of the conclusion.

In order to highlight the point just made, let us envisage the following situation. Suppose that, in a fashion analogous to a Turing test, we come across a certain 'inference machine' and we start playing a game with it. We feed it with several sets of true premisses and ask it to draw conclusions from them. Suppose also that in all (or most) cases the 'inference machine' draws true conclusions. To say the least, we would conclude that the 'inference machine' is (or is likely to be) reliable. We would also think that the 'inference machine' must operate according to some rules of inference in such a way that when the premisses are fed in it activates a rule and draws a conclusion. But *qua* machine, the 'inference machine' makes no assumptions about the rules it activates. It just activates them. And, given the success of the 'inference machine' in drawing true conclusions, can we protest that we should first identify the rules it activates, prove that they are reliable, and only then accept that the 'inference machine' is reliable? I think this would be unreasonable and, in any case, counter-productive. If the 'inference machine' started producing consistently false conclusions, we would have reason to start worrying. But in their absence, worrying is unnecessary.[6]

Pursuing the previous example, one might object that the issue is more complicated if we think, as we should, of reasoners as 'conscious inference machines'. For, the objector might note, the defence of the reliability of the rule of inference *does* matter for the *justification* that the reasoner might have for taking the conclusion to be correct (or, likely to be correct). This is really the point on which the allegedly vicious nature of rule-circularity turns. For whether or not the proof of reliability is required for justification will most likely depend on the epistemological perspective which one adopts. As is well known, *externalist* accounts sever the alleged link between being justified in using a reliable rule of inference and knowing, or having reasons to believe, that this rule is reliable. On such accounts, if the rule is reliable, then it thereby confers justification on a conclusion drawn using this rule, insofar as the premisses are true. Hence, given externalism, all we should require of a rule-circular argument is that the rule of inference employed *be* reliable; no more and no less than in any ordinary (first-order) argument. A rule-circular argument would be no more vicious than any other first-order application of the rule involved in it. Since first-order applications are not vicious, nor is the second-order application involved in the rule-circular argument. What is special with rule-circular arguments is what the conclusion says. It asserts that the rule of inference is reliable. But the correctness of this conclusion depends on the rule being reliable, and not on having any reasons to think that the rule is reliable. No less than the conclusion of any first-order ampliative argument, the conclusion of a rule-circular argument will produce a belief, this time about the rule of inference itself. This belief will be justified if the rule is reliable. But, if we keep with externalism, it is the truth of this belief and the (objective) reliability of the rule which generated it that matter. Justification requires no more than *reliability* and *truth*.

Rival *internalist* accounts of justification suggest that justification requires something over and above the fact, if it is a fact, that the rule *is* reliable, viz. knowing (or justifiably believing) that the rule of inference involved is reliable. So, if one took an internalist approach, then a separate justification of the reliability of the rule would be required for the overall warrant the reasoner might have for taking a belief issued by the rule to be true. On this understanding of justification, rule-circular arguments might appear to be vicious. For it seems that believing the conclusion of the rule-circular argument would be necessary in order to justifiably use the rule involved in it the first place. Hence, internalists would be likely to require an *independent* justification of the rule – that is, a justification of the kind that a rule-circular argument cannot possibly offer.

So, the issue of whether rule-circular arguments are vicious turns on the theory of justification one adopts. Realists should have to be externalists if they take NMA seriously. And their critics will have to argue for internalism, if the charge of vicious circularity is to go through. Given an externalist perspective, NMA does not have to assume *anything* about the reliability of IBE. Consequently, it does not have to assume anything about the reliability of IBE that anyone else (the critics of realism, in particular) *denies*. To be sure, the proponents of NMA have to assume an externalist theory of justification that some critics of realism might deny. But that is a different matter. That battle can be fought on general epistemological grounds which have nothing to do with the issue of circularity.

The point just made may give rise to further objections. One such might be that, even if we grant externalism, NMA does rely on the assumption that IBE is reliable. For, if the NMA does not presuppose or assume this, why should it employ an IBE in its defence of realism? Why not rely on some *other* type of inference? And if NMA does rely on this assumption, realists surely need to defend it in an independent way, would they not? Another objection might be that, if externalism is assumed, why should realists bother to offer NMA in the first place? By offering this argument, do they not implicitly assume that we need reasons to believe in the reliability of IBE? That is, do they not grant what the internalists have argued for all along? Let us take these objections in turn. Providing the answer to the first is a straightforward matter; but the second objection will not be met without some more work.

Why should NMA rely on an IBE in its defence of realism? Does that not imply that it assumes IBE to be reliable? I do not think it does. If one knew that a rule of inference was unreliable, one would be foolish to use it. This does not imply that one should first be able to prove that the rule is reliable before one uses it. All that is required is that one should have no reason to doubt the reliability of the rule – that there is nothing currently available which can make one distrust the rule. The defenders of NMA are 'guilty' of something: we would not use IBE if we had reasons to consider it unreliable. But we have no such reason. There is nothing vicious in admitting all this. If someone denied that abduction is reliable, they should have to give some reasons why this is so. This debate can go on independently of the issue of circularity. It will turn on arguments which aim to show that IBE should not be trusted. (Such arguments will be dealt with in Chapter 9.) But an analogy, due to Frank Ramsey (1926 [1978: 100]), will bring the present point home. It is only via memory that we can examine the reliability of memory. Even if we were to carry out experiments to examine this, we would still rely on memory: we would have to remember the outcomes of the experiments. But there is nothing vicious in using memory to determine and enhance the degree of accuracy of memory. For there is no reason to doubt its overall reliability.

Let us now focus on the second objection above: by offering the NMA, are realists not implicitly offering *reasons* to believe in the reliability of IBE? And, if so, should not these be independent reasons? I have two points against this objection.

1   The objection misunderstands what the NMA aims to do. NMA does not *make* IBE reliable. Nor does it add anything to its reliability, if it happens to be reliable. It merely generates a new belief *about* the reliability of IBE which is justified just in case IBE is reliable.
2   But, suppose we granted that NMA aimed to defend the reliability of IBE. This is certainly not excluded by externalism. It is just optional. Would the mere fact that the defence relies on a rule-circular argument make the attempted defence vicious – and hence lacking in rational force? I do not think so. If the rule-circularity of a defence is taken to be an outright vice, then we should simply have to forgo any attempt to explain or defend any of our *basic* inferential practices. What this implies is that even internalist defences, ultimately, will have to rely on rule-circular arguments. When it comes to the defence of our basic modes of reasoning, both ampliative and deductive, it seems that we either have no reasonable defence to offer or else the attempted defence will be rule-circular.

This dilemma shows up already in the case of deductive inference. It goes back to Lewis Carroll and his 'What the tortoise said to Achilles' that one cannot prove the soundness of *modus ponens* unless one ultimately employs *modus ponens*. We need *modus ponens* (and other deductive rules) because we need truth-preserving rules of inference – rules such that, whenever the premisses of an argument are true, the conclusion is also true. But can we prove that *modus ponens* is truth-preserving? The best we can do is to prove a meta-theorem that *modus ponens* in the object-language is truth-preserving. This meta-proof, however, requires that the meta-language already has *modus ponens* (or other deductive rules) as a rule. Intuitively, the idea is that any kind of proof (even the proof that *modus ponens* is truth-preserving) requires some rule of inference in order for it to go through. In the case of *modus ponens*, the required rule must also be truth-preserving. But do we not need a proof that *this* rule is truth-preserving? And so on. A typical reply, expressed vividly by Salmon (1965: 54), is that we *should* trust *modus ponens* because we do not have any reason to doubt that it is truth-preserving: we can 'reflect' on instances of *modus ponens* and realise the inconceivability of the situation in which all of the premises are true and the conclusion is false. Whether this is exactly right is still debatable. Van McGee (1985) and William Lycan (1994), for instance, have suggested that there are counter-examples to *modus ponens*. That is, there are instances of arguments which instantiate *modus ponens*, and yet have true premises and a false conclusion.[7] I do not want to enter this interesting debate here, but the typical response to these counter-examples shows that the defence of the soundness of *modus ponens* is a far from trivial (and presupposition-less) exercise. The typical reply to these counter-examples, discussed by Kornblith (1994), is that if we just define *modus ponens* using the standard meaning of the logical connective for conditional statements of the form 'p q', (where the conditional is true either when the antecedent is false or the consequent true), then there is *no* room for counter-examples: any purported counter-example is dismissed on the grounds that it should not be formalised as a purported instance of the schema $\{p; p{\rightarrow}q; \text{therefore } q\}$. The issue here is not whether this dismissal is correct (Lycan 1994a, for instance, doubts that it is). Rather, the issue is that no justification of *modus ponens* is possible which does not rest on some presuppositions. All we can do is engage in a process of *explanation* and *defence*. By reflecting on *modus ponens* (and other deductive rules we use), we aim to systematise it, to explain to ourselves the ways in which we should use it, and to show that, *given* the meaning of the logical connectives and the truth-tables, it delivers its goods – it is truth-preserving.[8]

A similar, if more complicated, situation arises when it comes to inductive reasoning. Inductive rules are non-truth-preserving. However, it is wrong to apply deductive standards to inductive reasoning. While deduction is concerned with truth preservation, induction is concerned with learning from experience. The fact that induction is not deduction shows nothing other than that each should be treated as a distinct mode of reasoning. But how can the very possibility of rational learning from experience be defended, if not by a rule-circular argument? Carnap's work can help us address this issue in a systematic way. Carnap's major problem was to establish which kinds of inductive argument in his systems of inductive logic are valid, in the sense that they license conclusions with high inductive probability (or degree of confirmation). In particular, he wanted to find out which among a number of ampliative rules (straight rule, Laplace's rule, c^*, $c^\dagger$, etc.) can best represent inductive learning from experience. But, we all know that one cannot defend the validity of inductive arguments without using *some* form of inductive reasoning. Reflecting on this question, Carnap (1968: 265–267) suggested that the circularity involved in an attempt to vindicate inductive reasoning is both indispensable and harmless. Here is a reconstruction of his argument.

Reasoners are either *inductively blind* – where 'inductively blind' refers to reasoners who make no inductive inferences and who are not disposed to make any – or they are not. If the reasoners are inductively blind, then we cannot possibly show them when an argument is inductively valid and when it is not. For learning to discriminate between these two cases, and therefore learning to recognise inductively valid arguments and to discard invalid ones, requires an 'inductive intuition'. This intuition should not be confused with the Cartesian idea of an infallible source of knowledge. Rather it should be seen as some sort of *disposition* to use inductive reasoning and to fallibly recognise that an argument is inductively valid. If there were such (unfortunate) inductively blind persons, they would be inductively blind precisely because they lack this disposition to learn from experience. When it comes to *our* attempts to persuade them why learning from experience is reasonable, we can rely only on some inductive argument – we have to rely on the past successes of inductive reasoning. What we are doing is indispensable, because no other argument could show them that learning from experience is reasonable. Yet being engaged in rule-circular reasoning also is harmless because, being induction-blind, nothing could persuade our interlocutors to reason inductively. If, on the other hand, the reasoners are not inductively blind – if they already operate within a network of dispositions to learn from experience – it is also both indispensable and harmless to engage in rule-circular reasoning in an attempt to explain to them the circumstances under which an inductive argument is or is not valid. It is indispensable because no non-inductive argument is available, and it is harmless because, in this case, it is an instance of a self-clarificatory procedure.

So, in either case, in our attempt to vindicate learning from experience, being engaged in rule-circular reasoning is both indispensable and harmless. The situation is totally analogous to the defence of deductive reasoning. There is no way in which one can persuade a *deductively blind* person of the soundness or rationality of deductive arguments. However, all those who operate in a network of deductive intuitions – e.g. who have internalised the meaning of the logical connectives, etc. – can be made to discriminate between valid and invalid arguments.

Carnap's argument suggests a wholly new perspective on the issue of what exactly we do when we offer arguments in defence of our basic inferential practices. In one sense, no inferential rule carries an absolute rational compulsion, unless it rests on a framework of intuitions and dispositions which takes for granted the presuppositions of this rule (truth preservation in the case of deductive reasoning, learning from experience in the case of inductive reasoning, searching for explanations in the case of abductive reasoning). When we attempt to vindicate or defend certain rules of inference (e.g. certain deductive, inductive or abductive rules), this is not because we want either to justify them without any assumptions, or to prove that they are rationally compelling for any sentient being. It is because we want to evaluate our existing inferential practices: to reflect on the rules we use or are disposed to use uncritically, and to examine the extent to which and in virtue of what these rules are reliable. Such evaluations cannot be made from a neutral epistemological standpoint. They, too, have to employ some methods. In the final analysis, we just have to rely on some basic methods of inquiry. The fact that we make recourse to rule-circular arguments in order to defend them, if defence is necessary, is both inescapable and harmless.[9]

By parity of reasoning, if one is disposed to reason abductively one should have no special problem with using NMA in defence of the reliability of IBE. NMA is no worse than attempts to defend *modus ponens* and inductive rules. In fact, the class of reasoners who use abductive reasoning is much broader than the class of committed realist epistemologists who reflect on the reliability of IBE and defend it by offering the NMA. This class will most certainly include non-realists – those who do not take sides on the realism debate. But it will also include those critics of realism who employ abduction, but disagree with the conclusion of NMA, the thesis that scientific theories are approximately true. As I noted above, that this class is not empty follows from the fact that at least some critics of the realist NMA try to show that there are better potential explanations of the success of science than the realist one. If sound, NMA can have rational force for all of them.

So, NMA has not been shown to be viciously circular. That being so, I do not know what the problem with NMA is. In any case, Fine (1986: 115) is mistaken in maintaining that NMA is 'of no significance'.

Fine has, however, launched another criticism against EDR, what he calls 'a deep and . . . insurmountable problem with the entire strategy of defending realism' (1986: 114). He grants, for the sake of the argument, that EDR may be successful in convincing someone who already employs abductive reasoning about the truth of realism. Then he asks: 'should that not be of some solace, at least for the realist?' (ibid.: 117).

Fine thinks that EDR should give no comfort to realists. For one must demand that the proofs of one's meta-theories be more stringent than the proofs in one's theories. To this end Fine appeals to Hilbert's programme of showing the consistency of mathematical theories by using only the most stringent and secure means – in particular, means which fall outside the proof-theoretic tools of the theory under consideration. Fine argues:

> Hilbert's idea was, I think, correct even though it proved to be unworkable. Metatheoretic arguments must satisfy more stringent requirements

than those placed on the arguments used by the theory in question, for otherwise the significance of reasoning about the theory is simply moot. I think this maxim applies with particular force to the discussion of realism.

(1986: 114)

From a naturalist viewpoint, it is of great relevance to the debate if a requirement has proved to be utopian. It is plain from Goedel's second incompleteness theorem that there cannot be a stringent proof, in Hilbert's sense, of the consistency of Peano arithmetic. In particular, any consistency proof for such an axiomatic formal theory is – at least in some sense – less elementary than the formal methods which the axiomatic theory formalises. Hilbert's requirement might be in principle correct. Yet, it is unreasonable to demand that a philosophical theory must satisfy a requirement that mathematics, with an accurate notion of proof and a strict and rigorous deductive structure, fails to satisfy. Fine's demand (1986: 115) that a realist theory of science employ 'methods more stringent than those in ordinary scientific practice' is unnaturally strong and unnaturally non-naturalistic.

Are there better explanations of the success of science?

What needs to be shown also is that NMA's conclusion is indeed the best explanation of the instrumental success of science. This is crucial because otherwise NMA cannot adequately defend the reliability of abduction; moreover Fine has argued that there is a better non-realist explanation of the success of science. In fact, Fine (1986a: 154) defends the rather bold thesis that anything which realists can do instrumentalists can do, and in a better way.

Fine's claim is that some notion of *instrumental reliability* of scientific theories best explains the success of science, where 'instrumental reliability' is a feature of scientific theories in virtue of which they are 'useful in getting things to work for the practical and theoretical purposes for which we might put them to use' (1991: 86). However, Fine's strategy faces a general problem. Suppose that he uses IBE in order to infer the *truth* of instrumentalism. Then he seems to admit that abduction *is* reliable, yet it just happens that, contrary to what realists expect, realism is not the best explanation of the success of science: rather, instrumentalism is. But then Fine would have to concede that abduction is reliable.

So Fine's use of IBE must be different. It should not, that is, be seen as an inference to the *truth* of the best explanation – the latter being, according to him, that science is instrumentally reliable. In fact, Fine has spoken of 'an instrumentalist version of the inference to the "best" explanation' (1991: 83). This version should still favour the best explanation, but it should assert that the best explanation is *empirically adequate* rather than true. Instrumentalism would get accepted as empirically adequate, *à la* van

Fraassen. Yet there would still, I think, be a problem. For even if instrumentalism were shown to be the best explanation of the instrumental success of science, it could not be more empirically adequate than realism. Realism and instrumentalism are equally empirically adequate. They both entail the empirical success of science. And note that for most instrumentalists empirical adequacy is the only epistemic virtue of a potential explanation – the only feature that contributes to its belief-worthiness *qua* explanation. If Fine accepted this common instrumentalist tenet, then even if instrumentalism were a better explanation of the success of science, it would be no more belief-worthy than realism, since they would be equally empirically adequate. If, however, Fine thought that certain explanatory virtues could, alongside their empirical adequacy, make one explanation more belief-worthy than another, then he would move away from an instrumentalist version of IBE and would defend instrumentalism only at the cost of conceding a major point to realism, viz. that explanatory virtues are ultimately epistemic virtues.

Let me, however, leave aside these qualms and focus on the central question: is the instrumentalist explanation of the success of science better than the realist one? Fine (1986a: 153–154; 1991: 82–83) contrasts two forms of (simplified) abductive explanations of the success of science:

(a)	(b)
Science is empirically successful	Science is empirically successful
∴ (probably) theories are instrumentally reliable	∴ (probably) theories are approximately true

Fine suggests that pattern (a) is always preferable to (b) on the grounds that if the explanandum is the empirical success of scientific methodology, then we do not need to inflate the potential explanation with 'features beyond what is useful for explaining the output' (1991: 83). So Fine thinks 'the instrumentalist, feeling rather on home ground, may suggest that to explain the instrumental success we need only suppose that our hypotheses and theories are instrumentally reliable' (1991: 82–83).

I think Fine's argument rests on the hidden assumption that an appeal to the (approximate) truth of background scientific theories goes beyond the features that are useful for explaining the instrumental success of science. In his essay 'Unnatural Attitudes' (1986a: 153), he has in fact suggested that admitting anything more than instrumental reliability 'would be doing no explanatory work'. His argument goes like this. When realists attempt to explain the success of a particular theory, they appeal to the approximate truth of a theoretical story as the best explanation of the theory's success in performing certain empirical tasks. But if this explanation is any good at all, they must 'allow some intermediate connection between the truth of the theory and success in its practice. The intermediary here is precisely the pragmatist's reliability' (1986a: 154). So, Fine suggests, the job that truth allegedly does in the explanation of the success of a theory is actually done by this intermediate *pragmatic* reliability. Truth seems explanatorily redundant. Moreover, if pragmatic reliability is substituted for truth in the realist account of success, one gets an alternative account in terms of instrumental reliability (ibid.: 154). Fine concludes: 'since no further work is done by ascending from that intermediary to the realist's "truth", the instrumental explanation has to be counted as better than the realist one. In this way the realist argument leads to instrumentalism' (ibid.). On the basis of this argument, Fine proves a meta-theorem: 'If the phenomena to be explained are not realist-laden, then to every good realist explanation there corresponds a better instrumentalist one' (ibid.).

There are two strange aspects to Fine's argument.

1   It is not at all obvious that there is anything like a *pragmatic* notion of reliability which realists have to take into account in their explanation of the success of science. Between successful empirical predictions and theories there are methods, auxiliary assumptions, approximations, idealisations, models and probably other things. Let us suppose that this stuff is what Fine calls the 'pragmatic intermediary'. Let us also suppose that these things alone could be summoned to account for the empirical success of a theory. Would this make claims concerning the truth of the theory explanatorily superfluous? Surely not. For one also wants to know why some particular model represents successfully the target physical system whereas others do not, or why one model represents the target physical system better than others, or why the methods followed generate successful predictions, or why some idealisations are better than others, and the like. When realists argue for the approximate truth of background scientific theories, they, in effect, want to explain the success (or instrumental reliability) of this intermediary stuff. Approximate truth would be summoned in order to explain the successful constraints which theories place on model-construction as well as the features of scientific methods in virtue of which they produce successful results. So, if Fine meant this stuff when he spoke of a pragmatic intermediary between the (approximate) truth of theory and its success in practice, the existence of *this* pragmatic intermediary would not render approximate truth explanatorily superfluous.

2   Even if we assume that there is some other *pragmatic* notion of reliability to be interpolated between approximate truth and empirical success, and even if we equate this notion with Fine's instrumental reliability, that it has any real explanatory import would be open to doubt. Instrumental reliability is nothing but a summary statement of the fact that the theory performs successfully practical tasks. If we then try to explain the theory's empirical success by saying that background theories are instrumentally reliable, we simply paraphrase what needs to be

explained. It is immaterial whether we phrase the explanandum as 'Theories are successful' or as 'Theories are instrumentally reliable'. No explanation is thereby offered, only a paraphrase of theories' success in terms of theories' instrumental reliability. The situation here is totally analogous with an attempt to 'explain' the fact that hammers are successful in driving nails into a wall by saying that hammers are instrumentally reliable for nail-driving. Recall that what is at stake is whether an instrumentalist explanation is better than the realist one. It turns out that, despite all the manoeuvring, it is not an explanation at all.

Fine has implicitly recognised that instrumental reliability is a rather poor explanation. For he has recently (1991) suggested a way to make claims of instrumental reliability potentially explanatory. He has outlined a dispositional understanding of the instrumental reliability of science. On this view, instrumental reliability involves a *disposition* to produce correct empirical results. Fine claims that this dispositional explanation of the success of science is 'an explanation of outcomes by reference to inputs that have the capacity (or "power") to produce such [i.e. instrumentally reliable] outcomes' (1991: 83).

This new understanding of instrumental reliability *is* potentially explanatory: it accounts for empirical success by an appeal to a *capacity*, or disposition, that theories have in virtue of which they are empirically successful. Although certainly in the right direction, this account is incomplete. Not because there are no dispositions, or powers, in nature, but rather because one would expect also an explanation of why and how theories have such a disposition to be instrumentally reliable; in particular an explanation that avoids the troubles of Moliére's 'explanation' of why opium sends somebody to sleep in terms of its 'dormitive power'. Is it a brute fact of nature that theories – being paradigmatic human constructions – have the disposition to be instrumentally reliable? This seems hardly credible. If dispositions of this sort need grounding, then there is an obvious candidate: the property of being approximately true would ground the power of scientific theories to be instrumentally reliable. Since Fine would certainly deny this account, he owes us an alternative story of how this disposition is grounded. Else, should this disposition need no grounding, he needs to show how can this be so.

I conclude, then, that Fine has failed to prove his meta-theorem in favour of instrumentalism. The realist account is the best overall explanation of the empirical success of science.

Could we not just deflate our quest for explanation?

There is an aspect of the *intuitive* epistemic thrust of Fine's critique of realism with which I have not yet dealt: that somehow 'going beyond the data' to posit 'theoretical entities' is more problematic than abandoning some forms of intuitively attractive abductive reasoning. A defender of Fine's critique of realism in particular might suggest that a deflationary account of explanation as licensing retrodiction and prediction might do just as well, without taking extra risks about theoretical commitments. Here is how. Suppose that someone accepts the foregoing distinctions between premiss-circularity and rule-circularity as well as the existence of abductive, or explanatory, intuitions. He might, therefore, acknowledge the *prima facie* force of the demand for an explanation of the reliability of scientific methodology. But instead of accepting the realist's explanation, he identifies explanation with retrodiction and prediction, and offers the following (Quinean) second-order induction about abduction as an epistemic justification of abductive practices in science: past abductive inferences have generated empirically successful theories; hence, based on a second-order *induction*, it is reasonable to expect that abductive inferences will keep providing empirically successful theories. So he concludes that one can be equipped with inductive generalisations about the instrumental reliability of abductive scientific methodology on the basis of which one can predict or retrodict the instrumental reliability of scientific methodology in particular cases. But, he stresses, these inductive generalisations do not commit one to the existence of unobservable entities, nor do they entail that abductive reasoning is a reliable guide to theoretical truth. All that they entail is that one can rely on abductive reasoning to get instrumentally reliable theories, but nothing more. I shall call this 'the induction-about-abduction' move.

I think this move is in the spirit of Fine's dispositional account of instrumental reliability discussed at the end of the previous section. In fact, the suggested inductive generalisations about the instrumental success of scientific methodology might be offered as a way to ground claims about the disposition of this methodology as instrumentally reliable. Two responses, which work in tandem, are available. First, that these generalisations do not really explain why scientific methodology is reliable; and, second that these generalisations are not free of theoretical commitments. Let us take them in turn.

Take the (second-order) generalisation that abductive reasoning generates instrumentally reliable theories. Let us call it A. A can be paraphrased as the conjunction of the following two claims:

A_1: abductive reasoning has generated instrumentally reliable theories in the past and present; and

A_2: abductive reasoning will generate instrumentally reliable theories in the future.

Now remember what needs to be explained: the instrumental reliability – past, present and future – of scientific theories. It is, then, not difficult to see that A_1 & A_2 is merely a paraphrase of what needs to be explained. More specifically, we can question whether this generalisation, as it stands, is suitable for prediction and retrodiction. If we use A ($= A_1$ & A_2) to *predict* a future instance of instrumental reliability, we need to assume that A (= A_1 & A_2) is already well-confirmed, which means that we need to assume what is really at issue: that A_1 on its own provides good inductive evidence for A_2. What exactly makes it the case that A_1 supports A_2? It may well be the case that hitherto instrumentally reliable theories fail when they are extended in new domains; unless, of course, we assume that they are truth-like. This appeal to truth-likeness would explain why theories are (or tend to be) instrumentally reliable, and would also warrant the projection to future instrumental reliability. On the other hand, if we use A (= A_1 & A_2) to *retrodict* the past instrumental reliability of scientific theories (A_1), we will have to appeal, implicitly, to their future reliability (A_2), a fact as much in need of explanation and grounding as is A_1. In any case, positing the approximate truth of scientific theories would offer a more satisfactory and highly non-trivial way to predict and retrodict their instrumental reliability: it is in virtue of theories being approximately true that we can

- retrodict their instrumental success in certain cases;
- predict future successes; and
- confirm the generalisation that abductive reasoning generates empirically successful theories.

This last claim would be in accord with the confirmation of empirical generalisations in scientific practice. Empirical generalisations are considered well confirmed mainly when they are embedded in larger theoretical structures which explain how the properties involved in the generalisation co-vary and how the generalisation gets connected with other well-supported ones. A framework which is (approximate) truth-linked plays precisely this role when it comes to the explanation of the instrumental reliability of scientific methodology and the instrumental successes of scientific theories.

At any rate, it is highly dubious that the 'induction-about-abduction' move can altogether avoid theoretical commitments. Boyd has in fact considered a similar objection to his attempt to defend the reliability of abductive reasoning (cf. 1984: 68–70; 1985: 236–241). The point is straightforward. Prior to performing the induction on past empirically successful scientific theories, we must naturally accept that instrumental success constitutes evidence for the truth of the inductive generalisations about observables made by these theories. But this judgement is not independent of all theoretical commitments. From myriad generalisations that involve observables, scientists pick only some as genuinely empirically supported and confirmed. Their choice is theory-dependent: theories suggest connections between hitherto unrelated observable phenomena; they determine which predicates are projectible, and which collections of individuals form natural kinds. But if ordinary judgements concerning inductive generalisations about observables involve theoretical commitments, any attempt to have an induction-about-abduction that is free of theoretical commitments will be seriously impaired.[10]

Can Darwin help?

Van Fraassen has offered a different explanation of the success of science. It is this:

> The success of science is not a miracle. It is not even surprising to the scientific (Darwinist) mind. For any scientific theory is born into a life of fierce competition, a jungle red in tooth and claw. Only the successful theories survive – the ones which *in fact* have latched on to actual regularities in nature.
>
> (1980: 40)

On this account, there is no surprise in the fact that current theories are empirically successful. For the Darwinian principle of the survival of the fittest has operated. Current theories have survived because they were the fittest among their competitors – fittest in the sense of latching on to universal regularities. Clearly, this is an elegant and simple explanation of the fact that current theories are successful. But does it undermine the realist explanation?

If we unpack van Fraassen's story, we find that it is *phenotypical*: it provides an implicit selection mechanism according to which entities with the same phenotype, i.e. empirical success, have been selected. But a phenotypic explanation does not exclude a *genotypic* account: an explanation in terms of some underlying feature which all successful theories share in common; a feature which has made them successful in the first place. The realist explanation in terms of truth provides this sort of genotypic account: every theory which possesses a specific phenotype, i.e. it is empirically successful, also possesses a specific genotype, i.e. approximate truth, which accounts for this phenotype. In order to see the point more clearly, compare van Fraassen's story with this (due to Peter Lipton): Each in a group of people has red hair. This is no surprise; but is explained by the fact that this group is comprised of members of the club of red-haired persons. (The club is, in a sense, a mechanism which selects only persons with red hair.) But this observation does not explain why George (or, for that matter, anyone of them taken individually) has red hair. A different, most likely genetic, story should be told about George's colour of hair.

Notice here that the realist explanation is *compatible* with van Fraassen's Darwinian account. Yet, the realist's is arguably preferable, because it is deeper. It does not stay on the surface – that is, it does not just posit a selection mechanism which lets through only empirically successful theories. It rather tells a story about the deeper common traits in virtue of which the selected theories are empirically successful.

As Lipton (1991: 170ff.) has suggested, there is another reason for preferring the genotypic to the Darwinian explanation: all that the phenotypic explanation warrants is that theories which have survived through the selection mechanism have not yet been *refuted*. There is no warrant that they will be successful in the future. Any such warrant must be external to the phenotypic story. For instance, this warrant can come from a combination of the phenotypic explanation with the principle of induction. On the other hand, the genotypic explanation has this warrant up its sleeve: if a theory is empirically successful because it is true, then it will keep on being empirically successful.

To sum up, then, there are no better explanations of the success of science than the realist one. Not that the discussion so far has exhausted all arguments levelled against IBE and its role in the realism debate. More is to come on this in Chapter 9, when I discuss van Fraassen's position. Additionally, there is a seemingly powerful argument against NMA which needs to be rebutted. It is the so-called 'pessimistic induction', enunciated by Laudan. Its thrust is that NMA cannot possibly be taken seriously because it flies in the face of the (alleged) fact that the history of science is the graveyard of supposed 'best explanations' of the evidence.

Part II will be devoted to defending realism against the pessimistic induction (Chapters 5 and 6), after which an attempt will be made to rebut the argument from the 'underdetermination of theories by evidence'.

Part II
Sceptical challenges

5 Resisting the pessimistic induction

The explanationist defence of realism (EDR) has suffered a rather serious blow from Laudan's contention that the history of science itself destroys the credibility of realist explanation of the success of science. For it is full of theories which were once empirically successful and yet turned out to be false. Laudan's argument[1] against scientific realism is simple but powerful. It can be summarised as follows:

> The history of science is full of theories which at different times and for long periods had been empirically successful, and yet were shown to be false in the deep-structure claims they made about the world. It is similarly full of theoretical terms featuring in successful theories which do not refer. Therefore, by a simple (meta-)induction on scientific theories, our current successful theories are likely to be false (or, at any rate, are more likely to be false than true), and many or most of the theoretical terms featuring in them will turn out to be non-referential.
>
> Therefore, the empirical success of a theory provides no warrant for the claim that the theory is approximately true. There is no substantive retention at the theoretical, or deep-structural, level and no referential stability in theory-change.

Laudan has substantiated his argument by means of what he has called 'the historical gambit': the list that follows – which, Laudan says, 'could be extended *ad nauseam*' – gives theories which were once empirically successful and fruitful, yet were neither referential nor true. These theories were *just* false:

- the crystalline spheres of ancient and medieval astronomy
- the humoral theory of medicine
- the effluvial theory of static electricity
- catastrophist geology, with its commitment to a universal (Noachian) deluge

- the phlogiston theory of chemistry
- the caloric theory of heat
- the vibratory theory of heat
- the vital-force theory of physiology
- the theory of circular inertia
- theories of spontaneous generation
- the contact-action gravitational ether of Fatio and LeSage
- the optical ether
- the electromagnetic ether.

If Laudan is right, then the realist's explanation of the success of science flies in the face of the history of science: the history of science cannot possibly warrant the realist belief that currently successful theories are approximately true, at least insofar as the warrant for this belief is the 'no miracle' argument. In what follows, I analyse the structure of Laudan's argument and show how scientific realism can be defended.

Laudan's *reductio*

The 'pessimistic induction' is a kind of *reductio*. The target is the realist thesis that:

(A)   Currently successful theories are approximately true.

Laudan does not directly deny that currently successful theories may *happen* to be truth-like. His argument aims to discredit the claim that there is an *explanatory connection* between empirical success and truth-likeness which warrants the realist's assertion (A). In order to achieve this, the argument compares a number of past theories to current ones and claims:

(B)   If currently successful theories are truth-like, then past theories *cannot* have been.

Past theories are deemed not to have been truth-like because the entities they posited are no longer believed to exist and/or because the laws and mechanisms they postulated are not part of our current theoretical description of the world. Then, comes the 'historical gambit':

(C)   These characteristically false theories were, nonetheless, empirically successful.

So, empirical success is not connected with truth-likeness and truth-likeness cannot explain success: the realist's potential warrant for (A) is defeated. As Laudan put it:

Because they [most past theories] have been based on what we now believe to be fundamentally mistaken theoretical models and structures, the realist cannot possibly hope to explain the empirical success such theories enjoyed in terms of the truth-likeness of their constituent theoretical claims.

(1984a: 91–92)

Hence, the pessimistic induction 'calls into question the realist's warrant for assuming that *today's* theories, including even those which have passed an impressive array of tests, can thereby warrantedly be taken to be (in Sellars' apt image) 'cutting the world at its joints' (Laudan 1984b: 157).

No realist can deny that Laudan's argument has *some* force. It shows that, on inductive grounds, the whole truth and nothing but the truth is unlikely to be had in science. That is, all scientific theories are likely to turn out to be, strictly speaking, false. This is something that realists seem to have to concede. However, a false theory can still be *approximately true*. The notion of approximate truth is discussed in detail in Chapter 11. For the time being, let me note that a theory is approximately true if it describes a world which is similar to the actual world in its most central or relevant features. So, what realists need to show is that past successful theories, although strictly speaking false, have been approximately true. This is the defensive line in which realists regroup and start their counter-attack.

Laudan's immediate challenge is that a theory cannot be said to be approximately true unless it is shown that its central terms refer (1981: 33). This requirement seems plausible. But one should be careful here. The intended realist claim is that from the genuine empirical success of a theory one can legitimately infer that the entities posited by the theory are real – they inhabit the world we live in. Without this assumption we cannot adequately explain the empirical success of a theory. There is, however, no way in which any proponents can 'step outside' of their theories and check whether these entities exist. We should simply have to rely on our theories as our best guide to what the furniture of the world is. What Laudan observes is that, given the past track-record of science, we simply cannot do that: the radical changes in the central ontological claims made by theories over the centuries suggest that any such claim is as likely to go as any other. None of them, in other words, enjoys any privilege over any other. Mary Hesse has put the same thought in the form of the 'principle of no privilege', which, she says, follows from an 'induction from the history of science'. According to this principle, 'our own scientific theories are held to be as much subject to radical conceptual change as past theories are seen to be' (1976: 264). In order to rebut the 'principle of no privilege', realists should show that:

1   the theoretical discontinuities in theory-change were neither as widespread nor as radical as Laudan has suggested;

2   instead, there has emerged a rather stable and well-supported network of theoretical assertions and posits which is our best account of what the world is like; and

3   theoretical terms that can be legitimately taken to have been central in past theories can still be referential, i.e. they can still be taken to refer to entities which feature in science's current theoretical ontology.

In sum, realists should try to reconcile the historical record with the realist claim that successful theories are typically approximately true. How can this be done?

Realist gambits

Before discussing this, let me make two preliminary points. First, one should note that scientists are not prone to acquire only false beliefs. As science progresses, they accumulate more evidence, further and fresh empirical data, which they can then use to update and modify their beliefs and theoretical commitments. Besides, scientists can come to know how to better test their theories and, in particular, how to identify those methods of theory-construction which are likely to generate false and unwarranted beliefs. Hence, they can form better-supported theoretical beliefs. They can learn how to gauge the requisite evidence for their beliefs, how to improve their methods, and how to avoid unreliable methods. There is no guarantee, of course, that this process of learning from past experience will lead from false to truer theories. However, if scientists can positively learn from past experience, they are in a better position to abandon false theoretical claims in favour of new ones that are better supported by the evidence. Hence, these claims have a better chance of being truth-like than did those now abandoned. Second, even a quick glance at current science suggests that there is a host of entities, laws, processes and mechanisms posited by past theories – such as the gene, the atom, kinetic energy, the chemical bond, the electromagnetic field etc. – which have survived a number of revolutions to be retained in current theories. That is, one can quickly see that Laudan has overstated his case against scientific realism. In its crudest form, the pessimistic induction boils down to the claim that, as science grows, we can certify only the accumulated theoretical falsehoods, while we invariably have no good reasons to believe that we have hit upon some theoretical truths. But this is far-fetched and implausible.

Success too-easy-to-get

It is now time to attempt a conclusive refutation of Laudan's *reductio*. In light of the structure of his argument outlined earlier, one way to block Laudan's *reductio* is to target the 'historical gambit' or premiss (C). One can substantially weaken premiss (C) simply by reducing the size of Laudan's list. If we manage to restrict the meta-inductive basis, it no longer warrants the conclusion that genuine success and approximate truth are unconnected. Therefore, the 'historical gambit' is neutralised.

The form of Laudan's 'historical gambit' is this. It claims that all past theoretical conceptualisations of the several domains of inquiry $T_1, \ldots, T_n$ Laudan has sampled have been empirically successful yet false, and it concludes, inductively, that *any* arbitrarily successful scientific theory T_{n+1} is likely to be false (or, at any rate, more likely to be false than true).

This kind of argument can be challenged by observing that the inductive basis is not big and representative enough to warrant the pessimistic conclusion (cf. Devitt 1984: 161–162; McMullin 1984: 17). The basis for Laudan's induction can be eroded by querying whether all of the listed theories were, as a matter of fact, successful and whether they were representative of their disciplines at stages of development sufficiently advanced as to be reckoned theoretically mature.

One can dispute the claim that all theories in Laudan's list were successful. Laudan suggests that a theory is successful 'so long as it has worked reasonably well, that is, so long as it has functioned in a variety of explanatory contexts, has led to several confirmed predictions, and has been of broad explanatory scope' (1984a: 110). To be sure, he thinks that this is precisely the sense in which realists claim scientific theories to be successful when they propose the 'no miracle' argument (ibid.). However, the notion of empirical success should be *more* rigorous than simply getting the facts right, or telling a story that fits the facts. For any theory (and for that matter, any wild speculation) can be made to fit the facts – and hence to be successful – by simply 'writing' the right kind of empirical consequences into it. The notion of empirical success that realists are happy with is such that it includes the generation of novel predictions which are in principle testable.[2] Consequently, it is not at all clear that all theories in Laudan's list were genuinely successful. It is doubtful, for instance, that the contact-action gravitational ether theories of LeSage and Hartley, the crystalline spheres theory and the theory of circular inertia enjoyed any genuine success (cf. McMullin 1987: 70; Worrall 1994: 335). A realist simply would not endorse their inclusion in Laudan's list. On the contrary, the real question for a realist is this: are theories which were *genuinely* successful characteristically false?

Given the centrality of novel predictions in my defence of realism, it is prudent to analyse this notion a bit further so that it becomes clearer and certain misunderstandings are avoided. A 'novel' prediction is typically taken to be the prediction of a phenomenon whose existence is ascertained only *after* a theory suggests its existence. On this view a prediction counts as novel only if the predicted phenomenon is *temporally* novel, that is, only if the predicted phenomenon was hitherto unknown. This, however, cannot be the whole story. For one, theories also get support from their ability to explain already known phenomena. For another, why should the provenance of the predicted phenomenon have any bearing on whether or not the prediction supports the theory? One can easily imagine a case in which, unbeknown to the theoretician whose theory made the prediction of a temporally novel phenomenon, the phenomenon had already been discovered by some experimenter. Would or should this information affect the support which the predicted fact confers on the theory? If we thought that *only* genuine temporally novel predictions can confer support on theories, then we would have to admit that once we were aware that the fact was known, the predicted fact would become impotent to support the theory. In order to avoid these counter-intuitive pitfalls, the notion of novelty should be broader than what is meant by 'temporal novelty'. Following Earman (1992: Chapter 4, section 8) we should speak of 'use novelty', where, simply put, the prediction P of a known fact is use-novel *relative to a theory T*, if no information about this phenomenon was used in the construction of the theory which predicted it.[3]

But how exactly are we to understand the claim that a theory T makes a use-novel prediction of a known phenomenon? I think that in order to appreciate the issue at stake, one must follow Worrall (1985; 1989c) and provide some analysis of the ways in which a known fact E can be accommodated in a scientific theory T. Generally, there are two such ways:

- Information about a known fact E is used in the construction of a theory T, and T predicts E.
- A phenomenon E is known the time that a theory T is proposed, T predicts E, but no information about E is used in the construction of T.

Tidal phenomena, for instance, were predicted by Newton's theory, but they were not used in its construction. Let me, then, call *novel accommodation* any case in which a known fact is accommodated within the scope of a scientific theory, but no information about it is used in its construction. Let me, moreover, contrast novel accommodation with *ad hoc accommodation*. Although the Lakatosian school has produced a fine-grained distinction between levels of ad hocness, (cf. Lakatos, 1968: 399; 1970: 175; Zahar, 1973: 101), I shall take the most general case, namely:

Conditions of ad hocness: A theory T is ad hoc with respect to phenomenon E if and only if either of the following two conditions is satisfied:

1 A body of background knowledge B entails the existence of phenomenon E. Information about E is used in the construction of a theory T, and T accommodates E.

2 A body of background knowledge B entails the existence of phenomenon E. A certain already available theory T does not predict/ explain E. T is modified into theory T' so that T' predicts E, but

the *only* reason for this modification is the prediction/explanation of *E*. In particular *T'* has no other excess theoretical and empirical content over *T*.[4]

Given this analysis, novel accommodation (or use novelty) of known facts can be explicated as follows:

> *Use novelty*: A prediction *P* of a phenomenon *E* is use-novel with respect to a theory *T* if *E* is known before *T* is proposed, *T* does not satisfy either of the ad hocness conditions and *T* predicts *E*.

The real issue then is whether use novelty and temporal novelty have different bearings on the empirical support of a theory. I do not want to enter here the subtleties of this debate, for my purpose is to contrast novel accommodation with ad hoc accommodation. But, briefly, my view is that both use novelty and temporal novelty, so long as they are sharply distinguished from any ad hoc accommodation, are *complementary* aspects of theory confirmation. For, one can demand that a theory should accommodate known phenomena in a *non* ad hoc way, and *in addition* to this that it must yield temporally novel predictions. When, however, it comes to the *support* that use-novel and temporally novel predictions confer on a theory, that is, when it comes to the degree to which they confirm a theory, we may well assign different weights to these two sorts of prediction. It is natural to suggest that any temporally novel predictions which obtain carry an *additional* weight, because a theory that suggests new phenomena takes an extra risk of refutation. For there is always the possibility that a known fact can be 'forced' into a theory, whereas a theory cannot be forced to yield an hitherto unknown fact. Hence, predicting a new effect – whose existence falls naturally out of a theory – makes the theory more risky and susceptible to extra experimental scrutiny which may refute it.[5]

In sum, I want to stress that it is important *not* to contrast use novelty and temporal novelty, but both are to be contrasted with ad hoc accommodation. For, if anything, there is at most a difference in *degree* between use novelty and temporal novelty, whereas, there is a difference in *kind* between novel accommodation and ad hoc accommodation.[6]

Besides making the notion of empirical success more rigorous, another way to reduce the size Laudan's list is to suggest that *not all* past theoretical conceptualisations of domains of inquiry should be taken seriously. Realists require that Laudan's list should include only *mature* theories; that is, theories which have passed the 'take-off point' (Boyd) of a specific discipline. This 'take-off point' can be characterised by the presence of a body of well-entrenched background beliefs about the domain of inquiry which, in effect, delineate the boundaries of that domain, inform theoretical research and constrain the proposal of theories and hypotheses. This corpus of beliefs gives a broad identity to the discipline by being, normally, the common ground that rival theories of the phenomena under investigation share. It is an empirical matter to find out when a discipline reaches the 'take-off point', but for most disciplines there is such a point (or, rather a period). For instance, in the case of heat phenomena, the period of theoretical maturity was reached when such background beliefs as the principle of impossibility of perpetual motion, the principle that heat flows only from a warm to a cold body and the laws of Newtonian mechanics had become well entrenched. If this requirement of maturity is taken into account, then theories such as the 'humoral theory of medicine' or the 'effluvial theory of static electricity' drop out of Laudan's list. Once Laudan's list is restricted to those past theories which were *mature and genuinely successful*, then it is no longer strong enough to warrant the pessimistic conclusion.

Although it is correct that realists should not worry about all of the past theories that Laudan suggests, the present move is not enough to defeat the 'pessimistic induction': for it does not account for the fact that at least *some* past theories which pass both realist tests of maturity and success are nevertheless considered false. Relevant examples are the caloric theory of heat and the nineteenth-century optical ether theories. If these theories are false, despite their being both distinctly successful and mature, then the intended explanatory connection between empirical success and truthlikeness is still undermined. How then can we defend this explanatory connection?

The *divide et impera* move

The crucial premiss in Laudan's *reductio* is (B) (see p. 102): if we hold current theories to be truth-like, then past theories are bound not to be truthlike since they posited entities that are no longer believed to exist, and posited laws and theoretical mechanisms that have now been abandoned. Without this premiss the pessimistic conclusion does not follow.

Can we defeat (B)? Here is a suggestion: it is enough to show that the success of past theories did not depend on what we now believe to be fundamentally flawed theoretical claims. Put positively, it is enough to show that the theoretical laws and mechanisms which generated the successes of past theories have been retained in our current scientific image. I shall call this the *divide et impera* move. It is based on the claim that when a theory is abandoned, its theoretical constituents, i.e. the theoretical mechanisms and laws it posited, should not be rejected *en bloc*. Some of those theoretical constituents are inconsistent with what we now accept, and therefore they have to be rejected. But not all are. Some of them have been retained as essential constituents of subsequent theories. The *divide et impera* move suggests that if it turns out that the theoretical constituents that were responsible for the empirical success of otherwise abandoned theories are those that have been retained in our current scientific image, then a substantive version of scientific realism can still be defended.

This move dissociates genuine empirical success from characteristic falsity. Moreover, it paves the way for the 'right kind' of explanatory connection between success and truth-likeness. Laudan, realists should say, has taught us something important: on pain of being at odds with the historical record, the empirical success of a theory cannot issue an unqualified warrant for the truth-likeness of everything that the theory says. Insofar as older realists have taken this view, they have been shown to be, to say the least, unrealistic. Yet, it would be equally implausible to claim that, despite its genuine success, everything that the theory says is wrong. The right assertion seems to be that the genuine empirical success of a theory does make it reasonable to believe that the theory has *truth-like constituent theoretical claims*.

Moreover, if the theoretical constituents that were responsible for the empirical successes of past theories have been retained in subsequent theories, then this gives us reason to be more optimistic about their truth-likeness: that all these theoretical constituents have been shown to be invariant and stable elements of our modern scientific image; they have survived several 'revolutions' and have contributed to the empirical success of science. I think realists should follow Philip Kitcher's lead (1993) and suggest that the best way to defend realism is to use the generation of stable and invariant elements in our evolving scientific image to support the view that these elements represent our best bet for what theoretical mechanisms and laws there are.

This preamble for the *divide et impera* move may resonate with two recent reactions to the 'pessimistic induction', those of Kitcher (1993) and of Worrall (1989; 1994). Both have defended the analogous view that realists should characterise which kinds of statement are abandoned as false and which are retained. Kitcher suggests a distinction between 'presuppositional posits' and 'working posits', while Worrall draws the line between the 'content' of a theoretical statement, which gets superseded, and its 'structure', which is retained. The position I defend is akin to Kitcher's, although some differences will be discussed shortly. However, the *divide et impera* move is not meant to reflect or capture Worrall's distinction between structure and content. The latter distinction and Worrall's position deserve a more detailed discussion and criticism, to which Chapter 7 is devoted.

How should realists circumscribe the truth-like constituents of past genuinely successful theories? I must first emphasise that we should really focus on the specific successes of certain theories, like the prediction by Fresnel's theory of diffraction that if an opaque disk intercepts the rays emitted by a light source, a bright spot will appear at the centre of its shadow; or Laplace's prediction of the law of propagation of sound in air by means of the hypothesis that sound's propagation is an adiabatic process. Then we should ask the question: how were these successes brought about? In particular, which theoretical constituents made essential contributions to them? It is not, generally, the case that *no* theoretical constituents contribute to a theory's successes. Similarly, it is not, generally, the case that *all* theoretical constituents contribute (or contribute equally) to the empirical success of a theory. (What, for instance, was the relevant contribution of Newton's claim that the centre of mass of the universe is at absolute rest?) Theoretical constituents which make essential contributions to successes are those that have an indispensable role in their generation. They are those which 'really fuel the derivation' – to use one of Laudan and Leplin's recent expressions (1991: 462).

When does a theoretical constituent H indispensably contribute to the generation of, say, a successful prediction? Suppose that H together with another set of hypotheses H' (and some auxiliaries A) entail a prediction P. H indispensably contributes to the generation of P if H' and A alone cannot yield P and no other available hypothesis H^* which is consistent with H' and A can replace H without loss in the relevant derivation of P. Clearly, there are senses in which all theoretical assertions are eliminable, if, for instance, we take the Craig-transform of a theory, or if we 'cook up' a hypothesis H^* by writing P into it. But if we impose some natural epistemic constraints on the potential replacement – if, for instance, we require that the replacement be independently motivated, non ad hoc, potentially explanatory, etc. – then it is not certain at all that a suitable replacement can always be found. Worrall has recently noted that whenever a theory is replaced by another, 'the replacing theory alone offers a constructive proof of the "eliminability" of the earlier one' (1994: 339). There should be no doubt that the old theory as a whole gets eliminated. Yet, Worrall's observation does not establish the eliminability of the specific theoretical constituents that contributed to the empirical successes of the superseded theory. If the *divide et impera* move is correct, then these constituents are typically those that 'carry over' to the successor theory (admittedly, sometimes, only as limiting cases of the relevant constituents of the replacing theory).

So, when it comes to explaining the specific successes of a theory by means of the claim that the theory has truth-like constituent theoretical claims, realists should argue that the truth-like constituents are (more likely to be) those that contribute essentially to, or 'fuel', these successes. Realists need care only about those constituents which contribute to successes and which can, therefore, be used to account for these successes, or their lack thereof. Analogously, the theoretical constituents to which realists need not commit themselves are precisely those that are 'idle' components, impotent to make any difference to the theory's stake for empirical success.

What is required to successfully perform the *divide et impera* move? The key to this question lies in the careful study of the structure and content of past genuinely successful theories. What is needed are careful case-studies that will

- identify the theoretical constituents of past genuine successful theories that made essential contributions to their successes; and

• show that these constituents, far from being characteristically false, have been retained in subsequent theories of the same domain.

If all kinds of claims that are inconsistent with what we now accept were essential to the derivation of novel predictions and in the well-founded explanations of phenomena, then one cannot possibly appeal to their truth-likeness in order to explain empirical success. Then, Laudan wins. However, if it turns out that the theoretical constituents which were essential are those that have 'carried over' to subsequent theories, then the 'pessimistic induction' gets blocked. Settling this issue requires detailed study of some past theories that qualify as genuinely successful.

The good news for realism, as we shall see in detail in the next chapter, is that relevant studies of the several stages of the caloric theory of heat and the nineteenth-century optical ether theories suggest that both of the foregoing requirements can be met. However, as regards the *general* argument thus far, the details of these studies – illuminating though they may be – are not necessary. This argument has aimed to show that if realists successfully perform the two tasks outlined above, then a case can be made for scientific realism; it has also indicated how these tasks can be performed, in particular, what role the suggested case-studies are to play, what issues they should focus on and how they are relevant to settling the argument between scientific realism and the 'pessimistic induction'.

Is the *divide et impera* move perhaps too close to Kitcher's approach? Could one not simply identify the idle constituents of a theory with Kitcher's 'presuppositional posits' and the essentially contributing constituents with his 'working posits'? These identifications may be pertinent. However, there are differences. My distinction between idle and essentially contributing constituents is meant to capture how the successes of a theory can differently support its several theoretical constituents. Kitcher's distinction between presuppositional and working posits, however, is meant to capture the difference between referring and non-referring terms. Working posits are said to be 'the putative referents of terms that occur in problem-solving schemata', while presuppositional posits are 'those entities that apparently have to exist if the instances of the schemata are to be true' (Kitcher 1993: 149). But, so put, the distinction is problematic. For, in effect, we are told that the success of a problem-solving schema does support the existence of the referents of some of the terms featuring in it, but it does not support the existence of a putative entity the presence of which is required for the truth of the whole schema. But unless one shows how it is possible that the empirical success of the theory can lend support only to some, but not all, existence claims issued by the theory, then Kitcher's contention seems to be just grist to Laudan's mill. Kitcher suggests that the putative referents of presuppositional posits, such as the ether, were apparently only presupposed for the truth of the relevant schemata; in fact, they turned out to be eliminable without derivational loss (1993: 145). This suggestion is retroactive and open to the charge that it is ad hoc: the eliminable posits are those that get abandoned. Yet, as we are about to see, the *divide et impera* move can improve on Kitcher's views by avoiding this charge.[7]

A central objection to my line thus far is the following: with the benefit of hindsight, one can rather easily work it out so that the theoretical constituents that supposedly contributed to the success of past theories turn out to be those which were, as it happens, retained in subsequent theories. So, the realists face the charge that they are bound to first identify the past constituents which have been retained and then proclaim that it was those (and only those) which contributed to the empirical success and which enjoyed evidential support. Can realists do better than that? Retention aside, can we independently identify the theoretical constituents that contribute to the successes of a given theory and show that it is only those that we deem truth-like?

In response to this objection, it should be pointed out that eminent scientists do the required identification all the time. It is not that realists come, as it were, from the future to identify the theoretical constituents of past theories that were responsible for their success. Scientists themselves tend to identify the constituents which they think were responsible for the success of their theories, and this is reflected in their attitude towards their own theories. This attitude is not an all-or-nothing affair. As we are about to see in some detail, scientists do not, normally, believe either that everything a successful theory says is truth-like or conversely that, despite its success, nothing it says is truth-like. Rather, the likes of Lavoisier, Laplace and Carnot – to mention just a few – had a differentiated attitude towards their theories (in this case the caloric theory), in that they believed in the truth-likeness of some theoretical claims while considering some others to have been too speculative, or too little supported by the evidence, to be accepted as truth-like. This differentiated attitude was guided by the manner in which the several constituents of the theory were employed in the derivation of predictions (e.g. Laplace's prediction of the correct law of the propagation of sound in air) and in well-founded explanations of phenomena (e.g. Carnot's explanation of the fact that maximum work is produced in a Carnot-cycle). So, theoretical claims which were not essential for the success of the theory were treated with suspicion, as for instance was the case with the assumption that heat is a material fluid; and those claims which 'fuelled' the successes of the theory were taken to enjoy evidential support and were believed to be truth-like, as for instance was the case with the claims that heat can remain in latent form, or that the propagation of sound in air is an adiabatic – rather than an isothermal – process.

My claim is that it is precisely those theoretical constituents which scientists themselves believed to contribute to the successes of their theories (and hence to be supported by the evidence) that tend to get retained in theory change. Whereas, the constituents that do not 'carry-over' tend to be those that scientists themselves considered too speculative and unsupported to be taken seriously. If this view is right, then not only is the *divide et impera* move not ad hoc, but it actually gains independent plausibility from the way scientists treat their theories, and from the way they differentiate their commitments to their several constituent theoretical claims. If, therefore, there is a lesson which scientists should teach realists it is that an all-or-nothing realism is not worth fighting for.

In the next chapter, I try to substantiate these general philosophical points by means of two detailed case-studies. They concern the two controversial items on Laudan's list: the caloric theory of heat and the optical ether theories of the nineteenth century. Let me here just summarise the main points that these studies will raise and defend.

The study of the *caloric theory of heat* shows that the caloric representation of the cause of heat as a material fluid was not as central, unquestioned and supported as, for instance, Laudan (1984a: 113) has claimed. Caloric was not a putative entity to which the most eminent scientists had committed themselves as the real causal agent of heat phenomena. More importantly, the empirical success of the caloric theory was not essentially dependent on claims concerning the existence of an imponderable fluid which caused the rise (fall) of temperature by being absorbed (given away) by a body. The laws which scientists considered well supported by the available evidence and the background assumptions they used in their theoretical derivation were *independent* of the hypothesis that the cause of heat was a material substance: no relevant assumption was essentially used in the derivation–prediction of these laws. So, the laws which scientists considered to be well supported by the evidence and to generate the empirical success of the caloric theory did not support, nor did they require, the hypothesis that the cause of heat was a material substance. What this study suggests is that the parts of caloric theory which scientists believed in were well supported by the evidence and were retained in subsequent theories of heat, whereas the hypotheses that were abandoned were those which were ill-supported by the evidence. Hence, the point which the first case-study will highlight is this: when the laws established by a theory turn out to be independent of assumptions associated with allegedly central theoretical entities, it makes perfect sense to talk of the approximate truth of this theory, despite the recognition that not all of its theoretical terms refer.

The second case-study – which discusses the *dynamical optical ether theories* of the nineteenth century – aims to offer a different service to realism. It suggests that the most general theory – in terms of Lagrangian dynamics and the satisfaction of the principle of the conservation of energy – which was the backbone of the research programme around the dynamical behaviour of the carrier of light-waves has been retained in the subsequent framework of electromagnetism. This general theory was employed in the study of the *luminiferous ether* which was taken to be the dynamical structure which underlies light-propagation and which was such that it sustained the light-waves, and stored their energy (*vis viva*), during the time between their leaving the source and until just before reaching the receiver. Given that the carrier of light-waves was a dynamical structure of unknown constitution, the application of Lagrangian dynamics to study its behaviour enabled the scientific community to investigate its most general properties (e.g. its general laws of motion) leaving out the details of its constitution. The investigation of the possible constitution of the carrier of light-waves was aided by the construction of models (e.g. Green's elastic-solid model of the ether), where this model construction was based on perceived analogies between the carrier of light-waves (e.g. its ability to sustain transversal waves) and other physical systems (e.g. elastic solids). It was mostly these models that were abandoned later on. This case-study will show that a reading of the nineteenth-century theories of optics which suggests that the content of these theories was exhausted by the elastic solid-like models confuses the model and the actual, yet concealed, dynamical system the behaviour of which scientists were trying to understand. The advocates of the pessimistic induction would simply make an illegitimate move, if they appealed to those past failed models which scientists took to be heuristic devices, in order to infer that any current or future physical theory is likely to be false.

One of the points that the second study raises relates to the status of the abandoned theoretical term 'luminiferous ether'. It is hard to deny that the postulation of a medium for the propagation of light – denoted by the term 'ether' – underwrote the development of optical theories during the nineteenth century. Yet, the term 'ether' has been seen as an exemplar of a non-referring scientific term. Does it, then, follow that the whole range of dynamical theories of optics in which ether had a central function cannot possibly be approximately true? Discussion of that issue is postponed until Chapter 12, where attention turns to theories of the reference of theoretical terms. There I motivate a causal–descriptive theory of reference and defend the view that it is plausible to think of 'luminiferous ether' as referring to the electromagnetic field.

6 Historical illustrations

Heat as an imponderable fluid or heat as motion?

The core problems of the theories of heat in the late eighteenth and the early nineteenth century were the following: the cause of the rise and fall in the temperature of bodies; the cause of the expansion of gases when heated; the change of state; and the cause of the release of heat in several chemical interactions, and especially in combustion. It was in this problem-nexus that scientists such as Joseph Black, Antoine Lavoisier and Pierre-Simon Laplace introduced the causal–explanatory model of caloric.

Caloric was taken to be a theoretical entity and 'caloric' was the theoretical term purporting to refer to a material substance, an indestructible fluid of fine particles, which causes the rise in temperature of a body which absorbs it (cf. Lavoisier 1790: 1–2). Heat was taken to be the observable effect of the transportation of caloric from a hot body to a cold one (ibid.: 5). Being a material substance, caloric was taken to be conserved in all thermal processes. In 1780s, Lavoisier used caloric as an important element in his anti-phlogiston system of chemistry (ibid.: Part I; also Lilley 1948). Moreover, the assumption that heat was conserved played an important role in the development and theoretical exploitation of experimental calorimetry (see Laplace and Lavoisier 1780: 156). In dealing with the change in the state of a substance (e.g. the vaporisation of water), where, although a large quantity of heat is needed, this change takes place at constant temperature, Black (1803) assumed that heat can exist in a latent form, too. Lavoisier had already suggested that caloric can exist in two forms: either free (*calorique sensible*) or combined. Combined caloric was thought to be 'fixed in bodies by affinity or electric attraction, so as to form part of the substance of the body, even part of its solidity' (1790: 19). So, the existence of latent heat was explained by means of caloric in combined form.

However, a dynamical conception of heat had been the rival of the caloric theory ever since the latter was put forward. According to the dynamical theory, the cause of heat was not a material fluid. Instead, it was the motion of the particles which constitute a substance. So, heat was taken to be nothing over and above the result of the motion of the molecules of a body. Laplace and Lavoisier give the following account of the dynamical theory: '[H]eat is nothing but the result of the insensible motions of the molecules of matter. . . . According to the hypothesis we examine [i.e. the dynamical theory] the heat is the *vis viva (force vive)* which is the result of the insensible motions of the molecules of bodies' (1780: 151–152).

The dynamical representation of the cause of heat was less developed than the caloric theory. But, it could also explain the transmission of heat and the restoration of equilibrium between unequally heated bodies put in contact (ibid.: 152 and 154). Most proponents of the caloric theory considered the dynamical theory as a serious but, given the available evidence, less probable competitor (see Black 1803: 44). The main reason why the dynamical account attracted the attention of scientists was that it could explain the production of heat by friction. Davy (1799: 9–23) listed a series of experiments which constituted, as he said, a *reductio ad absurdum* of the thesis that heat was a material substance, since matter could not be produced or created by motion, that is, for instance, by rubbing two things together. So, this empirical fact was taken to undermine the claim that the cause of heat was a material substance which was never created or destroyed. Count Rumford (Benjamin Thomson) (1798: 70) took up Davy's misgivings against the caloric theory and performed several experiments in which heat was produced by friction. He also suggested that the cause of heat could not be a material substance since heat could be produced by friction in an *inexhaustible* manner, and no material substance can be inexhaustible. On the contrary, he said, if heat was motion, as the advocates of the dynamical theory suggested, then its generation by friction would be easily explained.

Most caloricists, however, were unmoved by Count Rumford's challenge because, after all, only a finite quantity of heat could ever be obtained before the bodies used for the production of heat by friction were rubbed away. Hence, their claim was that the production of heat by friction could not be inexhaustible. Besides, the dynamical representation of heat was physically and mathematically undeveloped and did not attract any significant attention until Clausius and William Thomson showed that this representation is compatible with the Carnot–Clapeyron theory of work and the basic laws of the caloric theory.

Yet, the caloric representation of heat was not without problems. Probably its most important difficulty was related to the problem of the weight of caloric. According to both the critics and the advocates of the theory, if caloric were a material substance, then it should have mass and weight. Up to 1785, all experiments performed had shown that a heated substance did not weigh more than when it was unheated. The absence of weight from caloric was an important problem for the caloric theory. Reviewing several experiments, Black (1803: 45) stated:

It has not, therefore, been proved by any experiment that the weight of bodies is increased by their being heated, or by the presence of heat in them. This may be thought very inconsistent with the idea of the nature or cause of heat that I . . . mentioned [i.e. that the cause of heat is a material fluid]. It must be confessed that the afore-mentioned fact may be stated as a strong objection against this supposition [i.e. that the cause of heat is a material fluid].

Starting from 1787 and lasting until late 1790s, Count Rumford performed a series of experiments in order to calculate 'the weight ascribed to heat'. Rumford examined whether liquids change in weight when they lose heat by just cooling down. The results obtained were negative. So he concluded that the caloric theory could not explain away the absence of weight from caloric, unless it assumed that caloric 'is so infinitely rare, even in its most condensed state, as to baffle all our attempts to discover its gravity'. On the contrary, he argued, if one adopted the theory that 'heat is nothing more than the intestine vibratory motion of the constituent parts of heated bodies', then it would be clear that 'the weight of bodies can in no wise be affected by such a motion' (1799: 100). So, whereas the caloric theory had to perform an artificial manoeuvre in order to accommodate the absence of weight from caloric, the competing dynamical theory could accommodate this fact more naturally.

Does the superiority of the caloric representation of heat at this early stage suggest that scientists believed that the caloric theory was true? What I will show is that most of the eminent supporters of the theory were very cautious in expressing their attitude to the *epistemic value* of the theory. Let us consider the following points:

1   Most of the eminent proponents of the caloric theory were aware of the difficulties that this theory faced.
2   They knew the advantages of the alternative representation of heat, especially in explaining the production of heat by friction.
3   They were aware also of the shaky experimental evidence, and of the inaccuracy of most of the experimental results available.

Such factors made most of the eminent scientists working within the caloric theory of heat to be very careful in their statements and very cautious in their epistemic claims. Probably the example most illustrative of this behaviour concerns Black. In his lectures, Black presented *both* contemporary theories of heat. He emphasised moreover that '(O)ur knowledge of heat is not brought to the state of perfection that might enable us to propose with confidence a theory of heat or to assign an immediate cause of it' (1803: 42). He noted that 'the supposition' that heat was a material fluid appeared the 'most probable', but he added that 'neither of these suppositions [i.e. the material and the dynamical] has been fully and accurately considered by their authors, or applied to explain *the whole facts and phenomena* related to heat. They have not, therefore, supplied us with a proper *theory* or *explication* of the nature of heat'.

Black was cautious in his attitude towards the caloric theory, in fact towards both theories of heat available at his time, because neither could adequately explain *all* the then-known phenomena of heat. He went on to say that most of the ways that caloricists followed in order to develop their theories in the light of recalcitrant experience were ad hoc. Black gives the following excellent account of ad hoc modifications:

> Many have been the speculations and views of ingenious men about this union of bodies with heat. But, as they are all hypothetical, and as the hypothesis is of the most complicated nature, being in fact a hypothetical application of another hypothesis, I cannot hope for much useful information by attending to it. *A nice adaptation of conditions will make almost any hypothesis agree with the phenomena.* This will please the imagination, but does not advance our knowledge.
>
> (1803: 46)

This attitude towards the hypothesis that the cause of heat is a material substance, which amounted to a suspension of judgement until better evidence came in, was not just Black's idiosyncratic behaviour. After presenting both theories, Laplace and Lavoisier also suggested that the theory of experimental calorimetry was independent of the considerations concerning the cause of heat. Here is their own account:

> We will not decide at all between the two foregoing hypotheses [material v. dynamical theory of heat]. Several phenomena seem favourable to the second [the dynamical theory of heat], such as the heat produced by the friction of two solid bodies, for example; but there are others which are explained more simply by the other [material theory of heat] – perhaps they both hold at the same time. So . . . one must admit their common principles: that is to say, in either of those, *the quantity of free heat remains always the same in simple mixtures of bodies*. . . . The conservation of the free heat, in simple mixtures of bodies, is, then, independent of those hypotheses about the nature of heat; this is generally admitted by the physicists, and we shall adopt it in the following researches.
>
> (1780: 152–153)

Their account suggests two things: on the one hand, the principle of conservation of heat was not adhered to because it was a consequence of the claim that the cause of heat is a material substance, but rather because it was taken to be a *theoretical generalisation* stemming from the experiments in calorimetry. On the other hand, since calorimetric laws were independent of considerations about the cause of heat, they could not be used to test either of the theories of the cause of heat.

Lavoisier repeated his reservations about the caloric representation of heat in his monumental *Traite Élémentaire de Chimie* (1789). Although in this work he put forward the material theory of heat as a candidate for the cause of heat phenomena, he was careful to qualify his commitments: 'Strictly speaking, we are not obliged to suppose this to be a real substance; it being sufficient, as will more clearly appear in the sequel of this work, that it is considered as the repulsive cause, whatever that may be, which separates the particles of matter from each other' (1790: 5).

What follows from all this is that the scientists of this period were not committed to the truth of the hypothesis that the cause of heat was a material substance. Therefore, caloric was not as central a posit as, for instance, Laudan has suggested (1984a: 113). Equivalently, the theoretical attempt to discover the cause of heat did not revolve around the unquestioned belief that caloric was the wanted cause. Most scientists' cautious attitude was the product of some important methodological considerations:

1 The caloric theory faced anomalies which could not be explained easily.
2 An alternative theory was available, which could account for some of the anomalies that the caloric theory faced.
3 The hypothesis that the cause of heat was a material substance was not essentially and ineliminably involved in the derivation and explanation of the laws of calorimetry.
4 The modifications to which the caloric theory was subjected in order to overcome some anomalies were rather artificial and ad hoc.
5 Most of the work in experimental calorimetry was conducted independently of any theory of heat.

However, it would be wrong to infer that the scientists' attitude towards the caloric theory was instrumentalist. Rather, using current philosophical terminology, I would claim that: *semantically*, the scientific community's attitude towards the theory was realist. 'Caloric' was a putative referring term which stood for a material fluid whose transportation from one body to another caused changes in temperature. *Epistemically*, the scientists' attitude was one of cautious and differentiated belief. Their epistemic attitude was not an all-or-nothing matter, but rather was determined by the evidence which supported the several theoretical constituents of the theory.

Laplace's prediction of the speed of sound in air

One of the most notably successful predictions attributed to the caloric theory is Laplace's prediction of the speed of sound in air. In 1816 Laplace published a memoir in which he suggested that the transmission of sound takes place in an adiabatic way, thereby correctly predicting the speed of

sound. This was an amazing success, for Laplace corrected Newton's calcu-
lation of the speed of sound in air. Unlike Newton, who had assumed that
the expansions and contractions of a gas, as sound passes through it, take
place isothermally, Laplace suggested that the propagation of sound was an
adiabatic process. He assumed that there was some quantity of latent heat
which was released from the compression of the air. This quantity of heat
is normally diffused in the gas. But, for Laplace, 'since this diffusion takes
place very slowly relative to the velocity of the vibrations, we may suppose
without sensible error that during the period of a single vibration the quantity of heat remains same between two neighbouring molecules' (1816: 181).
He then approximated sound-propagation by an isothermal compression of
the gas and followed by heating the gas at constant volume.

Laplace suggested that Newton had failed to appreciate the effect of the
second process on the pressure (or elasticity) of the gas. For Laplace 'it is
clear that the second cause [heating the gas at constant volume] should
increase the velocity of sound since it increases the elasticity of the air'
(ibid.). He was then able to show that the speed of sound is represented by
the formula

$$v^2 = (c_p/c_v) \, dP/d\rho,$$

where c_p is the specific heat of air under constant pressure, c_v is the specific
heat under constant volume, P is the pressure and ρ the density of air.[1] The
result obtained was 345.18 m/sec. Laplace attributed the difference from
the experimental value to 'the uncertainty in experimental measurements'
(cf. 1816: 181). In fact, he was right, since he took $\gamma (= c_p/c_v) = 1.5$ based
on the quite off-the-mark calculations by Delaroche and Bérard.[2]

Was this successful and novel prediction in any way dependent on the
hypothesis that heat is a material substance? Laplace's account does not
explicitly rest on any particular representation of heat, although he happened
to be an advocate of the caloric theory. It is also noteworthy that Laplace's
explanation of the propagation of sound in terms of an adiabatic process is
essentially correct and has been retained in the subsequent theoretical
accounts of heat.

In 1823, Poisson established by theoretical means the general law which
governs adiabatic processes, that is, PV^γ = constant, where γ is the ratio of
the two specific heats of a gas under a certain temperature (cf. 1823:
328–329). Here again, however, this law was shown to be *independent* of
any specific hypothesis about the cause of heat. To be sure, Poisson did
rest his derivation on the hypothesis that the quantity of heat absorbed or
released by a body is a *state function* of three macroscopic properties of
the body – pressure P, temperature T, and volume V. And, it is worth
observing, the assumption that the quantity of heat involved in a process is
a state function of the macroscopic parameters (pressure, temperature and
volume) should be taken as the fundamental hypothesis of the mature caloric

theory. For if such a function of heat did exist, it would follow that, in a complete cycle from (V_1, T_1) back to (V_1, T_1), the quantity of heat absorbed was equal to the quantity of heat released, irrespective of the way that the changes took place; that is, it would follow that heat was a conservative quantity. After Clausius's work in thermodynamics, it was recognised that heat is not a state function of the macroscopic properties of a gas. On the contrary, the quantity of heat released or absorbed by a body depends on how the process happens. More specifically, when work is produced in a thermal cycle, the quantity of heat involved in this cycle does not uniquely depend on the initial and final states in which the substance undergoing the changes is found. As a result, heat is not conserved in all thermal processes.

However, Poisson's derivation of the theoretical law of adiabatic change, is approximately correct. For although heat is not a function of the state of a gas, one can approximate infinitesimal changes in the quantity of heat of a gas, such as those occurring in an adiabatic process, by the method employed by Poisson, that is by analysing an infinitesimal change in heat in terms of the partial derivatives of two macroscopic parameters (cf. Fermi 1936: 20, 21–26). So, although in the advanced caloric theory the hypothesis that the cause of heat is a material substance was made concrete by the assumption that heat can be mathematically represented as a state function, Laplace's account of the propagation of sound did not depend on this hypothesis. Moreover, Poisson's theoretical derivation of the law of adiabatic change was approximately correct despite the use made by the derivation of the mathematical representation of heat as a state function.

Carnot and caloric[3]

Let me now move on to discuss the role of the caloric theory in Carnot's work. Carnot devotes his 'Reflections on the Motive Power of Fire' to the theoretical study of the work which can be produced by a gas undergoing specific changes so that it returns to its initial state (i.e. it traverses a complete – and reversible – thermal cycle).

In his theoretical account of the motive power of heat, it seems as though Carnot had accepted the principle of the conservation of heat and the existence of a state-function. For instance, he wrote (although in a footnote of his text) that '(t)his fact [i.e. the conservation of heat] has never been called in question. It was first admitted without reflection, and verified afterwards in many cases by experiment with the calorimeter. To deny it would be to overthrow the whole theory of heat to which it serves as a basis' (1824: 19/76).[4]

However, Carnot was also aware of the difficulties faced by the hypothesis that heat is conserved in any process whatsoever. Even in his published paper, he questioned the soundness of the supposed central axiom of the caloric theory. He remarked:

The fundamental law [i.e. that heat was a state function] which we proposed to confirm seems to us however to require new verifications in order to be placed beyond doubt. It is based on the theory of heat as it is understood today, and it should be said that this foundation does not appear to be of unquestionable solidity. New experiments alone can decide the question. Meanwhile, we can apply the theoretical ideas expressed above, *regarding them as exact,* to the examination of different methods proposed up to now for the realisation of the motive power of heat.

(1824: 46/100–101; emphasis added)[5]

Concerning the motive power of heat, Carnot stated that the work produced in a steam engine was due to the *redistribution of caloric* among the parts of the engine. So, he took it to be the case that the steam produced in the boiler of an engine was used to transport caloric to the condenser, thereby producing mechanical work, without any quantity of heat being consumed in this process. The hypothesis that heat is a material substance entailed this thesis: if caloric was a substance, then it had to be indestructible; then it could produce work in a heat engine without being consumed, but by its mere redistribution.

However, Carnot was very careful not to employ the hypothesis of conservation of heat. In order to support this claim let us look at the demonstration of the theorems relating to the well-known Carnot's cycle. Carnot considers two bodies A and B kept at different, but constant, temperatures, T_1 and T_2 respectively, where $T_1 > T_2$ (see Figure 6.1). The working substance is a gas contained in a tank $abcd$, the top side, cd, of which is movable with a piston. Carnot studied a process which consisted of four steps (Carnot 1824: 17–19/74–76):

1   The gas is brought in contact with body A, at the constant temperature T_1, and is slowly left to expand, at a constant temperature T_1, to the position ef (i.e. isothermal expansion from V_1 to V_2).
2   Body A, then, is removed from the gas, and the latter is left to expand from the position ef to the position gh, where its temperature becomes equal to that of the body B, i.e. T_2 (i.e. adiabatic expansion from T_1 to T_2).
3   Then, the gas is brought in contact with body B, at a constant temperature T_2, and is compressed from gh to cd, at a constant temperature T_2 (i.e. isothermal compression from V_2 to V_1).
4   Body B is removed, and the gas is compressed from cd to ik, its final temperature being again T_1. Finally, the gas is brought to its initial state ab by contact with the body A (i.e. adiabatic compression from T_2 to T_1).

The process can be repeated indefinitely, by repeating the four steps in the same order.

Using his cycle, Carnot demonstrates the following propositions:

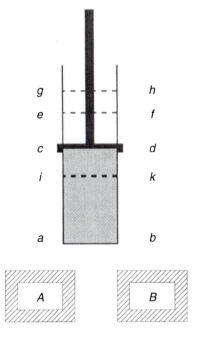

Figure 6.1 Carnot's cycle
Source: Adapted from Carnot 1824

(1) The maximum quantity of work can be produced when and only when a substance undergoes transformations in a Carnot cycle (see 1824: 19/76).

The demonstration of this theorem is most interesting since Carnot appeals to well-established independent background knowledge. Suppose, Carnot says, that more work W' is produced in some cycle C' than the amount of work W produced in a Carnot cycle C. Were this so, it would be possible to create perpetual motion. For one could first subject the substance to the transformations of cycle C', *then* direct the excess motive power $W'-W$ from the condenser (the cold body) to the boiler (the hot body), and finally subject the substance to the transformations of the Carnot cycle C. But '. . . this would be not only perpetual motion, but an unlimited creation of motive power without consumption of either caloric or of any agent whatever. Such a creation is entirely contrary to ideas now accepted, to the laws of mechanics and of sound physics' (1824: 12/69). So, Carnot establishes that $W' - W$ must be negative or zero in order to avoid perpetual motion. Hence, W is the maximum work that can be produced in a reversible cycle.

(2) The work produced in a cycle is independent of the substance used and, for a given quantity of heat, depends only on the difference in temperature of the bodies between which the cycle works.[6]

For Carnot the crucial factor in the process of generating mechanical work is the difference in temperatures between the boiler and the condenser of a steam engine. Hence, he correctly suggests that the work produced in a cycle is independent of the working substance involved. Carnot suggests also that the work produced in a cycle is *a function of the quantity of heat* transferred from (the hot) body A to (the cold) body B during the process. That is, the work produced in a complete cycle C is $W(C) = g(Q^{tr}, T_f - T_i)$. The demonstration of the second theorem appears to be tied to the wrong hypothesis that heat is conserved in a Carnot cycle. For, despite his doubts concerning the conservation of heat, we have seen Carnot assuming that the work produced in his cycle is due to the *redistribution* of caloric between bodies A and B. This can be taken to mean that the quantity of heat Q_A released from body A is equal to the quantity of heat Q_B absorbed from body B and that, therefore, all heat gets transferred from body A to body B. So, one may assume that Carnot's proof rests on the equation: $Q_A = Q_B = Q^{tr}$. This is a conservation statement, and it might appear that it is essentially employed in Carnot's derivation. Yet, Carnot was again very careful. In presenting his cycle, he never explicitly said that the quantity of heat released by body A was *absorbed* by body B. In the crucial step (4) of his cycle (see Figure 6.1 and the text preceding it), Carnot said only that 'the compression is continued till the air acquires the temperature of the body A' (1824: 18/75). This is correct, and by no means does it entail that $Q_A = Q_B = Q^{tr}$. Hence, Carnot did not appeal to any assumptions about the conservation of heat in order to establish his law.[7]

In order to make this last point more forceful we must jump slightly ahead and see Émile Clapeyron's account (1834) of Carnot's cycle. Clapeyron was the first to put Carnot's theory in its well-known diagrammatic form. But during the crucial step (4), where the gas, after being compressed isothermally in contact with the cold body B, is allowed to compress adiabatically, Clapeyron stated that 'the compression continued till the heat released by the compression of the gas and absorbed by the body B is exactly equal to the heat communicated by the source A to the gas, during its expansion in contact with it in the first part of the operation' (1834: 76–77). This *is* a clear conservation statement. So, in *interpreting* Carnot's cycle, Clapeyron demanded that $Q_A = Q_B = Q^{tr}$, i.e. he demanded that heat was conserved in a Carnot cycle.

In light of the foregoing analysis of Carnot's theorems and their demonstrations, it transpires that they do not depend on the hypothesis that heat is conserved in a Carnot cycle. In fact, in his posthumously published notes – which were written not long after his memoir – Carnot suggested that the caloric theory should be abandoned. He stressed that within the caloric theory, it 'would be difficult to say why, in order to develop motive power by heat, a cold body is required; why motion cannot be produced by consuming the heat in a heated body' (1986: 187). Carnot suggested that the hypothesis of the conservation of heat broke down when it was called upon to explain the production of work by heat.[8] He also stressed that the caloric theory of heat was undermined by a series of experimental results, mostly related to the production of heat by friction (1986: 185–186). From his posthumously published notes, one can also see that sometime between 1824 and his early death in 1832 Carnot countenanced a dynamical theory of heat.[9]

Localising relations of evidential support

Stated in an anachronistic way, the attitude of the most eminent scientists towards the caloric theory of heat, in the light of the well-founded laws of experimental calorimetry, the law of adiabatic change and Carnot's theory of work, was this: the probability of these laws, given the hypothesis that heat is a material substance, is not high, and moreover it is not overwhelmingly greater than the probability of these laws, given the falsity of this hypothesis.

My account thus far has rested on the premise that it is both in principle and in practice possible to *localise* the relations of evidential support, and to show which parts of a theory are supported by the evidence at hand, or at any rate, which parts are better supported than others.[10] However, Laudan (1981: 26–27) has commented that realists must be holists in confirmational matters, for otherwise they cannot maintain that the deep-structural claims of a theory are well supported. He also seems to think that realists must accept the view that observational evidence for a theory is evidence for everything that a theory asserts. Laudan's allegations about realist commitments seem to rest on a rather misleading account of evidential support, according to which empirical evidence cannot give support to some of the theoretical claims involved; instead empirical evidence supports a theory as a whole and, therefore, it supports each and every one of its theoretical claims.

Laudan's claim stems from a bad reading of Boyd (1981), according to whom the support which empirical evidence lends to a theory extends all the way to the deep-structural claims of the theory. Boyd's point, however, is meant to deny the empiricist contention that the empirical evidence supports only the empirical claims made by the theory. He rightly stresses that evidence for the empirical adequacy of a theory can be evidence also for the truth of a theory, and in particular for the truth of its theoretical claims. Boyd's position, however, does not commit the realist to holistic confirmation. All it says is that confirmation extends all the way to the theoretical claims, and does not just stay at the observational level. Yet, there is no reason to think that empirical evidence cannot lend a different credence to the several theoretical constituents of the theory. Nor is there any reason to think that all parts of a theory are equally well supported by the evidence. Empirical evidence may well extend to the theoretical elements of a theory, and yet support some of them better than others, or remain silent about yet other theoretical claims. As this study of the caloric theory of heat has shown, in actual scientific theories there are those deep-structural claims which are warranted by the evidence, and others which are not.

Let me highlight some ways in which the evidence supports some theoretical claims only weakly.

- Some piece of evidence may be in conflict with some particular theoretical claims.
- In the light of recalcitrant experience, some theoretical claims are modified in an ad hoc way in order to conform to the unfavourable new evidence.
- Some theoretical claims are such that the evidence does not make them any more likely than alternative and incompatible claims.
- Some theoretical claims are 'neutral' with respect to sound background beliefs, in that the latter do not increase their probability of being true.

As I stressed in Chapter 5, not all the deep-structural claims of a theory play the same role in the derivation of predictions and in providing well-founded explanations of observable phenomena. Some theoretical claims may be essential to the derivation of predictions and explanations of the phenomena; some others may be 'idle'. Some theoretical claims may be mere visualisations of underlying causes, and as such unusable in the generation of testable predictions or, at any rate, in specifying circumstances under which they can be thoroughly tested. Given that deep-structural claims may be supported by evidence to different extents – conferring probabilities that range from high to low – it is a good empirical constraint on any confirmation theory to localise the praise and blame for the successes and the failures of a theory, and to differentiate the degrees of support of the several theoretical constituents. So, it is entirely consistent to stress that empirical evidence sends its support all the way up to the theoretical level, while recognising that it does not do so indiscriminately and without differentiation.

In sum, the realist answer to Laudan's allegations about holistic confirmation should be this: if scientists entertain some theoretical beliefs it is because empirical evidence, together with other sound background beliefs, renders them well confirmed. This position leaves space for a localised theory of confirmation. For empirical evidence surely extends right to the deep-structural claims. Yet, on its way there, it may confirm them differentially. Realists need not commit themselves to unwarranted theoretical claims; yet they have good reason to commit themselves to theoretical claims, insofar as the latter are well supported by evidence and other sound background beliefs. Evidence can be such that it shows which theoretical claims are likely to be true, and which we must discard or suspend our judgement about. So, scientific realists need not accept a theory in its entirety. Instead, realism requires and suggests a *differentiated attitude to*, and *differentiated degrees of belief in*, the several constituents of a successful and mature scientific theory. The degree of belief one has in a theory is, in general, a function of the extent of its support by the available evidence. Since different parts of a theory can be supported to different degrees, realists should place their bets on the truth of a theory accordingly. So, let me just emphasise that belief can be the right epistemic attitude towards scientific theories, but belief admits of degrees. Hence belief in a theory, and in its several theoretical constituents, is often a matter of degree.

From the caloric theory to thermodynamics

One main conclusion of the case-study thus far is that the laws of the caloric theory can be deemed to be approximately true independently of the referential failure of 'caloric', i.e. irrespective of the absence of a natural kind as the referent of the term 'caloric'. So, a point worth highlighting is that when the laws established by a theory turn out to be independent of assumptions involving allegedly central theoretical terms, it can still make perfect sense to talk of the approximate truth of this theory.

The existence of a significant truth-content in the caloric theory is not a conclusion that we draw by hindsight. I shall now turn my attention to Clausius, one of the founders of modern thermodynamics, in order to show the sense in which the caloric theory of heat was taken to be approximately true by the proponents of the new theory of thermodynamics.

Rudolf Clausius concentrated his research on the capacity of heat to produce work. He made the following observations:

1   Joule's experimental principle of the equivalence of heat and work, i.e. the principle that a certain quantity of heat must be consumed in the production of a proportional amount of work, strictly contradicts Carnot's 'subsidiary statement' that no heat is lost in a thermal cycle where work is produced.
2   Joule's principle is strictly compatible with Carnot's 'essential principle' that heat always flows from a warm to a cold body (Clausius 1850: 112).

According to Clausius, during the production of work it may be the case that both a quantity of heat is consumed in the generation of work *and* a quantity of heat passes from the warm to the cold body, so that both quantities stand in a definite relation to the work produced. So, in place of the one hypothesis of the caloric theory which, as such, contradicts Joule's experimental finding that heat is consumed during the production of work, Clausius issued two distinct but compatible hypotheses.

Analysing the Carnot cycle, Clausius introduced the new concept of the 'internal energy' of a gas, which 'has the properties which are commonly assigned to the total heat, of being a function of V and T, and of being therefore fully determined by the initial and final conditions of the gas . . .' (1850: 122). The internal energy is a function of the macroscopic parameters of the gas and, therefore, it is conserved in a complete cycle. Clausius suggested that the so-called 'total quantity of caloric' absorbed by the gas (or the working substance in general) consists, in fact, of two parts: (i) the internal energy of the gas which has the properties which the advocates of the caloric theory erroneously attributed to the 'total quantity of heat' and (ii) the quantity of heat consumed for the generation of work, the amount of which depends on the course of change the gas undergoes. So, it is important to note that according to Clausius, 'caloric' was a partially referring term. It did not refer to any material substance, but, under its mature formulation, it could be seen as referring partially to the internal energy of a substance.

Clausius went on to derive the first law of thermodynamics, which asserts that the quantity of heat received by a gas during very small (infinitesimal) changes of volume and temperature is equal to the increase in the internal energy of the gas plus the heat consumed for the work done by the gas. He notes (1850: 133–134) that despite the fact that Carnot was far from proving the first law of thermodynamics, his theorems were independent of the assumption that no heat was lost in a Carnot cycle. They follow from the physical impossibility of perpetual motion.[11] Clausius concluded:

> It seems therefore to be *theoretically* admissible to retain the first and the really essential part of Carnot's assumptions [i.e. that 'the equivalent of the work done by heat is found in the mere transfer of heat from a hotter to a colder body'] . . . [And it is similarly admissible] to apply it as a second principle in conjunction with the first [i.e. the first law of thermodynamics]; and the correctness of this method is, as we shall soon see, established already in many cases by its *consequences*.
>
> (1850: 132, 134)

The reader will have noted that Clausius' derivation from Carnot's theory rests on a distinction between an *essential* and a *subsidiary* part. But, what is the justification for this distinction? I shall not repeat what I have already said about the alleged centrality of the assumption that the cause of heat is a material substance. The point I want to make is that by pointing to the reasons why the community upheld this distinction, we can see why this distinction was justified. Let us then see what these reasons were.

1   A shared desideratum of the community was to keep as much as possible of Carnot and Clapeyron's mathematical machinery and successful predictions.
2   The (for Clausius) essential parts of Carnot's theory were those which were best supported by the evidence.
3   Helmholtz, Clausius and William Thomson showed that the disputed principle of the conservation of heat was unnecessary for the derivation of Carnot's law.

4   The sound laws which had been established within the caloric theory were readily deduced and accounted for in the new theoretical framework of thermodynamics.
5   No alternative theory was ever produced which dictated the total rejection of Carnot's theory.

Hence, we may conclude that Clausius' justification for the distinction between essential and subsidiary principles of Carnot's theory reflected the *theoretical and methodological desiderata* of the scientific community.

Having thus completed my brief account of the transition from the caloric theory to thermodynamics, I must stress one last point: the development of the dynamical representation of heat was constrained by the successes of the caloric theory. The latter were such that any alternative account of heat should have been able to accommodate them. Not only did the dynamical representation of heat after 1850 provide a truer account of the causal mechanisms involved in the thermal processes, but it also succeeded in accommodating the sound parts of the previous theory within the bounds of the new causal account of the nature of heat. The important point here is that this was the practice of the main scientists working in the field: they located and preserved the well-supported content of the caloric theory of heat by replacing the erroneous hypothesis of conservation of heat by two independent and compatible hypotheses and by retaining the rest of the sound laws. It is in this sense that the caloric theory can be said to be approximately true, despite the referential failure of 'caloric'.

One may even suggest that if the term 'caloric' was not so loaded, it could have been retained in order to refer to the internal energy of a substance. As we saw, the latter, like caloric, is a function of the macroscopic properties of a substance even within the new theory of heat. Hence, there is a sense in which 'caloric' may be seen as referring to the internal energy.[12] Be that as it may, the relevant moral about the reference of abandoned theoretical terms is that: not all cases of abandoned terms are troublesome. The serious cases concern terms which were indeed central in some genuinely successful theory; *central* in the senses that

•   descriptions of the putative referent of the terms were indispensable in the derivation of predictions and in the well-founded explanations of phenomena; and
•   the advocates of a theory took the theory's successes to warrant the claim that there were natural kinds denoted by these terms.

It is only about such terms that the issue of preservation of reference is pressing. If such terms turn out to be vacuous, then there seems to be no connection between empirical success and the successful reference of a theory's theoretical terms. But not all abandoned terms have been this central. When some abandoned term had not been central, realists should not be required to show how it can possibly be referential. 'Caloric', simply, was not such a central term.

NINETEENTH-CENTURY OPTICS: THEORIES AND MODELS

Abstract dynamics versus concrete models

One of the prime objectives of theoretical research in optics during the nineteenth century was the formulation of a dynamical theory of light-propagation, which aimed to yield the laws of the behaviour of light from general dynamical principles concerning the carrier of light-waves, known as the 'luminiferous ether'. This research programme was developed by Augustin Louis Cauchy, George Green, James McCullagh and George Gabriel Stokes. Within the framework of the new electromagnetic conception of light, it was pursued further by James Clerk Maxwell and his followers.

Although, thanks to the pioneering research of Augustin Fresnel, the luminiferous ether was known to be a conservative system which sustained transversal waves, it is important to stress that its physical constitution and its internal connections were unknown. In view of this, theoretical research in optics was developed on the basis of an interplay between general dynamical theories and concrete models of the constitution of the ether.

The theoretical framework that scientists adopted was Lagrangian dynamics. They considered the carrier of the light-waves as a dynamical system whose general behaviour could be studied by Lagrangian dynamics and aimed to derive, within this framework, the most general laws of light-propagation. This was taken to be sufficient for the development of a dynamical account of light-propagation. The use of Lagrange's method enabled the scientific community to investigate the general dynamical properties and functions of the carrier of the light waves, leaving 'out of account altogether the details of the mechanism, whatever it is, that is in operation in the phenomena under discussion' (Larmor 1893: 399). The subsumption of light-propagation under Lagrangian dynamics required the specification of the kinetic-energy function and the potential-energy function. While the form of the dependence of the kinetic energy on the velocity of the moving bodies is in all cases the same and can be known, the form of the dependence of the potential energy on the position of bodies cannot be generally stated: it depends on the special nature and characteristics of the system under consideration. Hence, the prime task of theorists was to specify a potential-energy function which could adequately describe the behaviour of the ether. To this end, they had to employ several modelling assumptions about the nature and characteristics of the ether.

It was exactly at this point that particular theoretical models of the ether proved to be very useful. As we shall see in detail in the sections that follow, these models aimed to specify the potential-energy function of the ether. Having formulated such a potential-energy function, the next task was to correlate it with some of the known properties of light – amplitude, intensity and others. Then, the resulting theory was put to the test by examining whether it yielded the known laws of light-propagation. For the purpose of offering a dynamical basis for light-propagation, no further specification of the nature of the carrier of light waves was needed. For the specification of the potential-energy and kinetic-energy functions was suffcient to subsume light propagation under the domain of dynamics; and then it was possible to examine whether the resulting laws of motion could yield the known laws of light-propagation. For the purposes of this investigation, the significant issue here is that the advancement of dynamical theories of light-propagation did not require scientists to *believe* that the ether was constituted in the way implied by the specific model in use.[13]

However, the models employed for the specification of an energy function did also stand for *possible* candidates for the constitution of the carrier of light-waves. For instance, the model that Green (1838) and Stokes (1849; 1862) employed rested on the assumption that the energy function of the otherwise unknown ether could be associated with that of an ordinary elastic solid. Then a model based on the dynamics of an elastic solid (henceforth, an elastic-solid model) was used in an *heuristic* way to investigate whether the constitution and internal connections of the ether could be mapped on those of an elastic solid. Such a procedure was heuristically valuable for the discovery of what ether could be, and what ether is not.

The heuristic value of an elastic-solid model – as opposed, for instance, to models based on the dynamics of liquids – was based on certain *positive analogies* between an elastic solid and the otherwise unknown carrier of light-waves. In particular, after Fresnel's work, scientists settled for the view that light-waves were uniquely transversal. This fundamental discovery suggested that the carrier of light waves had to possess properties in virtue of which it could sustain transversal waves.[14] A model of such an otherwise unknown carrier of light-waves could be constructed on the basis of the propagation of a disturbance through an elastic solid. For the latter exhibits properties, such as capacity to sustain transversal waves, which are analogous to the known properties of light-propagation. In view of this fact, most scientists started attacking the problem of the dynamical foundations of light-propagation 'through the analogy with the propagation of elastic waves in solid bodies' (Larmor 1893: 392). They used the features of the propagation of a disturbance in elastic solids as a set of assumptions about the constitution of the carrier of light-waves.

Despite its usefulness, the elastic-solid model of the constitution of the ether was not taken to reveal the real constitution of the ether. Here part of the problem lies with the fact that an elastic solid can also transmit longitudinal waves. In fact – and this was the touchstone for the elastic-solid model – it follows from the laws of mechanics that when a transversal wave strikes the interface of two media, it gives rise to a transversal *and* a longitudinal component. Since light-waves were known to be purely transversal, the emergence of the longitudinal component presented an important *negative analogy* between the elastic-solid model and the propagation of light. As we shall see shortly, the successful neutralisation of the longitudinal component turned out to be the most important problem that the elastic-solid model faced as a plausible candidate for the constitution of the carrier of light-waves. However, even when the elastic-solid model was modified so that the longitudinal component was neutralised, the modified model could not yield the known laws of light-propagation.

In any case, what is worth noting is that models were used as heuristic devices, and that their construction and choice were guided by both background theory and material analogies. They were based on the background belief that the carrier of the light-waves, whatever its detailed constitution, is a conservative system with certain properties, e.g. capacity to sustain transversal waves. Then, Lagrangian dynamics provided the general framework for the theoretical description of light-propagation. It was within this framework that specific models were deployed. Having thus outlined the general framework of the relations between theories and models in the nineteenth-century optics, let us see three more concrete cases of theoretical modelling.

Green: modelling the unknown ether

The scientist most closely associated with the development of the elastic-solid model was Green.[15] It was he, however, who suggested the difference between the investigation of the general dynamical behaviour of light in terms of Lagrangian dynamics and the particular models which may be called forth in order to help uncover the constitution of the ether. He pointed out:

> We are so perfectly ignorant of the mode of action of the elements of the luminiferous ether on each other, that it would seem a safer method to take some physical principle as the basis of our reasoning, rather than to assume certain modes of action, which after all, may be widely different from the mechanism employed by nature.
>
> (1838: 245)

Based on the positive analogy between the propagation of elastic disturbances in a solid and the propagation of light, Green set out to investigate the former in order to find out the extent to which it can give rise to an adequate dynamical model of the latter. His objective was the specification of the potential-energy function ϕ of the propagation of disturbances in elastic solids (1838: 245). To this end, he applied the Lagrangian method to the dynamical system underlying the propagation of elastic waves in solids, and determined the most general equation of wave-motion in solids. Having chosen an ordinary elastic solid as his model, Green assumed that the value of ϕ for a volume element $d\tau$ ($= dx\,dy\,dz$) was a function of its *deformation*, i.e. of the change of form (shape/volume) of $d\tau$. He then specified the equation of motion in the case where the disturbance struck the interface of two media. For the Cartesian component u of the displacement vector $\mathbf{r}$, this has the well-known form

$$\frac{d^2u}{dt^2} = B\nabla^2u + (A - B)\,\text{grad}_x\,\text{div }u$$

where A and B are constants (cf. 1838: 255–256).

The foregoing wave equation gives two solutions, one corresponding to a transversal wave propagated with velocity $\sqrt{B}$, and another corresponding to a longitudinal wave propagated with velocity $\sqrt{(A - B)}$. In view of the fact that light-waves are purely transversal, Green suggested that if this equation were to describe the propagation of light, he would have to specify the coefficients A and B so that the part responsible for the 'generation' of the longitudinal component of the wave-motion becomes ineffective. He took it that A tends to infinity, and B is much smaller than A. Hence, $A - B \approx A$. Then, since $\sqrt{(A - B)} \approx \sqrt{A}$, it follows that longitudinal waves are transmitted with infinite velocity, and hence that they are undetectable (1838: 246). Green had therefore shown a kind of modification to which the elastic-solid model could be subjected in order for the longitudinal wave to be neutralised – but not to be eliminated. Yet, apart from this ad hoc way of fixing the coefficients, no adequate explanation of the neutralisation of longitudinal waves was offered. As Stokes (1862: 176) stressed in his report on the dynamical theories of optics:

> Although [Green's] theory is perfectly rigorous . . . the equations [determining the constants A, B] are of the nature of forced relations between the constants, not expressing anything which could have been foreseen, or even conveying when pointed out the expression of any simple physical relation.

Be that as it may, the real problem that the elastic-solid model faced was its inability to yield the known laws of the propagation of light, in particular Fresnel's laws of reflection.[16] Hence, it was unable to provide a set of assumptions constituting a dynamical basis for these laws (cf. Doran 1975: 156; Whittaker 1951: 142). This meant that, whatever the character of the carrier of the light-waves, it could not be an elastic solid of an ordinary sort (cf. Glazebrook 1885: 169; Larmor 1893: 395). The set of assumptions that this model employed, in particular its energy function, could not offer a true description of the physical system underlying the propagation of light. Green's model, however, was heuristically valuable in suggesting what the ether was not: whatever else it was, it could not possibly have the internal constitution and dynamical connections of an elastic solid.

McCullagh's rotational ether

McCullagh (1839), independently of Green, suggested that the Lagrangian method can be used for the description of the dynamical behaviour of light. He also developed the characteristic equation of motion for the propagation of light, which in vectorial notation has the form

$$\int \left(\frac{d^2 R}{dt^2} \right) \delta R \ d\tau = \int \delta V \ d\tau, \tag{A}$$

where $d\tau$ is a volume element $dxdydz$, and V is such that its integral over a volume element is the potential energy of the system, and the density ρ is taken as unity.

McCullagh's aim was the specification of the potential-energy function V for the physical system underlying the propagation of light-waves. However, the set of modelling assumptions he used were different from Green's. He first defined an abstract vectorial quantity L ($= X, Y, Z$) such that $L = \text{curl}R$, where R is the well-known displacement vector (i.e. Green's r). He then focused on the propagation of light in crystalline media, and assumed that L is a function of (i) the *angle of rotation* of a volume element $d\tau$ of the carrier of light-waves with respect to a co-ordinate system set along the principal axes, or axes of elasticity, of the crystal and (ii) the *angle of deformation* of a volume element $d\tau$. So, he determined the characteristic energy-function V (as a function of L):

$$V = - 1/2 \ (a^2 X^2 + b^2 Y^2 + c^2 Z^2) \tag{B}$$

McCullagh then stated:

> Having arrived at the value of V, we may now take it for the starting point of our theory, and dismiss the assumptions by which we were conducted to it. Supposing, therefore, in the first place, that a plane wave passes through a crystal, we shall seek the laws of its motions from equations (A) and (B), which contain everything that is necessary for the solution of the problem.
>
> (1839: 156)

So, McCullagh made the important observation that once the energy function was determined, one could dispense with the actual details of the constitution of the system underlying the propagation of light and, instead, attempt to describe its behaviour by means of some general dynamical principles.

McCullagh was indeed successful in deriving the laws of reflection and refraction, thereby offering the first dynamical account of these laws. The general feature of his theory, however, was that the carrier of light-waves whose dynamical behaviour he had described could *not* be modelled by an ordinary elastic solid (cf. also Harman 1982: 26; Whittaker 1951: 142–143). For, the vector **L**, representing the light-disturbance, could not possibly be modelled as the displacement in a medium which transmits vibrations by elasticity in the manner of an ordinary elastic solid. As we saw in the previous section, the potential-energy function (Green's function ϕ) which characterises the vibrations in an ordinary elastic solid depends on the deformation in shape and size of a volume element $d\tau$ of the medium. McCullagh's potential energy function V was dependent on the rotation of a volume element $d\tau$ of the medium, i.e. it is an energy function uncharacteristic of ordinary elastic solids. Consequently, McCullagh's dynamical account of the propagation of light could not be modelled by the set of modelling assumptions pertaining to the description of an elastic solid. The elasticity involved in McCullagh's account was purely rotational: it could not possibly be the elasticity of an ordinary elastic solid.

Although McCullagh's theory yielded the correct laws of optics, he was unable to provide a known physical system which could illustrate the rotational medium to which he was committed. As Larmor observed, this led to the neglect of the theory of rotational ether (1894: 415). What is noteworthy is that prior to Maxwell's mature theory of the electromagnetic field, the provision of an actual physical situation which exemplified the properties of the carrier of light waves was taken as *sine qua non* for the adequacy of any account of the propagation of light. However, McCullagh's theory was recovered later by G. F. FitzGerald (1878; 1880) who noted that the energy-function V was analytically identical with the one advanced by Maxwell himself. As soon as this was observed, McCullagh's theory fell in as a chapter of Maxwell's theory, facilitating the latter in the derivation of the laws of optics within the new electromagnetic theory of light. In fact, the physical system that could model McCullagh's ether was none other than Maxwell's electromagnetic field (cf. FitzGerald 1878; Stein, 1982: 315).

Stokes and the elastic jelly

Stokes, too, worked within the elastic-solid model. Yet, he was aware of the fact that an important *neutral analogy* between the elastic-solid model and the ether could be best accounted for within the otherwise inadmissible fluid models. This neutral analogy related to the motion of solid bodies through the ether: if the all-pervading ether was modelled on the basis of an elastic solid, then it would be difficult to accommodate the translatory motion of planets through it. How can a solid body – such as a planet – without resistance penetrate another solid?

In a series of papers on the possible constitution of the ether, Stokes tried to address this issue on behalf of a physically realisable elastic-solid model. The problem was this: was the ether like an ordinary fluid or did it possess some properties not present in ordinary fluids? (cf. 1848: 8). If the ether were treated as a fluid, then the mathematical model would have to be such that internal pressures of the medium are normal to the common surface of two portions whose mutual action was considered. If the ether were treated as an elastic solid, the internal pressures would have to be in general oblique, and hence they would always have a component tangential to the interface of two portions (cf. 1849: 281).

Stokes noted that in view of the well-established fact that light-waves were uniquely transversal, he had to adopt modelling assumptions based on the propagation of elastic waves in solids, but only 'so far as the motions which constitute light are concerned' (ibid.). This meant that he was 'absolutely obliged' to suppose the existence of a tangential force during the propagation of light-waves. Yet, he observed, this obligation did not entail 'that the ether is to be regarded as an elastic solid when large displacements are considered, such as we may conceive produced by the earth and planets, and solid bodies in general, moving through it' (ibid.). How could there be a medium which possesses some properties known to be present in an elastic solid and others which are incompatible with an elastic solid? It is at this point that the usefulness of physically realisable models becomes clear. For, if there were a realisable physical system which possessed these seemingly contradictory properties, then Stokes could argue that there was nothing physically inadmissible in having a carrier of the light-waves which shared some properties of an elastic solid and yet also exhibited fluid-like properties.

The physical system which can model the seemingly contradictory properties that the carrier of light-waves should have is an elastic jelly. Yet Stokes was quick to warn his readers that 'the following illustration is advanced, not so much as explaining the real nature of the ether, as for the sake of offering a plausible mode of conceiving how the apparently opposite properties of solidity and fluidity which we must attribute to the ether may be reconciled' (1848: 12). So, Stokes warned his readers not to take his model as explanatory, but rather as illustrative of the physical admissibility of such a medium. His construction was as follows. Take a piece of an elastic jelly. This jelly is an elastic solid, in that it possesses rigidity and elasticity. Dissolve the jelly in a little water and then keep watering it down. In the course of this process, the jelly becomes thinner and thinner and eventually it will be fluid. 'Yet', Stokes points out, 'there seems hardly sufficient reason for supposing that at a certain stage of the dilution the tangential force whereby it resists constraint [i.e. the characteristic of its solidity] ceases all of a sudden' (ibid.). So, the diluted jelly would be solid enough to resist deformation and fluid enough to permit the motion of solid bodies through it. Given this model, 'we may conceive the ether to be, a fluid as regards the motion of the earth and planets through it, an elastic solid as regards the small vibrations that constitute light' (1848: 13).

In view of this physically realisable situation, Stokes had shown how a neutral analogy can turn into a positive one. But it would be contrary to what he stated to claim that he took the carrier of light-waves to be an elastic jelly. In fact, he called for a 'suspension of judgement' as to the real constitution of the carrier of light-waves, since no adequate evidence was yet available (1848: 12). In 1862, thirteen years after his first papers on the dynamical behaviour of light, Stokes referred to the ether as a 'mysterious' entity, 'of the very existence of which we have no direct evidence' (1862: 172), thereby emphasising the important heuristic role of models in the investigation of its constitution. He stressed that, from a mathematical point of view, all theorists in optics, including himself, had treated the ether 'as a single vibrating medium' (ibid.: 180). He therefore emphasised the difference between a general dynamical theory of this single vibrating medium and the *particular models* which may be used to disclose its structure by means of positive analogies.

Maxwell's theory of the electromagnetic field

The main thread connecting the Maxwellian electromagnetic framework for optics and the theories I have examined thus far is the use of the Lagrangian method in the theoretical description of the dynamics of the electromagnetic (EM) field. The whole theoretical work describing the general dynamics of the carrier of light-waves was 'carried over' to Maxwell's theory, while the material that was superseded and eventually rejected related to the mechanical models. The electromagnetic field emerged as the physical system which underlies the propagation of light-waves: it plays the same role in the propagation of light as does the luminiferous ether, yet it is not reduced to any particular mechanical model.

Maxwell and his followers made clear two important points. First, there is a substantial distinction – a difference in kind – between the *explanatory* role that Lagrangian dynamics is called to play in the propagation of light and the *illustrative* role played by mechanical models. Second, the electromagnetic field has an independent physical reality: its behaviour can and should be understood without the assistance of mechanical models.

As stressed in previous sections, the first of these two points had been already made, yet not so sharply, by the pre-Maxwellian optical theorists. The second point, however, really was innovative. It suggests that scientists could deal straightaway with the dynamical properties of the carrier of light-waves, without trying to specify a mechanical configuration to which it could be reduced. What I want to stress, then, is that in the transition from the luminiferous ether to the EM field, the fundamental conceptual shift related to the role of mechanical models in the study and understanding of optical and electromagnetic phenomena. Let me elaborate.

Maxwell was concerned primarily with the theoretical understanding and description of electric and magnetic phenomena. Optical phenomena became his concern only after the fundamental discovery that light was nothing but an electromagnetic wave (cf. 1864: 42). To be sure, this fundamental discovery was facilitated by Maxwell's use of mechanical models. One of them – known as the 'idle wheels model' – models magnetic action by means of molecular vortices whose axes coincide with Faraday's 'lines of force', and electric action by molecular currents running tangential to these vortices (cf. 1861–62[1890]: 489 ff.). This model was heuristically valuable in that the very same structure was shown to satisfy some features of the propagation of light-waves as well as of electric and magnetic disturbances. This suggested that electric interactions can be represented in a medium-based manner, rather than as actions-at-a-distance. As Maxwell put it: 'light consists in transverse undulations of the same medium which is the cause of electric and magnetic phenomena' (ibid.: 500).

Maxwell was as cautious as anyone can be in stressing that his model was not supposed to display 'a mode of connexion existing in nature', but rather to suggest 'a mode of connexion which is mechanically conceivable and easily investigated' (ibid.: 486). So, Maxwell pointed out, it is one thing to use a model to investigate a physical system, but quite another thing to *identify* the model with the physical system under investigation. More generally, although he used models and analogies, he was careful to point out that no model – no matter how suggestive and useful – was a real surrogate for 'a mature theory, in which physical facts will be physically explained' (1855[1890]: 155). The sought-after 'mature theory' was put forward in his *A Dynamical Theory of the Electromagnetic Field* (1864), where Maxwell introduced the concept of the electromagnetic field. The electromagnetic field is 'the space in the neighbourhood of the electric and magnetic bodies' (1864: 34). Its most important property was its capacity for sustaining energy, or, as Maxwell put it elsewhere, its 'becoming a receptacle of two forms of energy': potential and kinetic (1873: 432). Maxwell identified potential energy with the electrostatic energy of the field and kinetic energy with the electrokinetic energy (cf. 1873: Chapter XI). This is what Maxwell called the 'intrinsic energy of the Electromagnetic Field' (1864: 41). Showing his commitment to the importance of this energy-based approach, he invited his readers to understand 'literally' his claims about the energy of the field (ibid.: 70). But when it came to the mechanical models he had offered, he called on his readers *not* to take them literally. He stated that he 'wish[ed] merely to direct the mind of the reader to mechanical phenomena which will assist him in understanding the electrical ones. [That is,] all these phrases [i.e. related to mechanical representations] . . . are to be considered as illustrative, not as explanatory' (ibid.).

Maxwell's mature dynamical theory of electromagnetic field rests on the general principles of dynamics and is independent of any particular model concerning the carrier of light-waves (cf. Maxwell, 1873: Chapters 5–9; see also Klein 1972: 69–70). Maxwell perceived correctly the essence of the whole research tradition in optics, viz. that Lagrangian dynamics allowed him to investigate into the most general laws of behaviour of the electromagnetic field without committing him to any particular hypothesis about its constitution, which was unknown. He stressed:

> We know enough about electric currents to recognise, in a system of material conductors carrying currents, a dynamical system which is the seat of energy, part of which may be kinetic and part potential. The nature of the connexions of the parts of this system is unknown to us, but as we have dynamical methods of investigation which do not require a knowledge of the mechanism of the system, we shall apply them to this case.
>
> (1873: 213)

So, he applied Lagrangian dynamics to a system of circuits carrying electric currents, the latter standing for the generalised co-ordinates of the system. He formulated the kinetic and potential energies of the system in terms of electric and magnetic magnitudes, and then proceeded to the derivation of the laws of motion of this system, thereby deriving the equations of the EM-field (1873: 233).[17]

What is worth stressing is that Maxwell's strategy suggests a cautious process of theory construction. The new theory of electromagnetic phenomena was to be built up slowly, in response to the evidence available and background knowledge of the physical world. In view of the fact that the evidence at hand could not suggest positively any hypothesis about the constitution of the electromagnetic field, the theorists had to restrict themselves to the description and explanation of its general laws of behaviour. This they did by connecting the kinetic and potential energies of the field with the electric and magnetic field variables, while postponing the completion of the rest of the picture until adequate evidence came in. As Maxwell puts it, theorists had to proceed without 'making any [further] assumption not warranted by experimental evidence' (op. cit.: 218). Maxwell's frequent appeals to evidence and to what theoretical constituents are supported by it reinforces the point I have already stressed: that scientists have a differentiated attitude towards the several parts of a theory in view of what evidence supports them.[18] Maxwell was confident that he was on the right track when he used general dynamical principles for the explanation of the dynamical laws of the electromagnetic field.

One can then draw the following conclusion relevant to the argument from the pessimistic induction. The most general theory – in terms of Lagrangian dynamics – which underwrote the research programmes associated with the dynamical behaviour of light-waves was retained in the new framework of electromagnetism. The relevant scientific beliefs about the carrier of the light-waves stretched as far as the available evidence could warrant. The latter could not support the formation of firm accounts of its constitution. It could, though, support the formation of sound explanations of its most general dynamical behaviour. Hence, Laudan is wrong to cite the ether theories among the mature scientific theories which have, allegedly, been shown to be false. The parts of 'luminiferous ether' theories which were taken by scientists to be well-supported by the evidence and to contribute to well-founded explanations of the phenomena were retained in subsequent theories. What became paradigmatically abandoned was a series of models which were used as heuristic devices for the possible constitution of the carrier of light-waves.

Theories and models: the analogical approach

In this section, I shall try to offer a more detailed account of the role of models in scientific theorising and the difference between theories and models. As the reader will surely know, there is a new approach to scientific theories – the so-called *semantic* view of theories – which suggests that theories are best understood as families of models. This is not the place to discuss this approach. (However, I say more about this approach in Chapter 11.)[19] In what follows here, I focus on a particular class of models, the so-called analogical models, and defend a certain view about them, which I call 'the analogical approach'.

The analogical approach, which can be traced back to Achinstein (1965; 1968) and Hesse (1953; 1966), focuses on models of physical systems. The prime problem scenario in model construction is taken to be the following. Scientists want to investigate a set of phenomena or, more generally, to find out about the behaviour of a target physical system X (e.g. the carrier of the light-waves). To this end, they construct a *theoretical model* of X: they employ a set of assumptions (normally of a complex mathematical structure) – let us call them modelling assumptions – which provide a starting-point for the investigation of the behaviour of X. So, the well-worn billiard balls' model of gases is a set of assumptions about the motion and collisions of an aggregate of gas molecules (target system X).

Far from being arbitrary, the choice of modelling assumptions for X is guided by *substantive similarities* between the target system X and some other physical system Y. It is in the light of these similarities that Y is chosen to give rise to a model M of X, that is to be the source of a set of assumptions on the basis of which the behaviour of X is to be investigated. So, for instance, the elastic-solid model of the carrier of light-waves was chosen on the basis that the propagation of light-waves (target system X) was, to a certain extent and in certain respects, similar to the propagation of elastic waves in solids (source system Y).

I call this approach to model-construction 'the analogical approach'. I attempt to capture the dependence of model construction on substantive similarities between two physical systems X and Y by adopting the locution 'model M of (target system) X based on (source system) Y'. But in order to ward off a possible source of confusion, it is important to distinguish clearly a model M of a system X based on system Y from system Y itself which, being to some extent similar to X, is the source of theoretical assumptions for the construction of model M. A theoretical model M of X is a set of assumptions about X. The system Y is employed, in a way that will become clear in a moment, to give rise to this set of assumptions. Yet, Y is a distinct physical system which is similar to X in some respects. So for instance, the elastic-solid model is based on some substantive similarities between the propagation of light-waves (system X) and the propagation of elastic waves in solids (system Y). But whereas system Y is an elastic solid, the model of the carrier of light-waves based on it is a set of assumptions about the propagation of light-waves and not about elastic solids.

Following Hesse (1966: 8–9), I take it that the relation between the source system Y and the target system X is characterised by the existence of

(a) some *positive* analogies, i.e. properties, or relations between properties, that both Y and X share;
(b) negative analogies, i.e. properties, or relations between properties, in respect of which X is unlike Y; and
(c) some neutral analogies, i.e. some properties about which we do not yet know whether they are positive analogies, and which may turn out either positive analogies or negative ones.

It is these positive and neutral analogies between Y and X which can give rise to a model of X based on Y. These analogies suggest that Y can play an *heuristic role* in unveiling some of the properties of a physical system X. For instance, by trying to explore the space of neutral analogies (i.e. by trying to find out whether or not X possesses more of the properties of Y) we end up with a better knowledge of what X is and what it is not. It should be then clear that although the existence of negative analogies between Y and X prohibits the identification of Y and X, it does not block the heuristic role of a model M of X based on Y. While distinct from X, Y can offer a set of modelling assumptions for X; that is, Y can give rise to a model M of X (see Figure 6.2).

According to the analogical approach, models are indispensable means of scientific theorising, their heuristic value being based on substantive similarities and analogies between different physical systems. As Hesse (1966: 68) stresses, these substantive similarities (or analogies) are of two sorts: formal and material.

A *formal* analogy between two systems X and Y relates to the mathematical structures which represent the behaviour of X and Y. In many cases the construction of a model M of X based on Y is tantamount to applying Y's mathematical description to X. That is to say, a model M of X based on Y is a set of assumptions which transfers the mathematical description

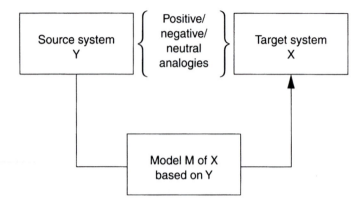

Figure 6.2 The heuristic role of analogical models

of system *Y* to system *X*. One must note here that in such a case one need not assume any sameness in properties between *X* and *Y*. All that is required is that some elements of *X* stand in the same relation to each other as do the corresponding elements of *Y*. Such a model *M* of *X* based on *Y* can be useful for understanding *X*. It may, for instance, suggest embedding the description of *X* in a broader mathematical structure. Or it may suggest further connections between the elements of *X* in view of connections which already hold between the corresponding elements in the mathematical description of *Y*.[20]

Material analogies relate to sameness or similarity at the level of properties. A set of material analogies between two physical systems *Y* and *X* alludes to the possibility that one of the systems, say *X*, can be described, in certain ways and to a certain extent, from the point of view of *Y*. In particular, it suggests that *Y* and *X* may be similar in more respects than just these latter (being in the space of neutral analogies). Therefore, the perceived similarities form a basis for supposing that further similarities can be discovered. Hence, they can furnish a basis for deriving predictions about possible properties of *X*.

At this point it may be useful to inquire into the relation between a model of a system *X* and a theory of *X*. Along with Hesse (1953: 203) and Achinstein (1968: 215, 217), I take it that, in principle, a theory is a set of literally understood statements which purports to describe correctly – truly – the behaviour of a particular physical system *X*. With models, however, things are not so clear-cut. When a theoretical model *M* is employed to provide a set of assumptions about the physical system *X*, one does not start off with the belief that *M* provides a literal description of *X*. As I said before, a theoretical model *M* of *X* based on *Y* is an heuristic tool for the study of *X*. One can, typically, employ a model even though one believes it to be only an approximation, or even a simplified, inaccurate and, at any rate, literally false representation, of *X* (Achinstein 1968: 217). To explore an expression of Giere (1988: 81) a model *M* of *X* based on *Y* represents *X* only in certain respects – specified by the positive analogies between *X* and *Y* – and to certain degrees – specified by the conditions of approximation and the idealisations employed in the model.

One may rightly object here that theories, like models, may also be seen as approximate, simplified and restricted descriptions/explanations of the phenomena. I think there is some leeway here. The point worth stressing is that the difference between a model of *X* and a theory of *X* is one of degree; in fact a difference of degree of *belief.* One may say even that the difference between a model and a theory may be seen as an intentional one, i.e. a difference relating to our having different attitudes towards their epistemic value. A model of *X* comprises a set of assumptions which are not yet believed to describe *X*. On the contrary, a theory of *X* is the end-product of scientific theorising. When something is advocated as a theory of *X*, the degree of belief that it correctly describes/explains *X* is, generally, high.

Models, heuristics and realism

Before I end this chapter, let me connect the approach to models just described with the details of the second case-study presented. One reason for doing so is that the development of nineteenth-century research in optics is quite characteristic of the research patterns in theoretical physics. Generally, the end of scientific theorising is the production of theories which describe and explain some phenomena under investigation. But, in view of what my second case-study showed, scientific theorising is a complicated process which rests on the interplay between, on the one hand, background theoretical frameworks and theoretical principles and, on the other hand, models which attempt to concretise and enrich these principles with a view to incorporating the phenomena under investigation into the theoretical framework.

As the research strategies of Green, McCullagh and Stokes suggested, theoretical physicists start with a network of general physical and mathematical principles – expressing their current background beliefs about the physical world – in an attempt to describe the most general behaviour of the target physical system *X*. These principles, however, need concretisation and filling in, both of which tasks are effected by the choice of specific modelling assumptions. Different scientists may employ different modelling assumptions. Green and McCullagh, for instance, modelled the potential-energy function of the carrier of light-waves by employing different assumptions about its internal organisation. But, as the analogical approach to model construction has suggested, the choice of modelling assumptions is not arbitrary. It is based on substantive similarities between the behaviour of the target system *X* and other physical systems which exemplify this general behaviour. So, the choice of a family of elastic-solid models, instead of a family of fluid models, was based on the presence of substantive similarities between the propagation of elastic waves in solids (source system) and the propagation of light through the ether (target system).

The resulting models of the target system X are then tested against the phenomena to be explained. Failure to square with known laws of the phenomena, as for instance was the case with ordinary elastic-solid models of the ether, renders them inadequate representations of the behaviour of the target system. But, even then, models have played a rather significant heuristic role. They have shown what the behaviour of the target system X is *not* like. They have, therefore, opened up the way for alternative representations. When, on the other hand, a model succeeds in yielding the known laws of the phenomena under investigation – as, for instance, in the McCullagh case – it promotes understanding of the behaviour of X, even though that understanding may stretch only to a certain extent and to a certain degree.

Having said all this, one may ask the following question: Does the view explored in my study entail that one can *never* be a realist about a theoretical model? – where by realism about a theoretical model I mean that one believes that a model M correctly represents a physical system X. To be clear, the upshot of my second case-study is that, for the scientists involved in this research programme, there were no good empirical and theoretical grounds for taking a realist stance towards the particular models they employed. From this, it does not follow that models should always be thought of in an *as-if* fashion. Nor does it follow that there can be no circumstances under which models offer adequate representations. The point is simply that in the presence of particular *empirical* and *theoretical* factors such as the existence of persistent negative analogies (Green), or the ad hoc nature of the suggested modifications (Stokes), or the lack of independent support for the modelling assumptions (McCullagh), the scientists did not adopt a realist stance towards their models.

Hence, I think one can, in principle, take a realist stance towards particular models. For, although scientists do not start off with the assumption that a particular model gives a literal description of a physical system X, there may be circumstances in which a model M of X offers an adequate representation of X. These circumstances relate to the accuracy with which a given model represents the target system. So, for instance, when testing a model M, it may happen that the neutral analogies between the target physical system X and the source system Y turn out to be positive. The finding of more positive analogies, matched with a persistent lack of negative analogies, may be a good starting-point for checking the possibility that model M correctly represents system X. Amassing more evidence, such that novel correct predictions for X derived from M, may be enough to show that M represents X correctly. In sum, taking a realist attitude towards a particular model is a matter of having evidence warranting the belief that this model gives us an accurate representation of an otherwise unknown physical system in all, or in most, causally relevant respects.

These thoughts complete my defence of scientific realism against the pessimistic induction. A more detailed study of the only theories in Laudan's 'historical gambit' against realism which realists should take seriously – being past mature and genuinely successful theories – has suggested that not only were they not outright false and abandoned, but that those theoretical constituents which enjoyed empirical support and contributed to their successes were carried over to the successor theories. There is, therefore, much more substantive theoretical continuity in theory-change than Laudan allows. Realists can ground their epistemic optimism on the fact that newer theories incorporate many theoretical constituents of their superseded predecessors. As a result, a rather stable network of theoretical principles and explanatory hypotheses emerges, which survives revolutionary changes and becomes part and parcel of our evolving scientific image of the world.

Keeping all this in mind, we can now turn our attention to Worrall's recent attempt to motivate an intermediate realist position: *structural realism*.

7 Worrall's structural realism

Worrall's answer to the pessimistic induction is a species of the *divide et impera* strategy defended in Chapter 5, but with some very interesting variations.[1] Worrall too tries to identify the parts of past abandoned theories which get retained in theory change, but argues that these parts relate to the *mathematical structure* of a theory rather than to its theoretical content.

Worrall's starting-point is the claim that the pessimistic induction is correct in suggesting a radical discontinuity in scientific theories at the theoretical level, i.e. at the level of the description of unobservable entities, underlying mechanisms and causes of the phenomena. Yet, he is also unwilling to admit that, as science grows, the only continuity that obtains is at the level of empirical laws. He therefore motivates a philosophical theory which aims to have the best of both worlds: a position which will accommodate both the radical *discontinuities* at the theoretical level and some substantive *continuity* at a level in between empirical laws and theoretical accounts of mechanisms and causes (cf. Worrall 1989: 111). What he has dubbed 'structural realism' suggests that most of the mathematical content of superseded mature theories has been retained in the successor theories, and that this retention marks an important non-empirical continuity in science. In a sense, Worrall aims to establish a philosophical position which saves as much of scientific realism as it is possible, given the possibility of scientific revolution. This position is said to be 'the only hopeful way of *both* underwriting the no miracles argument *and* accepting an accurate account of the extent of theory change in science' (ibid.: 117).

In order to illustrate and vindicate his position, Worrall has developed a particular case-study which involves the retention of the mathematical form of the Fresnel Laws in Maxwell's theory. He then argues that from Fresnel onwards the identification of the *structure* of light has remained unaltered, whereas there have been different theories or descriptions of its *nature*, i.e. of what light *is*. As he puts it: 'There was a continuity or accumulation in the shift, but the continuity is one of *form* or *structure*, not of content' (ibid.: 117).

Structural realism relies on a distinction between the *nature* of an entity, or process, and its *structure*, and claims that the latter is captured by the mathematical equations describing the behaviour of an entity, while the former somehow 'lies beyond' what can be quantitatively described. This is a view which I aim to challenge. The thesis I shall motivate and defend is that Worrall's attempted reconciliation of the pessimistic induction and the no miracle argument is not best captured by the structure versus content distinction.

Structural versus scientific realism

It is an undeniable fact that, in the transition from old to new theories, many mathematical equations have been retained, either as they were or as fully determined limiting cases of other equations which feature in the new theories. Examples of this sort can be produced at will: the mathematical form of Newton's laws is a limiting case of relevant laws of the special theory of relativity; the mathematical form of most of the laws of the caloric theory of heat – as we have already seen in Chapter 6 – has re-appeared within thermodynamics; and similarly for other past scientific theories. This fact seems immediately to suggest a type of continuity in theory change: a continuity at the formal-mathematical level. Yet, in many cases, the full physical interpretation of the mathematical symbols involved has changed radically. Hence, one may note, while the mathematical form of many laws has remained unaltered, their content – the physical processes and entities whose behaviour they purported to describe – has changed. Howard Stein has made this point clear when he states:

> What is in fact 'recognisable' is a distinct relationship, from older to newer theory, of *mathematical forms* – not a resemblance of 'entities'. This has always seemed to me the most striking and important fact about the affiliations of scientific theories. I do not suggest a philosophical 'explanation' of this fact; I cite it, on merely historical evidence, just as a fact.[2]

(1987: 393)

This important continuity in theory change can be fully accommodated within scientific realism. Scientific realists can explain the fact that mathematical equations have been retained in theory change by saying that they form an integral part of the well-supported and (approximately) true theoretical content of theories. But they would deny that *all* of what is retained is empirical content and (uninterpreted) mathematical equations. Not only is some theoretical content also retained, but scientists now have good reason to believe that the content of current theories – what they predicate of the world – is better supported by the evidence, and, hence, more likely to be true. So, scientific realism can be seen as defending the following theses:

1   Some parts of the theoretical interpretation of a mathematical equation have been retained as parts of the new theoretical interpretation of this

equation. For instance, as was seen in Chapter 6 in relation to the theories and models of nineteenth-century optics, not only has the wave-equation (which was taken to describe the propagation of a light-wave in the luminiferous ether) been retained in the electromagnetic theory of light (now describing the propagation of an electromagnetic wave in the field), but many of the substantive properties which an ethereal wave was supposed to possess – for instance transversality, ability to sustain potential and kinetic energy, finite velocity of propagation and others – have been retained as properties of an electromagnetic wave. The main point here is that when an entity is posited to play a certain causal role, it is assigned a number of properties in virtue of which it is supposed to play the role it does: (descriptions of) these properties are part and parcel of the theoretical interpretation of the terms employed to refer to this entity and of the laws which are supposed to govern its behaviour. There may be changes in the properties attributed by a new theory to a certain posited entity. Yet there may be substantive continuity with past theories in that some (or most) of the properties attributed to this putative entity by past theories are still taken to characterise the entity posited by the new theory.

2   The theoretical interpretation of the retained mathematical equations in the new theory is better supported by current evidence than was the full theoretical interpretation of the same equations in the superseded theory. For instance, the existence of electromagnetic fields is better supported (by means of variable and independent evidence) than the existential claims about a material substratum, associated with 'luminiferous ether'.

3   The current theoretical interpretation of the retained equations is more likely to be true than false. So, for instance, given the current evidence, it is more likely to be true than false that the wave equation correctly describes the propagation of electromagnetic waves in the field.

Worrall is unwilling to accept the foregoing full-blown realist position. His structural realism is meant to be different from the position above. But structural realism cannot be the mere recording of the fact that there is a continuity at the mathematical level when theories change. As a philosophical thesis, it must offer an *explanation* of this recognisable and important feature of theory change in science. Besides, as Stein (1987: 383) has hinted, this feature of theory change is compatible with instrumentalism. Hence, if structural realism is to be taken as a *realist* position, it must be so interpreted that it takes distance from instrumentalism.

I suggest therefore that structural realism is best understood as issuing an *epistemic constraint* on what can be known and on what scientific theories can reveal. In opposition to scientific realism, structural realism restricts the cognitive content of scientific theories to their *mathematical structure together with their empirical consequences*. But, in opposition to instrumentalism, structural realism suggests that the mathematical structure of a theory does reflect the structure of the world (i.e. it reflects *real relations* between unobservables). Structural realism thus can be seen to defend the following theses:

(a) Scientific theories can, at best, reveal the structure of the unobservable world by virtue of their own mathematical structure.
(b) Mathematical equations which get retained in theory-change express real relations among entities for which we know nothing more than that they stand in these mathematically expressed relations to each other.
(c) Different ontologies (and hence different theoretical interpretations) may satisfy the same mathematical structure, but there is no reason to accept that one of them is better supported by the evidence than any other, nor is there any reason to believe in one of them as the correct one.

This is a reasonably strong position. I take it to be *this* position that Worrall wants to endorse. Here is how Worrall describes his view: the structural realist 'insists that it is a mistake to think that we can ever "understand" the nature of the basic furniture of the universe' (1989: 122). Instead, what we, like Newton, can discover are 'relationships between phenomena expressed in the mathematical equations of [the theories], the theoretical terms of which should be understood as genuine primitives' (ibid.). Referring to the empirical success of quantum mechanics, Worrall states: 'The structural realist simply asserts [that] . . . the structure of the universe is (probably) something like quantum mechanical' (1989: 123).

Poincaréan preludes

Historically, the structural realist position can be traced back to the work of Henri Poincaré around the beginning of the century.[3] Poincaré was well aware of the force of the argument from the falsity of past scientific theories, which in turn-of-century France took the form of a debate about the 'bankruptcy of science'. In his address to the 1900 Congress of Physics (1900: 14–15; 1902: 173) he noted:

> The man of the world is struck to see how ephemeral scientific theories are. After some years of prosperity, he sees them successively abandoned; he sees ruins accumulated on ruins; he predicts that the theories in vogue today will in a short time succumb in their turn, and he concludes that they are absolutely in vain. This is what he calls the bankruptcy of science.

He then goes on to say: 'His scepticism is superficial; he does not understand either the aim or the role of scientific theories; without this he would understand that ruins can still be good for something' (ibid.).

Poincaré suggested that this argument has no force against those who take theories to be mere instruments for the co-ordination of empirical laws and the prediction of phenomena (ibid.). If theories do not aim to correctly describe the furniture of the world, then it is no problem that their theoretical parts, the unobservable entities and mechanisms they postulate, are mere speculations which subsequently get abandoned. As he noted, 'Fresnel's theory enables us to [predict optical phenomena] as well as it did before Maxwell's time' (1900: 15; 1902: 173).

Yet, as we have already seen in Chapter 2, a purely instrumentalist construal of scientific theories flies in the face of the genuine and novel empirical successes of theories. So, Poincaré opted for an intermediate position. He rejected the view that scientific theories are mere 'practical recipes'. Instead, he argued that successful scientific theories can tell us something about the unobservable world. But what exactly?

Scientific theories, Poincaré maintained, can tell us something about the relations in which unobservable entities stand to each other. Taking a neo-Kantian line, Poincaré equated the unobservable entities posited by science with the (Kantian) things-in-themselves, and deemed them unknowable. Still, however, he thought that the success of science could tell us something about the relational structure of a world populated by these, otherwise unknowable, unobservable entities: 'Still things themselves are not what [science] can reach as the naive dogmatists think, but only relations between things. Outside of these relations there is no knowable reality' (1902: 25).

The best indication of what the relational structure of the unobservable world is like, Poincaré thought, can be found in the mathematical structure of an empirically successful theory. In particular, those mathematical equations which survive conceptual revolutions and radical theory change, he thought, express real relations among unobservable entities. Here is his argument:

> [T]hese equations express relations, and if the equations remain true, it is because the relations preserve their reality. They teach us, now as then, that there is such and such a relation between this thing and some other thing; only this something formerly we called *motion*; we now call it *electric current*. But these appellations were only images substituted for the real objects which Nature will eternally hide from us. The true relations between these real objects are the only reality we can attain to, and the only condition is that the same relations exist between these objects as between the images ... which we are forced to replace.
>
> (1900: 15; 1902: 174)

And elsewhere he stated:

> [I]f we look more closely [at the history of abandoned scientific theories], we see that what thus succumb are the theories properly so called,

those which pretend to teach us what things are. But there is in them something which usually survives. If one of them taught us a true relation, this relation is definitely acquired, and it will be found again under a new disguise in the other theories which will successively come to reign in place of the old.

(1905: 182)

So, Poincaré – and, following him, Worrall – suggest that although the nature of the unobservable entities cannot be known, successful scientific theories can still tell us something about the structure of the unobservable world.[4]

Before we critically examine this view it is worth reminding the reader that we have already encountered (see the last section of Chapter 3: Empiricism and realism-without-the-tears?) a version of structural realism advocated by Grover Maxwell, and attributed to Frank Ramsey and the Ramsey-sentence approach to scientific theories. The Worrall–Poincaré position stems from a certain *epistemological* need: to reconcile some form of realism with the argument from the pessimistic induction. The structuralist metaphysics which accompanies it is then best seen as a direct consequence of their preferred answer to the pessimistic induction. On the other hand, Ramsey-style structural realism stems from the Russellian view that the world has a certain logico-mathematical structure which is reflected in (or can be inferred from) the logico-mathematical structure of our best scientific theories. The claim that only the logico-mathematical structure of the unobservable world can be known is taken by Ramsey-style structural realism to be the required compromise between the empiricist demand that science should stay as close to experience as possible and the realist view that science does discover something or other about the causes of the phenomena. I do not want to argue that there are fundamental differences between the two structural realist styles. Perhaps, if there are differences, one could describe them as motivational. In fact, presented as a position which asserts that only the structure of the unobservable world can be known, Worrall–Poincaré structural realism finds in the Ramsey-style framework its canonical formulations. If so, all arguments levelled against the Ramsey-style structural realism also hold against the Worrall–Poincaré position.[5]

Structural realism and the pessimistic induction

On the face of it, the structural realist position is attractive. What else should one expect of a realist position, given the pessimistic induction? It turns out, however, that structural realism faces some important problems. Let me suppose, as I should, that there is a well-motivated distinction between the formal-mathematical structure of a theory and its content (or interpretation). For it is clear that there can be two identical formal-mathematical structures which nonetheless have different interpretations. The issue I shall concentrate on is the following: can retention at the formal-mathematical level (the level of mathematical equations) be enough to form a basis for a realist answer to the pessimistic induction? In other words, is structural realism strong enough to answer the pessimistic induction?

As we have seen already, Worrall argues against Laudan that at least *some* non-empirical content is retained when theories change. His main argument for this is that mathematical equations are retained in theory change. Yet, Laudan has anticipated such a response. He has observed that one 'might be content with capturing only the formal mathematical relations' of the superseded theory T_1 within the successor theory T_2 (1981: 237). But he rejects this view as a viable realist position since, he contends, it amounts to the response of 'closet' positivists' (ibid.).

I think Laudan is right in pointing out that, without further argument, the appeal to mathematical continuity would do little to establish Worrall's position as realist. Worrall certainly needs an independent argument that mathematical equations *represent* the structure of the world, and hence that their retention in theory change marks a sense in which the superseded theory was right about the structure of the world.

The need for such an argument becomes apparent if we take into account the following alternative explanation of the mathematical retention in theory change. One might argue simply that retention at the level of equations is merely a pragmatic feature of scientific practice: the scientific community finds it just convenient and labour-saving to build upon the mathematical work of their predecessors. This predeliction for mathematical equations, the argument would go on, signifies just the conservativeness of the scientific community rather than anything about real relations in the world. In order to block this move, Worrall needs an argument to take him from the fact that mathematical equations are retained to the conclusion that this retention tells us something about the *structure* of the world; in particular to the conclusion that the retained mathematical equations represent real relations between otherwise unknown, (or, worse, unknowable), physical entities. I am not aware of such an argument in Worrall's (and Poincaré's) writings.[6] I do not believe it is impossible to give such an argument, but prior to its enunciation, no case for structural realism can be sustained.

The best candidate for the missing argument is nothing other than a version of the no miracle argument. Worrall cannot be pleased with the full-blown version of NMA (discussed in Chapter 4), since it aims to establish much more than he intends to accept. It aims to establish that genuinely successful scientific theories should be accepted as approximately true, where (approximate) truth pertains not only to relations among otherwise unknown entities, but to what these entities are. Comparing the wave-theory of light with our current theories of light, Worrall states: 'the classical wave theory is . . . "to a large degree empirically adequate" – yes; "to some degree *structurally* accurate" no doubt; but "approximately true" – no' (1990b:

343). Hence, the structural realist should go for a 'structural version' of NMA. Here is a possibility. The structural realist might argue that, from the vantage-point of the successor theory, the best way to explain why the abandoned theory was empirically successful is to suggest that the retained mathematical equations express real relations among unobservable entities in the world. So, the structural realist might present argument (W) as follows:

(W) Predictive success is cumulative: subsequent theories capture the confirmed empirical content of their predecessor theories. But mathematical structure is also cumulative: subsequent theories incorporate the mathematical structure of predecessor theories. Hence, there is a correlation between the accumulation of mathematical structure and the accumulation of empirical success. Since successful predictions suggest that the theory has somehow 'latched on to' the world, one may expect that the 'carried over' mathematical structure of the theory has 'latched on to' the structure of the world.

I do not for a moment doubt that a successful defence of realism requires explanatory arguments of the above sort. For central to their position is the claim that some salient features of science, notably its impressive predictive success, cannot be adequately explained unless one admits that theories have got the world right in some ways. Poincaré himself used such arguments frequently.[7]

Note, however, that argument if (W) is to lend any credence to structural realism, then it must be the case that the mathematical structure of a theory is somehow exclusively responsible for the predictive success of the theory. Only then would a structural realist be entitled to admit that the predictive success of a theory supports solely the claim that the mathematical structure of a theory expresses (or captures) the structure of the unobservable world. Worrall seems to defend this view when he says:

It is true – and importantly true – that many of the mathematical equations supplied by the wave theory of light still live on in science; and it is true – and importantly (if rather obviously) true – that repeatable (and repeated) experiments do not change their results, so that all the correct empirical consequences of the wave theory are still, of course, correct. Nonetheless, at the theoretical level there has been radical, ineliminable change.

(1990b: 342)

What is not true, however, is that mathematical equations alone – devoid of their theoretical content – can give rise to any predictions whatsoever. Predictions require theoretical hypotheses and auxiliary assumptions. The mathematical equations used for the derivation of a prediction are already theoretically interpreted – they have theoretical content. Hence, when a prediction is fulfilled, and when it thereby lends credence to the hypotheses which generated it, it is unfair to give all the credit to the mathematical equations. Some credit has to go the theoretical content of these equations as well as to the auxiliary assumptions. Even if one were to give all the credit to the equations together with the auxiliaries, since any theoretical hypothesis can serve as an auxiliary assumption in a given context, each and every theoretical hypotheses which contributes to the generation of predictions can get *some* credit from the ensuing empirical successes. So, if structural realists were to use a version of (W) in order to claim that retained mathematical equations reveal real relations among unobservable entities, they would also have to admit that some theoretical content, not necessarily empirical and low-level, is well-supported by the evidence. In particular, they would have to admit that some hypotheses/claims about these entities also get supported by the evidence, since they contributed to the empirical success no less than the mathematical equations which they 'flesh out'. If the empirical success of a theory offers any grounds for thinking that some parts of a theory have 'latched on to' the world, those parts cannot be just some (uninterpreted) mathematical equations of the theory, but must include some theoretical assertions concerning some substantive properties as well as the law-like behaviour of the entities and mechanisms posited by the theory. These theoretical parts include, but are not exhausted by, mathematical equations. Later on, I shall defend this thesis by looking into the case that Worrall has studied in some detail: Fresnel's equations and their retention in Maxwell's theory. For the time being, let me just stress the main point: if one admits that there is *substantive* (not just formal) retention at the structural–mathematical level, then one should admit that some theoretical content, too, gets retained. But such an admission would undercut the claim that predictive success vindicates only the mathematical structure of a theory.

So, a 'structural version' of NMA warrants more than the structural realist wants to accept. Capitalising on the fact that mathematical equations alone cannot generate any predictive success, nor can they explain it, a scientific realist should claim that what best explains the predictive success of theories is that some theoretical components of the theory (posited theoretical mechanisms as well as substantial properties and law-like behaviour ascribed to the entities) are, relevantly, correct. Any attempt to pin the credit for the predictive success on mathematical structure alone is neither necessary nor legitimate. Besides, structural versions of NMA involve no less epistemic risk than do the full-blown versions. The only difference is one of degree: *how much* non-empirical content one is willing to accept as relevantly correct. But it is not the case that a scientific realist is committed to the view that *all* non-empirical claims made by a theory are equally justified. Nor is it the case that a different kind of belief is involved when one asserts that one knows the structure of a process than when one claims that one knows what this process *is*.

To sum up, the fundamental insight Worrall has, i.e. that the predictive success of a theory points to the theory's being correct in some of its claims about the unobservable world, cannot be best served by a distinction along the lines of structure (or mathematical equations) versus nature (or theoretical content). As I argued in Chapter 5, the best place to draw the relevant line is between essentially contributing theoretical components and 'idle' ones. This last distinction, however, is orthogonal to Worrall's distinction between structure and nature.

Structure versus nature?

Worrall is somewhat ambiguous on what exactly the distinction he wants to draw is. Sometimes, he talks about a distinction between the structure of a theory and its theoretical interpretation. But on occasion he talks about a distinction between the structure of an entity (or process) and its nature. Witness, for instance, the following statement: '[I]t seems right to say that Fresnel completely misidentified the *nature* of light, but nonetheless it is no miracle that his theory enjoyed the empirical predictive success that it did; it is no miracle because Fresnel's theory, as science later on saw it, attributed to light the right *structure*' (1989: 117). As for the first distinction, it was noted in the previous section that Worrall requires some argument in order to show that structural retention can be the basis for a realist position and that, so long as this argument is a version of the NMA, it can license more theoretical continuity than Worrall is willing to admit. When it comes the second distinction, it is doubtful that it is well-motivated. The question is this: can we draw a distinction between the *nature* of an entity and its *structure* such that we can claim to know its structure but not its nature? In this section, I shall enunciate two theses: first, that the nature and structure of an entity form a continuum; and, second, that the nature of an entity, process, or physical mechanism is no less knowable than its structure.

Is the nature of a theoretical entity something distinct from its structure? Equivalently, can one usefully conceive of the physical content of a mathematical symbol (that is, of the entity or process it stands for) as distinct from the totality of the interpreted mathematical equations in which it features, (that is, from the totality of laws which describe its behaviour)? When scientists talk about the nature of an entity, what they normally do – apart from positing a causal agent – is to ascribe to this entity a grouping of basic properties and relations. They then describe its law-like behaviour by means of a set of equations. In other words, they endow this causal agent with a certain causal structure, and they talk about the way in which this entity is structured. I think that talk of 'nature' over and above this structural description (physical and mathematical) of a causal agent is to

hark back to the medieval discourse of 'forms' and 'substances'. Such talk
has been overthrown by the scientific revolution of the seventeenth century.

I shall try to make this point more concrete by considering the case of
mass. The traditional idea of mass is the 'quantity of substance' possessed
by a body. Accordingly, the nature of mass (that is, the nature of a theoretical entity) is something to do with the substance of a material body. But
after the scientific revolution, this traditional idea has been slowly replaced
by the concept of *inertial* mass, which is described as the property in virtue
of which the body resists acceleration, its description being given by
Newton's second law – the equation $m_i = F/a$. Hence, mass is understood
as being a structural property in virtue of which a body resists acceleration
when some force is exerted upon it. 'Structural property' may not be a nice
term, but it seems to me that it can convey the point that by discovering
more about the properties of mass we discover more about its nature, i.e.
about what mass *is*. Likewise, the gravitational mass of a body is described
by the law of universal gravitation as the property of the body in virtue of
which it is accelerated in a gravitational field of another massive body M.
This property is 'captured' quantitatively by the equation $m_g = Fr^2/GM$.
Moreover, it has been established that these two properties are in fact one
and the same: the property in virtue of which the body resists acceleration
is the property in virtue of which it is accelerated in a gravitational field.
That is, $m_g = m_i$. By equating these two properties, more structure, so to
speak, was added to *mass*, and knowledge about what mass *is* was increased.
So, knowing what mass is involves knowing what kind of property it is,
which laws it obeys, and in particular, the equations it satisfies within a
scientific theory.

It is certainly arguable that knowing which laws an entity obeys does
not exhaust knowing what this entity *is*. But one should be careful how to
interpret this claim. It is certainly possible that some of the properties in
virtue of which a certain entity plays a causal role may not be specifiable
in terms of mathematically formalisable laws and descriptions. It is also
true that, at any given point in time, we may not know all of the properties which an entity possesses, or that we may be wrong about some of
those properties. But these are empirical claims to be discovered and established by natural science itself. They do not guarantee that there is always,
so to speak, an 'excess nature' in every entity which cannot be captured by
further investigation into the laws that this entity obeys. On the contrary,
the actual scientific practice urges that improvements in our knowledge
of what an entity is involve further knowledge of the laws of behaviour of
this entity.

To recapitulate: to say what an entity *is* is to show *how this entity is
structured*: what are its properties, in what relations it stands to other objects,
etc. An exhaustive specification of this set of properties and relations leaves
nothing left out. Any talk of something else remaining uncaptured when
this specification is made is, I think, obscure. I conclude, then, that the

'nature' of an entity forms a continuum with its 'structure', and that knowing the one involves and entails knowing the other.

The case of light

Let us now consider the case of light, which Worrall and Poincaré have taken as illustrative of their thesis that there is a dichotomy between nature and structure. After citing the 'structural similarity' between Fresnel's laws and Maxwell's laws, Worrall appeals to Poincaré and argues that the discovery that light consists in vibrations of the electromagnetic field does not reveal the nature of light. Instead, one should understand this claim as saying that 'Maxwell built on the relations revealed by Fresnel and showed that further relations existed between phenomena hitherto regarded as purely optical on the one hand and electric and magnetic phenomena on the other' (1989: 120). Elsewhere he notes:

> Both Fresnel's and Maxwell's theories make the passage of light consist of wave forms transmitted from place to place, forms obeying the same mathematics. Hence, although the periodic changes which the two theories postulate are ontologically of radically different sorts – in one material particles change position, in the other field vectors change their strength – there is nonetheless a structural, mathematical continuity between the two theories. Something importantly more than merely correct empirical content, there is a carry over at the theoretical level too, but one of *structure* rather than content.
>
> (1990a: 21)

Is it correct to say that it was only 'structure' (i.e. uninterpreted mathematical equations) that was carried over in the transition from Fresnel to Maxwell? I shall now try to show that fundamentally correct *theoretical principles* about the propagation of light and some properties attributed to the carrier of light waves were also carried over.

Take a light-ray which strikes the interface of two media. Fresnel (1823: 773–774) set out to calculate the amplitude and intensity of the reflected and refracted (i.e. transmitted) rays with respect to the amplitude, intensity and state of polarisation of the incident ray. He discovered that the amplitude of the reflected and transmitted rays depend on the polarisation of the incident ray, and in particular on whether the incident light is polarised perpendicularly to or parallel with the plane of incidence. Fresnel took it that, generally, the vibrations constituting light are propagated perpendicularly to the plane of polarisation. His well-known laws have the following form:

The incident ray is polarised along the plane of incidence. Then,

$$R_{par} = \frac{-\sin (i - i')}{\sin (i + i')} I_{par} \tag{1}$$

where: R_{par} is the amplitude of the reflected ray polarised (as mentioned above)

I_{par} is the amplitude of the incident ray, i is the angle of incidence/reflection and

i' is the angle of refraction (transmission).

The incident ray is polarised perpendicularly to the plane of incidence. Then

$$R_{per} = \frac{-\tan (i - i')}{\tan (i + i')} \, I_{per} . \tag{2}$$

In his proof, Fresnel made use of the following assumptions:

(a) A *minimal mechanical assumption* that the velocity of the displacement of the molecules of ether is proportional to the amplitude of the light-wave. To be precise, one has to add here that for Fresnel the velocity of the propagation of light in an optical medium was inversely proportional to the square root of the density of the medium.

(b) The *principle of conservation of energy* ('*forces vives*') during the propagation of light in the two media. Applying the principle of the conservation of energy to the effective components of light in the interface of the two media, he arrived at a general relation of the form $\sin i' \cos i (1 - R^2) = \sin i \cos i' \, T^2$, of which he noted: 'This is the equation that results from the principle of conservation of *vis viva* and it must be satisfied in all cases, irrespective of whether the incident ray had been polarised parallel or perpendicularly to the incident plane' (1823: 772: my translation).

(c) A *geometrical analysis* of the configuration of the light-rays in the interface of two media. Then, by instantiating the principle of the conservation of energy for the components of the rays active in each case, he derived the two laws, (1) and (2) above. Finally, by taking the intensity of the light-wave to be a function of the square of its amplitude, he derived similar laws for the intensities of light-waves (cf. 1823: 775ff.).

It is worth noting that in his proof, Fresnel did not appeal to any specific mechanical model of the ether in order to derive his laws. What I have called a 'minimal mechanical assumption' (i.e. that the amplitude of the light-wave is proportional to the velocity of the displacement of the ether) was a subsidiary assumption in the proof, its sole purpose being to set up the principle of the conservation of energy. This claim is reinforced when we take into account Fresnel's general way of demonstrating 'the exclusive existence of transversal vibrations in light rays' (1822: 490). There too, Fresnel took the amplitude of vibrations as being 'proportional to the amplitude of the oscillations of the molecules of ether' (1822: 491). Instead of employing any specific mechanical model, Fresnel took it that the velocity of the ethereal molecules could be represented as a *vectoral quantity*, and analysed it in three components, along the Cartesian co-ordinates. He then noted that 'whatever the nature of the oscillations executed by the molecules of the ether, we can regard them as resulting from the combination of three series of rectilinear oscillations, the directions of which follow these three rectangular axes' (1822: 492; my translation). The point which Fresnel made was that no specific assumptions about the trajectories of the ethereal molecules were necessary. Rather, it was enough for the formulation of the principle of the conservation of energy to take energy as a function of the square of the amplitude of the light-waves, irrespective of how exactly this amplitude is realised (ibid.: 493).

The foregoing account of the discovery of Fresnel's laws motivates the following observation. There is no sense in which Fresnel was 'just' right about the structure of light-propagation and wrong about the nature of light, unless of course one understands 'structure' so broadly as to include the principle of the conservation of energy and the theoretical mechanism of light-propagation. But the issue is not terminological. The theoretical mechanism of (exclusively) transversal propagation is as structural – and as natural – as are rectilinear propagation, diffraction, interference, finiteness of the velocity of propagation, and satisfaction of the principle of the conservation of energy. At any rate, all of these properties of light-propagation were carried over in Maxwell's theory, even though Maxwell's theory dispenses for good with ethereal molecules.

We are therefore in a position to tell where Fresnel has been right and where wrong, without appealing to any distinction between structure and nature. For, even if we granted that Fresnel believed that light was an ultimately mechanical process, we can clearly say that he was right about *some* of the fundamental properties of the light-waves, and wrong about some others, especially those related to the alleged mechanical character of the propagation of light. He was right in saying that the transmission of light is a process which needs a carrier (what we, nowadays, call the 'electromagnetic field'), but wrong about the supposed molecular constitution of this carrier. He was right about the transverse character of the oscillations which constitute light, but wrong about their mechanical underpinning. He was right in stating that the propagation of light satisfies the principle of the conservation of energy, but wrong in reducing the amplitude of the light-wave to the velocity of molecular displacements. He was right in suggesting that light can be represented as a vectorial physical quantity but wrong in identifying the vectorial components with ether displacements. Therefore, unless 'structure' is so understood as to include whatever properties attributed by Fresnel to the light-waves were retained in Maxwell's theory, it is not correct to say that Fresnel discovered the structure and 'just' misidentified the nature of light.[8]

Maxwellian insights

Before I conclude this chapter, I wish to state a way in which one can draw
a methodologically useful, but not a sharp, distinction between nature and
structure, which goes back to James Clerk Maxwell. Maxwell (1890a: 763ff.)
distinguished between the geometrical character of the process of light-
propagation and the physical quantity which constitutes light. By 'geometrical character' of light-propagation, he meant all the properties of this
process which were independent of the exact physical quantity involved in
it. Given what he knew, Maxwell stressed that light could be 'a displacement, or a rotation, or an electrical disturbance, or indeed any physical
quantity which is capable of assuming negative as well as positive values'
(1890a: 766) – that is, it can be represented as a vector. All these different
physical quantities have in common a *structural* or *geometrical pattern*:
their propagation can be expressed by (one-dimensional) equations of the
form

$$V(x,t) = A \cos(nt - px + a),$$

where: A is the amplitude of the oscillations
the time $2\pi/n$ is the period and
the factor $(nt - px + a)$ is the phase.

Solutions to this equation represent waves with specific wave-lengths and
velocities of propagation (ibid.: 766). Taken on their own, the geometrical
features of this process cannot determine exactly what physical quantity is
propagated. Maxwell's point is that one can study and discover facts about
the physical process of light-propagation without being initially committed
to any physical quantity being constitutive of light.

I take it that the above distinction is methodological, for it creates no
sharp dichotomy between the structure of a process and the quantity (physical magnitude) involved in it. Maxwell's insight was that since the evidence
currently available to theorists could not definitely support a view as to
what physical quantity constitutes light, while it was possible to discover
and study many other properties of light-propagation without being
committed to any specific view about its constitution, one had better do the
latter while, at the same time, seeking for further evidence which can determine the former. But, after this evidence came in, Maxwell was ready to
affirm that 'light itself is an electromagnetic disturbance in the form of
waves propagated through the electromagnetic field according to electromagnetic laws' (1864: 42).

Yet, even before this fundamental discovery, Maxwell had not placed in
opposition the geometrical features of the propagation of light and its nature.
For instance, in citing interference, transversality and the like as features
of the process of propagation, Maxwell comments that: 'A further insight

into the physical nature of the process is obtained from the fact that ...'
(1890a: 766). And, later, he presented some evidence in favour of the electromagnetic theory of light, that is, in favour of the theory that light *is* 'an
electric displacement and a magnetic disturbance at right angles to each
other' (ibid.: 766, 772). So, although the geometrical features of light-
propagation do not uniquely determine the nature of light – what kind of
physical quantity light is – the latter can be found and known no less than
can the geometrical features.

Maxwell's insight can be generalised as follows.

It is a substantial discovery about the physical world that, on some
occasions, one can isolate and study some physical phenomena, without
being, right from the start, committed to what exactly physical quantity is involved in them. One may have abundant evidence about (what
Maxwell calls) the 'geometrical features' of a process, and yet one
may initially be ignorant about what exactly is the physical quantity
that possesses these geometrical features. There is no reason to think
that one will never be able to penetrate further into the physical magnitudes whose many geometrical features one knows. On the contrary,
when sufficient evidence is amassed, one can claim that one has come
to know what these entities are. But, the lesson to be drawn is that
we are better off if we let the evidence tell us what, at any given stage
of inquiry, we should be confident about and to what degree.

As Stein puts it, we must distinguish, as far as we can, 'between what is
known with some security, or held at least with some probability, and what
is bare and even implausible conjecture' (1989: 62).

The significance of Maxwell's (and, I should add, Worrall's) insight for
the realism debate is that scientific realism is not an all-or-nothing doctrine,
in the sense that one must either believe to an equal degree everything a
scientific theory predicates of the world or else believe in nothing but
(perhaps) observable phenomena. If scientific realism is to be plausible and,
as most realists would urge, in agreement with actual scientific practice,
then it must go for differentiated commitments to scientific theories, and
what they entail about the world, in accordance with the evidence which
supports them, as a whole and in parts. Structural realism, to the extent that
it rests on a sharp dichotomy between structure and content, and insofar as
it makes only structure knowable and attainable, cannot be adequately
defended. But, we must acknowledge that, after Worrall's attempt to motivate structural realism, we are wiser as to what the scientific realism versus
instrumentalism debate should involve. This in itself is testimony to the
substantial contribution made by Worrall (and Poincaré, and Stein) to this
debate.

8 Underdetermination undermined

Realists suggest that acceptance of a mature and genuinely successful theory should be identified with belief that the theory is approximately true. Some empiricists, however, counter that there is a simple argument against the realist thesis: the argument from the underdetermination of theories by evidence (henceforth, UTE). It goes like this: two theories which are observationally indistinguishable, i.e. they entail exactly the same observational consequences, are epistemically indistinguishable, too, being equally well supported by the evidence. Hence, the argument concludes, there are no positive reasons to believe in one rather than the other. This conclusion is what Laudan very aptly has called *the egalitarian thesis* (1996: 33). Since, the argument goes on, for any theory which entails the evidence there are incompatible but empirically indistinguishable rivals, it follows that no theory can be reasonably believed to be (approximately) true.

This argument has become a classic weapon in the attack against realism in science (cf. Duhem 1908; Putnam 1983a; Quine 1975; van Fraassen 1980). Its consequences – as well as several ways of responding to it – have been much discussed in the relevant literature (cf. Bergstrom 1984; Glymour 1971, 1976, 1980; Horwich 1982, 1991; Jardine 1986; Kukla 1994a; Laudan 1990a, 1990b; Laudan and Leplin 1991; Newton-Smith 1978, 1981, 1987; Sklar 1974, 1985; Worrall 1982).

Currently, the argument from UTE is employed centrally by Bas van Fraassen. He suggests that UTE shows that there are no reasons for believing more in one than the other of a pair of empirically equivalent theoretical descriptions. Instead of believing a theory to be true, he recommends that the best we can do is *accept* a theory as *empirically adequate*. Since two empirically equivalent theories are equally empirically adequate, van Fraassen points out, if we decide to accept one rather than the other, our decision is based not on epistemic grounds but rather on pragmatic ones. Acceptance, for van Fraassen, involves more than belief in empirical adequacy. It takes into account 'virtues' such as parsimony, explanatory power, etc. But these are *pragmatic* virtues, he says: they have nothing to do with the truth of the theory; nor should they be reasons to believe a theory. It should be clear, then, that if realists are to defend the view that theories can be accepted as approximately true, they have to block UTE.

Before we analyse the structure of UTE, we should notice that the argument capitalises on two well-known tenets of theory-construction:

1 A given finite segment of observational data does not uniquely entail a hypothesis which accounts for it.
2 There are alternative theoretical formulations which entail the same body of observational data.

The first tenet is a version of the so-called 'problem of induction'. The second says that the hypothetico-deductive method cannot warrant that there is only one hypothesis entailing the evidence available. Both tenets assert that there is leeway between a body of evidence and a theory employed to account for it. However, these near platitudes do not challenge the reliability of ampliative inferential practices in science. It is entirely reasonable to subscribe to both tenets, and yet to believe that the evidence confirms one theory more than the other – even though both theories entail the same evidence. It all depends on the account of confirmation which one adopts. For instance, on standard Bayesian accounts of confirmation, the mere fact that inductive inferences from a finite segment of data do not entail law-like generalisations does not show that a particular segment of data does not inductively support one law-like generalisation more than another (cf. Howson and Urbach 1989). Similarly, the mere fact that two alternative theories entail the same evidence does not imply that the evidence supports these theories equally well. Nor does it imply that *no* future evidence can favour only *one* of the two theories.

Although UTE capitalises on these two platitudes, it stretches far beyond them. It stretches beyond (1) for it challenges the reliability of ampliative inferences. UTE is not just a variant of ordinary inductive scepticism. In fact, advocates of UTE are, typically, not inductive sceptics. They are willing to grant that when it comes to observable phenomena induction works reliably. What they challenge is the possibility of theoretical knowledge in science. More specifically, UTE challenges the reliability of ampliative (abductive) inferences which go beyond the phenomena and posit unobservable entities and processes. The point it raises is that the theories which get licensed by these methods are not objectively better than those that do not. Hence, defending and showing the reliability of abductive inferences, a task which was dealt with in Chapter 4, is part and parcel of the realist rebuttal of the argument from underdetermination. What is also worth stressing is that UTE also stretches far beyond (2) above. For UTE, as routinely understood, intends to establish that two empirically congruent theories – that is, two theories that entail the same observational consequences – are *equally well supported* by these consequences.

The structure of UTE

UTE rests on two premises:

(a) The *empirical equivalence thesis* (EET): for *any* theory T and *any* body of observational evidence E, there is another theory T' such that T and T' are empirically equivalent in respect to E; and
(b) The *entailment thesis* (ET): the entailment of the evidence is the only epistemic constraint on the confirmation of a theory.

If UTE is to be blocked, at least one of the two premises must de defeated. The good news is that realists can find some comfort in the recent work of Laudan (1996). This work will be the backdrop to the discussion which follows.

Let us first concentrate on the first premiss. EET is certainly a bold claim, but there is a sense in which its proof is trivial. Given any theory T, one can construct another theory T' by just adding any statement one likes to T, or by just permuting two theoretical terms of T (e.g. 'electron' with 'proton', etc.). One can also create an empirically equivalent theory by taking the Craig(T) of T; or, by just accepting the 'theory' T^* that 'All observable phenomena are *as if* T is true, but T is actually false'. Clearly, T and T^* are logically incompatible but observationally equivalent by construction.

However, none of the alternatives mentioned above are really serious challengers. T^*, for instance, is not a proper theory. It is just the denial of the claim that there are theoretical entities. But, as I have already noted, the issue currently at stake is not the reality of unobservable entities but the correctness of their theoretical descriptions. Hence, the advocates of UTE need to show that there are, or can be, proper empirically equivalent scientific theories – theories which refer to theoretical entities but make incompatible claims about them.

Laudan has rightly pointed out that, apart from the foregoing piecemeal strategies, there is 'no algorithm for generating genuine theoretical competitors to a given theory' (1996: 61). Yet, there is a general feeling that the so-called Duhem–Quine thesis offers a constructive proof of EET. Put briefly, the Duhem–Quine thesis starts with the undeniable premiss that all theories entail observational consequences only with the help of auxiliary assumptions, and states that it is always possible that a theory together with suitable auxiliaries can accommodate *any* recalcitrant evidence. A corollary, then, is that for any evidence and any two rival theories T and T', there are suitable auxiliaries such that T' & *suitable auxiliary assumptions* will be empirically equivalent to T together with its own auxiliaries. If the Duhem–Quine thesis is true, then it follows that no evidence can ever tell two theories apart.

What is worth emphasising is that, if true, the Duhem–Quine thesis does create some genuine problems to a falsificationist (Popperian) account of theory testing. This is the view that theories are tested by attempting to refute them, in particular by examining potential falsifiers. The Duhem–Quine thesis suggests that any theory can be made compatible with any evidence by means of suitable adjustments to auxiliary assumptions. So, in effect, any theory can be saved from refutation. If so, then there is a serious problem for falsificationism. For if 'attempted refutations' are the sole test of theories (cf. Popper 1963: 37), then two incompatible theories which are not refuted by the evidence end up being equally well tested by it (cf. Jardine 1986: 85).

Even if true, however, the Duhem–Quine thesis does not create a similar problem for an inductivist, or confirmationist. For the fact that any theory can be suitably adjusted so that it resists refutation does not show that all theories are equally well confirmed by the evidence. An inductivist can always argue that the empirical evidence does not lend equal *inductive* support to two empirically congruent theories, especially when one of them has been 'cooked up' to eschew refutation. More specifically, the inductivist can argue that not all adjustments to auxiliary assumptions which are necessary to save a theory from refutation are themselves equally well supported by the evidence. Since it is reasonable to think that the degree of support lent by the auxiliary assumptions associated with a theory is reflected in the degree of support there is for the theoretical system as a whole, it follows that not all theoretical systems end up equally well-supported by evidence, although they entail the same evidence.

Is the Duhem–Quine thesis true? The standard rejoinder is that it is not at all certain that *non-trivial* auxiliary assumptions can always be found (cf. Grunbaum 1960, 1962; Laudan 1990a; Laudan and Leplin 1991; Worrall 1982).[1] Hence, the apparent force of the Duhem–Quine thesis remains, at best, a promissory note. Insofar as the recipe for constructing empirically equivalent theories rests on the Duhem–Quine thesis, it is no good.

Laudan has recently noted that we may be able to do better than that. One can turn the Duhem–Quine argument on its head: it is precisely the fact that the so-called observational consequences of a theory can be determined only with the aid of auxiliaries which shows that *diachronic* empirical equivalence cannot be guaranteed (1996: 57–59). Suppose that two rival theories T and T' share the same class of empirical consequences at time t. Given that all theories entail observational consequences with the help of auxiliaries, there is no guarantee that this class will increase monotonically, nor that it will remain the same for both theories in future times. As the two rival theories get conjoined to other – hitherto unavailable – auxiliaries, new empirical consequences may arise which are able to discriminate between the two theories and break the observational tie.

Laudan's move enjoys historical support, as can be evinced, for instance, from the case of the once-upon-a-time observational tie between the particle- and the wave-theory of light. But in all its generality, it is as conjectural as its opponent: the Duhem–Quine thesis. In fact, advocates of this thesis are bound to argue that Laudan's move does not discredit their claim. They will say that just as there may be auxiliaries which help disentangle observational ties, there may well be others that will ensure the re-appearance of a tie. Of course, this is just a re-iteration of the initial Duhem–Quine assertion. But it does suggest that Laudan's argument can work only in tandem with the standard claim, viz. that the advocates of the Duhem–Quine thesis have not proved the existence of non-trivial auxiliaries capable of accommodating any rival evidence. Whose is the burden of proof here I do not really know. So if we do not want to engage in an exercise of mere philosophical doubt, we should more carefully look at real cases of empirical congruence and examine the prospects of their resolution.

Are there any genuine cases of empirically indistinguishable theories? A standard example is the following: Let *NM* stand for Newtonian Mechanics, *R* be the postulate that the centre of mass of the solar system is at rest with respect to absolute space, and *V* be the postulate that the centre of mass is moving with velocity *v* relative to absolute space. Then *NM* & *R* and *NM* & *V* will be empirically indistinguishable given any evidence concerning relative motions of bodies and their absolute accelerations (cf. van Fraassen 1980: 46–47). However, this is a poor example. For *NM* & *R* and *NM* & *V* involve exactly the same ontology and ideology for space, time and motion. Hence this is not an interesting case of theoretical underdetermination. The difference between postulates *R* and *V* is immaterial (cf. Earman 1993).

However, there *are* some interesting cases of empirically indistinguishable theories. For instance, flat four-dimensional formulations of *NM* are empirically indistinguishable from a theory which avoids gravitational force in favour of a non-flat affine structure (cf. Earman ibid.). Moreover, there is the classic example of empirically indistinguishable theories concerning the physical structure of space (cf. Poincaré 1902, Chapters 4 and 5). Figure 8.1 gives a sketchy illustration of his point. Suppose that two-dimensional beings inhabit the surface of a hemisphere and they cannot escape from it. (A cross-section of their world is given in *A*). They try to discover the physical geometry of their world. They use rigid rods to measure distances such as *CD* and *DE* and they find them equal.

They triangulate their world, and they find that the sum of the angles of a large triangle is more than that of the two right angles. Soon, they come to the conclusion that they inhabit the surface of a semisphere. However, an eccentric mathematician of this world suggests that they are collectively mistaken. His hypothesis is that their world is a plane (cross-section B), not the surface of a semisphere (cross-section A). He proposes that there is a *universal force*, i.e. a force which affects everything in this world in the same way. In particular, this force makes all moving rods contract as they move away from the centre and towards the periphery. So, he says, the 'corresponding' distances *C'D'* and *D'E'* are not really equal. They appear to be equal because the measuring rod has contracted upon transportation

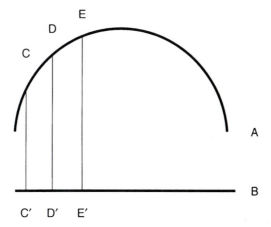

Figure 8.1 Empirically indistinguishable theories concerning the structure of space
Source: Adapted from Poincaré

from $D'E'$ to $C'D'$. (For instance, the interval $D'E'$ is, say, three times as long as the measuring rod. When they measure $C'D'$ it also appears to be three times as long as the measuring rod. They conclude that $D'E'$ is equal to $C'D'$. But this is not really so. $C'D'$ is shorter than $D'E'$, but because, unknown to them, the measuring rod has contracted, the rod appears to fit exactly three times to the smaller interval $C'D'$.) So, the eccentric mathematician says, the inhabitants of the world have come to the conclusion that their world is semispherical because they have not taken account of the deformation of moving rods. Here we have two empirically indistinguishable hypotheses. How can the inhabitants of this world decide between them? All observable phenomena are *as if* the shape of the world is spherical. But the observable phenomena would be exactly the same if the world was flat and a universal force acted on all bodies.

This science-fiction story can be easily extended to more realistic cases. As Reichenbach (1958: 33, 66) has shown, we may choose a model of Euclidean geometry as the physical geometry of the universe. Then we can create all and only the empirical consequences of the general theory of relativity provided that we postulate universal forces which make moving bodies (e.g. moving rods) contract accordingly. So, roughly, the theories $T_1 =$ (rigid rods and non-Euclidean geometry) and $T_2 =$ (contracting rods and Euclidean geometry) are observationally indistinguishable (cf. also Carnap 1966: 157). Hence, even though the strong thesis – for any theory there are interesting empirically indistinguishable alternatives – is implausible, a weaker thesis that there are some interesting cases of empirical equivalence is correct.[2]

How can realists react to this last claim? They can happily accept the existence of some theories that are empirically equivalent. For this fact creates no serious problem for realism. Actually it shows that, if anything, the force of the first premiss of UTE is *local* rather than *global*. Suppose that there are some theories which share the same class of observational consequences. This fact would create no serious problem for the rationality of scientific inquiry. All that follows is that some domains of inquiry may be beyond our ken. It would not show that no evidence and no application of any method can possibly make us accept a theory as approximately true. More generally, the existence of empirically equivalent theories can create a genuine problem only if it is shown to be a global phenomenon. This is what UTE should demonstrate if it is to ditch any hope of discovering the blueprint of the universe. But, there is no relevant evidence for this. In fact, it has been frequently the case that some hitherto empirically congruent theories are to be told apart by certain empirical evidence. For instance, the wave and the corpuscular theories of light were clearly distinguished on empirical grounds by Foucault's 1853 experiment, concerning the velocity of light in air and in water; Ptolemy's theory and Copernicus's theory were told apart when the latter was embedded in the framework of Newtonian dynamics. If such resolutions become available, then no serious case of UTE emerges.[3]

Evidence and entailment

Before I deal with the second premiss of UTE, the *entailment thesis*, let me make a quick digression. Not surprisingly, the logical empiricists found UTE non-disturbing. They thought that the dispute concerning two empirically equivalent theories T and T' was purely verbal, a quarrel over words: the empirically equivalent rivals were taken to be merely different languages ('equivalent descriptions') which describe the same totality of facts (Carnap 1966: 153; Reichenbach 1958: 35). Their general attitude was that the question, which of two empirically equivalent theories is true?, must be meaningless. This conclusion followed naturally from their criterion for meaningfulness: that the meaning of a statement lies in the method of its verification. Verification answers to observational evidence. Hence, if two theories entail the same observational consequences, nothing empirical can make a meaningful distinction between them. Therefore, the questions which of them is true?, and hence which may we believe?, are meaningless (cf. Carnap 1966: 150).

Naturally, the logical positivists did not think that all empirically equivalent theories are equally scientifically acceptable. But they thought that the choice of the better scientific theory was a matter of *convention*. In particular, they thought that judgements of simplicity could play a central role in the preferment of one theory over another. Carnap, for instance, insisted that the non-Euclidean geometry was to be preferred because it increases 'the overall simplicity of the total system of physics that would result from the choice' (1966: 164; cf. also Reichenbach 1938: 374–375; 1958: 34–35). But since these judgements were taken to be conventional, they lack confirmational power. Hence they cannot bear on the truth of the preferred theory. The cash-value of the positivists' attitude towards UTE is that only belief in the shared observational consequences of two empirically equivalent theories is a meaningful epistemic attitude.

As we have already seen (Chapter 1), the positivist criterion of meaningfulness cannot offer adequate semantics for scientific theories. Semantic realism – that is, the claim that scientific theories should be understood literally – has now replaced empiricist semantics. Hence, the positivists' 'solution' to UTE is clearly inadequate. The rub, of course, is that, on the face of it, a literal understanding of scientific theories seems to make UTE more rampant. For if two genuinely incompatible scientific theories are empirically equivalent, and if the argument from underdetermination is true, it follows that we simply cannot have any epistemic reasons to prefer one to the other.[4]

Well, a realist can always opt for what Newton-Smith (1978) has called the 'ignorance response'. That is, the realist may choose to hang on to a realist metaphysics, expressed by the claim that one of the two empirically congruent theories is true, but endorse a sceptical epistemology, captured by the claim that we shall never be in a position to know which of the two theories is true. This response does indeed secure realist metaphysics since it grants that there is a fact of the matter as to which theory is true of the world. If UTE is a local phenomenon, then it might be sensible for a realist to adopt the 'ignorance response' *vis-à-vis* the domains of inquiry in which no evidence and no application of any method can distinguish between two empirically congruent theories. But admitting that the 'ignorance response' is a viable realist answer to UTE is tantamount to conceding the main point that realists need to defend: that there is space for rational belief in one of the two empirically congruent theories. Instead of addressing the real challenge that UTE poses to realism – that there is no possibility of warranted belief in one of the two theories – the 'ignorance response' simply sidesteps it. So, it really is imperative that realists show how there can be epistemic reasons to prefer one theory to the other. This can be done by directly challenging the second premiss of UTE; that the entailment of the evidence is the only epistemic constraint on the confirmation of a theory – what I have called the entailment thesis (ET) (see p. 164).

Here is exactly where Laudan's recent work has lent realists a helping hand. For Laudan correctly suggests that when it comes to testing scientific theories, observing their consequences is neither necessary nor sufficient for empirical support.[5] Not all logical consequences of a hypothesis are potentially supportive, and conversely a hypothesis can be supported by evidence that is not among its logical consequences.

Hypotheses are not necessarily confirmed by their empirical consequences. Here, the point has been brought home by the literature on the infamous Ravens' Paradox. Bayesian solutions have stressed that one can consistently deny that positive instances of a hypothesis necessarily confirm the hypothesis. Laudan's own examples are even better (1996: 68). Quick recovery from a common cold after the patient has prayed for three days is a positive instance of the hypothesis that praying for three days makes the cold go away. Yet, we would not be willing to say that it confirms the hypothesis at hand, since the evidence offers no support to the hypothesis: the evidence would be what it is, even if the hypothesis was false (as in fact it is); the evidence can be easily explained without any loss by a readily available alternative hypothesis, etc. The point of this counter-example is this: it is precisely because scientists recognise that not all positive instances of a hypothesis are confirming instances that they put additional conditions on the admissibility of evidence, e.g. variability, control for spurious correlations, etc.

Conversely, *hypotheses can be confirmed by empirical evidence that does not logically follow from them.* A typical example here is that Einstein's account of the Brownian motion was widely taken to confirm the atomic theory although it was not among its consequences. More generally, suppose that a piece of evidence E is entailed by a hypothesis H which in turn can be embedded in a more general theory T. Suppose also that T entails another hypothesis H'. E can be said to *indirectly* support H' although it is not a logical consequence of H'. In sum, two theories with exactly the same observational consequences may enjoy differing degrees of evidential support: either because only one of them is indirectly supported by other relevant evidence, or because one of them is not really supported by its positive instances. So, the second premiss of UTE, the *entailment thesis* (ET), is defeated.[6]

Incidentally, it might appear that Laudan is committed to accepting both Hempel's (1945) Converse Consequence Condition (that if e confirms H, and T entails H then e confirms T) and the Special Consequence Condition (that if e confirms T, and T entails H', then e also confirms H'). But do not these two conditions taken together imply the notorious absurdity that any piece of evidence confirms any hypothesis whatsoever? It should be clear, however, that Laudan can easily avoid the foregoing absurdity. In line with his central point that entailment of the evidence is not sufficient for confirmation, he can deny that CCC is sufficient to bestow confirmation on the 'larger' theory T: there are cases in which e confirms H, T entails H, but T is not thereby confirmed. Such are, plausibly, the cases that give rise to the foregoing absurdity. Recall that the absurdity is generated as follows. Take any piece of evidence e and any hypothesis h. (1) e entails e, therefore e confirms e (by Hempel's entailment condition). (2) e confirms e, $h\&e$ entails e, therefore e confirms $h\&e$ (by CCC). (3) e confirms $h\&e$, $h\&e$ entails h, therefore e confirms h (by SCC). But Laudan can easily deny that in premiss (2) e confirms the 'larger' theory $h\&e$, by arguing that, although $h\&e$ entails e, e does *not* support $h\&e$. To be sure, as Laudan himself points out (private communication), he needs to specify precisely when entailed evidence is confirmatory and when it is not. More generally, since he has dissociated himself from the view that relations of evidential support mirror logico-semantic relations between hypotheses and evidence-statements, he needs to offer a rival account of evidential support. But even without such a fully-developed account – an account which Laudan would base on his view that all judgements of evidential support are comparative and hence should involve the evidence and at least two competing theories – it is plausible to argue that the evidence does not lend support to ad hoc hypotheses, i.e. hypotheses which are constructed so that they entail the evidence.

The role of theoretical virtues

As is well known, scientific realists typically suggest that when it comes to assessing the support which scientific theories enjoy, we should not examine only their empirical adequacy. This may be necessary but not enough on its own to make a theory well supported. We also need to take into account several *theoretical virtues* such as coherence with other established theories, consilience, completeness, unifying power, lack of ad hoc features and capacity to generate novel predictions. These virtues capture the *explanatory power* of a theory, and explanatory power is potentially confirmatory.

Take, for instance, two theories T and T' which entail the same body of data $e_1, \ldots, e_n$. Suppose that for every piece of data e_i ($i = 1, \ldots, n$) T' introduces an independent explanatory assumption T'_i such that T'_i entails e_i. But suppose T employs fewer hypotheses, and hence unifies the phenomena by reducing the number of independently accepted hypotheses. The claim is that because of this unification T is more confirmed than is T'. So, even if two theories are observationally congruent, they may not have equal explanatory power, and hence, they may not enjoy the same support. If these extra virtues are taken into account, it will not be at all easy to find more than one theory that satisfies them to an equal degree.

The rivals of realism, typically, deny that explanatory power has anything to do with confirmation and truth: theoretical virtues are pragmatic, rather than epistemic. Realists, typically, defend the view that these theoretical virtues have epistemic force because they are part and parcel of rational scientific judgement. McMullin (1987), for instance, suggests that explanation as well as predictive accuracy are the constitutive aims of science, and hence, it is only rational to choose the theory with the greatest explanatory power. He adds that those features which scientists use to characterise a 'good theory' are precisely those features which have been traditionally 'thought to be symptoms of truth generally'. As he puts it: 'The values that constitute a theory as "best explanation" are, it would seem, similar to those that would qualify a statement as "true"' (1987: 66–67). The problem, of course, is to show which explanatory virtues are connected with the likelihood of a theory's truth.

The required connection can be found in a combination of the insights of Boyd and Salmon. Boyd (1973; 1981; 1984) has suggested that the virtues which are constitutive of the explanatory power of a theory are, in a certain indirect sense, evidential. They guide scientists' judgements about the *theoretical plausibility* of competing theories. Among the many theories which may be, or become, available at any given time, scientists choose those which have the greatest explanatory power, relative to other background theories they accept. It is these background theories which rank the new theories in terms of theoretical plausibility. These background theories have themselves been accepted because they enjoyed evidential support and displayed similar theoretical virtues. Hence, their evidential support and theoretical plausibility are carried over, and reflected in, the new theories which they license. The virtues which constitute explanatory power become evidential precisely because they are present in theories which enjoy theoretical plausibility and evidential support.

Once this is accepted, all that remains is to show how exactly these virtues can bear on the degree of confirmation of the theories. Here is where Salmon helps. For he has argued persuasively that the past record of mature scientific theories can be used in assigning *prior probabilities* to current theories (cf. 1970: 85–86; 1985: 13; 1990: 186). The past record of scientific theories can be seen as the background knowledge in the light of which the plausibility of emergent scientific theories can be judged and estimated. More specifically, the suggestion is that, given two theories T and T' which have the same observational consequences but are differentiated in respect of some theoretical virtues, one should regard T more plausible than T' if, given the past record, theories which exhibit the virtues of T are more likely to be true than are theories like T'. So, for instance, if theories which have not been subjected to ad hoc adjustments have tended to be better supported by the evidence than theories with ad hoc features, then this consideration should be used in assessing the prior probability of other theories, in order to rank higher theories with no ad hoc features. Naturally, finding out which theoretical virtues have been associated with well-confirmed theories can be the outcome only of substantive empirical–historical research. This is in the spirit of *methodological naturalism*, which I explain and explore in the final section of this chapter.

Before I move on I wish to stress that Laudan's favourite rebuttal of the *entailment thesis* is very close to the realists' claim that theoretical virtues bear on confirmation. Arguing that theories can gain support from evidence they do not entail is, in effect, tantamount to saying that potential unifying power – a central theoretical virtue – can enhance the confirmation of a hypothesis. Here are two typical cases where a hypothesis can gain indirect support from evidence it does not directly entail.

(a) A hypothesis H is embedded in a broader theory T that enjoys strong evidential support. For instance, Lorentz's electron theory gained support from being embedded in Maxwell's theory, although the latter did not entail the former.

(b) A hypothesis *H* acts as a 'bridge' that connects, but does not entail, other apparently unrelated hypotheses H_1 and H_2. For instance, the atomic hypothesis acts as such a 'bridge' *vis-à-vis* the kinetic theory of gases and the molecular theory of the chemical elements, and gains support from both.

Both cases are instances of confirmation-via-unification. Conversely, arguing that entailment of the evidence is not sufficient for empirical support is, in effect, another way of saying that we should not accept a hypothesis merely on the basis that it entails the evidence, if that hypothesis is the product of an ad hoc manoeuvre, or if there is another hypothesis available which offers a better explanation of the evidence in the light of other independently acceptable background theories, etc. In both cases, the class of probative evidence for a certain hypothesis differs from the class of its observational consequences because we have to take account of its theoretical virtues in comparison to those of its rivals. These virtues are not just parasitic on the entailment relation between the hypothesis and its observational consequences, but rather constitute a function of the overall explanatory value of the hypothesis and its relation with the other accepted background theories.

In order to reinforce the suggested connection between theoretical virtues and evidential support, a small digression seems necessary. One should not fail to appreciate the service that can be done to realism by Glymour's 'bootstrap' theory of confirmation (1980). Glymour's important contribution to the debate is two-fold:

(1) he has shown that even if two theories entail the same observational consequences, there are still ways to show that they may be differentially supported by those consequences;
(2) he has argued that theoretical virtues, especially the explanatory power and unifying power, bear on the confirmation of a theory. As he puts it: 'Confirmation and explanation are closely linked ... ' (1980: 376).

So Glymour has brought together the two main lines of realist defence against UTE. Here is a simple example showing how one can block UTE (or, at least, some cases of it) (see Glymour 1980: 356–357). Suppose that a fundamental quantity *F* in a scientific theory *T* is analysed as the sum of two primitive quantities F_1 and F_2 (i.e. $F = F_1 + F_2$). One can then construct a theory *T'* which employs F_1 and F_2 instead of *F* and is clearly empirically equivalent to *T*. Are *T* and *T'* equally supported by the evidence? Surely there must be a scientifically significant reason for breaking up *F* into two components. One would normally require an independent argument as to how the individual values of F_1 and F_2 can possibly be computed.

If this is possible, then T' will have excess content over T, viz. the independently specifiable values of F_1 and F_2. Hence, some tests for the values of F_1 and F_2 might be feasible, which may differentiate T' from T. If, on the contrary, there is no scientifically significant reason for introducing F_1 and F_2, and if there is no way to calculate their individual values, then one can argue that T is better supported than T'. For T' has more untested hypotheses than T, while T is more unifying than T': it minimises the number of independently acceptable hypotheses and explains the same facts by using less hypotheses. But if there are good reasons to prefer T to T', although both T and T' entail the same observational consequences, then T and T' are no longer epistemically congruent. In effect, Reichenbach's recipe for creating empirically equivalent space–time theories as well as Poincaré's toy-world (see pp. 166–167) are instances of the currently discussed ad hoc technique and can be dismissed on precisely these grounds.

So far, I have argued that the conclusion of UTE can be effectively blocked. Where does that leave us *vis-à-vis* the scientific realism debate? Although realists can capitalise on Laudan's arguments, Laudan is not a professed scientific realist. In fact, he has been one of its most profound critics. He and the realists would agree that there is need for a richer account of the ampliative nature of the methodology of science than the one offered by the crude hypothetico-deductive method. In particular, they would agree that, given such a richer account, there are good epistemic grounds to choose between rival theories. Yet, they part company when it comes to scientific realism. To be sure, Laudan freely uses expressions such as 'evidential support', 'warranted assent' (1996: 56), 'adequate evidential warrant' (1996: 63). He talks of theory-acceptance, which is presumably distinct from acceptance as empirically adequate, since the latter stance would be the natural one to adopt, if someone endorsed the sceptical force of UTE. He even distances himself from those pragmatists who 'infer that only nonepistemic dimensions of appraisal are applicable to theories, and that, accordingly [theory appraisal] is not exclusively, nor necessarily, even preferential' (1996: 63). One here might well wonder how we should understand such claims as that a theory is well supported by the evidence, or that some theories enjoy more evidential support than do others. It seems natural to think that, if distinct from acceptance as empirically adequate, 'warranted assent' should be equated with belief in the approximate truth of the theory; or, at least, with the claim that this theory is our current best candidate for an approximately true description of its domain.

There can be little doubt that Laudan is unwilling to endorse the gloss I suggest. Two things show this. First, he is generally sceptical about truth and about science's ability to reach it. Such misgivings are tied to his own meta-methodology: 'normative naturalism'. I shall have to postpone showing that his 'normative naturalism' can warrant greater epistemic optimism about theoretical truth than he is willing to accept, until the next section. Second, his attempt to undercut UTE does not aim to defend scientific realism, but rather to defend the possibility of sound methodological judgements (cf. 1996: 20). For Laudan, methodology should be able to guide the comparative evaluation of *extant* rival theories and to show how rational *comparative* judgements are possible. If UTE is true, then clearly even this more modest aim cannot be fulfilled.

Once, however, the more modest aim is shown to be achievable, so too is the grander aim of showing that *absolute* judgements of approximate truth are rational. Suppose we have a theory which is better supported by the evidence than all its extant rivals. What else should we require in order to claim that this theory is (likely to be) approximately true? To put it in a different way, what else should we require in order to show that it is rational to believe in the theory? The sceptic would fall back on a version of UTE. He would suggest that the probability of a theory can never be high enough to warrant the belief, because it is possible that another theory, hitherto unthought of, may be at least as well supported by the evidence as is the current best. Laudan considers this move in what he calls the 'non-uniqueness thesis': the thesis that there may be another theory T' which is equally well supported as T with respect to certain ampliative rules and evidence (1996: 33, 53). He thinks that 'it is an open question' whether the non-uniqueness thesis is true, but reckons that it is possibly true (1996: 42–43). I do not think this can be shown on a priori grounds. In fact, the mere logical possibility of such a scenario should not worry us. Nor should it undermine the rationality of absolute judgements. To think otherwise is to suggest that ampliative reasoning should be infallible, and that only when a theory is proven to be true is it rational to believe in it. This may well be the demand of an outright sceptic, but if Laudan were to endorse that, he would also have to accept that comparative judgements cannot be rational. For even those are ampliative and fallible.

Is there not ample *empirical* evidence for the sceptical scenario? One may claim that Laudan more than anyone else (with the exception, perhaps, of Duhem) has provided relevant historical evidence and has consolidated the sceptical scenario in the form of the well-known, and previously discussed, argument from the pessimistic induction. But, as we have already seen in great detail (Chapters 5 and 6), the credentials of this argument have been seriously contested. If the arguments I presented there in defence of realism are sound, then this follows: the fact that our current best theory might be replaced by another which enjoys broader and better evidential support does not necessarily undermine the approximate truth of the superseded theory. All it shows is that (a) we cannot get to the truth all at once and (b) our judgements from empirical support to approximate truth should be more refined and cautious, in that they should commit us only to the theoretical constituents that do enjoy evidential support and which contributed to the successes of the superseded theory. To put it differently, amassing empirical evidence for the sceptical scenario does not undermine the possibility of absolute judgements of approximate truth of current best theories insofar as these judgements are focused on the constituents of those theories that *do* enjoy evidential support and to the extent to which these constituents *are* in fact retained in subsequent theories. Hence, absolute – but not crude – judgements of approximate truth can be rational. All the more so for someone who, like Laudan, builds his epistemology on the possibility of rational comparative judgements of evidential support. Perhaps then, and to the realists' delight, Laudan's demolition work on UTE can warrant greater epistemic optimism than he is willing to allow.

Normative naturalism without truth?

I noted above that Laudan is sceptical about science's overall ability to reach theoretical truth. In order to discuss this issue adequately, we need to examine in some detail Laudan's own meta-methodology: *normative naturalism*. To that task I devote this section.

The central component of Laudan's normative naturalism is *methodological naturalism* (MN): the view that methodology is an empirical discipline – the theory of 'the regularities governing inquiry' (1996: 110) – and that as such it is part and parcel of natural science. In particular, MN suggests the following.

1   All normative claims are *instrumental*: methodological rules link up aims with methods which will bring them about, and recommend that action which is most likely to achieve one's favoured aim.
2   The soundness of methodological rules depends on whether they lead to successful action, and their justification is a function of their effectiveness in bringing about their aims. A sound methodological rule represents our 'best strategy' for reaching a certain desired aim (see 1996: 103, 128ff.).[7]

Success and effectiveness in promoting aims cannot be evaluated a priori. Since they depend on contingent features of the world, they should be tested empirically 'in precisely the same way we test empirical theories' (ibid.: 133), that is, by looking for correlations, causal linkages (p. 17) and statistical laws (p. 134) between 'doing *x*' and 'achieving *y*'. After all, we want our methods to be effective in *this* world; that is, we want them to guide us to correct decisions and effective strategies for extracting information from nature. In this simple sense the methods we adopt must be amenable to substantive information about the actual world.

Laudan's instrumental account of methodology threatens to entail *relativism*. If methodology is concerned only with means–end relations and leaves the ends unspecified, if methodology is just about how to achieve whatever aims we happen to value most, then epistemic relativism seems to follow. If two communities, or two groups of enquirers, pose different aims of enquiry, is there any sense in which methodology can rationally adjudicate between them rather than merely *describe* the effectiveness of their respective 'best strategies'? And if there is a sense in which we can compare their respective 'best strategies', would not that presuppose a meta-perspective from which we methodologists can judge their comparative effectiveness? Such considerations have made the more mainstream episte-mologists unsympathetic to the naturalist project. Worrall (1988; 1989a) and Doppelt (1990), to name but two, have objected that methodological natu-ralism falls prey to relativism and fails to underpin the rationality of the scientific inquiry.

Laudan counters that MN does not endanger rationality and has definite normative–evaluative consequences. On the one hand, MN can offer 'warranted advice' (1996: 133) as to how someone can best achieve their favoured aims: given that method M promotes aim A, if someone wants to achieve A then they *ought* to do M. On the other hand, when it comes to evaluative comparison of rival methodologies, we can fall back on some principle 'which all the disputing theories of methodology share in common' (1996: 135). Laudan thinks that a suitable version of *enumerative induction* can be such a shared principle of evidential support, which he calls: (R): if method M has consistently promoted aim A in the past, and method N has failed to do so, then future actions based on the rule 'if you want A, then you ought to do M' are more likely to succeed than are actions based on the rival rule 'if you want A, then you ought to do N'.

This very move, however, entails that normative judgements cannot be purely instrumental. R offers the required 'quasi-Archimedean standpoint' (ibid.: 135) only if it is seen as part and parcel of a normative meta-perspec-tive on which all methodological appraisal ultimately rests. One central question is this: how is R itself to be evaluated? In particular, can it be eval-uated instrumentally? Is it itself warranted because it has been shown to be successful in promoting certain aims, whatever those may have been? Or is it warranted because it is a sound rule of ampliative reasoning? I do not wish to argue that we cannot evaluate the past performance of R empiri-cally. But two things are worth noting: (a) selecting the data pertaining to the evaluation of R, showing that past correlations are not spurious, estab-lishing that the predicates involved are projectible, etc., require the use of more sophisticated and controversial methodological principles; and (b) suppose that we can establish the authenticity of past successes of R; whether or not these successes warrant projections to the future, and hence whether or not they warrant acceptance of R as a sound principle, rest themselves on the soundness of inductive reasoning in general. But defending the sound-ness of inductive reasoning is an epistemic issue: it relates to showing that inductive reasoning is warranted in that it has the capacity to generate true conclusions when fed with true premises.

I would generalise this last point as follows. The *rationality of action*, it can be argued, is, to a first approximation, a means–end issue: rational action consists in following the 'best strategy' that will promote one's aims. But rationality of action cannot exhaust the content of rational judgement. Nor can it fully capture its normative dimension. An account of rational judgement should accommodate both the *rationality of belief* as well as the rationality of action. A purely instrumental story leaves the rationality of belief unaccounted for: when it is rational to hold a belief? Beliefs guide actions and support instrumental claims of the sort that the strategy followed to achieve a certain aim is the 'best'. When are these beliefs rational? When are they warranted by the available evidence? Judging their rationality and evidential warrant – and offering relevant normative advice – is an epistemic matter. It is a function of the epistemic relation between the evidence and the belief for which it is taken to be the evidence. And, similarly, it is a function of the soundness of the methods that produced and sustain these beliefs.

Laudan's methodological naturalism rightly suggests that the principles of sound ampliative reasoning cannot be laid out without using substantive empirical knowledge. It is equally right to point out that matters of justification are not a priori but are amenable to empirical investigation and knowledge. This is the invaluable insight of modern naturalism. This claim has also been defended by *reliabilist* epistemological theories à *la* Boyd (1981), Goldman (1986) and Papineau (1993). Their central point is that methodological and reasoning strategies should be evaluated by their success, or tendency to produce and maintain true beliefs, and that judging this success, or establishing the tendency, is open to empirical findings and investigation. Reliabilism, however, can easily account for the rationality of belief – as well as for the rationality of action – by arguing that a rational belief is a well-supported belief, where those beliefs are well-supported which are produced by reliable – truth-conducive and truth-maintaining – methods and processes. However, unlike Laudan's MN, reliabilist epistemology accepts that the aim of sound ampliative reasoning cannot be a matter of empirical investigation. Reasoning cannot be 'correct' if it consistently leads to false conclusions. Nor is it correct if it merely achieves the reasoner's aims. If this were the only requirement, then any fallacious mode of reasoning could be deemed 'correct' if it promoted the favoured aims of the relevant community of reasoners. Sound reasoning is intimately bound up with truth and the capacity to generate and maintain true conclusions from true premises. Truth emerges as the *basic cognitive virtue* of sound reasoning. Achieving true beliefs is the aim in light of which methodological and reasoning strategies should be evaluated. Reliabilism supplements methodological naturalism with a normative meta-perspective of truth-linked judgements.

These last considerations clearly separate Laudan's brand of naturalism *both* from other fellow-naturalists who accept a truth-linked axiology and a broadly reliabilist account of methodology *and* from non-naturalists, who rightly think that rationality, epistemic warrant and justification should answer to truth but argue that, on pain of vicious circularity, the naturalist project has no bearing on these issues. I think the right position lies some-where between the last two positions: the defence of rational methodological choices against relativists and subjectivists – who are Laudan's prime targets – requires a normative truth-linked meta-perspective, but, circularity notwith-standing, this defence can be firmly based on empirical considerations and the findings of the sciences. My naturalistic defence of inference to the best explanation in Chapter 4, shows how the charge of vicious circularity can be neutralised, while sticking to a truth-linked assessment of scientific methodology.

To be fair to Laudan, he does acknowledge that methodological natu-ralism should be coupled with a naturalised theory of axiology, that is a general theory about the constraints which 'govern rational choice of aims and goals' (1996: 17). He admits that no such general theory is now avail-able, but that, nonetheless, 'we now understand several of those valuative mechanisms pretty clearly' (ibid.). For instance, the goals should be 'in principle achievable' (p. 78); 'empirically realisable' and 'practically work-able' (p. 145). But, according to Laudan, aims are not normative requirements for the appropriate cognitive evaluation of science.

Aims can and do change, Laudan says. What, however, regulates these changes? What makes a change of aim rational and warranted? Laudan suggests that changes of aim should 'allow for the retention as scientific of much of the exemplary work currently and properly regarded as such' (ibid.: 158). This requirement turns out to be a central element of Laudan's concep-tion of axiology. Remember that the latter is supposed to be naturalised, and yet to preserve a normative element. In order to achieve this, Laudan introduces the idea of 'the canon of the Tradition' (op. cit.: 150), also known as 'the canon of great science' (ibid.: 156). This is a canonical representa-tion of the scientific past: the great historical moments, the important theoretical innovations, the classical experiments, in short the stable elements and great achievements of the modern scientific tradition. This 'canon', Laudan suggests, 'serve(s) as certifier and decertifier for new proposals about the aims of science' (ibid.: 162). So, a change of aim is warranted only if the new aim can preserve the canonical achievements of science under the new description of what the scientific inquiry is about.

How can this happen? I think there are only two possibilities: either the new and the old aims are consistent, or the 'canonical achievements' are independent of the specific aims that they were supposed to promote. In the former case, change of aim can be seen as a mere 'watering down' of existing aims. Abandoning certainty for high probability can be an instance of this. In the latter case, if Laudan does not want to abandon the view that 'canonical achievements' were supposed to promote some aims, he perhaps needs to acknowledge that although some subordinate (or explicit) aims may change, core (or implicit) aims remain intact and regulate the 'canon': what gets accepted in the 'canon' is what promotes the core aim – which I would describe as pushing back the frontiers of ignorance and error. Laudan is certainly reluctant to accept suggestions that refine axiology in terms of 'explicit/implicit aims' (cf. Worrall 1988) or 'secondary/primary aims' (cf. Leplin 1990; Rosenberg 1990). But I think he comes very close to endorsing something like this when he admits that 'although the older standards superficially appear to have been involved in producing the canonical achievements of the field, their actual role in producing those achievements was tangential and adventitious' (1996: 146).

No matter what else Laudan thinks about the aims of science, he is vehemently opposed to the view that truth (or truth-linked notions) should be the aim of inquiry. Using his axiological theory, he argues that truth is an exemplar of an unrealisable aim. He points out that truth is 'intrinsically transcendent' and 'closed to epistemic access' (1996: 78). He even endorses the epistemic version of Barnes and Bloor's 'symmetry thesis', on the basis that 'knowledge of a theory's truth is radically transcendent' – another way of saying 'radically inaccessible'. As he puts it: 'This transcendence entails the epistemic version of the symmetry thesis since we are never in a position to partition theories into the true and false and then proceed to explain beliefs in them differently on account of their truth status' (ibid.: 195). One of his main complaints against his opponents is that 'traditional epistemologists who . . . hanker after true or highly probable theories as the aim of science find themselves more than a little hardpressed to identify methods that conduce to those ends. Accordingly, normative naturalism suggests that unabashedly realist aims for scientific inquiry are less than optimal' (ibid.: 179).

What is so difficult about truth? Is truth epistemically inaccessible and utopian? First of all, note that Laudan's own arguments against the underdetermination of theories by evidence (UTE) do not fit well with his qualms about truth. As I argued in the last section, his rebuttal of UTE warrants greater epistemic optimism than he explicitly allows. Unless the non-uniqueness thesis is proven, and unless underdetermination is a global feature of scientific theorising, there is no reason to think that theoretical truth cannot be achieved. But neither of the above conditions are established by Laudan. Indeed his own arguments do so much to discredit generalised agnosticism about theoretical truth that one is bound to think that the possibility of achieving theoretical truth faces no damning objections.

Some philosophers' misgivings about truth (e.g. van Fraassen's) stem from the thought that science should simply aim for a different target, viz. empirical adequacy, or saving the phenomena. This thought cannot, on its own, undermine the view that science aims at the truth. Empirical adequacy is consistent with truth, and in fact is a necessary condition for it. The issue here is not a choice between two inconsistent aims, but rather why, in the absence of damning arguments against truth in relation to unobservable reality, we should opt for less. As far as I can tell, there is no independent argument for empirical adequacy, other than, that is, that theoretical truth is not achievable. But suppose that theoretical truth were indeed utopian as an aim. Is empirical adequacy less utopian? I deal with this issue in detail in the next chapter. For the time being, suffice it to note the following. There is certainly a difference between truth and empirical adequacy, but it is one of degree. Claims to theoretical truth exceed those of empirical adequacy because they involve the theoretical assertions made by scientific theories. But unless one thinks that there is a *special* problem with the cognition of unobservable entities and processes, reaching theoretical truth is just 'more of the same'. Van Fraassen would dispute this more-of-the-same line, because he thinks that claims which involve putative reference to unobservable entities are inherently undecidable. But Laudan does not seem to agree with this. He acknowledges that 'entities or processes originally introduced by theory frequently achieve observable or "empirical" status as experimental methods and instruments of detection improve' (1996: 57). To be sure, Laudan has offered his own arguments against science's capacity to unravel the deep structure of the world, but, as is well known, they are based not on our limitations in direct observation but on more sophisticated considerations concerning the allegedly poor track-record of science. As we saw in Chapter 5, these considerations are, however, hardly compelling. So, I conclude that Laudan's qualms about truth cannot be based on the possibility of an alternative – and more realisable – aim, viz. empirical adequacy.

Well, could truth be 'transcendent' because it involves this mysterious 'correspondence relation' that obtains between statements and facts? This line has been very popular among philosophers. I come back to this issue in Chapter 10, when discussing Fine's *natural ontological attitude*. But the following is worth noting. As Laudan rightly points out, the underlying thought of correspondence accounts of truth is that beliefs should be grounded in the world (cf. 1996: 79). I do not see how this perfectly sensible claim should make truth 'transcendent'. All it implies is that a belief is true if and only if its truth-conditions obtain. In particular, it is consistent with one of Laudan's central points that truth-conditions should not be confused with evidence-conditions (1996: 69–73). Truth-conditions are those which, when they obtain, make the belief true. Evidence-conditions are those which, when they obtain, make the belief warranted, or rational. The only remaining issue is this: can we be in a position to assert that the truth-conditions for an assertion obtain? In other words, can there be evidence for the claim that the truth-conditions for an assertion obtain?

Let me try to make this last point clearer. Let us bear in mind that Laudan also accepts that certainty in decision procedures is a utopian aim, and hence that it must be abandoned. If, however, one accepts that scientific assertions are short of certainty, one should have no special problem deciding their truth. In order to see this, consider the following question. Granted that truth is a non-recursive property, is it less decidable than other properties studied by science? What follows goes back essentially to Carnap (1945/6: 602).

Envisage a scientific group which wants to decide whether a certain substance is of a specific chemical constitution. They run relevant thorough tests and decide that the substance is, say, an acid. No amount of testing can decide with certainty – i.e. without any possibility of error – that the substance under consideration is an acid. Yet, there is a point at which the evidence is enough to warrant the belief in question. Now, let us grant that assertion *S*, 'Substance X is an acid', is decidable – that is, confirmable to a high degree – by some scientific procedures. As Carnap rightly observes, if *S* is confirmed to a degree *r*, then sentence *S'*, ' "Substance *X* is an acid" is true', is confirmed to exactly the same degree, since *S* and *S'* are equivalent, given the English language and the disquotational property of the truth-predicate. Carnap concludes that 'is true', and 'truth', are legitimate scientific notions, precisely on the grounds that sentences which state truth-values are confirmable. The truth of an assertion (or a belief) is neither less nor more confirmable than the assertion (or the belief) itself. There is no need for an extra assurance that a belief is true, over and above the assurance we get from the fact that this belief is the product of a reliable method. To be sure, it is perfectly possible that a belief issued by a reliable method is false. Reliable methods are fallible methods: the fact that a method is reliable does not logically guarantee that a belief issued by this method is true. The link between a reliably produced belief and a true belief is synthetic, not conceptual. But notice that fallibility does *not* entail actual falsity. All that it wards off is a conceptual identification of truth with epistemic notions such as warranted assertibility, ideal justification and the like. A warranted assertion or ideally justified statement may well be false: the very claim of warranted assertibility or ideal justification does not entail that the belief is true. However, unless one claims that no belief can be rationally said to be true unless it is shown that it is impossible for this belief to be false, it makes perfect sense to say that belief in truth is rational even though there is a logical possibility that the belief be false. In sum, if one is ready to abandon certainty in decision procedures, and to accept the disquotational property of the truth-predicate, there are no grounds for arguing that truth is undecidable, utopian and the like. The whole problem of the epistemic accessibility of the world relates to the reliability of our methods of interaction with it. The only extra burden on the scientific realist might be to show that our methods of investigating the world are indeed reliable. This is no small matter. But as we saw in Chapter 4, it is a matter that scientific realists can deal with adequately.[8]

Having thus defended realism against two major arguments levelled against it, viz. the argument from the pessimistic induction and the argument from the underdetermination of theories by evidence, it is now time to turn attention to some recent alternatives to scientific realism. This is going to be the task of Part III which I begin, in the next chapter, by discussing van Fraassen's *constructive empiricism*.

Part III

Recent alternatives to realism

9   Constructive empiricism
scrutinised

Realists are epistemic optimists. Based largely on the no miracle argument, they reason that science can and does attain theoretical truth no less then it can and does attain observational truth. More sceptical philosophers of science, however, stress that there is room to resist the realists' optimism. Agnostic empiricists grant semantic realism in order to *interpret* scientific theories. So, in this respect, they agree with scientific realists. Yet, unlike scientific realists, they challenge the *epistemic* status of *t*-assertions: they doubt that one can ever be in a position to warrantedly believe that the truth-conditions of *t*-assertions obtain. So, they want to motivate the view that the rational choice is suspension of judgement as to the truth of *t*-assertions.

Two things noted in the Introduction are relevant here. First, the 'epistemic optimism' of scientific realism should stress that it is *reasonable*, at least occasionally, to believe that science has achieved theoretical truth. In other words, realists stress that there is some kind of *justification* for the belief that theoretical assertions are true (or near true). This is precisely the role played by confirmation: confirmation of theoretical assertions – and not just of the observational consequences of the theories – provides the justification that realists need for their epistemic optimism. Second, it is worth distinguishing between two forms of agnostic empiricism: *naive* and *sophisticated*. This is necessary in order to accommodate van Fraassen's (1980 and especially 1989) constructive empiricism, which, I think, is subtler than naive agnostic empiricism. Van Fraassen's position differs from naive agnostic empiricism in the following way. He argues that even if it were shown that theoretical truth is attainable in a non-accidental way, realism would not be rationally compelling. For, he maintains, there is an alternative *empiricist* image of science in which the search for theoretical truth and belief in the truth of theories drop out of the picture without any loss for the practice of science. So, van Fraassen wants to defend the thesis that an agnostic attitude is no less rational than the realist attitude, even if it is not the only rational attitude as naive agnostic empiricists would have it. I discuss this position, which I shall call 'hypercritical empiricism', in great detail in this chapter. In the next section, I examine some general arguments in favour of agnostic empiricism and show that, given semantic realism, a selective agnosticism about theoretical truth cannot be maintained. To be sure, some of the rebutted agnostic arguments find their source in van Fraassen's own critique of realist epistemic optimism. Still, it is important to keep in mind for later that van Fraassen has a *positive* alternative to scientific realism on offer which builds on agnosticism, but has far-reaching consequences.

Against naive agnostic empiricism

Agnostic empiricists take theoretical discourse to be truth-conditioned. But they also note that when it comes to claims that putatively refer to unobservables one can never be in a position to assert that they are true (or likely to be true). Hence, they recommend suspension of judgement. But what exactly is involved in asserting that a statement is true (or likely to be true)? If one is ready to assert the statement S, then one should also be ready to assert that 'S' is true, and conversely. This much follows from the disquotational property of the truth-predicate, irrespective of whether one wants to endorse a minimalist account of truth (that is, to add to the above: 'And this is *all* there is to truth-ascriptions') or to defend a more substantive 'realist' account of truth (that is, to add to the above: 'Truth-ascriptions require that there is a *property* that all true statements possess, a property which one might call "correspondence with reality"'). An agnostic may have views as to how the concept of truth is to be understood. Van Fraassen, for instance, goes along with a 'correspondence' account of truth (see 1980: 197). But whatever the details of these views are, one's concept of 'truth' should satisfy the above disquotational schema. (Chapter 10 discusses the issue of truth-ascriptions in science in some detail.)

In this light, the issue of whether one can assert that a statement is true reduces to the issue of whether one can assert the statement (see also p. 182). Agnostics will take literally the theoretical assertions of the theory, e.g. that 'The gas in the flask is carbon monoxide', or that 'Neutrinos are produced during a β-decay', which, given semantic realism, have irreducible truth-conditions. Why exactly can they not assert statements such as the above (i.e. *t*-assertions), while making assertions which refer to observable entities, such as 'Jupiter has eight satellites' or 'Aspirin relieves headaches', or 'There is a silver–grey track in the cloud chamber' (i.e. *o*-assertions)? In order to sustain a sceptical attitude towards *t*-assertions, one should look for (and motivate) a relevant *epistemic* difference between *t*-assertions and *o*-assertions. This is exactly what the agnostic empiricist should argue for. For if there is a principled epistemic difference in the ways in which *o*-statements and *t*-statements come to be warrantedly asserted, then our semantic ascent to the truth of such statements should be guided by different standards.

This is precisely where trouble lurks for the naive agnostic. I take it that there are two candidates for the relevant epistemic difference: difference in the ways of *verification* and difference in the ways of *confirmation*. Yet neither can produce the *principled* difference which the agnostic is after. Verification is clearly too strong if it is understood to mean 'proving the truth'. Old empiricists saw that very clearly when they abandoned verificationism (see Chapter 1). Not only can we never be in a position to verify a universal generalisation which refers only to observables; singular statements, too, are, strictly speaking, unverifiable. If conclusive proof is required for accepting a claim as true, then one can conceive of all sorts of circumstances in which a singular *o*-claim (e.g. that the reader is now reading this paper) cannot be proved (see also p. 7). So if verification (in this strong sense) is accepted, the process of asserting *any* statement, be it an *o*- or a *t*-statement, cannot get off the ground.

Looking for differences in the ways of confirmation is more promising, because, to say the least, there should be no doubt that *o*-statements are confirmable. If *t*-statements are somehow *inherently* unconfirmable, then agnostic empiricists might latch on to a relevant (and valuable to them) *epistemic* difference. In what follows I take some time to show that there can be no *principled confirmational difference* between *o*-assertions and *t*-assertions. My point will be this: if, because of confirmability, belief in *o*-assertions is rational, and if there is no confirmational difference between *o*- and *t*-assertions, then belief in *t*-assertions, too, is rational.

How could it be that *t*-assertions are inherently unconfirmable? One option is to say that the evidence can *never* raise their probability. But it is not clear to me that there *is* a theory of confirmation which can achieve this feat. On the standard Bayesian account of confirmation, for instance, a theoretical hypothesis is confirmed insofar as its posterior probability is greater than its prior. This can be easily achieved whenever the probability of the evidence is less than *one*. So, all novel predictions – those whose probability is not equal to unity – do confirm a theoretical hypothesis which entails them. (I do not want to claim that only novel predictions confirm. 'Old evidence' does confirm too. But for the point at stake, it is enough to show that at least some evidence can confirm theoretical hypotheses.)

Well, one may adopt the view that theoretical hypotheses have *zero* prior probability. If so, no matter what the evidence is, their posterior probability cannot be raised; hence they cannot be confirmed. I understand this claim if it is meant to be the *definition* of the point that *t*-assertions are not confirmable: to say that *t*-assertions are not confirmable is to say that, by definition, they have *zero* prior probabilities. But if it is meant to be a substantive claim, then it is absurd. To give, by fiat, zero prior probability to all *t*-assertions amounts either to claiming that they are contradictions, where clearly they are not, or to adopting theoretical dogmatism. On the latter reading, no empirical fact forces empiricists to be agnostics: they simply choose a dogmatic policy which makes the confirmation of theoretical hypotheses impossible. In any case, a similar dogmatism can threaten the possibility of confirmation of *o*-statements. For agnostic empiricists should justify why their dogmatism is one-sided: why do they choose to give non-zero priors to claims about observables, and in particular to universal generalisations?

An agnostic empiricist may be willing to adopt van Fraassen's line that *t*-assertions have *vague* prior probabilities. The claim here is that the prior probability (*prob*(*H*)) of a *t*-assertion *H* which entails evidence *E* is *anywhere* in the closed interval [0, *prob*(*E*)]. Van Fraassen claims that 'for the most thorough agnostic *H* is vague on its probability from zero to the probability of its consequences, and remains so when he conditionalises on any evidence' (1989: 194). Two replies are available here.

First, the assignment of vague priors does not show that the evidence can have no impact on the probability of *t*-assertions. When the evidence is learned, i.e. when *prob*(*E*) = 1, the vagueness interval of the posterior *prob*(*H*/*E*) is increased to [0,1]. But this simply means that the evidence does bear on the posterior probability of *H*, because now this probability can be associated with values greater than those before the evidence rolled in. In actual practice, such changes in vague probabilities due to new evidence may make us change our attitude towards a hypothesis. Imagine, for instance, that I am told that the probability of surviving open-heart surgery is anywhere in the interval [0.1, 0.4]. But suppose that some new evidence comes in about the condition of my heart which changes the interval to [0.1, 0.8]. Surely, this new information would make me rethink my original decision to avoid the operation.[1]

The second reply goes as follows. Here again, as in the case of zero prior probabilities previously discussed, if vague priors were to offer any solace to an agnostic empiricist, they could prove too much. For, equally, one may give vague prior probabilities to *o*-assertions. So an agnostic empiricist would still have to show what the relevant difference is between *o*- and *t*-assertions in virtue of which only the latter have vague priors. An agnostic might be tempted to dismiss this point by saying the following. Suppose, for instance, that I enter a lab and I see a tube which seems to contain some stuff. Before I examine the tube, I can have a definite prior degree of belief that it contains a liquid, but the prior degree of belief that this liquid is hydrochloric acid can be vague. So, the agnostic might say, it is much more plausible to give definite priors to *o*-assertions than to *t*-assertions.

This answer will not do. Epistemically, the situations in which *o*- and *t*-assertions are involved is quite similar. One's evidence for there being a liquid in the tube is certain liquid-like impressions. Given these impressions, one has two options available. The first is to assign a vague probability to the hypothesis that there is a liquid in the tube – call it *H*. One then simply chooses to be an agnostic. Given that the probability of the evidence (the liquid-like impressions) is *prob*(*E*), the vague probability that one gives to *H* is anywhere in the interval (0, *prob*(*E*)). Alternatively, from the evidence – the liquid-like impressions – one can infer, perhaps not always explicitly, that there is a liquid in the tube. One thereby gives *H* a definite probability of *prob*(*H*). From *H*, one can then infer further predictions, e.g. that the stuff can be poured into a different tube, that it can be drunk, etc. Further testing may or may not confirm *H*. If it does, one can come to assert with some further confidence that there is a liquid in the tube. But these two options are equally available when it comes to theoretical assertions. One can choose to be an agnostic by assigning a vague probability to the further hypothesis that the liquid in the tube is hydrochloric acid – call it *H**. Alternatively, one can assign a definite prior probability to *H** and then subject *H** to further testing by deriving predictions. If these predictions are fulfilled, one becomes more confident of the truth of *H**. Clearly, *prob*(*H*) will be at least as great as *prob*(*H**), but what matters here is that testing *H** has led its own probability to increase. If this probability is high enough, one can assert *H** with some real confidence. It is because we rely on background beliefs as to what kinds of things can be in tubes, that we assign a definite prior probability that it is liquid. But we can similarly rely on background beliefs to assign a definite (if smaller) prior probability to the claim that this liquid is hydrochloric acid. Given this symmetry in the epistemic situation, agnostics should have to justify why they would assign vague prior probabilities only to *t*-assertions: if they choose not to assign vague priors to *o*-assertions, then it is hard to show why *t*-assertions should be given vague priors.

So far we have found no good reasons to say that *t*-assertions are not confirmable. But there is still the 'ultimate objection' to be dealt with. Agnostic empiricists may well say that *t*-assertions are not confirmable because they are *ultimately* about unobservable entities and the latter cannot be epistemically accessed. What makes this objection interesting is that it presupposes that claims about observables *are* confirmable. If agnostic empiricists denied *this*, then their agnosticism would concern not just theoretical assertions but any empirical claim whatsoever. What exactly is the relevant difference between *o*- and *t*-assertions which makes the former confirmable but the latter epistemically inaccessible? Van Fraassen, for instance, says of typical statements about observables: '[W]e can see the truth about many things: ourselves, trees and animals, clouds and rivers in the immediacy of experience' (1989: 178). 'My scepticism', he adds, 'is with general theories and explanations constantly handed out about all this … ' (ibid.). Presumably, the 'immediacy of experience' creates a big epistemic asymmetry because we do not see the truth of *t*-assertions (which are typically explanatory of experience) in our immediate experience. And how could we? But the metaphor is too vague, as it stands, to be evaluated. Different ways to flesh it out will yield radically different approaches to what can and what cannot be epistemically accessed.

Suppose that one allows 'immediate experience' to include only whatever is *actually* observed. Then the truth of assertions about observable entities is not seen in our immediate experience. What is actually observed *is* observable, but not the other way around. So there are (or can be) assertions about observable entities whose truth is not seen in immediate experience, narrowly understood. Notice that although van Fraassen asserts that '[e]xperience is the sole source of information about the world and [its] limits are very strict', he takes it that: 'experience can give us information only about what is both observable and actual' (1985: 253). So, van Fraassen allows experience to give us information, not just about what is actually observed but about what is observ*able*. Now, there may be a tension between van Fraassen's actualism and his characterisation of 'observable'. For the latter is a modal notion, hence it implicates the notion of *possibility*. This possible tension has been discussed by Rosen (1994) in some detail, so I shall leave it to an end note.[2] The point I want to press is that if we allow experience to reveal to us truths about observables, then we *ipso facto* endorse an understanding of the limits of experience which allows epistemic access to unobservables.

Let us, then, take the limits of experience to include observables, that is entities which *can possibly* be observed. Then a lot depends on how exactly we understand what can or can not be observed. We all agree that the mere *logical* possibility of observation is too liberal to characterise the bounds of experience. No theoretical entity (unless its very idea is contradictory) would then fall outside the limits of experience. If logical possibility is far too liberal for the empiricist, what other conceptions of possibility are available? We should certainly look to some notion of *nomological* possibility. But nomological possibility is a double-edged sword. What grounds that which it is nomologically possible to observe is *not* what we humans, with a certain biological make up, *can* actually observe. Surely, it is nomologically possible to observe the satellites of Saturn, even though no human being can actually be transported anywhere near Saturn to see them with the naked eye. Rather, what grounds the nomologically observable for us humans is what the *laws of nature* allow beings with our biological make-up to observe. They would allow us to observe the satellites of Saturn, had we had the technology to be transported near enough. And we are right in hoping that, because Saturn's satellites are supposed to be big enough relative to a human observer, some day some humans *will* see them with naked eye. But, surely, the laws of nature do allow us to see a virus (without using microscopes, that is), had we had the technology to massively enlarge them, or to reduce some humans to so minuscule a size as to fit inside a minute capsule and be injected into someone's bloodstream. Is that science fiction? If it is, so is, currently, transporting a human near Saturn. One science-fiction story may be easier to realise than the other, but should this technical (or, better, technological) problem have any bearing on epistemological issues?

If we call the satellites of Saturn 'observable' because we can imagine (that is, because it consistent with the laws of nature to imagine) technological innovations which, although still unavailable, can make us directly observe the satellites, then we should allow viruses to be *observable*. The point here is not that even if viruses are, somehow, observable, there may still be some entities which we could not possibly see with naked eye, no matter what. That may well be so. Rather, the point is that it is *enough* to say to agnostic empiricists that on the presently discussed liberalised understanding of the limits of experience, some *paradigmatic* cases of what they would call 'unobservable' entities would fall within these limits no less than some paradigmatic cases of what they call 'unobserved-but-observable' entities. So the equation 'unobservable = epistemically inaccessible' is suspect: 'unobservable' is simply not co-extensive with 'epistemically inaccessible'.

In the absence of an argument which makes *t*-assertions unconfirmable, I think we should be content with Hempel's dictum:

> [S]ince such theories [theories that are formulated in terms of unobservable entities] are tested and confirmed in more or less the same way as hypotheses couched in terms of more or less directly observable or measurable things and events, it seems arbitrary to reject theoretically postulated entities as fictitious.
>
> (1965: 81)

To sum up, this section has tried to rebut the following thesis, which I attributed to naive agnostic empiricism: (P) despite the fact that *o*-assertions and *t*-assertions are semantically on a par (they are both truth-conditioned), there is a relevant *epistemic* difference between them such that if one accepts that *o*-assertions are confirmable by evidence, one can use this relevant epistemic difference to *deny* that *t*-assertions also are confirmable. If the arguments offered are sound, then there is no relevant epistemic difference – that is, difference in their respective comfirmability – between *t*-assertions and *o*-assertions. So, it simply does not make sense for agnostics to direct their arguments solely against the confirmability of *t*-assertions. What follows from this is that since there is no relevant epistemic difference, the issue of how *t*-assertions are confirmable is no longer hard: it simply reduces to how any kind of assertion is confirmable (see Hempel, quoted above). The (important) details are left to the theory of confirmation, and need not worry us here.

Oz and Id: the tale of two worlds

It is now time to pay some systematic attention to van Fraassen's own alternative to realism, which he calls *constructive empiricism*. Van Fraassen *does* offer arguments in favour of agnosticism when it comes to his attempts to undercut the epistemic optimism associated with scientific realism. But his heart, as it were, lies elsewhere. His own constructive empiricism is an attempt to bypass the issue of whether or not we *should* be agnostic about theoretical assertions, and to replace it with the issue of whether or not we *need* to be epistemic optimists, as realists would be. To this end, van Fraassen wants to motivate a consistent philosophical image of science in which search for theoretical truth does not even feature as the aim of science.

Let me motivate the constructive empiricist alternative with a tale, a variant of which has been related by van Fraassen (1975), about abstract entities.

Once upon a time there were two possible worlds, Oz and Id. These worlds were very similar to one another, and very similar to the actual world – call this @. Both worlds enjoyed 'the paradise that Boyle, Newton, Mendel, Rutherford, Bohr and the rest have created' in @ (cf. van Fraassen 1994: 192). But there was one difference. In Id, the aim of science was to achieve theoretical truth, and when theories were accepted they were believed to be true. In Oz, the aim of science was to achieve empirical adequacy, and when theories were accepted they were believed to be empirically adequate. No presumption was made about the truth or falsity of what these theories said of the unobservable world. But, now imagine a philosopher who reflects on the actual science, i.e. 'the paradise that Boyle, Newton, Mendel, Rutherford, Bohr and the rest have created' in @. Is there anything in this 'paradise' @ which dictates that, when it comes to the philosopher's account of the epistemic and aim-theoretic characterisation of science in @, the philosopher should think that Oz is not possible or well-founded? In other words, does our philosophical reflection on science dictate that we (philosophers) should view science *as an activity which involves search for and belief in theoretical truth in order to account for its practice and for its success?* Do we *have to* view @ as Id, as realists suggest, or can we make sense of science if we take @ to be like Oz?

The moral that van Fraassen would like us to draw from the tale is that there is an alternative theoretical–philosophical image of science: one can see science as an activity or practice which is possible, intelligible and successful, without also accepting that science aims at, and succeeds in, delivering theoretical truth. He suggests that it is precisely *this* image that modern empiricism should juxtapose to scientific realism. His constructive empiricism – which I prefer to call *hypercritical empiricism* – is an attempt to show that Oz is well-founded and that therefore one *need not* go for Id, as realists do. If this is right, then whether or not @-science can attain theoretical truth becomes irrelevant. What matters is that there is an image of science which makes a realist understanding of @-science *optional*.

Two preliminary points are in order which should pre-empt possible misunderstandings and facilitate my exposition. In his exchange with Rosen (1994) and myself (1996), van Fraassen (1994; 1997) has insisted that his general epistemic and aim-theoretic account of science should not be seen as a summary statement of the epistemic and aim-theoretic attitudes of individual scientists, or of the 'abstract noun' *the* scientist. Rosen (1994) has shown conclusively that if van Fraassen's view is taken to describe the epistemic and aim-theoretic practices of actual scientists, then it could be empirically tested, and probably shown to be false. That is to say, if Oz and Id were taken to be alternative descriptions of the epistemic and aim-theoretic views of actual scientists in @, then we could empirically investigate which of the two, whether Oz or Id, offers the more accurate description of @-scientists. So, van Fraassen has insisted that constructive empiricism is a philosophical view about *science* – a view that empiricist philosophers should consider and accept – not about *scientists* and their (conscious or unconscious) *behaviour*.[3] Constructive empiricism offers an alternative philosophical characterisation of science. In particular, it is an image suitable for *agnostic empiricists*. Quoting Rosen with approval, van Fraassen says:

> 'The aim' of attempting to carry through the constructive empiricist interpretation of science is 'to show that even though he sees no reason to believe what they say, the [scientific agnostic] need not be driven out from the paradise that Boyle, Newton, Mendel, Rutherford, Bohr and the rest have created.'
>
> (1994: 191–192)

In order to facilitate subsequent discussion, however, I shall talk about a set of ideal practitioners of science. I call this set 'ideal' simply to avoid the risk of confusing the aim-theoretic and epistemic aspects of science with the attitudes of particular scientists. So, a set of ideal scientists will be a set of persons who impersonate, as it were, the aim-theoretic and epistemic aspects of science in Oz and in Id, respectively.

The other point of clarification concerns what exactly needs to be accounted for by a philosophical theory of science. Realists and their opponents would agree that it is not the behaviour of actual scientists. But, then, what is it? In one sense, it is the *phenomenology* of scientific activity. This phenomenology should not include the intentions and doxastic attitudes of scientists, but it should include the salient features of the activity they are engaged with – most importantly, some central features of its practice and its empirical success. Van Fraassen is in agreement here (cf. 1994: 191). His aim is to offer an interpretation of 'what we all come to agree on classifying as science', in particular, an interpretation which makes Oz possible and well-founded.

Before explicating the details of Oz-science, it is important that we take a systematic look at the issue of observability.

The vagaries of observability

Theories in Oz are understood literally. Theoretical terms, like 'electron' and 'proton', are not taken to be useful 'shorthands' for complicated connections between observables. Instead, they are taken to refer putatively to unobservable entities. As van Fraassen explains, 'literal does not mean truth-valued'. It rather means that theories are capable of being true or false

(1980: 10–11). Hence, it is a feature of Oz-science that scientific theories imply certain theoretical (ontological and explanatory) commitments. The theory of electrons, for instance, implies the existence of electrons. But, as we shall see shortly and in some detail, Oz-scientists refrain from asserting the existence of electrons because they refrain from asserting the truth of the electron theory. In a nutshell, Oz-science subscribes to semantic realism, but it refrains from going all the way on to epistemic realism.

The semantic realist understanding of theories in Oz has a broader philosophical significance. Oz-theories do not conform to the standard empiricist (Carnapian) two-language model (cf. Chapter 3). Van Fraassen agrees with realists that all observation is theory-laden. For him 'all our language is thoroughly theory-infected' (1980: 14). In fact, so theory-infected is it that if we started to chuck out the so-called theoretical terms, then 'we would end up with nothing useful' (ibid.). The novelty of van Fraassen's position consists in the fact that he has liberated empiricism from the need to split the language of science into two mutually disjoint sets: the set of *t*-terms and the set of *o*-terms. New empiricism proclaims that there is just one language, the language of scientific theories. Empiricism is no longer seen as a position about the stratification of the language of science; nor about the meaning of *t*-terms. Rather, it is seen as an irreducible commitment to the view that 'our opinion about the limits of perception should play a role in arriving at our epistemic attitudes towards science' (1985: 258).

Observability ('the limits of perception') is still being offered a privileged epistemic role. But this role is now linked with the origination and justification of one's beliefs. Observability is a property of an entity, and not a demand to describe an entity in terms of a special (the so-called 'observational') vocabulary. This is a key move. Empiricism is now understood to rest on a distinction between observable and unobservable *entities*. This distinction becomes a central epistemic tool, but it does not mirror the (old empiricist) line which separated theoretical from observational *terms* (cf. van Fraassen 1980: 14, 54). In Oz, observability should guide (in fact, determine) what is to be believed, but the description of the *content* of the belief can be given in a thoroughly theory-infected language.

An entity is called *observable* if suitably placed observers can perceive it by their unaided senses (van Fraassen 1980: 16). So, although Jupiter's satellites are currently observed only through telescopes, they count as observable entities because an astronaut near Jupiter could observe them with naked eye. Interestingly, van Fraassen argues that the distinction between observable and unobservable entities is not a philosophical distinction imposed on science. If it were, then the new empiricist position would not be so radically different from the old one. Where old empiricists imposed an artificial distinction between observational and theoretical terms and predicates in order to carry through their philosophical programme of making science stay as close to the observable world as possible, new empiricism would merely redraw the boundary of an artificial distinction so that it is now cast in terms of *entities* rather than *words*. Van Fraassen, therefore, insists that the distinction between observable and unobservable entities is an *empirical* distinction: it is science, in particular our current scientific theories, that delineates which entities are observable and which entities go beyond the limits of observability. He says: 'To delineate what is observable, however, we must look to science – and possibly to that same theory – for that is also an empirical question' (1980: 58).

Take, however, the theory of electrons. It does not say whether or not electrons are observable. It ascribes many properties to electrons, but not observability or its negation. It is a contingent fact of the world and of human physiology – and not an implication of the theory of electrons – that humans cannot directly observe electrons. For all we know, the electron theory could have been written by creatures who were able to observe electrons directly. So, whether or not an entity is observable is not dictated by the theories positing this entity. Still, van Fraassen has a fall-back position: the limits of observability are characterised by empirically discoverable facts about 'us *qua* organisms in the world, and these facts may include facts about the psychological states that involve contemplation of theories' (ibid.). It follows that the distinction between observable and unobservable entities is to be drawn from within our best theories of human biology, physiology and psychology. It is *these* theories that tell us that, qua organisms, humans cannot observe electrons, but can observe tables and *could* observe distant planets. It is these theories that tell us that we humans can see some big and bulky things, but not some little or minute ones.

This is all fine. But it does not sit particularly well with another aspect of Oz-science, viz. that theories are accepted as empirically adequate. The problem is this. Oz-scientists accept the best theories of human biology, physiology, etc. as empirically adequate. Hence, they accept that whatever these theories say about the observable world is true. These theories, however, are supposed to delineate what is observable to a human with a certain – standard – physiology. Hence, Oz-scientists have to accept that what is observable is delineated by theories whose empirical adequacy can be judged only if they know *in advance* which entities (and phenomena) are observable. In other worlds, Oz-observability is determined by empirically adequate Oz-theories. But whether or not these theories are empirically adequate *depends* on a prior account of Oz-observability. This circle needs to be broken at some point. But is there such a point?

There are two obvious ways out, both of which must be unappealing to van Fraassen.

1   The first way is to denounce the distinction between observable and unobservable entities altogether. If there is no such distinction, then there is no reason to draw it, and hence there is no reason to worry about how the realm of observable entities is delineated. But this move would clearly undermine an essential rationale for being a constructive empiricist.

2   The second way is to draw the distinction from *outside* science: there are some paradigm-cases of entities which should count as observable, and these offer the benchmark against which empirical adequacy and further theory-led delineations of observability should be judged. In this case, however, not only is the distinction *imposed* upon science by our pre-scientific *LebensWelt*. More importantly, it cannot be settled a priori that all paradigm-cases of observable entities will be such that they are rendered observable when the distinction is rationalised from within science.

 For instance, being a witch had been taken to be an observable property attributed to women in the Middle Ages, but it does not stand up any scientific rationalisation as an observable property, since it does not exist, anyway.

Here is another relevant worry. Van Fraassen should clearly include *properties* in the class of observable entities. In fact, this is what really counts for judging empirical adequacy. A theory is empirically adequate not just when what the theory says of the observable objects is true. Theories typically say of observable objects that have a number of unobservable properties: e.g. they say of tables that they have the theoretical property of being constituted by molecules. But constructive empiricists want to discount these claims as non-committal. What they take as committal are the observable properties ascribed to observable things – the colour of the table, or the pain of the stomach. To say of a theory that it is empirically adequate is to say that the observable things have the observable properties attributed to them by theories. Then, the following problem arises. Attributing to a certain entity the status of being observable is, basically, to ascribe yet another *property* to this entity. Is this property – the property of being observable – an observable one? Well, it cannot be because naked-eye observations are totally irrelevant to finding out whether an object possesses the property of being observable. I can see a table with the naked eye. I can attribute to it lots of observable properties: shape, colour, size, etc. But if I attribute to it the property of being observable, I do not do so on the basis of observations. Although I can observe the colour of the table and, hence say that colour is an observable property, I cannot observe the observability of the table. Observability is a *theoretical* property which, at best, can be operationalised by being taken to be indicated by the presence of a number of observable properties, e.g. colour, shape, size, etc. I say that the table is observable because I can see its size, shape, colour, I can sit at it, etc. Since observability is a theoretical property, it is no better than any other theoretical property whose presence is taken to be indicated by a number of observable properties (e.g. the property of having spin, which is indicated by the presence of deflected light-spots on a Stern–Gerlach screen).

 Van Fraassen insists that it is one thing to characterise those objects which are observable, but quite another to describe these objects. The description of an observable entity can be couched in theory-infected language, but this does not make the object anything other than an observable object. One can describe a table, using the terms of modern science, as 'an aggregate of interacting electrons, protons, and neutrons'. Yet, van Fraassen adds, a table *is* an observable thing. One can believe in the reality of the table, use theoretical language to describe the table, and yet remain agnostic about the *correctness* of its current description by science. Van Fraassen can consistently make all these claims, precisely because he is an agnostic, and not an eliminativist, about theoretical entities. He does not want to say that the entities posited by science do *not* exist. Nor does he want to say that current theoretical descriptions of observable entities are false. If he did say so, then he would be in all sorts of trouble. For if one asserted the falsity of the proposition 'A table *is* an aggregate of interacting electrons, protons, and neutrons', then one would no longer be entitled to use this proposition to describe tables. So what he says is that the fact that Oz-science uses the current descriptions to characterise observable objects does not imply either the truth or the falsity of these descriptions.

All this is fine, too. But there is a rather interesting twist. It relates to the means we employ to identify an object as some 'X'. Suppose that Oz-scientists want to find out whether a certain object is X. Suppose also that they have, one way or another, selected a set of entities which count as observable. If the issue is whether the object is, say, a table, then they will, typically, be able to figure that out without committing themselves to the correctness of their best theoretical descriptions of 'table'. Were the situation to be more complicated, were they for instance trying to find out whether the blood on the murder weapon was the blood of the defendant, then they would not rely on the observable properties of the blood stains: they would certainly have to rely on *theoretical* descriptions concerning human DNA found on the murder weapon in order to attempt the relevant identification. Intuitions here say that Oz-scientists would thereby accept the correctness of these descriptions, since if they were not confident in their theory-led methods to reliably indicate non-observable similarities and differences in the blood-stains they would not rely on them in order to form a judgement.

The natural rejoinder would be that Oz-scientists need assume only that these descriptions are empirically adequate, i.e. that they are such that they get all relevant observable phenomena right. But since there are no relevant observable (i.e. naked-eyed) differences between the two blood stains, Oz-scientists will have to go for a detour. They will have to rely on conditionals of the form: if the blood found on the defendant and on the murder weapon is the same, then the manipulation of the blood stains based on the theoretical description of the victim's DNA will yield certain observable results which are different from the results expected if the blood-stains are genetically different. So, Oz-scientists will have to accept that the theoretical descriptions of the DNA structure, though not necessarily correct, are empirically adequate in the sense that the observable results to which they give rise when the DNA structure is manipulated are exactly those which would be expected if these theoretical descriptions were correct. To most people, this would be an admission of defeat: surely these theory-led predictions do not prove the correctness of the relevant theoretical descriptions, but they should highly confirm them nonetheless. If the sole basis for expecting empirically adequate results is the correctness of the theory, then resisting the conclusion that the theory is, relevantly, correct is otiose. However, the whole idea of stopping at the level of empirical adequacy and declining to draw any conclusions from it is, for van Fraassen, what *constitutes* his own empiricist alternative. As such, it is a fall-back position: one can simply *choose* to stop at the level of believing the theory to be empirically adequate, and decline to take a stance on the issue of the correctness of a certain theoretical description. What then needs to be shown is that by adopting this attitude one stands to lose something. I postpone showing this to a later section.

For the time being it is important to note that whether or not a distinction between observables and unobservables can be drawn – and shown to be well-founded – the central philosophical issue concerns the use to which this distinction is put, and why. Sometimes, it can be useful to draw distinctions where perfect continua exist. But the line drawn must be plausibly useful. A standard way to interpret van Fraassen's argument in *The Scientific Image* is as suggesting that the observable–unobservable distinction draws the line between what is epistemically accessible and what is not: *all* statements about the unobservable world are undecidable in that no evidence can warrant belief in theoretical claims about the unobservable world. If correct, this point would at least motivate a (radical) empiricist epistemology: belief in theoretical assertions can never be justified because no evidence can sway the epistemic balance in their favour.

We have already seen that arguments to the effect that theoretical assertions are insupportable do not hold much water. What is worth adding are these two questions: Why should the fact that some things are visible to the naked eye, whereas others are not, have any *epistemic* significance at all? Why should it be the case that unobservability is tantamount to epistemic inaccessibility and observability is tantamount to epistemic accessibility?

One would expect of an empiricist to have answers to these questions. One answer could be that the unaided senses can decide claims about observables but not about unobservables. Yet, our senses alone, i.e. without the aid of instruments, can decide nothing but a tiny fraction of the things that scientists reasonably claim to know. Senses alone cannot decide even elementary processes such as measuring temperatures, apart from the crude sense that a body with high temperature 'feels' hot. One might, however, add that as far as observable phenomena are concerned, it is always possible that human beings can be in such a position as to decide claims about them by means of their unaided senses. The trouble with this suggestion is that it is generally incorrect. Unaided senses cannot even decide claims pertaining to the empirical adequacy of theories. For instance, our theories say that the temperature in Pluto is extremely low. But nobody can check this – even in the crude sense of 'feeling cold' – by being transported to Pluto, the reason being that no human being can possibly survive these low temperatures. So, a recourse to unaided senses is too poor a move to sustain the alleged epistemic relevance of the observable–unobservable distinction.

Besides, as Menuge (1995) has noted, it is wrong to suppose that beliefs about observables are somehow immediately justifiable (or, worse, in no need of justification) in a way that theoretical beliefs are not. Any plausible reason to think that a different *kind* of justification is always required for non-observational beliefs (e.g. beliefs based on instruments) would end up requiring *this* very kind of justification for observational beliefs as well. Suppose, for instance, one were to argue that in order for an instrument-based belief to be justified one must first be justified in believing that the given instrument operates reliably. But exactly the same requirement can be posed on the putative justification of eye-based beliefs, given that the human eye itself is a complex instrument known to be fallible. So, how can we argue that eye-based beliefs are immediately justifiable, while also holding the view that instrument-based beliefs require some extra justification? We should either consider both types of belief to be proximately justifiable, or else we should deny that observations with instruments always require a different *type* of justification. What Menuge rightly concludes is that there is no difference in quality between the evidence of the unaided senses and that of instruments. Both can warrant belief, and sometimes beliefs based on the unaided senses are less warranted than instrument-based beliefs (1995: 66–67).[4]

Such problems for van Fraassen's reliance on observability have been extensively discussed by many philosophers of science, including Churchland (1985), Hacking (1984) and Salmon (1985). The main point should be well-taken: the distinction between observables and unobservables is not well-founded epistemically. It transpires, however, that some such epistemic distinction between observable and unobservable entities is *constitutive* of what van Fraassen's takes empiricism to be. He says: '(I)f we choose an epistemic policy to govern under what conditions, and how far, we will go beyond the evidence in our beliefs, we will be setting down certain boundaries' (1985: 254). I think this is correct. What van Fraassen has failed to establish, though, is that these boundaries should include only claims about unobserved-yet-observable phenomena, and that they ought to exclude *all* claims about unobservables. This may be what he demands of his prescribed boundaries. But it is not necessarily what empiricism amounts to. For instance, as Salmon (1985; 1994a) has convincingly argued, Reichenbach's empiricism was consistent with his belief that unobservable entities exist and can be known.

At this point the general moral I want to draw is this. It is one thing to demand some caution in knowledge claims about the unobservable world, especially in the light of the fact that scientists have been in error in some of their beliefs about it. But it is quite another thing to adopt the radical position which excludes from knowledge any claim which goes beyond what can be observed by naked eye, or felt, etc. Empiricist philosophers – van Fraassen in particular – are right to point out the need for caution, but wrong insofar as their demand for caution leads them to ban any knowledge whatsoever of the unobservable world. To say that no evidence can warrant belief in a claim that refers to unobservable entities, to say that all claims about unobservables are inherently insupportable, is not to adhere to empiricism; it is dogmatism. It amounts to a desk-thumping position which declares that because something is too little, or too attenuated, to be visible to the naked eye it must lie forever beyond our epistemic reach.

Oz revisited

Let me highlight some of the central aspects of Oz-science. The criterion of success in Oz is not truth in every respect, but empirical adequacy. When a scientific theory is accepted, it is accepted as empirically adequate and not as true. Acceptance in Oz involves the belief that the theory has accomplished its aim, meets its criterion of success, i.e. is empirically adequate. Hence acceptance involves *some* belief, but it is belief in empirical adequacy as distinct from (theoretical) truth. But acceptance in Oz involves *more* than belief: it involves what van Fraassen has called 'commitment': 'a commitment to the further confrontation of the new phenomena within the framework of that theory, a commitment to a research programme, and a wager that all relevant phenomena can be accounted for without giving up the theory' (1980: 88). What it is very important to stress is that Oz-science is said to incorporate, in one form or another, every element of scientific practice that, realists would argue, speaks in favour of belief in theoretical truth (e.g. that theories are essentially employed in the interpretation of the phenomena, are used as the basis for explanation and prediction, that theoretical virtues are relied upon in theory-choice, etc.). Yet in Oz believing in the truth of the *t*-assertions, or even aiming at theoretical truth, is simply not part of the picture.

With all this in mind, the question before us is the following: are the conceptual resources present in Oz sufficient to account for all the salient features of actual science? In the next two sections, I try to show two things: first, that an Oz-attitude towards theories makes sense only if we assume some form of verificationism; second, that there is a central aspect of scientific practice, the 'conjunctive practice', which does not make good sense in Oz.

Commitment as potential belief

Paul Horwich (1991) has argued that, *qua* psychological states, belief and acceptance are one and the same. Belief, he notes, is a psychological state with a certain causal role. 'This would consist in such features as generating certain predictions, prompting certain utterances, being caused by certain observations, entering in characteristic ways into inferential relations, playing a certain part in deliberation, and so on' (1991: 3). One could also add that beliefs stand, typically, as causal intermediaries between one's desires and one's actions to satisfy them. But, Horwich notes, acceptance of a statement with assertoric content is individuated (as a psychological state) by exactly the same causal role. Hence, he concludes, acceptance can be no different from belief: it *is* belief.

I think this argument is sound as far as it goes. But it does not go very far against van Fraassen, the reason being that van Fraassen *defines* Oz-acceptance in such a way that there is a property of belief which is *not* a property of acceptance. To be sure, Oz-acceptance is tantamount to belief when it comes to assertions about observables. But there is a divergence when it comes to theories (or individual assertions) which make reference to unobservables. In this case, Oz-acceptance involves belief that the theory is empirically adequate *and* commitment to the theory. But although Oz-commitment to the theory is pretty much like belief in the theory, it does not involve belief in the *truth* of the theory. So Oz-acceptance, unlike belief, does not entail belief in truth, when the accepted statement make reference to unobservables. (I can simplify this by saying that Oz-acceptance does not entail belief in theoretical truth.)

How could we restore the thrust of Horwich's argument against van Fraassen's *intended* position? We should start by noting that Oz-acceptance involves two elements, one being cognitive, the other said to be non-cognitive. The cognitive element is *belief*: belief in empirical adequacy. As van Fraassen has noted: 'If you accept a theory, you must at least be saying that it reaches its aim, i.e. meets the criterion of success in science (whatever that is)' (1983: 327). Given that in Oz the criterion of success is empirical adequacy, Oz-acceptance commits at least to the belief that the theory has 'latched on to' some truths, viz. truths about observables. The supposed non-cognitive element of Oz-acceptance is *commitment*. I have already quoted van Fraassen on 'commitment'. Here is another relevant passage:

> In addition, the acceptance involves a commitment to maintain the theory as part of the body of science. That means that new phenomena are confronted within the conceptual frame of the theory, and new models of the phenomena are expected to be constructed so as to be emdeddable in some models of that theory. It should go without saying that, even when acceptance is unqualified, it need not be dogmatic; fervent and total commitment need not be blind or fanatical.
>
> (1985: 281)

So, commitment is what Oz-acceptance involves, on top of belief in empirical adequacy. Elsewhere, van Fraassen has compared commitment to 'taking a stand' (1989: 179). Take, for instance, one of his own examples: 'It seems likely to me that we have evolved from lesser organisms' (ibid.). This is a statement which involves reference to unobservable entities (lesser organisms) and processes (evolution). Van Fraassen suggests that in making this judgement, one (he?) need not report a belief; one just takes a stand. He notes that judgements such as the above do not 'state or describe, but avow': they express 'propositional attitudes' (ibid.).

One could try to drive a *definitional* wedge between ordinary acceptance and Oz-acceptance, by adding a non-cognitive element to the latter. But the difficulty with this move is that it is not at all clear in what sense a commitment is different from a belief, and hence, in what sense it is a non-cognitive attitude. The phenomenology of commitment (described in the passages quoted above) is identical to the phenomenology of belief. Besides, if commitments express propositional attitudes, they are no less truth-evaluable than are beliefs and other such attitudes. Calling the attitude one of expressed 'avowal' is of no help. It is hard to see what exactly is involved in belief that is not involved in 'avowal', and conversely. If someone told me that he doubted that we have evolved from lesser organisms, I could reply to him 'I avow that we do'. And if I *avow* that we have evolved from lesser organisms, I am ready to act on this avowal in no different a way than if I *believe* that we have evolved from lesser organisms. But, perhaps the key to the issue is the 'as if' operator: to say that 'I avow that p' *should* be understood as 'I believe that things are *as-if* p'. To believe *that* p is not, arguably, the same as to believe *that* things are *as-if* p. But what exactly is the difference?

Here is a suggestion. The 'as if' operator 'brackets' the truth-value, in particular the truth, of the belief: an 'as-if' belief has all the characteristics of belief except that the truth of the belief is 'bracketed'. It therefore seems to me very tempting to say the following. One can characterise Oz-acceptance as *potential* belief, since Oz-acceptance involves – via belief in empirical adequacy *and* commitment – whatever is involved in belief *minus* holding the theoretical assertions of the theory to be true. So, Oz-acceptance is to be contrasted with *actual* belief in that the latter involves, in addition, holding the theoretical assertions of the theory to be true. If this characterisation is right, then the following question suggests itself: once the theory is Oz-accepted, what else would be required in order to hold the theory true? In other words, once all the elements of *potential* belief – via commitment and belief in empirical adequacy – are present, what would or could turn potential belief into actual belief?

An immediate reply could be that being in the state of potential belief is enough for explaining scientific practice. But this would be too quick. If all we are concerned with is finding the minimal explanation, then one could further restrict the cognitive aspect of Oz-acceptance, relegating even more to 'mere' non-cognitive commitment. Oz-acceptance could incorporate in its cognitive dimension solely the belief that the theory saves the phenomena only on the working days – let us call that 'working empirical adequacy'. This attitude is certainly weaker than belief in empirical adequacy *simpliciter*, hence we might just assume belief in 'working empirical adequacy' in order to explain the practice of science. Alternatively, Oz-acceptance may involve only the belief that the theory is unrefuted, and relegate the stronger belief that the theory is empirically adequate to a mere non-cognitive commitment. What this suggests to me is that if the cognitive dimension of Oz-acceptance can be further restricted, then we simply have to accept that what is minimally required for the explanation of scientific practice should not dictate one's philosophical reconstruction of science.

The rejoinder here might be that if the cognitive dimension of Oz-acceptance were further restricted, then the account offered would not be in accord with some salient feature of scientific practice in @, viz. that acceptance involves belief in empirical adequacy and not mere belief in the theory being unrefuted, or being '(working) empirically adequate'. Such accounts of acceptance would be 'revisionary', as Rosen (1994: 155) has put it. And certainly, it is part of the rationale of a philosophical account of @-science that it should not be revisionary: it should not aim to reform salient aspects of science, but instead it should account for them. Yet, what exactly should Oz-acceptance involve in order not to be revisionary? Should it involve *just* belief in empirical adequacy, or should it involve *at least* such belief? If it is the former, why is that a non-revisionary claim? To say that anything more or less than belief in empirical adequacy would be revisionary would not do, unless one had already established that the non-revisionary cognitive dimension of acceptance should implicate *just* belief in empirical adequacy. If it is the latter (that is, if Oz-acceptance should involve *at least* belief in empirical adequacy), then it is left open that Oz-acceptance may involve belief in truth as well. (Note here that I am not talking about the epistemic attitudes of the scientists, but rather, in the spirit of van Fraassen's demand, about philosophical accounts of what acceptance should involve.) Why then should we take it for granted that Oz-acceptance should involve *just* belief in empirical adequacy and *nothing* more? To say that anything more is explanatorily redundant will not do, for so can be belief in empirical adequacy, as opposed to weaker belief in theories being unrefuted. I leave this point as a challenge, for the time being. In the next section, I offer a more sustained argument why belief solely in empirical adequacy will not do.

So, let me return to my main point: what would or could turn potential belief – exemplified in Oz-acceptance – into actual belief – exemplified in Id-acceptance? Frankly, I see no other candidate than the following: what is required to turn a potential belief in the theory into an actual belief is a *proof* that the theory is true. Then, given that no proof of the truth of the theory is possible, a potential belief in the theory could not possibly turn into actual belief. But this answer would commit van Fraassen to verificationism. That is certainly unwelcome. For, if what is required for believing the theory is a proof that the theory is true, then – by the very same token – proof should be the requirement for the belief that the theory is *empirically adequate*. Since no such proof is forthcoming, belief in truth is no more precarious than belief in empirical adequacy. This point is defended in detail in the concluding sections of this chapter.

Belief in truth is better

In this section I intend to show that if Oz-scientists (that is, the ideal practitioners of Oz-science) aim merely at empirical adequacy, and if they accept their theories merely as empirically adequate, they are going to be worse off than their Id counterparts – even by their own lights.

What the Oz tale shows, van Fraassen might say, is that belief in the truth of *t*-assertions is 'supererogatory'. On the one hand, it is unnecessary for the functioning of science: Oz-science proceeds on the basis of belief in the empirical adequacy of theories and does exactly as well. On the other hand, belief in truth fosters the illusion that one takes an extra risk by believing the theory to be true (cf. 1985: 255). But there is no such extra risk involved, because we can have evidence for the truth of the theory only via evidence for its empirical adequacy. We can never have more reasons to believe in the truth of a theory than to believe in its empirical adequacy. Since the truth of the theory entails its empirical adequacy, it follows from the probability calculus that the probability that a theory is true is less than or equal to the probability that it is empirically adequate. In line with the anti-metaphysical Occam's razor, belief in the truth of the theory is redundant (ibid.).

Let us try to evaluate the above argument. All that the probability calculus entails is that if we are to assign probabilities to a theory's truth and a theory's empirical adequacy, then the latter should be at least as high as the former. However, the probability calculus does not dictate how high or how low the probability of a theory's truth may be. In particular, it does not dictate that the probability of the theory's truth is not (cannot be) high, or at any rate high enough to warrant the belief that the theory is true. This is a crucial issue. Realists do not deny that the probability of the observational consequences of the theory being true is at least as great as the probability of the whole theory being true. As we have seen, what they emphatically deny is that the theoretical assertions of theories are somehow inherently insupportable; that they can never be likely (or never more likely to be true than false). Agnostics should then need precisely to show that the likelihood of a theory can never be high (or higher than 0.5). This, as

I have argued, is something that has not been shown. Nor are there good prospects that it can be done (see pp. 186–191).

Is there a real risk involved in believing a theory to be true, or is the risk only illusory? To conclude the latter would be somewhat hasty. Realists argue there is something to be gained by believing the theory to be true. Envisage two theories T_1 and T_2 which are accepted as true. One can form their conjunction $T_1 \& T_2$ and claim that, since T_1 and T_2 are true, so is $T_1 \& T_2$. One then comes to believe $T_1 \& T_2$ and starts applying it to the explanation of the phenomena. Is it only explanation that can be gained, though? In general $T_1 \& T_2$ will entail more observational consequences than T_1 and T_2 taken individually. So there is certainly something to be gained, something extra, by believing the theories: extra observational consequences that would not have become available if the theories had been taken in isolation. Besides, as Friedman (1983: 244–247) has argued persuasively, these extra consequences boost the confirmation of T_1 and T_2 taken individually. Over time, T_1 and T_2 have received two confirmational boosts: one on their own and another as parts of $T_1 \& T_2$. This argument has become known as the 'conjunction argument'.

There is a crucial difference between truth and empirical adequacy. Although truth is preserved under conjunction, empirical adequacy is not, at least not necessarily. So although 'T_1 is true' and 'T_2 is true' entail that '$T_1 \& T_2$ is true', 'T_1 is empirically adequate' and 'T_2 is empirically adequate' do *not* entail that '$T_1 \& T_2$ is empirically adequate'. The conjunction of two empirically adequate theories may even be inconsistent. The model-theoretic explication of empirical adequacy makes this apparent. To say that T_1 is empirically adequate is to say that there is a model ϕ of T_1 such that all phenomena of type P are embedded in ϕ – let us abbreviate this as $\exists\phi(P)$. Similarly, to say that T_2 is empirically adequate is to say that there is a model ψ of T_2 such that all phenomena of type Q are embedded in ψ – i.e. $\exists\psi(Q)$. However, $\exists\phi(P)$ and $\exists\psi(Q)$ do not entail $\exists\chi(P \& Q)$, i.e. that there is a model χ of $T_1 \& T_2$ such that all phenomena of types P and Q are embedded in χ. There should be no doubt that, after the conjunction of the two theories has been effected, the constructive empiricist can always accept $T_1 \& T_2$ as empirically adequate (as opposed to believing that it is true). But the whole point is that the eventual decision to accept $T_1 \& T_2$ as empirically adequate is *parasitic* on the following process: accepting *T1* to be true and T_2 to be true, and then forming their conjunction $T_1 \& T_2$.[5]

An immediate reaction to the 'conjunction argument' is to say that, although it is sound, it is irrelevant. For the conjunctive practice involved in the argument is not a salient feature of scientific practice, and hence we need not account for it. This much seems to be implied by van Fraassen's initial reaction (see 1980: 83–84). He has claimed that in actual practice, theories are not conjoined in a straightforward manner, but they are so corrected. Even if true, this point is exaggerated. First of all, when theories are put together with other auxiliary theories and hypotheses to derive predictions, there is no correction process involved, merely conjunction. For instance, when some optical theory is conjoined with elementary fluid mechanics in order to test a prediction about the velocity of light in a medium, no process of correction is involved. Second, although it is certainly true that *some* processes of conjunction involve the prior correction of one of the theories, the conjunction will now involve the new corrected theory T_1^* and the theory T_2. Hence, the original argument still goes through (cf. Hooker 1985).

So, the conjunctive practice is a feature of science that does need to be accounted for. If belief in truth is involved in accepting a theory, then there is no problem. So, there is no problem to account for this practice if we go for Id-science. Let us compare this with what happens in Oz. As we have already seen, science in Oz aims only at empirical adequacy; and Oz-acceptance implicates only the belief that the theory is empirically adequate. Hence, the conjunctive practice cannot be immediately 'rationalised' in Oz, unless it is parasitic on belief in truth.

What it is important to note is that the 'conjunction argument' can be developed into a *diachronic argument* for belief in (the truth of) theories. Because they hold their theories to be true, Id-scientists (i.e. ideal practitioners of science in Id) are diachronically better off than their Oz-counterparts. They can routinely conjoin these theories with *whatever* auxiliary assumptions (or other theories) are available or become so in the future, and so are able to derive extra observational consequences which their Oz counterparts would have missed because, *ex hypothesis*, they accept theories as only empirically adequate. This argument does not refer merely to currently available auxiliary assumptions (or theories), but also to those that will become available in the future. The claim is that belief in theories is a better way to guarantee that scientists will not miss out on hitherto unknown observational consequences which their theories will yield when they are conjoined with hitherto unavailable auxiliary assumptions. What this argument implies is that, in a sense, 'the paradise that Boyle, Newton, Mendel, Rutherford, Bohr and the rest have created' cannot be fully re-created in Oz, unless conjunctive scientific practice in Oz is parasitic on belief in the truth of theories.

Precisely because constructive empiricists cannot legitimately argue that the conjunctive practice is not an actual feature of scientific practice, I want to consider carefully another possible reply that they might want to offer to this diachronic argument for realism. This goes as follows.

Although Oz-acceptance implicates only belief in empirical adequacy, Oz-science has developed the 'conjunctive practice' none the less. However, the *justification* offered is different. After philosophical reflection on this practice, it is noted (or, rather, the constructive empiricist spokesman of Oz notes) that the justification is inductive (of the second order): when theories T_i and T_j were conjoined in the past, the resulting new theory $T_i \& T_j$ yielded more predictions than its individual predecessors, and was more likely to be empirically adequate. Oz-scientists, therefore, have endorsed this practice because, on (second-order) inductive grounds, it is more likely that this practice which was successful in the past will yield empirically adequate theories if it is followed persistently in the future than if it is not.

The inductive argument under consideration relies on the premiss that, in the past, the conjoined $T_i \& T_j$ has tended to be more empirically adequate than its individual predecessors T_i and T_j. This invites the following objection. The actual (second-order) inductive argument should be much more complicated. Given the finite amount of evidence available at *any* time, the argument should proceed in *two* steps. It should rely initially on a first-order induction in order to move from the claim that the conjoined theory $T_i \& T_j$ is unrefuted to the claim that $T_i \& T_j$ is empirically adequate. It is only then that one can perform the second-order induction in order to move from the claim that conjoined theories have been empirically adequate in the past, to the claim that the practice of conjoining theories tends to generate theories with greater empirical adequacy. The difficulty lies mainly with the first step, i.e. with the first-order induction. For, as Boyd (1985) has tellingly argued, ordinary inductive projections from a theory's being unrefuted to a theory's being empirically adequate depend on theory-generated *judgements of projectability*. Among the many theories that are unrefuted at any given moment of time only a few are projected to be empirically adequate. The selection of those which are projectable cannot be based on just observational evidence, since clearly all unrefuted theories tally equally well with the observational evidence available. Those that are selected are precisely those which are considered theoretically plausible by their proponents, e.g. those that are licensed by other background theories and relevant background beliefs. If, however, first-order inductions are theory-led and theory-informed, then they carry with them several theoretical commitments which cannot be simply brushed aside. Ideal practitioners of Oz-science who need to perform these first-order inductions in order to move on to the second-order induction about the practice of conjoining theories end up being no less committed to theories than their Id-counterparts.

Well, one might argue, in Oz these so-called theoretical commitments are merely 'pragmatic virtues'. Hence, commitment to the truth of the theory which guides and informs projectability judgements may still be avoided. To which I reply as follows. The ultimate problem with the attempt to justify the conjunction practice by a second-order induction is that it leaves the original point of the diachronic conjunction argument untouched. Even if one conceded that after a while it became apparent that the practice of conjoining theories pays off in terms of empirical predictions, one should still want to know what exactly was involved in conjoining the first few theories. For prior to learning from experience that conjoined theories tend to be more empirically supported, increased empirical adequacy could not have been a good enough motive. This can be shown by the following consideration.

Take any two theories T_i and T_j. Suppose that they are unrefuted and that one has fixed probabilities $prob(T_i)$ and $prob(T_j)$ that each of them is empirically adequate. This information on its own implies nothing at all about the crucial probability $prob(T_i \& T_j$ is empirically adequate). There is no definite probabilistic relation that obtains between $prob(T_i$ is empirically adequate), $prob(T_j$ is empirically adequate) and $prob(T_i \& T_j$ is empirically adequate). Hence there is not even a lower bound for $prob(T_i \& T_j$ is empirically adequate). *Prob*($T_i \& T_j$ is empirically adequate) might be *anywhere* in the interval [0,1]. So, if it is expected that $prob(T_i \& T_j$ is empirically adequate) has a definite value at all, let alone that it is greater than the probability of each of the two theories being empirically adequate, this judgement must be based on something other than estimations of probabilities of theories empirical adequacy. This judgement is, in fact, parasitic on ascribing *truth* to the theories *before* the conjunction takes place. The relevant judgement should be something like: T_i is true; T_j is true; hence $T_i \& T_j$ is true; if $T_i \& T_j$ is true, $T_i \& T_j$ is going to be empirically adequate; hence $prob(T_i \& T_j$ is empirically adequate) is now anywhere in the interval [$prob(T_i \& T_j)$, 1]. We may still lack a definite connection among $prob(T_i$ is empirically adequate), $prob(T_j$ is empirically adequate) and $prob(T_i \& T_j$ is empirically adequate) but this should no longer worry us. Once we switch to taking theories as true, what matters is that there is a definite motive to conjoin: that the conjoined theory will, as a rule, yield more observational consequences, and that therefore the scientists will be in a better position to test whether or not it is empirically adequate.

Recently, André Kukla (1994) has suggested that there may be a way to account for the conjunctive practice from an empiricist point of view. He concedes that the 'conjunction argument' is telling against constructive empiricism, but notes that *conjunctive empiricism* is immune to this argument. When a conjunctive empiricist accepts a theory, he accepts its *T#* version, where *T#* says that the empirical consequences of *T*, *in conjunction with whatever auxiliary theories are accepted*, are true. Belief in *T#* is stronger than belief that '*T* is empirically adequate', but Kukla notes, it is also weaker than belief in *T* itself. Hence, belief in *T#* may be the right way to reconstruct Oz-attitude towards theories.

Is conjunctive empiricism any better than constructive empiricism? One plausible thought is that the ability of *T#* to yield correct observational consequences makes sense only if it is accepted that *T* is true. For, simply, there is nothing other than the truth of *T* which can guarantee that *T* will yield correct observational consequences when it is conjoined with any auxiliaries which might become available in the future. To take seriously the possibility that T may be characteristically false but that it yields correct predictions and that it will *keep yielding* them when conjoined with hitherto unavailable – and God-knows-what – auxiliaries, is no more credible than to believe that a coin heavily biased in favour of tails will *fail* to systematically yield tails when the tosses are made under God-knows-what hitherto unspecified circumstances. This is possible, but very unlikely.

A stubborn empiricist, Kukla reacts, would find the essence of the above argument question-begging. For, in effect, it suggests that the best – if not the only – explanation of $T\#$'s ability to keep yielding correct predictions is that T is true. This need for explanation, Kukla insists, is what a stubborn empiricist would deny. So let us leave this argument to the one side. What I now show is that, despite its promise, conjunctive empiricism falls foul of the original argument against constructive empiricism. Moreover, the conjunctive empiricists' belief in $T\#$ is *doubly parasitic* on belief in the truth of T and belief in the truth of all auxiliaries that might become available in the future. Let us see how this is so.

There are two defining moments of conjunctive empiricism. First, that when one accepts $T\#$, one accepts that the 'phenomena will also confirm all the empirical consequences that follow from the conjunction of T with other accepted theories' (Kukla 1994: 959). Second, that once the switch to $(T_i)\#$s is effected, the inference of $(T_1 \,\&\, T_2)\#$ from $(T_1)\#$ and $(T_2)\#$ is 'unobjectionable' (ibid.). Let us examine carefully these $(T_i)\#$s. In order to get them, conjunctive empiricists have to conjoin T with other accepted theories A. They thereby have to form $T \,\&\, A$. It is only *then* that they can withdraw to believing only $T\#$ – that is, believing that the phenomena will confirm all the empirical consequences that follow from the conjunction of T with A. But, given the original 'conjunction argument', the process of forming the subject of the conjunctive empiricist's belief (i.e. $T\#$) is parasitic on believing in the truth of T and A taken separately. Suppose otherwise. That is, suppose that the conjunctive empiricists' premises are that (1) T has true observational consequences; and (2) that A has true observational consequences. From these two premises it does not follow that all of the observational consequences of $T \,\&\, A$ are true. It might simply be the case that $T \,\&\, A$ entail an extra observational consequence which is false. So, $T\#$ does not follow from the conjunctive empiricists' premises, unless T and A are taken to be true.

But let us suppose that conjunctive empiricists have come up with their $(T_i)\#$s. Can they conjoin them freely, as Kukla says, even though they are not taken to be true? Is the inference of $(T_1 \,\&\, T_2)\#$ from $(T_1)\#$ and $(T_2)\#$ 'unobjectionable'? As I will show, this inference is guaranteed to be valid only if it is parasitic on belief in truth. Let Cn stand, as usual, for the set of the logical consequences of a set of axioms. Recall that Kukla's $(T_i)\#$ is short for the set of the observational consequences of $T_i \,\&\, A_i$, where T_i is a theory and A_i is a set (any set) of auxiliary assumptions. The inference that Kukla calls 'unobjectionable' rests on the assumption that $Cn((T_1)\# \& (T_2)\#) = Cn(T_1 \& T_2)\#$. But it should be by now clear that the formula $Cn((T_1)\# \& (T_2)\#) = Cn(T_1 \& T_2)\#$ may fail. This is, to repeat, because the consequences of conjoining the observational consequences of $(T_1 \& A_1)$ with the observational consequences of $(T_2 \& A_2)$ are a proper subset of the consequences of the conjunction $[(T_1 \& A_1) \& (T_2 \& A_2)]$. The latter conjunction entails extra consequences, some of which might be observational. The only way in which it is guaranteed that the above formula will not fail is to take the $(T_i)\#$s to be true.

But perhaps I have been unfair to Kukla. For there is, after all, a way in which the formula $Cn((T_1)\# \& (T_2)\#) = Cn(T_1 \& T_2)\#$ will hold good, even though the $(T_i)\#$s are not true. This will happen if, as Earman (1978) has implied, $(T_1)\#$ and $(T_2)\#$ are *complete* with respect to observational consequences; that is, if for *any* sentence S in the language of $(T_1)\#$ that draws only on the observational vocabulary, either $(T_1)\#$ entails S, or else it entails its negation (and similarly for $(T_2)\#$). Now, Kukla might just have assumed that his $(T_i)\#$s are, by definition, *complete* in the above sense. But Earman has rightly dismissed this option, because 'it cannot be expected to hold for interesting scientific theories'. The reason is simply that the observational consequences of scientific theories will typically be conditionals of the form $S_1 \rightarrow S_2$, and 'the theory by itself will not decide the truth of either S_1 or S_2' (Earman, 1978: 198). The same goes, I should add, for auxiliaries and other concomitant theories A. I see no justification for the expectation that there are *always* going to be auxiliaries which, being parts of Kukla's $(T_i)\#$s, will decide either all the antecedents or all the consequents of the observational conditionals $S_i \rightarrow S_j$ implied by scientific theories. That the $(T_i)\#$s are complete in the Earman sense is at best a 'promissory note' with no hope that it can be cashed. I then conclude that insofar as the conjunctive empiricists' inference is 'unobjectionable', it is because it is *doubly parasitic* on belief in truth. Only predication of truth guarantees that the inference from $(T_1)\#$ and $(T_2)\#$ to $(T_1 \& T_2)\#$ is valid.

So, what has gone wrong? I think all that Kukla has noted is that belief in $T_i\#$s is the 'fall-back' position that empiricists should accept. But belief in $(T_i)\#$s, although stronger than belief in empirical adequacy, does not solve the original 'conjunction problem': it accentuates it. There should be no doubt that *after* $T \& A$ is accepted, its probability is going to be less than, or equal to, the probability of $T\#$. But this does not show that we need not believe in $T \& A$ before we choose to believe $T\#$ instead. Whether or not the degree of belief in $T \& A$ is high enough to warrant belief is an open (empirical) issue. But there is no argument which says it will never be high, or high enough. Whether or not, after one forms $T\#$, one throws away the degree of belief in $T \& A$ and sticks to the belief in $T\#$, the fact remains that the latter degree of belief was made possible *because of* the former.

What can we conclude from this? If my arguments are right, then, from a diachronic point of view, belief in truth is a more rational attitude towards theories than mere belief in empirical adequacy. Even if, at the end of the day, the aim for which one develops and conjoins theories is increased empirical adequacy, this aim is better achieved via belief in the truth of theories. Oz-science shoots itself in the foot.

On van Fraassen's critique of abductive reasoning

Theoretical beliefs in science are formed by means of abductive reasoning. But so are most of our every-day commonsense beliefs. Realists have exploited this fact in order to argue that if one has no reason to doubt commonsense abductive reasoning, then one should have no reason to doubt abduction in science. The pattern of reasoning, as well as the justification, are the same in both cases. So, suppose that one hears strange noises in the wainscoting. One also sees some mouse-droppings; some piece of cheese left outside the fridge the night before has gone missing, etc. One then reasonably infers that there is a mouse in the wainscoting. The mouse is unobserved. But its presence in the wainscoting implies certain things which if observed will improve our confidence in its existence. For instance, it implies that more mouse-droppings will be found. It implies that when a mouse-trap is installed, there is a reasonable chance that the mouse will be caught, given its liking for cheese. Our belief in the presence of the mouse – and not of something else – makes us act in a certain way, which would be odd, if not inexplicable, had we not inferred the presence of a mouse. For instance, we decide to borrow the neighbour's cat, although we might hate cats. Well, the mouse is observable; something that can be seen, killed by a cat, caught in a mouse trap. But suppose that no one will ever see the mouse, not even the cat, because the mouse decided to leave the house after it found out that the particular brand of cheese favoured by the residents was not to its liking. So, we have no chance to observe further marks of its presence. Still, it is reasonable to posit its existence: no mouse, no sense to be made of all the relevant findings. In the event that we see no further evidence for the presence of the mouse, we might think harder. Our confidence in its presence might drop a little. Or we might look for another account of the absence of further findings: it was a one-off phenomenon; the mouse left after it had its single meal.

Whatever the reason, positing the presence of the mouse is well justified. It is based on good reasons. Our confidence in its presence may go up or down as new evidence rolls in. But the positing itself has been reasonable. We formed potential explanations of the findings and we picked the best, given our background knowledge. Once the explanation has been adopted, i.e. once the presence of the mouse has been accepted, we may look for further evidence in its support depending on how confident we have been about our explanation, how thorough the search has been for other potential explanations, how well they stand to scrutiny, etc. In commonsense abductive reasoning, we have internalised these procedures by having formed (and having learned to acquire) reliable background knowledge: certain findings are typically explained by the presence of mice. What really matters, however, is that the whole process of reasoning is inferential, rather than directly perceptual. The reasoning process involved in such cases is nothing other than abductive.

Suppose, now, that a scientist observes that in the standard account of β-decay, the principle of the conservation of energy is violated. The energy of the decaying neutron is not commensurate with the energy of the emerging proton and electron. What needs to be explained here is not mouse-droppings, but sure enough, something needs to be explained. Pauli's positing of the neutrino (a particle with no charge and mass, but with spin) is just another instance of abductive reasoning. When the neutrino's energy is taken into account, there is no need to abandon the principle of conservation of energy during β-decay. The degree of confidence in the existence of neutrino will depend on many factors. But, sure enough, accepting its existence will guide looking for further experimental and theoretical confirmation. Pretty much like the mouse-case, the presence of neutrino in a β-decay implies certain further predictions of neutrino-related phenomena.

Abductive reasoning is so pervasive in both science and every-day life that it hardly needs pointing out. So, the point I am trying to stress is not that it is a psychologically real reasoning process. Rather, to repeat, the point is that if abductive reasoning is ontologically committing in everyday life, then there is no reason not to be so committing in science.[6]

Abduction and commonsense reasoning

Well, van Fraassen disagrees. But he has been somewhat ambiguous. One way to read some of his arguments in *The Scientific Image* is as follows. He seems to accept that abduction (henceforth Inference to the Best Explanation – IBE) can operate as a mode of inference in science, although he insists that the conclusion of such an inference, i.e. the hypothesis endorsed on the grounds that it is the best explanation of the evidence, is accepted only as empirically adequate (that all observable phenomena are as the hypothesis says they are), as opposed to approximately true. Here is a relevant passage:

> [E]xplanatory power is certainly *one* criterion of theory choice. When we decide to choose among a range of hypotheses, or between proffered theories, we evaluate each for how well it explains the available evidence. I am not sure that this evaluation will always decide the matter, but it may be decisive, in which case we choose to accept that theory which is the best explanation. But, I add, the decision to accept is a decision to accept as empirically adequate. The new belief is not

that the theory is true (nor that it gives a true picture of what there is and of what is going on plus approximately true numerical information) but that the theory is empirically adequate.

(1980: 71–72)

Plug into this the premiss that when the theory is solely about the observable world, empirical adequacy and truth coincide. It follows that when the explanatory hypothesis arrived at by IBE is about observables, the claim that this hypothesis is empirically adequate amounts to saying that this hypothesis is true.

What this quick argument suggests is that van Fraassen does not doubt that IBE operates reliably in many 'ordinary cases' which involve reference to unobserved-but-observable entities, like the case of the mouse in the wainscoting (see 1980: 19–20, 21). It appears then that for van Fraassen the problem with IBE arises when the potential explanation involves reference to unobservable entities. Then empirical adequacy and truth no longer coincide. Whereas '"there is a mouse in the wainscoting" and "all observable phenomena are as if there is a mouse in the wainscoting" are totally equivalent; each implies the other (given what we know about mice)' (1980: 21), the propositions 'there is an electron in the cloud chamber' and 'all observable phenomena are *as if* there is an electron in the cloud-chamber' are not equivalent. Still, on the same reading of van Fraassen's position, in an abductive problem-situation involving some unobservables the best explanatory hypothesis should be the one that is chosen, but it must be entertained as at best empirically adequate. No pretension about its likely truth is warranted, nor should be made.

It is a natural thought (that I have certainly had in the past) that van Fraassen sustains a selective attitude towards IBE: the latter *is* a means to go beyond the realm of what has been actually observed and so form warranted beliefs about *unobserved* things or processes; yet IBE is *not* a means by which to form warranted beliefs about the realm of *unobservable* things or processes. I still think that this is a correct interpretation of van Fraassen's writings and shall try to persuade you of this. But van Fraassen and his co-authors deny that it is (cf. Ladyman, Douven, Horsten, and van Fraassen, 1997). They argue that van Fraassen objects to IBE *simpli-citer*, irrespective of whether the abduced hypothesis is about observables or unobservables. His example of the mouse in the wainscoting serves a different purpose, we are told. It motivates the claim that realists cannot justify their reliance on abductive reasoning in science on the basis that abductive reasoning is a pervasive element of commonsense reasoning. How is that?

Van Fraassen and his co-authors (Ladyman *et al.* 1997) argue that commonsense abductive reasoning can be seen as either of two empirically indistinguishable forms of reasoning: IBE and as-if IBE. An as-if IBE is such that the conclusion is accepted *as-if* it was true. Since, however, empirical adequacy and truth coincide when it comes to judgements about unobserved-observables, as-if IBE and IBE are empirically indistinguishable modes of inference when unobserved-observables are involved. If this is so, how can we possibly find out whether commonsense abductive reasoning is IBE or as-if IBE? And if we cannot find that out on empirical grounds, how can the realist argue that common sense abductive reasoning is IBE as opposed to as-if IBE? The intended conclusion is that the realist cannot simply transfer the legitimacy of common sense abductive reasoning to scientific abductive reasoning, since the former can be seen as an instance of as-if IBE.

I find this argument spurious. If, as van Fraassen and his collaborators claim, the conclusions of an as-if IBE and of an IBE are equivalent when it comes to claims about observables, then there is *no* need to choose between them: if as-if IBE is reliable in its conclusions (in the restricted set of claims about observables), so is IBE. If one doubts the reliability of IBE when it comes to claims about observables, then one should also doubt the reliability of its rival which, as van Fraassen once put it, is 'apt in an anti-realist account'. Conversely, if one trusts the reliability of as-if IBE when it comes to claims about observables, then one should also trust the reliability of IBE. In any case, one cannot simply have different epistemic attitudes towards IBE and as-if IBE when claims about observables are involved. If, then, different epistemic attitudes crop up when their respective conclusions involve reference to unobservables, this difference surely reflects a selectively sceptical attitude towards unobservables entities: we can abduce to unobserved-but-observable mice, but we should not abduce to unobserved-but-unobservable neutrinos.

Strictly speaking, however, the conclusions of an as-if IBE and an IBE are not equivalent, even when only observables are the referents: 'there is a mouse in the wainscoting' and 'all observable phenomena are as-if there is a mouse in the wainscoting' are *not* equivalent. The former does entail the latter, but not conversely. Just consider the case where our pet cat Tom realised that we are about to dump him and determines to make us think that there is a mouse in the wainscoting so that we decide to keep him. So, even at the level of observables, we cannot just stay indifferent between 'all observable phenomena are as-if there is a mouse . . . ' and 'there is a mouse'. We need to stick our necks out and endorse, after we balance things, the best explanatory hypothesis on which to base our future action: shall we punish Tom or, instead, install a mouse-trap? The point is simply that as-if IBE is a myth: we decide to install the mouse trap because we know that an as-if mouse is not caught in a mouse-trap.

The fact of the matter is that if commonsense abductive reasoning is abandoned, commitments to unobserved-but-observable entities (e.g. an unobserved-but-observable mouse in the wainscoting) would be left unsupported. Surprisingly, van Fraassen and his collaborators agree with this conclusion: 'the scepticism entailed by a rejection of IBE in general is simply accepted by van Fraassen' (Ladyman *et al.* 1997: 319). However, van Fraassen and his collaborators also endorse the view that 'a philosophical position which leads to scepticism reduces itself to absurdity' (ibid.: 317). Van Fraassen is said to accept the scepticism entailed by the rejection of any kind of IBE – be it about observables or unobservables – yet he is also said *not* to be a sceptic about things whose truth we can see 'in the immediacy of experience' – hence not a sceptic 'of the Cartesian variety' (ibid.: 319). Such a position leaves him with *very little* about which he is not a sceptic. To repeat a central point already made (see pp. 189–191): suppose that we do 'see' the truth about observed things in our experience. Do we also see truths about unobserved-observables in the immediacy of experience? If anything, immediate experience is about observed things, not about unobserved-but-observable ones. When we posit unobserved-but-observable entities (e.g. when we claim that your own copy of this book exists when you leave the room), we need to perform some kind of inference (rudimentary and unconscious though it may be) from what we immediately experience to an unobserved-but-observable thing that causes or sustains our immediate experiences (past *and* future). Similarly, positing extinct animals is surely reasonable (although they are 'observable' only in a very loose sense of the term). The truth of such claims is by no means seen in the immediacy of experience of, say, fossils. If IBE is generally abandoned, then we are left with a poor epistemology that admits only judgements about observed things. Cartesian scepticism may well be evaded, but Humean scepticism is in the offing.

At this point van Fraassen and his collaborators retrench: they claim that even if IBE about observables may, after all, be acceptable, it is problematic when it comes to unobservables because in the former case, but not in the latter, 'we do not routinely introduce new ontological commitments' (Ladyman *et al.* 1997: 316). This is contentious. IBE about observables *does* involve the introduction of a new type of entity. For instance, positing an extinct type of animal is *both* an instance of IBE *and* introduces new 'ontological commitments'. And IBE about unobservables *does* involve the introduction of instances of known types, e.g. instances of the HIV-virus. At any rate, there is no reason why our epistemic attitude towards a posit should relate to whether it introduces instances of a new type of entity or instances of a known type. What matters, in either case, is that the posit is introduced to causally cement our 'immediate experiences'.

That is not all, I am afraid. Van Fraassen has recently produced two interesting arguments that truth is not attainable, even if scientists are able to specify and choose the best explanation. Let me examine them, and try to refute them, in turn.[7]

The argument from a bad lot

Van Fraassen's first argument – which may be called *the argument from the bad lot* – goes like this:

> Let us grant that scientists have effected an ordering of a set of theo-
> ries $T_1, \ldots, T_n$ each of which offers a potential explanation of the
> evidence e and that they have sorted out which is the best explana-
> tion of e, say T_1. In order for them to say that T_1 is the approximately
> true account of e, they must take 'a step beyond the comparative judge-
> ment that $[T_1]$ is better than its actual rivals'. They must take 'an
> ampliative step'. This step involves belief that the truth is already more
> likely than not to be found within the set of theories available to them.
> But our best theory may well be but 'the best of a bad lot'. So, in
> order for the advocates of IBE to argue that IBE leads to truth, they
> must *assume* a principle of privilege. That is, they must assume that
> 'nature predisposes us to hit on the right range of hypotheses' (cf.
> 1989: 142–143).

What does van Fraassen mean when he says that our best theory may well
be 'the best of a bad lot'? I take it he means one of the following three
things.

1   He may mean that it is logically possible that our best theory is the
    best of a bad lot. Clearly, any sensible model of abduction must allow
    for this possibility. For surely there is no a priori warrant that scien-
    tists will invariably have hit the truth. But one of the issues at stake
    here is this: should one first eliminate the possibility that the truth may
    lie outside the theories that scientists have come up with *before* one
    argues that there are good reasons to believe that the truth lies within
    this range of theories? If this is what van Fraassen demands, then I
    must say that he operates with a very strong notion of warrant. In fact,
    it is such a strong notion that it renders unwarranted even beliefs about
    empirical adequacy. For, given the finite evidence currently available,
    it is also logically possible that any currently unrefuted theory is not
    empirically adequate. Would van Fraassen say that unless this possi-
    bility is excluded, no belief in the empirical adequacy of any given
    theory is ever warranted? There is nothing wrong with such an answer
    apart from the fact that it would lead to bald scepticism: very few
    beliefs, if any, can be warranted if the notion of warrant involves elim-
    ination of the possibility that the belief be false. I do not think van
    Fraassen can afford to have such a strong notion of what constitutes
    belief-warrant without being an outright sceptic.
2   A second way to interpret van Fraassen's claim that our best theory
    may well be 'the best of a bad lot' is this: although it is logically
    possible that that our best theory is 'the best of the bad lot', it is in
    fact unlikely that it is. For obvious reasons, he cannot really mean this:
    this is just the intended realist position.

3   Van Fraassen may mean that it is likely (or, more likely than not) that our best theory is 'the best of a bad lot'. This is, I think, the only reasonable interpretation of van Fraassen's argument. If true, this claim would threaten realist optimism about IBE. So I take it that van Fraassen's point is that unless an unwarranted privilege is appealed to, *it is more likely that the truth lies in the space of hitherto unborn hypotheses.*

Let me say straightaway that there is a point that the friends of abduction must concede. As we saw in Chapter 5, the history of science suggests that the whole truth (whatever that means) regularly lies outside the range of theories scientists consider at a given period. Even our best-supported theories can be held to be only approximately true. But, this admission – sound though it is – does not undermine abduction. All that it concedes is that, at given stage of the scientific inquiry, scientists have come up with only part of the truth and further truths are to be discovered. What the friends of abduction – normally scientific realists – need to show, then, is that, contrary to van Fraassen's suggestion, the best explanatory hypothesis can be warrantedly believed to be approximately true. How may they do this?

I think the best defence of IBE is to go on the offensive. In response to van Fraassen the realist can state that there *is* a sense in which we are privileged and warrantedly so. This is what I call the appeal to *background knowledge privilege*. Let me elaborate.

One should observe that the argument from a bad lot works only on the following assumption: scientists have somehow come up with a set of hypotheses each of which entails the evidence – their only relevant information being that these hypotheses just entail the evidence – and then they want to know which of them, if any, is true. If this situation were representative of what goes on in an abductive problem-situation, then, admittedly, scientists would not have the slightest clue as to whether any of these theories is likely to be approximately true. Even if they could specify which theory is the best explanation of the evidence, according to some criteria of 'bestness', they could not associate the best explanation with the likeliest one. However, as Boyd (1984; 1985) and Lipton (1991; 1993) have persistently argued, and as I have tried to show in Chapter 4, it is at least dubious and at most absurd that theory choice operates in such a knowledge vacuum. Rather, theory choice operates within and is guided by a network of background knowledge. An actual scientific example can illustrate this claim.

After the discovery and successful explanation of the phenomena of interference and diffraction, the wave theory of light began to supersede the emission theory in explanatory power. Light was believed to consist of waves, but the wave theory left it open whether the waves were longitudinal or transversal, or, in fact, both. In particular, given the successful wave theory of sound, it was taken, for instance by Young and Poisson, that light-waves were longitudinal, like sound-waves. Before the discovery of the phenomenon of polarisation of light the hypothesis that light-waves are longitudinal accounted for some phenomena of light-propagation. But the phenomenon of polarisation forced upon scientists the belief that light-waves exhibit sidedness, which could not be explained unless one accepted the hypothesis that light-waves have at least a transversal component.

In 1816, Arago and Fresnel (see 1819) discovered that two light-rays polarised at right angles to each other do not interfere, whereas two light-rays polarised parallel to each other exhibit fringes of interference. According to Arago and Fresnel, given the background wave theory of light, this phenomenon could be explained on the assumption that light-waves are purely transversal. However, there was an alternative hypothesis that entailed the evidence, namely that light consists of both transversal and longitudinal waves. This hypothesis provided a potential explanation of the phenomena, but this explanation was poorer than that offered by the hypothesis that light-waves are exclusively transversal – poorer because, although it entailed the observed phenomena of interference, by positing longitudinal waves it also created new and intractable explanatory difficulties. As Fresnel later stated:

> We [Arago and Fresnel] both felt that these facts would be explained very simply, if the vibrations (oscillatory movements) of the polarised waves took place in the plane itself of these waves [i.e. if they are transversal]. But, what became of the longitudinal oscillations along the light beams? How were these oscillations destroyed by the polarisation phenomenon and why did not they reappear when the polarised light was reflected or refracted obliquely on a glass plate?
>
> (1866: 629)

What Fresnel stressed was, in effect, that the hypothesis that light-waves have both a transversal and a longitudinal component would also have to account for the disappearance of the longitudinal wave after the light-wave had gone past the polariser. On the other hand, the hypothesis that light-propagation is a purely transversal process would not have this extra burden: it explained the phenomenon of polarisation more simply, more completely and without need of any ad hoc manoeuvre. Hence, Fresnel accepted what he called 'the fundamental hypothesis', namely that the propagation of light is a uniquely and exclusively transverse process (1866: 786). This hypothesis was singled out as the best explanation of the phenomenon of polarisation and was accepted as the correct account. As we saw in Chapter 6 (see pp. 130–137), Fresnel's 'fundamental hypothesis' became itself part of the new background knowledge that constrained explanations of other light-phenomena.

This case drives home two important aspects of what I earlier called 'the background knowledge privilege'. The first aspect is that background knowledge can drastically narrow down the space in which hypotheses can provide a potential explanation of the evidence at hand. (In the foregoing case, Fresnel ended up with two potential explanations of the Arago–Fresnel effect.) The second aspect is that when the background knowledge does not suggest just one theoretical hypothesis, then explanatory considerations – which are part and parcel of scientific practice – are called forth to assist the selection of the best from among the hypotheses which entail the evidence. (In the foregoing case, Fresnel's explanatory considerations dramatically favoured the hypothesis that light-waves are uniquely transversal.) I think both aspects of the 'background knowledge privilege' make it plausible that, contrary to van Fraassen's claim, scientists can have strong evidence for the belief that the best explanation is also the correct account of the phenomena.

Van Fraassen could challenge the appeal to background knowledge in abductive problem-situations on the ground that the background beliefs might not be approximately true after all. Again, he could say, they might have been the best of a bad lot. However, van Fraassen's challenge would rest on a dubious and, I think, incorrect assumption, viz. that evidence can never guide scientists to form (approximately) true theoretical beliefs. As we saw in Chapters 5 and 6, even though evidence does not entail theoretical hypotheses, it can support some theoretical hypothesis to a high degree, so that it is unlikely that the hypothesis could be plain false *and* the evidence be what it is – as it happened in the example discussed. It is true that the probability (and, I think, the degree of confidence) of a theoretical belief will be *at most* as high as the probability of the evidence it entails. And it is also true that the probability associated with a theoretical belief can hardly ever be unity. But, to repeat a central point (see pp. 204–205), this does not mean that this probability can never be high. The fact that the probability of a theoretical claim can at most be as high as the probability of the evidence it entails does not mean that scientists can never have a warranted high degree of confidence in a theoretical claim in the light of the supporting evidence. Those beliefs for which scientists acquire overwhelmingly supportive evidence augment the mass of warranted background beliefs and become the pivots for new warranted beliefs.[8]

At this point, the reader might object that it is as if I have somehow begged the question of background knowledge. That is, the reader might think that the issue at stake is *whether* in fact scientists do operate within an environment of approximately true background beliefs, and that my arguments have just begged this question.

By way of addressing this objection, it seems to me relevant to distinguish between (a) the *general* sceptical (Humean) worry of how one goes about vindicating an ampliative mode of inference such as induction or IBE in a non question-begging way – given that a kind of circularity is involved in any such vindication – and (b) van Fraassen's *particular* sceptical worry that in order to have the cake of abductive reasoning and to eat it (i.e. show that it tends to generate approximately true beliefs) the friends of abduction must grant themselves an unwarranted privilege.

I have dealt with worry (i) already, in Chapter 4, where I defended the general reliability of abductive reasoning. When it comes to van Fraassen's argument from a bad lot, the issue at stake between van Fraassen and the realists is not whether scientists operate at all within an environment of correct background beliefs; it is rather the issue of the *extent* of their correct background beliefs. Even van Fraassen needs background beliefs in order to support his claims about empirical adequacy. So, I think my arguments to date in the debate with van Fraassen do not beg the question. All they suggest is that scientists are more privileged than van Fraassen considers them to be.

In order to see that the issue at stake *is* the extent of scientists' background knowledge, let me ask the following question: is the background knowledge privilege excess baggage that only a realist seems to need to take on board? Or do van Fraassen's claims about empirical adequacy also require some similar sort of privilege?

Let us recall that the privilege a realist needs is that part of the truth lies already in background beliefs in relation to which scientists are to choose their best explanatory theory. Let us now move back to Oz-world. There, scientists are not interested in choosing the most likely-to-be-true theory, but the most likely-to-be-empirically-adequate one. How can they know that the theory which they have selected as the best is not the most seemingly empirically adequate theory of a bad lot? In other words, how can they know that the empirically most adequate theory does not lie in the spectrum of the hitherto unborn theories?

There is a *symmetry* between the realist's position and the constructive empiricist's position in respect of the argument from a bad lot. The constructive empiricist's notion of adequacy is that a theory is empirically adequate if and only if it saves all phenomena, past, present and future, and squares with all actual and possible observations. It is perfectly possible that the best theory available now, which squares nicely with a finite number of actual observations and phenomena, may cease to do so with future phenomena, or with possible observations in space–time regions in which it has not yet been tried, or with possible data on which it has not yet been tested. In light of these possibilities, would constructive empiricists say that a theory which saves the data that *has been* tried is empirically adequate *simpliciter*? If they did, they would violate their own understanding of empirical adequacy. So in order for them to claim that the best currently available theory is empirically adequate, they need an ampliative claim, asserting that scientists have already hit upon an empirically adequate theory. In particular, they would have to claim that it is unlikely that a theory which squares with the observations to date will cease to do so in the future, or in space–time regions yet to be tried. They would have to appeal to the existence of universal regularities between phenomena, and to some principle of privilege which asserts that the theory has hit upon them. They would then have to claim that it *is* in virtue of this fact that the theory which saves a given range of phenomena *is* empirically adequate. In doing so, constructive empiricists would indeed appeal to a 'background knowledge privilege' of the kind they deny to their realist colleagues. Hence, constructive empiricists cannot afford to deny that there is a 'background knowledge privilege'. They have to concede that, to some extent, scientists operate in an environment of correct background beliefs. What they dispute is the *extent* to which scientists are privileged. It is in this sense that I think my arguments do not beg the question.

In order to avoid a possible misunderstanding, let me note the following. Ladyman *et al.* (1997) have objected to my point that since each theory has indefinitely many empirically equivalent rivals, it makes no sense to say that one of them is empirically adequate. Hence, they argue, there is no need to choose between them. But notice that when it comes to claims about empirical equivalence, all we might have is an argument that, in a certain family of theories, if T_i implies certain observational consequences, so does T_j $(i, j = 1, 2, \ldots)$. If T_i and T_j *are* empirically equivalent, then *if T_i is* empirically adequate, so is T_j. At *any* given time, however, there is only a finite amount of data from which each T_i can draw support. At *any* given time, what at best we know of all the theories in the family is that they are (a) unrefuted; and (b) a piece of evidence entailed by one of them is also entailed by any other. Van Fraassen suggests that a theory should be accepted as at best empirically adequate. But he has noted: 'If you accept a theory, you must at least be saying that it reaches its aim, i.e. meets the criterion of success in science (whatever that is)' (1983: 327). It should be, then, clear that accepting each and every theory in the above family as empirically adequate (given the finite set of data already available) *does* require some privilege: this family of theories has hit upon universal regularities by virtue of which each of its members can be projected as empirically adequate. This privilege is indefinitely strong too, given that there is an infinity of ways in which each T_i in the family can be refuted and an infinity of unborn theories which agree with each T_i on all *actual* data but entail different predictions about unavailable data. Does the realist claim that one of the T_is is approximately true require even more privilege? Whatever extra privilege it requires, it is of the same type. To assume that claims about unobservables require a different *type* of privilege *is* question-begging: it presupposes that coming to assert the truth of claims about unobservables is inherently different from coming to assert the truth of claims about observables.

Constructive empiricists might retrench here and argue that they indeed need some sort of privilege to ground their judgement that current theories are empirically adequate. But, they may argue, asserting *their* privilege involves less epistemic risk than asserting the realist privilege. In my inferential practices, van Fraassen could say, if I am to be hanged, why should it be for a sheep and not for a lamb? (see 1980: 72). Obviously, it takes less risk to assert that there are universal regularities between phenomena, and that if a theory has hit upon them it is going to be empirically adequate, than it does to assert that a theory is approximately true.

Problems of epistemic risk are interesting because they contrast with problems of security: the more one is willing to believe, the more numerous are the ways in which one can be in error. It is important that we should be secure about our beliefs, in the sense that we have good warrants for what we believe. But, it does not follow from this that one's belief in the approximate truth of background scientific theories is not secure. Although it will be at most as secure as are beliefs in mere regularities (since the approximate truth of background theories entails the existence of universal regularities), that can be secure enough to warrant the extra risk one takes in asserting that background theories are approximately true.

Note also that epistemic risk contrasts with ignorance: the less willing one is to believe, the lower one's probability of error – and the less one pushes back the frontiers of ignorance. Undeniably, realists take an extra epistemic risk when they say that background theories are approximately true; but taking an extra risk is the necessary consequence of aspiring to push back the frontiers of ignorance and to get to know more things, in particular about the unobservable causes of phenomena. In taking this extra risk, realists want to know more about scientific theories than do constructive empiricists. So the latter are unjustified in suggesting that this risk is not worth taking on safety grounds – for two reasons: first, they also take an inductive risk which goes beyond current evidence; and, second, if risk is the price to pay for pushing back the frontiers of ignorance, it is well worth the expense.

The argument from indifference

Let me now turn to van Fraassen's second argument against IBE (see 1989: 146). I call this *the argument from indifference*. It goes like this:

> Let us grant that we have chosen the theory T that best explains evidence e. A great many of unborn hypotheses inconsistent with T explain e at least as well as T. Only one theory, either T or one of the hitherto unborn theories, is true. All the rest are false. Since we know nothing with respect to T's truth-value other than it belongs to the (probably infinite) class of theories that explain e, we must treat it as 'a random member of this class'. But then we may infer that T is very improbable.

Responding to an earlier version of the argument from indifference, Armstrong remarked quite nicely: 'I take it that van Fraassen is having a bit of a fun here' (1988: 228). I think Armstrong is quite right. Van Fraassen's argument rests on a controversial assumption, viz. that the only thing we know about the best explanatory theory T is that it belongs to the (probably infinite) class of theories that explain e equally well. But this is absurd. Note that van Fraassen grants that T has passed several tests and has qualified as the best explanation of e. Then he claims that T (the best available explanation of the evidence) is as probable as all other *unborn*/potential explanations of e. In order to assert this, one must first show that *there always are* other potentially explanatory hypotheses to be discovered, let alone that they explain the evidence at least as well. But how do we know this in advance? Of course, it is no surprise to encounter the argument that there always are trivial alternatives to T that entail the evidence, e.g. notational variants of T, or theories that are formed by just tacking things on T. But this can hardly support the claim that T is as probable as any of these alternative hypotheses. At any rate, T would be as probable as those alternatives only if the sole thing that counted towards the probability of a theory is that it entails the evidence. Yet, as we saw in Chapter 8 (pp. 168–176), this is wrong. Relatedly, even if we granted that there always are unborn/potential explanations of e, what is to say that as explanations of the evidence they are as good as the one offered by T? If they are not, they should not be taken to be as probable as T.

It is only reasonable, I think, to demand that any alternatives to T should be scientifically interesting in the sense that the scientific community has independent theoretical reasons to accept them as genuine empirically equivalent rivals to T. For only then is there a serious issue as to whether and on what grounds scientists should believe in one theory rather than the other. Imagine, now, a case in which there are two serious rivals T and T' such that no current evidence and no explanatory consideration can distinguish between them. Then, *temporary* suspension of judgement is clearly the right attitude, while the search for further discriminatory evidence proceeds. But the argument from indifference goes far beyond this sound attitude. It intends to establish that *permanent suspension of judgement* is the right attitude towards a theory that provides the best explanation of the evidence on the grounds that there are unborn hypotheses that explain the evidence at least as well. This is, however, an assumption which cannot be simply taken for granted. Van Fraassen needs to *argue* for this. In particular, he needs to show that for any theory there is a non-trivial alternative such that the two theories are indefinitely indiscriminable by any evidence and the application of any method. No such argument, let alone proof, is available, as we saw in Chapter 8.

Van Fraassen could always appeal to his own theory of explanation to support his argument from indifference. He could first remind us of a difference between the informational and confirmational virtues of theories: the fact that theory T is more informative than theory T' does not make T more likely than T'. He could then argue that although explanatory power is indeed a virtue which stretches beyond a theory's ability to square with the phenomena and offers reasons to accept a theory, it is an *informational* virtue of a theory. So, since no informational virtue raises the belief-worthiness of a theory, neither does explanatory power (see van Fraassen 1983a: 166–169; 1985: 247, 280; 1989: 185, 192).

Such an attempt to sweep explanation under the carpet of information is, however, contentious. Van Fraassen is surely right to note that a potential explanation offers information about the putative causes of the phenomena, and that this fact does not *ipso facto* make an explanation likely. Nevertheless, acquiring this putative information is just the first step in scientists' quest for well-confirmed theoretical beliefs. If the explanatory hypothesis is sufficiently rigid, so that it cannot be the product of ad hoc adjustments, if it coheres with other background beliefs that are well-supported by the evidence, and if, moreover, it yields novel predictions or unites hitherto unrelated phenomena, then one can claim that this hypothesis is better supported than another which either remains silent or gives a poorer explanation.

Let us, for instance, consider a case where there are ten theories $T_1, \ldots, T_{10}$, each of which explains a single phenomenon e_i ($i = 1, \ldots, 10$). Let us also imagine that a scientist proposes a grand-theory T^* that unites all these diverse theories and explains all of the phenomena that they explained. T^* may also entail a great deal more than do the individual theories. T^* is surely more informative than any single individual theory, even more informative than their mere conjunction, and this is definitely a virtue of T^*. However, the facts that T^* unites hitherto unrelated phenomena (or domains) and yields novel predictions have also significant *confirmational value*. The fact that, on purely probabilistic grounds, the probability of T^* is less than or equal to the probabilities of each individual theory $T_1, \ldots, T_{10}$ (since T^* entails each of those) does not show that the probability of T^* cannot be high enough to warrant belief. So, it is not the mere fact that a theory tells an informative story that makes it likely. Rather, it is some of the features of the potential explanation which, having confirmational value, increase the theory's probability. Van Fraassen is too quick to sweep these features of an explanation under the carpet of informational virtues and to dismiss, out of hand, their relevance to confirmation.

It is also noteworthy that the argument from indifference, if interesting at all, is symmetrical with respect to both scientific realism and constructive empiricism. Suppose that one wants to have grounded judgements of empirical adequacy. In particular, suppose that one wants to claim that current theories are empirically adequate, yet wishes to suspend one's judgement as to their truth-value. However, judgements of empirical adequacy are no less susceptible to the argument from indifference than are judgements of truth. Suppose that we take the best theory T_{ea}, which we now *project* as empirically adequate. Of course, there is an infinity of other theories such that all are consistent with the finite data that T_{ea} saves. All these theories differ from T_{ea} only in some observable respects, e.g. T'_{ea} states that in the mouth of the first black hole to the west of our galaxy there is a white raven (or, indeed, T''_{ea} is a variant of T_{ea} that involves *gruesome* predicates). However, only one of these theories is really empirically adequate. Since, the only thing that we know with respect to the empirical adequacy of our best theory T_{ea} (or of the family thereof) is that it belongs to the (probably infinite) class of theories that save the available data, we may treat T_{ea} as a random member of this class and, hence we may conclude that T_{ea} is unlikely to be empirically adequate.

To be sure, if it is the case that a theory has many empirically equivalent rivals, then, clearly, if this theory is empirically adquate, all of its empirically equivalent rivals also will be. If such a situation arises, let us say that we have a family of empirically adequate theories. Yet, this situation would do nothing to protect constructive empiricists from the charge that the argument from indifference can be turned against them. For even if we talk of a family of empirically adequate theories we should not forget that this is a projection: given that at any given time there is only a finite amount of data available, we can project only that the family of empirically equivalent theories is, in fact, a family of empirically adequate theories. For, there will also be an infinity of theories which agree with each and every member of the family on all of the available data (that is, they will be unrefuted), but disagree with each and every member of the family on hitherto unavailable data.

Constructive empiricists would be no more at ease with the argument from indifference than would their realist colleagues, if they wanted to avoid bald scepticism and to have grounded judgements of empirical adequacy. They therefore need to resist the claim that the best available theory T_{ea} which currently saves the phenomena is just a random member of the class of theories (most of which are as yet unborn) which also save the phenomena. In order, however, to place T_{ea} in a privileged position *vis-à-vis* those unborn rivals which agree on the available data but disagree on the unavailable data, they must show that T_{ea} is much more likely to be empirically adequate than its unborn rivals. Yet such a judgement cannot be based solely on the available evidence since by hypothesis T_{ea}, like all of its unborn rivals, saves exactly the same evidence. So, the belief that T_{ea} is more likely to be empirically adequate than its unborn rivals should be based on the claim that T_{ea} possesses some potentially confirmatory theoretical virtue (e.g. simplicity or explanatory power) which its rivals do not possess. Constructive empiricists could claim that it is because of this fact that they are justified in believing that T_{ea} has latched on to universal regularities and, they could therefore use this claim to ground their judgement that T_{ea} *is* empirically adequate. But then how can they avail themselves of such theoretical virtues while denying the same benefit to their realist colleagues?[9]

I think the constructive empiricist's position *vis-à-vis* the argument from indifference differs from the realist's only in degree. The latter finds absurd the claim that the best available theory is as likely-to-be-(approximately)-true as all as yet unborn hypotheses, whereas the former finds absurd the claim that the best available theory is as likely-to-be-empirically adequate as all hitherto unborn hypotheses. But in order to have grounded judgements of the epistemic goods they demand from scientific theories, both need to appeal to some non-empirical yet potentially confirmatory theoretical virtues. As for the difference in the risk involved in their respective claims, I think I took care of that objection towards the end of the previous section.

I conclude, then, that the argument from indifference fails to establish that one should treat the best available explanation as a random member of the class of (mostly unborn) potential explanations of the evidence. In fact, it turns out that were this argument to be accepted as sound, it would prove too much. For it would be equally effective against van Fraassen's attempt to have grounded judgements of empirical adequacy.

New epistemology?

Van Fraassen has aimed to embed his constructive empiricism in what he has called a 'new epistemology' (1985; 1989). This 'new epistemology' differs from standard (or traditional) epistemology in that it is no longer concerned with the circumstances under which a belief is rational/warranted/justified. Instead, it now focuses on opinion, rather than belief, and the circumstances under which *change* of opinion is rational. As it has recently been put: '[Van Fraassen] is not interested in warrant (i.e. the rationality of beliefs), but in the rationality of changes of belief' (Ladyman *et al.* 1997: 315). A complete discussion of van Fraassen's philosophy would certainly require a detailed critical examination of this 'new epistemology'. But this will have to await a different project.

I end this chapter with some general and cursory remarks. In the debate between scientific realism and constructive empiricism, it seems, the aim of the new epistemology is to allow constructive empiricists to move between their rejection of IBE in general and the ensuing scepticism about anything other than observed posits: IBE can go; grounded judgements of empirical adequacy, too, can go; one does not *have to* even believe in the empirical adequacy of the theory, while remaining agnostic about its truth. Yet scepticism is not forthcoming, because under the new epistemology beliefs need not be justified to be rational (cf. Ladyman *et al.* 1997: 315).

What I want to suggest is that a full explication of rationality cannot deal just with belief change. It is perfectly reasonable to argue that not all beliefs are equally rational, even though their professors might update them, say, via Bayesian conditionalisation. A creationist scenario is not, at least for some of us, of a rationality (warranty) equal to that of evolutionary theory, and it should be part of the task of epistemology to explain why it is more rational to believe in the latter than it is to believe in the former. Take one of the central lines of 'new epistemology': 'what is rational to believe includes anything that one is not rationally compelled to disbelieve' (ibid.: 315). We still need to know what kinds of things one is rationally compelled to disbelieve, i.e. what kinds of beliefs are not warranted. A full theory of rational belief should certainly be open-minded and endeavour to avoid dogmatism. But it should also allow for *comparative judgements*: some beliefs are more rational than others. Belief in the existence of middle-sized material objects should certainly be evaluated as having a more rational basis than belief in the existence of sense-data and constructs of them. Whatever else it does, the 'new epistemology' should make this comparative judgement available. But if explanatory considerations contribute to elevate the rationality of belief in material objects, so much the better for my molecules.

10 NOA, cognitive perfection and entity realism

Arthur Fine has defended a neutral stance in the scientific realism debate. He has famously called his position the 'natural ontological attitude' (NOA). Fine's claim is that both realist and anti-realist approaches are 'unnatural attitudes' to science, extraneous attachments to the body of science rather than its natural garb (see Fine 1986a). But Fine's own 'natural attitude' to science is not unproblematic. A point that has repeatedly been made is that Fine's NOA is inherently unstable: under close inspection, it collapses either to realism or to its rivals. Van Fraassen (1985: 246), for instance, thinks that, 'with minor modifications', NOA would be compatible with constructive empiricism, and Devitt (1991: 45) wonders how NOA differs from his own understanding of realism.

In the first few sections of this chapter I discuss what I think is the major element of Fine's NOA, viz. his deflationist approach to the concept of truth and to philosophical debates about the concept of truth. Advertising NOA, Fine says:

> [A] distinctive feature of NOA that separates it from similar views currently in the air is NOA's stubborn refusal to amplify the concept of truth by providing a theory or analysis (or even a metaphorical picture). Rather, NOA recognises in 'truth' a concept already in use and agrees to abide by the standards rules of usage.
>
> (1986: 133)

Fine argues that the realism versus anti-realism debate attempts to inflate the concept of truth 'already in use'. He suggests that no such inflation is necessary and that philosophers should simply live happily with the fact that all there is to be said about truth in science is captured by the notion 'already in use'. 'The general idea', he says, 'is to accept entrenched uses but to refrain from the project of seeing those uses as grounded in the 'nature of truth', some deep truth-making properties, or the like. Thus, NOA does not think that truth is an explanatory concept, or that there is some general thing that makes truths true' (1986a: 175). Explaining his stance more recently, he notes: 'NOA argues that the concept of truth cannot be rejected but sees [it] as operating openly in local and specific contexts and hence as resistant to the kinds of general theories (or 'interpretations' or 'meta-narratives') that long have constituted the bread and butter of philosophy of science' (1996: 174).

What exactly does Fine say on truth? What exactly does he deny and what does he affirm? Passages such as the above (and the overall spirit of his relevant writings) do not make his position clear enough, so I think we are in need of some interpretive work. In particular, we need to extract some position from Fine's writings which is detailed enough to be thoroughly evaluated. I suggest that there are two readings of Fine's account of truth, which I call the 'negative attitude' and the 'positive attitude' respectively. The *negative attitude* starts with the assumption that there is a concept of truth 'already in use' in science but questions whether truth has a deeper nature that admits of further philosophical investigation and analysis. The *positive attitude* seeks to say something more specific about the operative concept of truth. It can be interpreted as implying that a minimalist–deflationist account is enough to characterise it adequately.

In analysing these two sides to Fine's account, I argue for four theses.

1   If NOA is right in arguing that there is a concept of truth 'already in use' in science, then NOA is inconsistent with some traditional forms of (positivist) anti-realism.
2   What Fine calls the 'core position' in the realism–anti-realism debate, viz. that the results of scientific investigations are true, if at all, 'on a par with more homely truths', is not about the concept of truth at all.
3   A *correspondence* theory of truth adequately explicates the concept of truth 'already in use'.
4   NOA's philosophical minimalism goes against the very possibility of doing epistemology of science.

Fine's deflationism

Fine's 'deflationist' account of science has been motivated by two considerations:

1   Both realism and anti-realism inflate the concept of truth 'already in use' in science. Realism gives an 'outer direction' to scientific truths: it renders them truths *about* a mind-independent world. Anti-realism, on the other hand, adds an 'inner dimension' to scientific truths: it reduces truth to human-oriented epistemic notions; it restricts truths within the confines of human epistemic reach (1986: 133; 1986a: 150).
2   Philosophical theories, be they realist or anti-realist, are unnatural attachments to science. They try to 'authenticate' science. In particular, realism aspires to provide an 'outside' authentication of science: science is *about the world*. Anti-realist positions, on the other hand, aspire to provide

an 'inward' authentication of science: science is *about us humans* and our relations with the observable world.

To these inflationary and 'hermeneutic' philosophical attitudes, Fine opposes his own deflationism. NOA recommends: 'Try to take science on its own terms, and try not to read things into science' (1986: 149). And again: 'NOA tries to let science speak for itself, and it trusts in our native ability to get the message without having to rely on metaphysical or epistemological hearing aids' (ibid.: 150).

NOA, according to Fine, rejects *'all* interpretations, construals, pictures, etc., of truth', be they based on some correspondence relation, or on some acceptance relation, or what have you (1986: 149). Instead, it recognises in 'truth' a fundamental semantic concept 'already in use' in science (as well as in everyday life) and abides by 'the standard rules of usage' (1986: 133). These rules involve the usual 'Davidsonian–Tarskian referential semantics' and support 'a thoroughly classical logic of inference' (ibid.). Fine thinks that ascriptions of truth in general, and of scientific truth in particular, are to be understood 'in the usual referential way so that a sentence (or statement) is true just in case the entities referred to stand in the referred to relation' (1986: 130).

Consequently, NOA adheres to the standard criterion of ontological commitment: those who accept a statement as true are committed to 'the existence of the individuals, properties, relations, processes and so forth referred to by the scientific statements that [they] accept as true' (ibid.). More specifically, NOA is happy to sanction commitments to the existence of unobservable entities, if the presumed-true scientific statements involve reference to unobservables. As for the epistemic attitude towards scientific theories, NOA contends that the degree of confidence in the truth of a given scientific theory will determine the degree of belief in the existence of the entities posited by this theory, where the former is 'tutored by ordinary relations of confirmation and evidential support, subject to the usual scientific canons' (ibid.).

The 'standard rules of usage' of the concept of truth 'already in use' must, no doubt, include the usual disquotational property: for any statement 'P', 'P' is true if and only if P. Besides, given Fine's explicit endorsement of the usual 'Davidsonian–Tarskian referential semantics', this concept is understood in connection with the concept of reference, where the semantic value of a statement 'P' (its truth, in particular) is determined by the semantic values of its constituent terms and predicates. Hence, if one is ready to assert, for instance, that snow is white, one should also be ready to assert that 'Snow is white' is true (and conversely), and one should also be ready to assert that 'Snow is white' is true because the referred-to entity (snow) has the referred-to property (is white). For many philosophers, the position just described is nothing but Tarski's own 'semantic conception of truth', and this is taken to be explication of the intuition behind the so-called 'correspondence theory of truth'. Alan Musgrave, for instance, has noted in connection with Fine's view: 'I have always thought (with Tarski himself) that the semantic conception of truth is a version of the common-sense correspondence theory of truth' (1989: 37). He goes on to stress that 'Realists can think that Tarski gives them as much of a correspondence theory as they need' (ibid.: 38). But now we have reached an impasse. For it seems from Fine's sketch that the concept of truth 'already in use' is that which realists have all along thought to be their own. And if the notion of 'correspondence' is made precise in the way Tarski and Davidson have suggested (i.e. that a statement is true just in case the referred-to entities stand in the referred-to relations), then Fine's NOA has just paid a compliment to the realist account of truth.

Things, however, are rarely quite so straightforward. Fine does not think he has vindicated a realist account of truth. We have seen him insisting that realists, somehow, inflate the concept of truth that NOA endorses, that they add a special interpretation: 'a desk-thumping, foot-stamping shout of "Really"' (1986: 129). So, for Fine, the battle cannot be over so quickly. He insists that the concept of truth 'already in use' is neutral *vis-à-vis* the assorted interpretations added to it. I do not think this is entirely correct (I do think that Musgrave's points are definitely in the right direction). But before engaging with this issue, it is important to try to understand what Fine's position amounts to.

Theories of truth

Let us first analyse carefully the 'hermeneutic' conceptions to which Fine is opposed. Terms such as 'realism' and 'anti-realism' are multi-faceted and mean different things to different people. If, however, we focus on a truth-based characterisation of the realism–anti-realism debate – a characterisation that Fine attacks – things become concrete. A realist account of truth puts the following robust gloss on truth-ascriptions: they should be understood as non-epistemic claims in that the concept of truth employed in them is not linked conceptually to irreducibly epistemic notions such as 'conclusive verification', or 'warranted assertibility', or 'idealised justification'. The reason for this is that realists take seriously the following two ideas: (a) that assertions have truth-makers and (b) that, ultimately, what these truth-makers are hinges on what the world is like independent of our theorising and not on the criteria of epistemic appraisal we may use. A non-epistemic account of the concept of truth is motivated as the best way to capture the intuition that scientific discourse is about a 'mind-independent' world, that is a world whose structure and content are independent of the epistemic standards science uses to appraise theories. If 'truth' is, ultimately, an epistemic concept, there could not possibly be a divergence between a circumstance in which the relevant epistemic notion applied and a circumstance in which a certain assertion was true. So, for instance, if the favourite epistemic notion is 'ideal justification', then there can be *no* divergence in the circumstances under which an assertion is ideally justified and the circumstances under which it is true. Consequently, it would be impossible for an assertion to satisfy the epistemic condition (e.g. be ideally justified) *and* be false. It follows that what is true of the world could not possibly be different from the description of the world that gets licensed by the relevant set of criteria of epistemic appraisal: it *would be* what gets so licensed. The way the world is could not, therefore, be independent of a set of descriptions which meets the relevant set of criteria of epistemic appraisal.

In contrast to a realist conception of truth, anti-realism asserts that the concept of truth should be essentially epistemically constrained. In line with my remarks on p. xxi, I shall call this position *anti-realism*. It is associated mainly with the work of Dummett and Putnam. Dummett employs a notion of 'warranted assertibility', whereas Putnam talks of 'idealised justification'. Anti-realists too take assertions to have truth-makers. Where they differ from realists is that (a) they conceive of these truth-makers as a set of (ideal) epistemic conditions – the conditions which render a statement warrantedly assertible; and (b) they link the truth of an assertion with its knowability or recognisability. In typically anti-realist accounts, if an assertion cannot be known to be true, or if it cannot be recognised as true, then it cannot possibly be true. As Dummett once put it, a 'statement cannot be true unless we know it to be true, at least indirectly, or unless we have means to arrive at such knowledge, or at least unless there exists that which, if we were aware of it, would yield such knowledge' (1982: 108).[1] To be sure, the notion of 'warranted assertibility' is too weak, as Crispin Wright (1992) has shown, to capture intuitively compelling aspects of the concept of truth. Unlike dairy products, truth should *not* have 'a best-before date'. If something is true, it stays true whatever further information we might pile on and whatever further evidence we might gain. In Wright's words (1992: 45), truth is 'stable' (it cannot be defeated by any further evidence) and 'absolute' (it cannot be improved by any further information). 'Warranted assertibility', however, is both unstable (since further evidence could remove the warrant) and relative (since further information can improve on the warrant).

All this means that the required epistemic concept which anti-realists should use to reduce truth needs to be suitably strengthened so that the warrant which confers 'warranted assertibility' on a statement is both stable and absolute. Wright (1992) has proposed a notion of *superassertibility* which, by definition, meets these requirements. Important though it may be, this issue need not worry us here. For the preceding discussion has just aimed to get out of the way two points.

1   A realist non-epistemic account of truth, as well as its rival (anti-realist) epistemic accounts, understand truth-ascriptions in a *substantive* way, where truth requires truth-makers. Realists and anti-realists have different approaches towards the required truth-makers, yet they take it

that true statements have something substantive in common: the fact that their worldly truth-makers obtain – on a realist account – or the fact that their (super)assertibility conditions obtain – on an anti-realist account.

2   Understood as above, the debate between realism and anti-realism centres, ultimately, around the following issue: should the concept of truth be such that it guarantees (or, at least, allows) that assertions are made true by worldly truth-makers which are independent both of our means to theorise about the world and of the circumstances under which we come to 'warrantedly assert' our theories and opinions? The realist conception of truth is such that it makes this independence possible, whereas the anti-realist conception denies this independence by tying conceptually what is true of the world to what, ultimately, can be known of it.

There is, however, an alternative approach to the debate about the concept of truth. One can simply deny that truth is the kind of concept that admits of a substantive analysis, since one can claim that anything which can be said *with* the truth-predicate 'is true' can also be said *without* it. So, the alternative claim is that since the truth-predicate is gratuitous, or redundant, there is no need for a complex account of the concept of truth. How can that be? One can start with the observation that 'is true' is gratuitous in all occurrences of the schema '"P" is true', where 'P' is a statement, since, by the disquotational property of the truth-predicate, asserting that '"P" is true' is equivalent to asserting P (given the English language). So one can replace *all* occurrences of instances of the schema '"P" is true' by the statements themselves. (So, for instance, '"Snow is white" is true' is equivalent to 'snow is white'.)

If this were all there is to the use of the truth-predicate, the line under discussion says, then this predicate would be totally eliminable: talk which involved the truth-predicate could be paraphrased in terms of talk that did not, without any loss of information, since when we add 'is true' to a certain statement 'P' we would say precisely what we would have said, had we simply asserted the statement 'P' itself. But unfortunately, it goes on, there are occurrences of the truth-predicate in statements which cannot be so eliminated. For instance, we *cannot* replace statements of the form 'All valid arguments with true premises have true conclusions', or 'Whatever Plato said was true', with others which do not involve the truth-predicate. This is because we would have to replace each such statement with an infinite (or finite but very long) conjunction of assertions (e.g. Plato said p & Plato said q & ...). Without the predicate 'is true' the paraphrase of such assertions, e.g. 'Whatever Plato said was true', would be literally endless. And that is precisely why, on the present account, we need the truth-predicate in our language: we use it to express generalisations such as the above and solely for this reason. So the truth-predicate is restricted to being a quasi-logical device implicated only in the expression of certain generalisations which cannot be properly (or fully) stated without it. This is what is sometimes called the 'minimalist theory of truth' (cf. Horwich, 1990; Williams, 1986).[2] I come back to this account later, but it is important to keep in mind that it emphatically denies that truth is 'a complex property' which admits of a substantive theory or analysis. In particular, the minimalist account denies that there are deep truth-making properties.

To many, the debate outlined thus far is quite familiar and very important. But where exactly does Fine stand in it? He clearly denies that a substantive account of truth is (or should be) part and parcel of the concept of truth 'already in use' in science. He urges us to 'stop conceiving of truth as a substantial something – something for which theories, accounts, or even pictures are appropriate' (1986: 142) But there is an ambiguity in what exactly he wants to deny and what exactly he wants to assert. I think there are two readings of his position. The first is that he adopts a purely *negative* attitude, while the second suggests that he adopts a *positive* attitude, too. (Since these are consistent with each other, he might adopt both.) The negative attitude just assumes that *there is* a clear concept of truth 'already in use' in science and complains that realist and anti-realist theories perform an illegitimate move by trying to add some interpretative gloss to it. As he put it recently: NOA places 'emphasis on retaining the ordinary concept of truth' and rejects 'both sides of the standard dualisms – both realism *and* anti-realism . . . ' (1996: 174). In this negative mode, Fine seems to think that there is little that can (or should) be said about the concept of truth 'already in use'. He stresses that we should 'take "true" as primitive' and should not 'trade in so-called theories of truth, whether realist or anti-realist' (ibid.: 184).

However, it is also very tempting to interpret Fine as favouring the previously outlined minimalist account. Even here, though, there is some residual ambiguity. He himself notes 'Although I am sympathetic to the deflationary approach to truth defended by Horwich (1990), I still prefer a plain no-theory attitude' (1996: 184). What this 'no-theory' attitude is, if it is anything distinct from the aforementioned dismissal of interpretations, is unclear. When he first introduced this 'no-theory' conception of truth (see 1986a: 175), he depicted it along the lines of the minimalist conception of truth. For accepting, as Fine does, 'the usual logic and grammar of truth, (including its redundancy property)' while denying that there is such a thing as 'the nature of truth' or 'some deep truth-making properties', *is* what minimalists advocate when they 'fill in' the bare bones of their accounts (cf. Horwich, 1990).

I think some interpretive work is necessary. In line with what I have just noted, one may interpret Fine's position on truth either as *agnostic* or as *atheistic*. It is an agnostic position insofar as Fine suggests either that we do not (cannot) know whether the concept of truth has a deeper nature, or that it is philosophically pointless to enquire into the deeper nature of truth.

But it is an atheistic position insofar as Fine argues that the concept of truth has *no* deeper nature, but instead its content is exhausted by the foregoing minimalist (quasi-logical) account. In what follows, I examine in some detail these two interpretations (which correspond to what I earlier called Fine's 'negative' and 'positive' attitudes respectively).

The negative attitude

One of Fine's central contentions is that realists as well as anti-realists accept what he calls the 'core position' concerning truth, viz. the results of scientific investigations are true, if at all, 'on a par with more homely truths'. Yet, he says, realists 'add onto' this core position by saying that these truths are *made* true by, and are *about*, the world, while anti-realists 'add onto' this core position by arguing that they are true because of the right kind of epistemic condition (cf. 1986: 128–129). I think Fine's claim can be challenged on two grounds. First, Fine's 'core position' is at odds with some forms of anti-realism. Second, even if Fine's 'core position' is universally accepted (as it is by modern anti-realists as well as by realists), it is not about the *concept* of truth at all. Rather, it is about whether there is a relevant semantic difference between types of statement which may be accepted as true. If this last point is right, then it simply does not follow that any additions to the 'core position' are illegitimate, simply because these 'additions' concern the concept of truth, whereas the 'core position' on its own does not engender a concept of truth. Let me defend these two points in turn.

The 'core position' and positivist anti-realism

The apparent force of Fine's claim that there is a 'core position' on truth shared by all sides in the realism debate rests on an indifference to the development of the debates over the status of theoretical entities and theoretical assertions. Scientific realists have always taken scientists' claims about unobservable entities at 'face value'. Their point has always been that (a) the world is populated by the unobservable natural kinds posited by well-confirmed scientific theories and (b) well-confirmed scientific beliefs are true of the entities they posit for the very same reasons, and in the very same way, in which commonsense beliefs about tables and chairs are true of those objects. In fact, most current realists insist that ontological commitments to theoretical entities are just an extension of the ontological commitments to commonsense objects (cf. Devitt 1984; Newton-Smith 1989a).

However, as we have already seen in some detail in Chapters 1–3, these realist views have been challenged by instrumentalists, phenomenalists. reductionists, conventionalists, fictionalists and what have you. In or' distinguish these views from the anti-realism of Dummett and F may call them collectively *positivist anti-realism*. There is no reason to iterate these positions here. But in order to make my point clear, it is important briefly to remind the reader that positivist anti-realism has treated theoretical entities as abbreviating schemes for the description of the complex relationships between observables, hypothetical constructs, auxiliary devices, *façons de parler*, nothing-but-useful-fictions, etc. Similarly, positivist anti-realism has treated theoretical assertions as claims about the actual and possible behaviour of observable entities, instrumental steps, shorthand for classes of 'if–then' statements, reducible to sets of observational statements, and the like. More generally, positivist anti-realism has treated theoretical discourse either as having assertoric content, which is, however, reducible to observational content, or as being non-assertoric. Reductive empiricists, for instance, who take assertions about putative unobservable entities to be *reducible* to assertions solely about observable entities, may well accept that theoretical assertions can be true, insofar as the relevant observable circumstances obtain. But they would deny that the truth of theoretical assertions commits them to the independent (irreducible) reality of unobservable entities. Similarly, fictionalists would deny that theoretical discourse is assertoric (and hence truth-valuable) in the first place. It has been among this set of attempted (re-)interpretations of claims about unobservables that realists have taken a robust view of the truth of science's theoretical assertions and have defended the independent (and irreducible) existence of the referents of theoretical terms. The realist claim about independent existence grounds the view that assertions about theoretical entities should be taken 'literally', and hence the view that assertions concerning the truth of theoretical statements should be taken to have irreducible assertoric content. Similarly, the claim about the factual reference of theoretical terms grounds the distinction between what evidence there is for the empirical manifestations of theoretical entities and what is *true* of these entities.

With the possible exception of those who advocate the full reducibility of theoretical discourse, positivist anti-realist positions emphatically do *not* share with realism Fine's 'core position'. They do not even grant that theoretical assertions are truth-valuable, or that they are true, if at all, on a par with more homely truths. Fine thinks that the realist 'desk-thumping, foot-stamping' attitude exemplified in the claim 'Electrons *really* exist' is an inflation of the concept of truth 'already in use' in science. He notes with disdain that, in their attempt to explain the robust sense which realists attribute to their truth-claims, realists argue: 'There really are electrons, really!' (1986: 129). These claims, Fine goes on, are said to be about reality – 'what is really, really the case' (ibid.). However, the realists' alleged inflation of the concept of truth 'already in use' is more of a call to take science literally than anything else. As Smart (1963: 35) has pointed out, the 'real' or 'really' to which realists appeal is meant precisely to block the equation of theoretical entities with theoretical fictions (like lines of force), logical constructions (like the average height), or non-existent objects (like unicorns). To sum up, not only is the so-called 'core position' not universally accepted, but the realists' 'desk-thumping, foot-stamping' attitude has aimed precisely to motivate and defend the 'core position' which Fine places at the heart of NOA. If I am right, then NOA is incompatible with some forms of anti-realism: for positivist anti-realists deny one (of the few) thing(s) that NOA asserts.

What is the 'core position' about?

As noted above, however, the most important point to be made is that the 'core position', as Fine describes it, is *not* about the concept of truth at all. There is no doubt that, unlike positivist anti-realists, modern anti-realists take scientific theories literally. There is also no doubt that they accept Fine's 'core position' – that is, that the results of scientific investigations are true, if at all, 'on a par with more homely truths'. So is the philosophical debate between realism and anti-realism an illegitimate and unmotivated addition to the uncontested 'core position'?

If you look at the 'core position', as formulated by Fine, it becomes clear that it is *not* a position about what truth *is*. Rather, it is a position about which statements may be legitimately accepted as true and whether different types of statement should admit of different types of truth-evaluation. Two parties may take exactly the same set of assertions to be true and also agree that all types of statement within a discourse are subjected to the very same standards of truth-evaluation, and yet disagree as to what exactly each attributes to a statement when they say that it is true. So looking at the 'core position' does nothing to elucidate the issue of which concept of truth is operative in a discourse.

What is going on here should be quite clear: two concepts might agree on their extension, but be different concepts. Here we have two (or more) concepts which are candidates for the *concept* of truth. They may be co-extensive (which is what the 'core position', in effect, asserts), but whether they are the same concept, or whether they are all fit for the concept of truth, are issues that still need to be dealt with.

Let us focus on science. The 'core position' there is the following: there is no relevant semantic difference between statements couched in an observational (homely) vocabulary and statements couched in a theoretical (exotic) vocabulary. Take, now, realists and anti-realists. They apply different semantic standards, but they apply them uniformly. Realists would endow both homely and exotic statements with irreducible and independent truth-conditions. Anti-realists would go for evidence-constrained semantics: they would, for instance, endow both types of statement with (super)assertibility conditions and would say that they are true if and only if their (super)assertibility conditions obtain. Given that difference, both realists and anti-realists can agree (*contingently*) on the very same set as being the set of true statements. For instance, they would both agree that 'Neutrinos are emitted in a β-decay' is true and that 'Roses blossom in spring' is true. So what is their difference? Clearly, it is that they have different (although overlapping, given that both accept the features relevant to the disquotational property of the truth-predicate) concepts of truth. On the realist conception a statement may be (super)assertible without being true, and conversely. But on the anti-realist conception this is not an option. (As noted earlier in this chapter on p. 231, realists allow for a possible divergence in the extensions of the set of true statements and the set of (super)assertible statements, whereas the anti-realists do not.) Fine thinks that they 'add something' to the core position. They certainly do. But since the 'core position' is not about the concept of truth, what they add to it is a concept of truth which the 'core position' simply lacks. This addition should not be jettisoned as illegitimate. The 'core position' on its own does not engender a concept of truth, although it is compatible with different such concepts.

In several places, Fine takes the view that the 'core position' is, all by itself, sufficient for our philosophical reflections on science. He stresses: 'the core position [is] all by itself, a compelling one, one that we ought to take to heart' (1986: 130). And later he adds: 'NOA suggests that the legitimate features of [the realist and anti-realist] additions are already contained in the presumed equal status of everyday truths with scientific ones, and in our accepting them both as *truths*. No other additions are legitimate, and none are required' (ibid.: 133). I think this, at best, can be only partially true. It is certainly true that the shared 'core position' is enough to make both realists and modern anti-realists take seriously modern science and its truth-linked aspirations. But, on its own, the 'core position' gives us no clue as to what is ascribed to an assertion when it is said to be true. And it is exactly there that realists and anti-realists differ. Even if Fine were to take the strong (atheistic) view that *nothing* is ascribed to an assertion when it is said to be true, that would be just another philosophical theory which competes with both the realist and the anti-realist accounts.

A possible objection at this stage is that Fine's negative (or agnostic) attitude may well aim to show that this dispute about the concept of truth does *not* matter. But this does not follow from the fact that both realists and anti-realists agree on the 'core position'. Two parties may agree that they see a red rose, but they may well disagree on what is ascribed to the rose when it is called 'red', or on the basis of what property the rose is red, or in virtue of which relations it is classified alongside other red objects. So Fine is in need of further philosophical argumentation in order to defend his negative attitude. In any case, I wish now to argue that the philosophical debate about the concept of truth *does* matter, even if all parties (contingently) agree on which statements should be accepted as true. Unless we have already established that there is no deep truth-making property, be it (ultimately) the world or a set of epistemic criteria, it is theoretically important and challenging to examine whether truth has a deep nature. So, unless we have already shown that the concept of truth operative in a discourse is fully accounted for by a minimalist account, it is an open question whether or not truth is a substantive property. And if it is an open question, we (philosophers) should try to answer it by devising theories. The situation here is analogous to examining whether there is some deep(er) property in virtue of which all red things are red. This is a theoretical issue which is not to be settled by looking at whether we agree or not that a certain bunch of objects are all red. What we need are substantive theories about properties which, if present, would explain why all the objects in the bunch have a certain feature. That is how theoretical investigation proceeds and that is how progress occurs. In order for Fine to close off this issue (that is, in order for his negative attitude to be successful), some positive attitude towards the concept of truth is required, and not some positive attitude as to which statements we should take to be true. In particular, Fine's strategy requires defence of the claim that truth is *not* a substantive property, since if it is not there is no point in searching for a substantive account. So, all we are left with are several *theories* about the nature of truth, one of which is that truth is not a substantive property (apparently, Fine's view). The defence of any particular theory requires engagement with the philosophical issue of whether a substantive theory of truth can be correct. There seems to be no way out of it for Fine, no less than for anyone else.

I do not think Fine would so easily give up his negative attitude towards the philosophical debate about concept of truth. In fact, he occasionally seems to take the view that a literal understanding of the truth-ascriptions in science *exhausts* his so-called 'no-theory' conception of truth. For instance, he says that his 'no-theory' conception of truth is akin to what 'van Fraassen usually means by taking truth 'literally'; i.e. as an unanalysed term whose use is basic and well understood' (1986a: 175). And he remarks that '"literal" is meant to exclude the correspondence metaphors of realism' (ibid.: 157, n. 6). Against this, there is no point repeating that the 'core position', on its own, is not a concept of truth. So, I shall try a different route.

Suppose that Fine is right in suggesting that taking the truth of scientific assertions literally is based on a 'basic and well-understood' concept of truth which requires no further analysis. Then, by taking theories non-literally, all positivist anti-realists had failed to understand a basic concept. Hence, explaining this basic notion to them (even by thumping tables, so to speak) must have been a legitimate philosophical engagement. Now, if Fine is right in thinking that the concept of truth is 'unanalysable', what needs to be explained to positivist anti-realists is not the concept of truth itself, but *how to use* this concept. But this is hopeless. For their problem was not that they did not know how to *use* the concept. After all, they did use it, since they thought that observational discourse was truth-valuable. Rather, their problem was that the concept of truth (and cognate notions) was not appropriate for theoretical discourse. That is, they thought that the concept of truth did not *apply* to theoretical discourse, since they thought that theoretical discourse did not report (even putatively) anything about irreducible and independently existing entities. It should be clear, then, that persuading them to take theoretical discourse *literally* cannot rest on explaining to them how to use an 'unanalysable' (and 'already in use') concept of truth. Rather, it can rest only on *analysing* this concept and on showing that a consistent application of the concept of truth licenses assertoric theoretical discourse no less than it licenses assertoric observational discourse. The most appropriate way to proceed in this analysis is to argue that, no less than observational statements, theoretical statements should be allowed to have *truth-makers*: as observational assertions are about observable things and are true when the observable things are the way they are described to be, so theoretical assertions are about unobservable things and are true when the unobservable things are the way they are described to be.

So, the (innocent-looking) claim that theories should be understood literally implicates a concept of truth which at least makes it possible that theoretical assertions have truth-makers. To say that, if true, the assertion 'Neutrinos are emitted in a β-decay' is literally true is much more substantive than Fine thinks. For it at least commits its advocates to the view that, among the many possible interpretations of the statement 'Neutrinos are emitted in a β-decay', there is one that commits to neutrinos and β-decays. What makes *this* interpretation the literal one is, surely, a prior commitment to the claim that theoretical statements have irreducible truth-makers.[3] Realists and anti-realists simply disagree on whether or not these truth-makers are independent of the means by which we are able to know them.[4] But the point here is not which of them is right and which wrong. Rather, the point is that the very thought that theoretical assertions should be understood literally implicates a concept of truth which admits of further analysis; and that this concept is much more substantive than Fine thinks.[5] So, even were we to grant that the concept of truth 'already in use' in science is *just* the concept implicated in the literal understanding of scientific theories, then neither realists nor anti-realists would illegitimately inflate this concept.

To recapitulate: Fine's negative attitude cannot be maintained. The 'core position' is not about the concept of truth operative in science. But even if we force it to be the case that the operative notion of truth has whatever features are necessary for taking all types of scientific assertion literally, even then this notion of truth requires (and hence makes possible) that scientific assertions have truth-makers.

The positive attitude

We have already seen Fine claiming that he does *not* want to endorse a minimalist–deflationist theory of truth. Recall what he says: 'Although I am sympathetic to the deflationary approach to truth defended by Horwich (1990), I still prefer a plain no-theory attitude' (1996: 184). Yet Fine sometimes seems to argue against realism by advocating as the standard everyday conception, applicable to observational statements as well as to theoretical ones, a *thin* (minimalist–disquotational) conception of truth. So, for instance, he rejects the views that truth has an essence (see 1986: 142), that truth is an 'explanatory concept', that 'there is a some general thing that makes truths true' (1986: 175). Compare this with Horwich's claim that 'it is unjustified and false . . . [that] "is true" attributes a complex property, *truth* – an ingredient of reality whose underlying essence will, it is hoped, one day be revealed by philosophical or scientific analysis' (1990: 2). And again with this: 'unlike most predicates, "is true" should not be expected to participate in some deep theory of that to which it refers – a theory which goes beyond a specification of what the word means' (ibid.). Now, Horwich's minimalist–deflationist theory is nothing but the view outlined earlier (pp. 233–234): that the truth-predicate is a formal predicate which 'exists solely for the sake of a certain logical need' (1990: 2), viz. to construct generalisations of the form 'What Plato said was true' (see also Williams 1986). On this view, 'nothing more about truth needs to be assumed' (Horwich 1990: 6).

It may be that Fine does not want even to *assert* as much as Horwich does, but that he nonetheless wants to *deny* as much as Horwich does. For Horwich offers at least an account of the *meaning* (and the role) of a truth-predicate, whereas Fine seems keen to abstain even from this. Thus:

> If pressed to answer the question of what, then, does it *mean* to say that something is true (or to what does the truth of so-and-so commit one), NOA will reply by pointing to the logical relations engendered by the specific claim and by focusing, then, on the concrete historical circumstances that ground that particular judgement of truth. For, after all, there *is* nothing more to say.
>
> (Fine 1986: 134)

But this is hardly credible. For, as we have seen, Fine *does* have a few positive things to say about the concept of truth: that it respects the Tarski–Davidson semantics, the redundancy property of the truth-predicate, etc. And, in any case, discussing 'the concrete historical circumstances that ground [a] particular judgement of truth' has nothing to do with the issue of the concept of truth which is operative in a certain discourse. The only thing it relates to is the circumstance under which a particular judgement of truth took place, not which concept of truth was involved in this particular judgement.

Fine, however, might want to entertain the view that different concepts of truth operate in different cases in which a judgement of truth is made. But, if so, we are certainly in need of more philosophical argumentation. When it comes to scientific discourse, this means that we need some further argument that, for instance, on some occasions the operative concept of truth is realist, on some other occasions anti-realist, and on other yet different occasions a minimalist one. But it is up to Fine to produce such an argument. In any case, one could (plausibly) argue, along the lines of Wright (1992: 23), that once a truth-predicate satisfies the minimal properties that are required of it to function as a truth-predicate, it is an open issue whether the occurrence of a truth-predicate in different discourses has one or more than one substance (e.g. scientific discourse, moral discourse, aesthetic discourse, etc.). In this case, one would leave it open whether there is a uniform concept of truth applying over *different* discourses. But Fine's point seems different. For he implies that even within the *same* discourse, e.g. scientific discourse, there may be different concepts of truth operating. I do not see how this can be the case without an outright *relativism* resulting about the concept of truth. So, I think Fine needs to support this claim, if indeed he means to make it.

In what follows I assume that Fine's positive attitude advocates a mini-malist–deflationist account of truth in scientific discourse. And although, as we have seen already, Fine is not clear on this matter, I think that he would stand to gain in clarity were he to adopt the minimalist–deflationist account of truth. For if he did, he would not be in the uncomfortable position to deny that there is a uniform – but minimal – conception of truth operative in scientific discourse. Besides, by adopting explicitly the minimalist–defla-tionist account of truth, he would not compromise his 'no-theory' conception, since deflationists typically argue that their account does not add up to a 'heavyweight' theory of truth (cf. Williams, 1986: 223).

Note that thus far in this chapter I have not really taken sides in the realism versus anti-realism debate, although it should be clear that my heart lies with realism. I have refrained from taking sides because the main point to be made was that, contrary to what Fine says, there is still need for philo-sophical debate about the concept truth: it is still an open issue whether or not truth is a substantive concept. But, from now on, I intend to defend the realist cause, first by focusing on the debate between a realist 'correspon-dence' account and the deflationist view, and subsequently by challenging a few typically anti-realist accounts of truth.

The standard way to proceed when discussing a thin (minimalist) concep-tion of truth is to enquire whether such a conception of truth can explain *all* facts involving truth. The issue here is the *explanatory completeness* of a thin account. Horwich and other deflationists (e.g. Williams 1986) argue that their account is explanatorily complete: it explains everything that there is to know about the role of a truth-predicate in a language. Their oppo-nents, be they realist or anti-realist, argue that there are salient facts about truth that are not explained by a thin account (see Devitt 1984; Field 1972; 1992; Papineau 1993; Putnam 1985; Wright 1992). Given that this issue has been debated thoroughly in the literature, and that I have nothing much to add in defence of a thicker account of truth to whatever has been offered by the above philosophers, I want to proceed in a different way. My aim is to show that a thicker *correspondence* theory of truth can adequately explicate the concept of truth involved in Fine's suggestion that we 'treat truth in the usual referential way so that a sentence (or a statement) is true just in case the entities referred to stand in the referred-to relation' (1986: 130).

'Correspondence' and deflationist accounts of truth are 'half-rivals'. At a first level of approximation, they both take the concept of truth to be non-epistemic. Realists make this the defining feature of the concept of truth, whereas deflationists just take this as implied by their minimal concept of truth. Williams, for instance, notes that on deflationary views 'truth is no more an epistemic property than it is on a full-blooded correspondence theory' (1986: 224). He adds: 'Someone convinced that truth *must* be some kind of epistemic property might well think of the disquotational account as a kind of minimal realism' (ibid.). Besides, both realists and deflationists agree that there is a very close connection between saying, for instance, that 'snow is white' *is true* and saying *that* snow is white. So, the difference between deflationist accounts and 'more-than-minimal' realist accounts is whether or not a non-epistemic account should conceive of truth as a substantive property. In particular, their difference is whether or not statements such as '"snow is white" is true if and only if snow is white' implicate a more substantive 'correspondence' account of truth.

So-called correspondence theories of truth rely on the thought (or, the platitude, as Wright 1992: 25 puts it) that to say a statement *is* true is to say that things are as the statement describes them to be. Deflationists are perfectly happy with this thought. Both Horwich and Williams, for instance, try to accommodate this element of truth-ascription in their accounts. Horwich is perfectly happy with the idea that '"Snow is white" is true *because* snow is white' (1990: 111), and thinks that statements like this are enough to capture the intuitive pull of the idea that 'each truth is made true by the existence of a corresponding fact' (ibid.: 112); and Williams argues that deflationary accounts make available the 'minimal "correspondence"' expressed in the realist claim of correspondence between language items and extra-linguistic reality (1986: 233). But if the central thought behind 'correspondence' theories is so strong that even deflationists' accounts aim to capture it, what *is* the problem with the realist 'correspondence' account?

Wright complains that although deflationism may do justice to some correspondence 'phraseology' (1992: 27) Horwich's detailed account cannot capture the robust sense in which realists talk of correspondence to reality (ibid.: 83). According to Wright, the realist conception of correspondence takes seriously the idea that 'the truth of a statement consists in its representation of something external, in its holding up a mirror to the world' (ibid.). Williams would certainly agree with Wright's complaint. For he himself argues that the deflationists' 'minimal correspondence' is not enough to capture the realist claim of 'physical correspondence or any other substantial theory' (1986: 233).

I am not at all sure how to understand metaphors such as 'holding up a mirror to the world'. But I intend to argue that a story of the form '"Snow is white" is true *because* snow is white' *is* robust enough to capture the intended realist sense of 'correspondence'. Wright's complaint against Horwich is that in order for stories such as this to capture the realist notion of correspondence it has to be the case that 'a state of affairs (snow's being white)' should be 'the *source* of the truth of the sentence "snow is white"' (Wright 1992: 26). He may well be right that Horwich's own deflationist account fails to capture the idea of a *source* of truth. In fact, if Horwich managed to capture this idea, that he was offering a non-substantive account of truth would be a matter of doubt. But there is no reason to think that a substantive conception of correspondence should admit anything more than (a variant of) what Wright has just pointed out, viz. that snow's being white is the source of the truth that 'snow is white'. I think this is all that it should admit. The realist idea that 'correspondence' gives a substantive account of truth is fully captured by claims of the form: the source of the truth of a sentence '*P*' is *P*. Add to this the Tarskian notion of satisfaction (reference) which allows the semantic properties of the parts of the state-ment, i.e. the denotation of terms and the extension of predicates, to determine truth-conditions. What you get is a thick-enough conception of truth. Why should realists strive for more? On reflection, what we have thereby reached is an account of truth where the source of the truth of a statement '*P*' is that the referred-to entities stand in the referred-to rela-tions. What makes the referred-to entities standing in the referred-to relations the *source* of the truth of a statement is that the referred-to entities *do* stand in the referred-to relations – that snow has the property of being white, etc. A statement such that the referred-to entities *do* stand in the referred-to rela-tions 'corresponds' to reality. In sum, the realist 'correspondence' account of truth is nothing but a *summary* of the claim that statements are true whenever the entities being referred to have the properties, or stand in the relations, being referred to. If this line is right, then the realist 'correspon-dence' theory merely explicates the concept of truth involved in Fine's suggestion that we 'treat truth in the usual referential way so that a sentence (or a statement) is true just in case the entities referred to stand in the referred-to relation' (1986: 130).

The immediate objection here is that I have just shifted the focus from the concept of truth to the concept of *reference*. For what makes it the case that a certain entity rather than anything else is being referred to by a certain term or predicate? This is exactly where the whole issue turns. It is not about the explication of the realist conception of correspondence. This is easy. It is about the theory of reference that needs to be in place in order to make the realist notion of correspondence *thick*. And that is exactly where realists and deflationists disagree. Realists rely on a substantive theory of reference, most typically on the Kripke–Putnam causal theory, where the semantic properties of a language are fixed by means of causal chains that connect the linguistic atoms (terms and predicates) with their referents, and hence statements with their truth-conditions (cf. Field 1972: 366–367).

Deflationists, on the other hand, deny that there is a substantive theory of reference and put forward semi-formal accounts of how reference gets fixed (cf. Horwich 1990: 122–123). I discuss the causal theory of reference and defend a version of it which is suitable for realism in Chapter 12. For the time being, I simply rest my case by noting the following: if Fine's suggestion that we 'treat truth in the usual referential way so that a sentence (or a statement) is true just in case the entities referred to stand in the referred-to relation' (1986: 130) allows a substantive (causal) theory of reference to fix the semantic values of the linguistic items, then his suggestion is fully consistent with a thick realist 'correspondence' conception of truth. But I am not sure where exactly Fine stands in this debate. He systematically refrains from discussing this issue, but seems persuaded by Putnam's 'model-theoretic' argument against realism that the realists should 'reexamine [their] vague requirement of substantial epistemic access to features of the world structure' (1985: 157). Here again, however, Fine needs to say more.

Reciprocity and contamination

To be sure, Fine has attempted to offer a general philosophical argument against the *very possibility* of a substantive correspondence account of truth. He begins with the following questions: 'If we want to compare a statement with its corresponding state of affairs how do we proceed? How do we get at a state of affairs when that is to be understood realist-style, as a feature of the *World*?' (1986a: 151). He then makes two observations.

1 Since we causally interact with the world, it cannot be independent of us: there is a *reciprocal* relation between us and the world.
2 Whatever information we retrieve from such an interaction with the world is *contaminated* information about interacted-with objects.

But 'How then, faced with reciprocity and contamination, can one get entities both independent and objective?' (ibid.). There is a quick answer to the foregoing question, one which Fine entertains: 'the realist has no direct access to his World', and, therefore, the realist account of truth as a correspondence relation between statements and an independent world falls apart.

Once again, this argument admits of different interpretations. If all that Fine intends to stress is that there is a causal dependence of our theorising about the world on the world, then his argument poses no threat to a realist account of truth. In fact, it supplements it. Causal interaction does not forbid knowing things about the interacted-with entities. On the contrary, it is because our causal interaction with the world gives us reliable means with which to discover facts about it that we can have epistemic access to the world in the first place and can fallibly assert when the truth-conditions of our beliefs obtain. The information we conceptualise and theorise about is surely information about interacted-with objects, but what else could it be?

Insofar as causal interactions and connections are the source of our knowledge of the world, then there is no problem with our access to truths about the world. In any case, the central realist point about truth does not concern our causal give-and-take with the world. As already and repeatedly stressed, it is that truth is *logically* independent of human opinion: there is no conceptual or logical link between the truth of a statement and our ability to recognise it, assert it and the like. Our beliefs are about interacted-with objects – since they cannot be about *un*interacted-with objects. Yet, their truth – insofar as they are true – is logically independent of methods of verification, justification, etc.: their truth is not entailed by the fact that we are (ideally) justified to assert whatever we assert about the interacted-with objects. Similarly, for realists the interacted-with objects are simply the objects with which we causally interact. These objects are deemed independent of us, not in any causal sense, but only in a logical sense: they are not the outcome (whatever that means) of our conceptualisations and theorising. So interpreted, Fine's argument poses no problem to realism.

In light of this, Fine's argument may intend to imply that, as result of reciprocity and contamination, there is a logical–conceptual dependence of the world on our theorising about it. If so, his argument breaks his neutrality and leads him towards a non-realist account of truth. If Fine means to suggest that our conceptualisations and theorising of the information we receive somehow determine which objects we interact with – they make them what they are: the interacted-with objects – then this view would threaten the conceptual independence of truth from our epistemic capacities. As we have seen, Fine does not intend to motivate such an account of truth. But it is hard to see how he can avoid doing so if he takes 'reciprocity' and 'contamination' to generate a logical dependence of the world on our theorising about it. Immediately after his argument, Fine cites with approval the following excerpt from Kuhn (1970: 206): 'There is, I think, no theory-independent way to reconstruct phrases like "really true"; the notion of a match between the ontology of a theory and its "real" counterpart in nature now seems to me illusive in principle'. This suggests to me that, in his attempt to argue against the very possibility of a 'correspondence theory of truth', Fine may well be drawn towards a kind of epistemic or 'internal realist' account of truth.

Success and truth

It may be thought however, that my defence of a thick-enough conception of correspondence still falls short of showing that 'correspondence' marks a substantive property. Is this not, after all, exactly where realists and deflationists disagree? Is this not the point that, for instance, Williams makes when he contrasts the deflationists' 'minimal correspondence' with the realists' 'physical correspondence'? So, this section will defend a well-known argument in favour of a substantive 'correspondence' account of truth. This is the so-called 'success argument' offered by Hartry Field (1986; 1992) and others. Let me first give some background.

What is it to take seriously the realists' talk of truth-conditions? It is, as Field (1986: 59) put it, to think of truth-conditions as 'objective features of an utterance or thought-state, features which the utterance or thought-state could have whether or not we know it, and which it has in virtue of facts about the relations between the utterance or thought-state and the world around us'. Being committed to such objective features seems to be part of the realist understanding of truth. But, the thought may be, why commit oneself to all this 'heavy machinery' if it is an 'idle wheel', that is, if positing such objective truth-conditions plays no causal–explanatory role in our theorising about the world? The 'success argument' aims precisely to show that objective truth-conditions do play such a causal–explanatory role. Briefly put, the argument is that an appeal to truth-conditions is essentially involved in the explanation of why successful actions are successful. This explanation is based on the claim that the truth-conditions of the belief(s) on which successful actions were based have been realised. More specifically, it is based on the claim that all sorts of reliable beliefs are needed for success in various domains, and that for a belief to be reliable it should be such that it reliably indicates its truth-conditions (cf. Field, 1986: 90, 92–95).

Take for instance, a football team's defence. They want to force an attacking player of the rival team to be in an 'off-side' position. They have a set of (relevant) beliefs as to what this involves. Put simply, they believe *that*, when they see the opportunity arising, they have to co-ordinate their movements, move forward, and align themselves behind the attacking player. He is then 'off-side', the play stops and the attack falls apart. As football fans know very well, this is quite a delicate operation to perform. But when it *is* successful, as it very often is, what explains this success is that whatever conditions were required to make the defenders' relevant beliefs true were realised: they *co-ordinated* their movements, they all *aligned* themselves behind the attacker, etc. Such an explanation of success relies essentially on the use of truth-conditions. In the final analysis, it is because of the fact that the beliefs' truth-conditions are realised that actions based on those beliefs are successful. It is then but a short step to generalise the point by saying that agents tend to be more successful when the truth-conditions of their beliefs are realised. (Compare: what explains the efficacy of the physician's prescription in curing the disease is that the truth-conditions for his beliefs, e.g. that the patient is infected by such-and-such a virus and that this virus is killed by such-and-such an antibiotic, were realised.)

Deflationists are quick to point out that they can offer an explanation of each *particular* successful action in terms of their own minimal account. So, Horwich (1990: 23–24, 44–45), for instance, argues that he can explain each particular successful action as follows: to say that a belief which has guided a successful action is true, is merely to assert the *content* of the belief. Hence, he implies, no appeal to truth-conditions seems necessary. These explanations, he contends, 'will confirm the view that no account of the *nature* of truth ... is called for' (1990: 24; cf. also Williams 1986: 232). But I do not see how this conclusion follows. There are, I think, two points to make.

1   Even if each and every successful action is explained by just citing the content of the beliefs which guided them (and not their truth), it is not clear why this content is anything other than the truth-conditions of the beliefs, realist-style. Clearly, what deflationism needs is a theory of content which divorces the content of a belief from its truth-conditions. But this is still an open issue (cf. Field 1992: 328–329).

2   It seems perfectly legitimate to ask: what does each and every belief that guides particular successful actions have in common by virtue of which this systematic pattern of success is generated? Trying to block off any attempt to answer this question is hardly acceptable, unless one has already established that the answer is: nothing. But if such a negative answer has not been established, I see no problem in answering this question by saying the following. What all beliefs that guide particular successful action have in common by virtue of which they generate this systematic pattern of success is that their truth-conditions – the *referred-to entities standing in the referred-to relations* – have been realised. At least this is a systematic explanation of the sort that any scientific investigation into a matter looks for. What is interesting is that, given this explanation, one can paraphrase it by saying that the beliefs on which successful actions have been based 'correspond to reality'.[6] Call this 'correspondence with reality' a property that all these beliefs share in common and you get as substantive an account of the nature of truth as is possible. No illegitimate moves are involved in this. In any case, the move is no less legitimate than positing a common property of all coloured objects: that they reflect light-waves of specific frequencies and absorb all others. If NOA would be happy to attribute the above property to all coloured objects, then I do not see why it should not be happy to attribute to all true beliefs the property of correspondence with reality, understood as just explained. The above account of 'correspondence' should justifiably fall within the 'entrenched uses' of the concept of truth of which Fine approves (see 1986a: 175).

Need we do epistemology of science?

I want to conclude discussion of Fine's position by suggesting that there is a general issue which seems to separate NOA and those philosophers (be they realists or anti-realists) who disagree with Fine's outlook: whether or not we still need to do normative epistemology of science. I think Fine wants to *eliminate* this need. He certainly expresses disdain for 'the global interpretations, the "isms" of scientific philosophies', which appear to be 'idle overlays to science: not necessary, not warranted, and in the end, probably not even intelligible' (1986: 149). Fine's NOA is promoted as an antidote to all this.

The reader may think that it is Fine's naturalism which dictates his disdain for normative epistemic theories. For, a part of the tradition engendered by Quine's 'Epistemology Naturalised' does suggest that epistemology should be abandoned, or treated as within the domains of the special sciences. But two points are worth making. First, Fine denounces Quinean naturalism (see 1996: 176–177). Second, as we saw in Chapter 8, naturalism need not be eliminative. It is one thing to argue (rightly) that there is no epistemological method prior to science and that the epistemological inquiry should be continuous with, and dependent upon, the methods and findings of empirical science; it is quite another to argue (wrongly) that there is no space for normative judgements, evaluation and interpretation of science and of scientific practice. Recent work on naturalised philosophy of science, be it realist (Boyd 1989; Kitcher 1993; 1995) or not (Laudan 1996), suggests that naturalism can secure a place for normative and evaluative epistemological inquiry.

In order to show that Fine cannot eliminate the need to engage with normative epistemology of science, my focus here is on the issue of theory acceptance. One of the central concerns of modern epistemology of science has been to characterise what should be involved in accepting a scientific theory. Scientific realists suggest that acceptance should be equated with the belief that the theory is approximately true, and that this belief can be warranted and rational. Their opposition is not uniform. Anti-realists would go for the claim that acceptance involves belief in truth, but, as we have seen, they would put a certain epistemic gloss on the concept of truth. Constructive empiricists, on the other hand, have suggested, along the lines of the instrumentalist tradition, that acceptance should involve less than belief in approximate truth, and that belief in the approximate truth is neither warranted by evidence nor necessary for the deployment of scientific theories (see van Fraassen 1980).

In opposition to all this, Fine runs his own deflationary story. Here is a characteristic statement:

> [R]ealism requires two distinct elements. It requires belief and it also requires a particular interpretation of that belief. Thus anti-realism, in particular instrumentalism, pursues the following strategy. If it does not withhold belief, then it offers instead a non-realist interpretation of the belief. ... But the reader will no doubt notice that there is an interesting third way. For one can go along with belief, but then simply not add on any special interpretation of it – neither realist nor anti-realist. That is the way of NOA.

(1986a: 176)

But this unsatisfactory. Suppose that someone, like Fine (1996: 184) believes in electrons and in DNA and in dinosaurs. Suppose, more specifically, that by belief in such entities one means, like Fine (ibid.), that one 'accept[s] [these] entities', rather than questioning 'the science that backs them up'. What exactly it means to say that one *accepts* a scientific theory? It means different things to different philosophers (even to different scientists). Is it to accept the theory as empirically adequate? If so, then, unlike Fine, one does not assert the existence of electrons, DNA, etc. Nor does one believe in them. Is it to accept the theory as true? Then one, like Fine, *does* believe in the existence of electrons, DNA, etc. But, even so, it makes sense to ask: does warranted belief in the existence of electrons render it impossible that the electrons theory be false? This question admits of different answers, depending on whether one wants to advocate a realist or an anti-realist conception of truth. One cannot just sit on the fence. Sitting on the fence is not just non-committal. It is so ambiguous, one might say, as to have no content at all.

Fine may well want to get by with this ambiguity. He says: 'the ambiguity over the character of accepting in science that results from not raising the realism/instrumentalism question seems to be an ambiguity we can quite well live with' (1991: 93). Well, one can live with whatever ambiguities one chooses. But this does not entail that one ought not to remove the ambiguities. And that is exactly why doing epistemology of science is imperative: to pinpoint, examine, and possibly remove the ambiguities of ordinary scientific practice. But perhaps Fine thinks that the ordinary notion of theory acceptance in science is not a notion that admits of philosophical elucidation. For instance, he notes: 'With theories that stay around, questions about the character of acceptance (do molecules 'really' exist?) frequently drop out of the scientific discussion, assuming they were ever there to begin with' (1991: 94). Accordingly, 'NOA suggests that in general we can get along without regard to the question of what accepting the theory amounts to, unless the question is scientifically relevant' (ibid.).

When is the question of theory-acceptance scientifically relevant, and when is it not? Fine refrains from saying, perhaps, because, in the final analysis, it *always is* relevant. And how could it not be? It is one thing to accept a theory as true (or near true); it is quite another to accept it as empirically adequate – and it is altogether something else to say that acceptance answers not to beliefs about how the world (or even its observable part) is structured but instead to a bunch of social norms. In discussing briefly the scientific practice of acceptance of certain existential claims, Fine suggests that 'the decision to accept as true a particular existence claim is the decision to accept the complex network of judgements that ground it'. This existence claim 'will be accepted as true just to the extent in which the relevant scientific community goes along with the network of normative judgements and the concomitant ranges of theories' (1986: 153). And 'particular judgements of truth are anchored in a network of much more general judgements and the concomitant ranges of theories' (ibid.). I am not sure how to interpret these claims about the acceptance of theories and of existential claims. But such claims might be understood as a *theory*, albeit 'thin', of acceptance. In any case, Fine presents such claims as an *alternative* to the realist view that grounds existence claims in 'contact with reality'. So, I do not think it unjust to Fine to say that his main line is this: when scientific assertions are said to be true, their truth is certified by the norms, theoretical beliefs and practices of the relevant scientific community. Two things seem to follow, if Fine does advocate this last view. First, NOA does get involved in a major epistemic debate: it offers a theory of what is involved in accepting a scientific theory. Second, this theory is itself open to interpretation and evaluation. Suppose that the thrust of the theory is that the operative epistemic standards are just the prevailing standards of the community. Taken at face value, this view seems prone to slide towards a kind of a *constructivist anti-realist* view of acceptance: the standards of a scientific community, whatever they happen to be, fix all that is relevant to the epistemic evaluation of the community's beliefs, existence claims, etc. If so, there seems to be no room for normative questions such as 'Does the community have good reasons to adopt its relevant beliefs, existence claims, etc.?' For, simply, on this account, what it is for the community to have good reasons is to have the reasons it happens to have – those licensed by the prevailing standards. If these standards are moreover socially inculcated, then, ultimately, whatever epistemic force they may have is determined by social factors and is amenable to change whenever these factors change.

These are issues which I do not intend to discuss in any detail here. The only point I want to make is that the above constructivist reading is in the spirit of Fine's theory of acceptance. Fine can certainly avoid truth-relativism and radical forms of social constructivism since he never says that truth itself is definable in terms of the community's prevailing standards. (His position is, however, consistent with truth-relativism, since never does he say that truth is not definable in terms of the community's prevailing standards.) But, still, if epistemic norms are definable in terms of the community's prevailing standards, then a weaker form of relativism follows: one in which there is no space for considering whether each community's standards are right or wrong. NOA cannot just stay silent. Yet, if it says something positive, it engages in philosophical theorising (perhaps even in hermeneutics). If, on the other hand, it just denies dealing with the central epistemic issues that arise from and within science, then it denies the very legitimacy of doing epistemology of science. NOA's 'hands-off' attitude is just philosophically eliminative.

Should we then abandon NOA's ark? I am inclined to say yes. But I think we would be better off to know what we thereby abandon. The foregoing analysis has suggested that it is not clear what exactly we accept when we go for NOA, and what exactly we abandon when we leave it behind. I hope that my interpretive work has helped to elucidate this issue.

And I hope also that my positive arguments have shown why NOA's ark is sinking. In any case, NOA's vagueness refutes what Fine intended to show in the first place: 'how minimal an adequate philosophy of science can be' (1986: 133).

Mor(e) of NOA

NOA has found some allies within the realist camp. Newton-Smith, for instance, has attempted to formulate a favourable-to-realism version of NOA. He has called it 'MOdest Realism' (MOR). MOR differs from NOA in two essential respects: (1) MOR adds a blend of 'progressivism' in science, thereby admitting that 'some' notions of truth, approximate truth and convergence are legitimate (Newton-Smith 1989: 187–188). (2) MOR dismisses the 'hands-off science' attitude of NOA towards philosophy of science. According to MOR there are problems arising from the scientific game, such as the problem of underdetermination and the nature of ontological commitments in science, which need special philosophical treatment (ibid.: 187). Yet, MOR takes up what Newton-Smith thinks is a basic element of NOA: that the very same procedures of justification operate when it comes to judgements about observables as when it deals with unobservables. As he puts it: 'NOA and MOR see scientific discourse as being of a piece with ordinary discourse' (1989: 188).

On closer inspection, however, it is doubtful that NOA and MOR agree. MOR, for instance, accepts inference to the best explanation as a warranted way of forming beliefs about scientific unobservables, whereas NOA remains notably silent on this, and – more to the point – Fine has generally challenged the view that abductive reasoning can be defended as reliable. What is worth noting, though, is that MOR does inherit the general attitude associated with NOA, viz. that looking at the language-game of science as a form of life, it is unlikely that any general and enlightening description of the function of truth and belief is possible (Newton-Smith 1989: 188).

I argued in the previous sections that this pessimistic attitude is not warranted. Here, I want to make a few comments on a related matter. In another piece, Newton-Smith argues that MOR must not just treat truth as a notion 'already in use' in science, but should say something more about it (1989a: 45). What MOR says, however, is not very different from what a realist should say. MOR incorporates the Tarskian notion of satisfaction, and the causal theories of reference to fix the relations between words and the world. It also warns off epistemic conceptions of truth (1989: 188; 1989a: 45). The only visible difference from a standard non-epistemic conception of truth is that MOR accepts what Newton-Smith calls the 'generous proposal'. According to this, if the truth of a statement remains undecidable even for an observationally omniscient being (that is, a being who has access to *all* observable states of the universe), then truth is *not* at stake (cf. 1989a: 43–44). In other words, MOR's suggestion is that if no actual or possible observation can decide the truth of a statement, then there is no fact of the matter the truth of which science needs to establish.

One might wonder here whether realists would lose anything were they to accept the 'generous proposal'. After all, MOR does not take 'truth' to be an epistemic notion. It just denies that truth is *radically* non-epistemic. It does not tie truth to *our* capabilities to verify, recognise, justify and cognate notions. It just denies that there is a fact of the matter about, say, the truth of statement '*S*' when even an ideally placed observer – who has access to all relevant observations – could not establish it. However, one might equally wonder what realists would gain if they accepted the 'generous proposal'. The 'generous proposal' would not make their claims about truth more modest – at least in any noteworthy sense. The possibility of an 'omniscient state' of observational knowledge is no less metaphysically inflated than the possibility that there is a fact of the matter about the truth or falsity of '*S*', even though the state-of-affairs referred to by '*S*' triggers no discriminatory observations. So I submit that a realist theory of truth would be neither better off nor worse off after the incorporation of the 'generous proposal'. I do not see why one would be more of a realist if one believed that there was a fact of the matter as to the truth of the statement '*Everything in the universe was doubled in size yesterday at midnight*', whereas one would be less of a realist, if one believed that there was no fact of the matter as to whether the foregoing statement is true or false.

Having said that, I would opt for a cautious rejection of the 'generous proposal' on the following (modest) grounds. First, admitting that truth is radically non-epistemic gives a more uniform way in which to state the realist commitments, without imposing any *anthropocentric* division of assertions into those for which there is a fact-of-the-matter and those for which there is not. Second, I find it more plausible to believe that some aspects of reality may lie forever beyond the cognitive reach of any human being, even beyond the reach of someone with perfect observational knowledge, than to believe that if no observation can decide an assertion, it is meaningless to argue that it can still be true or false. Were I to choose, I would prefer to live with the possibility of some aspects of an independent reality being beyond our observational reach rather than with a-man-(or an omniscient being)-is-the-measure-of-everything theory.

The 'state of cognitive perfection'

Epistemic accounts of truth conceptually link truth with some *epistemic condition*, such as warranted assertibility, verification, ideal justification, etc. Hence, they deny typically realist claims that truth exceeds our capability to recognise whether the truth-conditions of a statement obtain, or that it outruns warranted assertibility, idealised justification and the like, in the sense that it is possible that a statement is, say, warrantedly assertible, and yet false.

Recently, several conceptions of truth as *idealised justification* of some sort have been advocated as explications of the concept of truth appropriate for scientific realism (see Ellis 1985; Jardine 1986). They typically tie truth to an *idealised state of scientific inquiry* such that all of the empirical evidence 'is in'. For Ellis, truth is 'what we should believe, if our knowledge were perfected, if it were based on total evidence, was internally coherent and was theoretically integrated in the best possible way' (1985: 68). Ellis recognises that the very notion of a state of perfection is difficult to explicate. Nonetheless he thinks that 'this is what truth, if it exists, must be' (ibid.). In an analogous fashion, Jardine takes truth to be 'the limit of human inquiry, the theory that would be converged on were human inquiry prosecuted indefinitely under sufficiently favourable circumstances' (1986: 14).

Ellis and Jardine's conception of truth is problematic on many counts. Newton-Smith (1989a) has offered a detailed criticism of their views, so I shall refrain from further detailed argumentation against them. I want only to stress three things, which I shall illustrate with reference to Ellis.

1   The main motivation of these epistemic accounts of truth is that truth should be human-oriented in order to be recognisable and useful. But the arguments for such accounts are far from conclusive. Ellis, for instance, cites the argument that epistemic notions of truth preclude scepticism, because, 'our epistemic values *must* be adapted to the end of discovering what is true, because *truth* is just the culmination of the process of investigating and reasoning about nature in accordance with these values' (1985: 69). If 'truth' is *defined* as the deliverances of our epistemic values, then the latter can be said to be adapted (or, better, predestined) to yield truths. But why should 'truth' be so defined? I think it would be a significant achievement if one could show – probably on evolutionary grounds – that our epistemic values are truth-conducive. This would not show that our epistemic values are infallible. But it would underwrite their reliability and so offer cogent arguments against the sceptic. However, to attach the label 'truth' to whatever our epistemic values license or lead, and then to say that *these* values are so adapted as to yield truths, is an ill-conceived way of making sure that at some point of the inquiry we will have truth and nothing but truth. Ellis beats the sceptics not by challenging their arguments, but by making truth fall, by default, within human reach.

2   The second point is that, appearances to the contrary notwithstanding, the epistemic conception under consideration inflates the notion of truth *no less* than does the standard non-epistemic account. For instance, Ellis's definition of truth in terms of a *state of cognitive perfection* (where all of the evidence is in and our theoretical system is integrated the best way) presupposes an a priori commitment to the view that there is a finite amount of observational states which can count as evidence

relevant to the truth or falsity of our theories. Or, alternatively, it presupposes a commitment to the view that there is a point in human inquiry where either all possible causal interactions with the world which can be relevant to the truth or falsity of our theories have obtained, or all unobtained interactions are identical to those already obtained, hence being impotent to refute the theory. These views are metaphysically more far-fetched than the realist view that it is logically possible for even that theory which we believe, under the state of perfection, to be false.

3   Even if we could envisage a state such that all the evidence 'is in', and such that our theoretical system were integrated in the best way, could we really tell whether we were in such a state? How do we know when we have reached this state of cognitive perfection? Could we compare what we think is true with what is true from the standpoint of the state of cognitive perfection? If the state of cognitive perfection is unreachable, then it cannot play its intended role: it cannot provide a link between epistemic values and truth, in which case its positing is useless and redundant. But if the state of cognitive perfection exists and is reachable, then one must show how it can be recognised as *the* state of cognitive perfection; for otherwise it cannot play its intended role, either.

So, what are the prospects of the currently discussed epistemic conceptions of truth? I think they are poor. Current conceptions of epistemic truth are either implausible or insufficiently differentiated from the non-epistemic conception. This is not accidental. My view is that any advocate of an epistemic notion of truth faces the formidable task of having to devise a notion of truth which, to use Jardine's words, is neither too *secular*, nor too *theological* (1986: 35). These views try to avoid the awkward dependence of truth on the vagaries of our evolving epistemic values, but they try also to link truth to *some* notion of epistemic justification. But in the attempt to break away from secular notions of truth and to make truth a standing property they move towards a theological notion: the justification procedures become so ideal that they lose any intended connection with humanly realisable conditions. All in all, epistemic conceptions of truth end up either secular, and then rather implausible because they engender relativism, or else theological, and then insufficiently distinct from the non-epistemic understanding of truth.

Entity realism?

Recently there has been an attempt to defend so-called 'entity realism', viz. the position that one may believe in all sorts of entities posited by scientific theories (e.g. electrons, genes, Higg particles, etc.), while one actually suspends or witholds belief in the theories in which descriptions of these entities are embedded. Entity-realism has been entertained by Cartwright (1983) and Hacking (1983). Introducing entity-realism, viz. the thesis that 'a good many theoretical entities do really exist' (1983: 27), Hacking says: 'But one can believe in some entities without believing in any particular theory in which they are embedded. One can even hold that no general deep theory about the entities could possibly be true, for there is no such truth' (ibid.: 29). As McMullin has, rather nicely, put it, entity-realism stresses that we can 'know *that* the electron is, even though there is no similar assurance as to *what* it is' (1987: 63).

A major motivation for entity-realism comes from laboratory life. For both Hacking and Cartwright, experimenters have good reasons to believe in specific unobservable entities, not because they accept the relevant theories but because they *do* things with these entities. They manipulate them, they jiggle them in order to produce several effects, they use them to interact with other entities. These phenomena of laboratory life would be inexplicable if these entities did not exist. As Hacking once put it for quarks: 'So far as I'm concerned, if you can spray them, then they are real' (1983: 23).

Entity realism is a realist position, sure enough, since it defends the reality of unobservable entities. But entity realism is a *selective* realist position, since it restricts warranted belief to entities only, and suggests to fellow-realists that they are wrong in claiming that the theoretical descriptions of these entities are approximately true. To a certain extent this scepticism about theories is motivated by none other than the argument from the pessimistic induction (see Hacking 1983: 27). Hopefully, the arguments I offered in Chapter 5 against the pessimistic induction will suffice to persuade the entity realist that greater epistemic optimism is warranted.

But the main point I want to make is different: the distinction between being realist about entities and being realist about theories is misconceived. It may well be the case that electrons exist, even though some (or most) of our descriptions associated with the term 'electron' are false. But the issue at stake is different. It is this: can we assert that electrons are real, i.e. that such entities exist as part and parcel of the furniture of the world, without also asserting that they have *some* of the properties attributed to them by our best scientific theories? I take it that the two assertions stand or fall together. Experimenters do not know what exactly it is that they manipulate, although they can know that they are manipulating something, unless they adopt some theoretical description of the entities they manipulate. It is by means of such theoretical descriptions that they make the relevant identifications and discriminations. What makes electrons different from, say, neutrinos is that they have different properties, and obey different laws. One should rely on these theoretical descriptions in order to manipulate these entities effectively and exploit their causal powers.

Constructive empiricists would re-interpret this practice by saying, roughly, that when a putative entity is taken to be manipulated, a theoretical story is told which interprets the observed and observable phenomena in such a way that they are brought under the scope of the story. Yet, they would suspend their judgement on both the reality of the posited entity *and* the correctness of the theoretical story which describes it. I have discussed the weaknesses of this position in Chapter 9. The interesting difference between entity realists and constructive empiricists is that the former want to be realists about the posited entity but wish to suspend their judgement about the correctness of its theoretical description. It is *this* combination that is problematic – on two counts:

(a) if it is not admitted that some theoretical descriptions of the causal powers of the entity are correct, then the mere positing of the entity cannot produce any sound expectations about which phenomena are due if and when this entity is manipulated;
(b) the very same process is involved in accepting the reality of an entity, and in accepting the (approximate) correctness of its theoretical description.

In both cases, it is a judgement based on explanatory considerations. The entity is posited in order to account for the phenomena observed, and the correctness of its theoretical description should be assumed in order to explain how the entity is successfully manipulated in order to produce phenomena that lie within the scope of its causal powers.

Hacking notes, for instance: 'We are completely convinced of the reality of electrons when we regularly set out to build and often enough succeed in building new kinds of device that use various well-understood causal properties of electrons to interfere in the more hypothetical parts of nature' (1983: 265). I take it that the just described process by which 'we are completely convinced' that electrons are real involves two steps. The first step is positing a natural kind – *electrons* – and the second is relying on the 'well-understood' causal properties of the members of the kind in order to predict, or produce, certain effects. Both steps presuppose the very same type of argument – *inference to the best explanation*. In both steps a hypothesis is adopted on the (perhaps implicit) ground that it best explains the relevant evidence. The first step requires the adoption of the hypothesis that there are electrons. If this hypothesis is accepted, it should be on the ground that it is a better explanation of the phenomena than saying, for instance, that the phenomena are uncaused, or that there are multiple and heterogeneous causes, or what have you. The second step requires the adoption of the hypothesis that electrons have certain causal powers. If this hypothesis is accepted, it should be on the ground that it offers a better explanation of the phenomena than other hypotheses about different causal powers that electrons may have. So: two steps, but one type of argument.[7]

To be sure, it may be pointed out that there are two versions of 'entity realism': one *thin*, the other *thick*. The thin version accepts the reality of causal agents behind the phenomena. The thick version – which is the more interesting and informative – ascribes causal properties to these agents on the basis of which they are further manipulated to produce certain effects. Given what I have said, the thick version should rely on an inference to the best explanation and should be committed to the view that at least some of the theoretical descriptions of these entities and of their causal properties are broadly correct. Hence, the thick version of entity realism collapses the original distinction between realism-about-entities and realism-about-theories. That the full electron theory might be wrong does not imply that it does not have truth-like theoretical constituents. Nor is it required for theory realism to be well-motivated that the whole theory be true. The thin version of entity realism, on the other hand, *may* motivate a distinction between entity realism and theory realism. For even if it is admitted that the thin version relies on an abductive strategy – after all, I do not see how else the putative causal agent could be posited – it may well be the case that the advocate of the thin version does not have to accept the essential correctness of any theories or theoretical descriptions of the posited entity. Be that as it may, the problems with the thin version are that it is not very informative and it does not have the right target. It is not very informative because just positing causal agent does not explain how they can be manipulated. This requires ascribing causal properties to them. And it has the wrong target because, although it may well be effective against eliminative instrumentalists and phenomenalists – who deny the reality of unobservable natural kinds – it remains silent when it comes to agnostic versions of empiricism which doubt that what these entities are can ever be known.[8]

These thoughts conclude Part III. In the next, and final, part our attention shifts to some central notions of the realist philosophical package: *approximate truth* and *reference*.

Part IV
Refilling the realist toolbox

11 Truth-likeness

Scientific realists standardly argue that our best scientific theories should be considered to be truth-like. Yet, a common challenge levelled against realists is that there is no coherent formal notion of truth-likeness, or verisimilitude. The implication is that the realist claim cannot be properly defended. This chapter reviews the truth-likeness saga. I argue, not surprisingly, that, up to now, all attempts to characterise formally the intuitive notion of truth-likeness have failed. This, however, is no reason for despair. For the intuitive notion of truth-likeness need not be formalised in order to be of use. In the final two sections of this chapter, I explain and defend the intuitions behind the realist notion of truth-likeness.

Popper on verisimilitude

The idea that, as science grows, new theories can be deemed to be more truth-like than their predecessors goes back to Karl Popper. As is well known, Popper (1959; 1963) adopted a falsificationist view of science, according to which theory testing proceeds through attempted refutations. At no stage, Popper claimed, are scientists warranted in believing in the truth of their theories. Such belief can be based only on the claim that the theory is well-supported, or well-confirmed, by evidence. But such a claim is inductive: it goes far beyond the currently available evidence for the theory. For Popper, however, induction and confirmation have no place in science. Instead, scientific theory-testing proceeds deductively. Theories, or theoretical hypotheses, are *conjectured* and, subsequently, are put to the test by checking the observational consequences derived from them. For Popper, when a theory is accepted, it is held to be corroborated; those theories are corroborated which (a) are unrefuted and (b) have stood up to severe testing.

The inadequacies of Popper's anti-inductivist views have been well thrashed out in the literature (cf. Worrall 1989b), so there is no need to repeat them here. What I intend to focus on is Popper's views on verisimilitude. Popper suggested that the aim of science should be the development of theories with higher degrees of *verisimilitude* (likeness to truth). One may well accept the view that all existing scientific theories are (likely to be) false, and yet also hold that they are closer to the truth than their predecessors. If, science as it grows, moves on to theories with higher verisimilitude, then there is a clear sense in which this process takes science closer to the truth (although, at any given point in time, we may not know how close to the truth science is). This is an important idea. But difficulty lies with its *formal* explication. Popper does offer a formal account, but one which, as we will see, is flawed. So it turns out that, using Popper's account, we *cannot* compare theories in terms of their verisimilitude. Let us see how this happens by looking, first, at Popper's definition of comparative verisimilitude (1972: 52):

Theory A is less verisimilar than theory B if and only if (a) their truth-contents are comparable and (b) *either* the truth-content of A is less than the truth-content of B and the falsity-content of B is less than or equal to the falsity-content of A; *or* the truth-content of A is less than or equal to the truth-content of B and the falsity-content of B is less than the falsity-content of A. The truth-content T_T of a theory T is the class of all true consequences of T, and the falsity-content T_F of T is the class of all false consequences of T.

Miller (1974) and Tichy (1974) proved (independently of each other) that Popper's definition is flawed. Here is the proof.

Assume that A and B are both false and distinct theories. According to Popper's definition, A is less verisimilar than B if and only if either

$$A_T \subset B_T \quad \text{and} \quad B_F \subseteq A_F \qquad (1)$$

or

$$A_T \subseteq B_T \quad \text{and} \quad B_F \subset A_F \qquad (2)$$

where: A_T and B_T are the truth-contents of A and B respectively;
$\quad\quad\quad A_F$ and B_F are their falsity-contents;
$\quad\quad\quad \subseteq$ stands for set-theoretic inclusion; and
$\quad\quad\quad \subset$ stands for proper inclusion.
It can be shown that the two conditions under (1) cannot be satisfied together, and similarly for the two conditions under (2).

Assume (1) that $A_T \subset B_T$ *and* $B_F \subseteq A_F$.

Then, B has at least an extra true consequence, say q (i.e. $q \in B_T$). Clearly, given that B_F is contained in A_F and is non-empty, there are some falsehoods common to both A and B. Take any of these false consequences common to A and B, say p (i.e. $p \in B_F$ *and* $p \in A_F$). Then, $p\&q$ is a false consequence of B (i.e. $p\&q \in B_F$), but clearly not of A (i.e. $p\&q \notin A_F$). Hence, there is at least one false consequence of B which is not a false consequence of A. So, contrary to our assumption, it is not the case that $B_F \subseteq A_F$.

Assume (2) that $A_T \subseteq B_T$ and $B_F \subset A_F$.

Then, A has at least an extra false consequence, say r (i.e. $r \in A_F$). Take any false consequence of A, say k (i.e. $k \in A_F$) which is also a false consequence of B (i.e. $k \in B_F$). Then clearly, $k \to r$ ($\equiv \neg k \lor r$) is a true consequence of A (i.e. $k \to r \in A_T$), but not of B (i.e. $k \to r \notin B_T$), since $r \notin B$. Hence, there is a true consequence of A which is not a true consequence of B. So, contrary to our assumption, it is not the case that $A_T \subseteq B_T$. QED

The thrust of the proof is that, using Popper's approach, we cannot compare false theories with respect to their relative verisimilitude. If we try to get a more verisimilar theory B from a false theory A by *adding* more truths to A, we also add more falsehoods to B, which are *not* false consequences of A. Similarly, if we try to get a more verisimilar theory B from a false theory A by *subtracting* falsehoods from A, we also subtract truths from A, which are *not* true consequences of B. Hence, Popper's definition is flawed.

Suppose that Popper's theory of verisimilitude did work. What it would show is that theories can be compared in respect of their observational consequences in such a way that it could be established that, as science grows, theories entail more true, or less false, observational consequences than did their predecessors. This would certainly show us something, viz. that, as science grows, theories can be compared *vis-à-vis* their observational truth-content. But, even if this worked, how much would it help the realist cause? Not much. For the realists claims are (a) that the truth-likeness of theories extends to their theoretical content and does not stop at the level of their observational consequences; and (b) that there are respects and degrees in which *current* theories are truth-like. Popper's account can defend neither of the above claims, and hence it is of no real service to the realists.

In Popper's theory there are no respects in and degrees to which current theories are truth-like. Their verisimilitude is said to be a function of the true observational consequences they entail, and not of their *overall fitting-ness* in the world. Popper's verisimilitude measure suggests that current theories are closer to the truth insofar as they entail more true consequences than did their predecessors. But, on this account, these theories may be as far from the truth as anything can be. In the Popperian account of scientific growth, a sequence of false theories may nonetheless constitute a march towards the truth by means of their increasing verisimilitude which – one hopes – tends, asymptotically, to the truth. But truth itself, and the truth-likeness of current theories, play, if anything, just a secondary role (see Popper 1972: 57–58).[1]

The refutation of Popper's account of verisimilitude has often been taken as a proof that scientific realists *cannot* have a notion of truth-likeness (cf. Laudan 1984: 91). Alas, even if Popper's theory stood intact, it would not be a theory that a scientific realist would have reasons to support. Scientific realists do not need a theory of truth-likeness which tells whether science moves closer to a truth that may lie millennia ahead; instead, realists seek a theory which can ground the judgement that current theories are close to the truth. Popper's theory remains silent on this.

The fact that Popper's definition of verisimilitude fails does not entail that any attempt to characterise formally the intuitive concept of truth-likeness is doomed. But, as we are about to see, the formal explication of truth-likeness has proven to be a notoriously difficult task.

The 'possible worlds' approach

The 'possible worlds approach' to truth-likeness, advanced by Graham Oddie (1986) and Ilka Niiniluoto (1987), characterises truth-likeness in terms of the distance between a possible world and the actual world. Let me explain the basics of this approach. A theory is characterised in terms of the basic states, or traits, it ascribes to the world. To each basic trait, there corresponds an atomic formula which says that an individual possesses this trait. Let us call them *atomic states*. Possible worlds correspond to all conceivable distributions of truth-values to atomic states. So, if there are n atomic states (corresponding to n basic traits), there are 2^n possible worlds W_i $(i = 1, \ldots, 2n)$, of the form

$$W_i = \bigwedge_{i=1}^{n} \pm p_i$$

where: p_i $(i = 1, \ldots, n)$ ranges over the basic states, and
   $\pm$ suggests that p_i occurs either unnegated (the corresponding atomic state is true in world W_i), or negated (the corresponding atomic state is false in W_i), but not both.

Every theory characterises (describes) a possible world W_i. The actual world W_A is one of these possible worlds. A theory T is *true* if and only if it describes the actual world W_A, and *false* if and only if it picks out another possible world. A theory T which is false of the actual world W_A may,

Table 11.1 Possible weather-worlds

	Hot (h)	Rainy (r)	Windy (w)
W_1	T	T	T
W_2	T	T	F
W_3	T	F	T
W_4	T	F	F
W_5	F	T	T
W_6	F	T	F
W_7	F	F	T
W_8	F	F	F

nonetheless, be *truth-like* in the sense that the possible world W_i it describes may agree on some atomic states with the 'target theory', i.e. the theory which describes truly the actual world. This partial agreement is employed to explicate the notion of truth-likeness.

Let us, for instance, envisage a simple weather-world which has three basic traits, i.e. hot (h), rainy (r) and windy (w). Then, as Table 11.1 shows, there are the following 8 possible worlds (including the actual one).

Let us say that W_1 is the actual world (a hot, rainy and windy world). The other seven possible worlds differ in some specifiable respect from W_1. Theories which pick out a possible world, e.g. W_3 ($h \wedge \neg r \wedge w$), are false, but nonetheless their closeness to the truth, i.e. W_1 ($h \wedge r \wedge w$), can be suitably specified.

The 'possible worlds' approach gives a nice and simple measure of the distance of each theory from the truth. A *proposition* is characterised set-theoretically as the set of possible worlds which the corresponding state-of-affairs holds. So, for instance, the proposition that it is hot (h) is the set $\{W_1, W_2, W_3, W_4\}$, whereas the proposition that it is not rainy is the set $\{W_3, W_4, W_7, W_8\}$. Truth-functional operations on propositions are defined in set-theoretic terms. So, the conjunction of propositions is defined as the intersection of the sets to which each conjunct corresponds. For instance, 'it is hot *and* it is not rainy' is $\{W_3, W_4\}$. Similarly, disjunction of propositions is defined as the union of the sets to which each disjunct corresponds. The truth-likeness of a proposition is, then, defined as a function of the ratio of *the sum of the distances between the actual world and the worlds in which this proposition holds* over *the total number of worlds in which this proposition is true*.

The distance (or symmetric difference) between a possible world and the actual world is a function of the basic states over which the two worlds disagree. In order to define the *distance function*, we assign weights t_i ($i = 1, \ldots, n$) to the n basic traits, such that

$$\sum_{i=1}^{n} t_i = 1$$

We then define the numerical distance between a possible world and the actual world as the sum of the weights of the basic states (traits) over which the two worlds disagree. Obviously, the distance between any possible world and the actual world takes values in the closed interval [0,1], where a totally false theory is at distance 1 from the actual world, and the true theory is at distance 0 from the actual world. Then, the distance of a proposition q from the truth is given as follows:

$$Dt(q) = \frac{\displaystyle\sum_{W_i \in \{q\}} Dt\,(W_i/W_A)}{|q|} \tag{1}$$

where: $Dt(W_i/W_A)$ is the distance between an arbitrary world W_i and the actual world W_A (i.e. the sum of the weights of the basic states on which the actual world W_A and the possible world W_i disagree); $\{q\}$ is the set of possible worlds in which q holds; and $|q|$ is the cardinality of this set.

The degree of truth-likeness of an arbitrary proposition q is given by:

$$Vs(q) = 1 - \frac{\displaystyle\sum_{W_i \in \{q\}} Dt\,(W_i/W_A)}{|q|} \tag{2}$$

Hence, we can get a numerical value for the verisimilitude of every proposition. Take, for instance, the weather-world, and assign equal weights t_i of 1/3 to each trait. Say we want to calculate the distance of proposition $\neg h$ from the truth. $\neg h$ holds in the set $\{W_5, W_6, W_7, W_8\}$. The cardinality of this set is 4. Then we calculate the distance between each world in which $\neg h$ holds and the actual world, and take their sum $Dt(W_5/W_1) + Dt(W_6/W_1) + Dt(W_7/W_1) + Dt(W_8/W_1)$. This is $(1/3+2/3+2/3+3/3) = 8/3$. This gives us the numerator of (1). We divide that by 4 (the cardinal number of the set in which $\neg h$ holds). Hence we get: $Dt(\neg h) = 2/3$. In one step, the whole process looks like this:

$$Dt(\neg h) = [Dt(W_5/W_1) + Dt(W_6/W_1) + Dt(W_7/W_1) + Dt(W_8/W_1)]/4$$

$$= (1/3+2/3+2/3+3/3)/4$$

$$= 2/3.$$

Hence, by means of (2), the verisimilitude of $\neg h$ is 1/3. Similarly, one can easily confirm that the verisimilitude of $\neg h \wedge r$ is 0.5, the verisimilitude of $\neg h \wedge \neg r$ is 1/6, the verisimilitude of $\neg h \wedge r \wedge w$ is 2/3, the verisimilitude of $\neg h \wedge \neg r \wedge \neg w$ is 0, and so forth.

The 'possible worlds' approach to verisimilitude is attractive. It avoids the major unpleasant feature of Popper's theory: it offers a neat way to compare different theories with respect to their truth-likeness. It also gives a quantitative (as opposed to a simply comparative) account of verisimilitude. Nonetheless, it faces some important problems. For one, as David Miller (1976) has pointed out, this approach is language-dependent: two logically equivalent theories turn out to have different degrees of verisimilitude. Let us sketch how this comes about.

We shall introduce two new weather-predicates: 'is Minnesotan' and 'is Arizonan', where a type of weather is defined as Minnesotan if and only if it is either hot and rainy or cold and dry, and a type of weather is defined as Arizonan if and only if it is either hot and windy or cold and still. So, the new predicate-letter 'm' is defined as $m =_{df} (h \wedge r) \vee (\neg h \wedge \neg r)$, and the predicate-letter 'a' as $a =_{df} (h \wedge w) \vee (\neg h \wedge \neg w)$. (Notice that $(h \wedge r) \vee (\neg h \wedge \neg r) \equiv (h \leftrightarrow r)$ and $(h \wedge w) \vee (\neg h \wedge \neg w) \equiv (h \leftrightarrow w)$.) It is easy to see that $h \wedge r \wedge w$ is logically equivalent to $h \wedge m \wedge a$, that is, that both statements are equivalent descriptions of the target theory. If the target theory (the actual world W_1) is $h \wedge r \wedge w$, then the statement $\neg h \wedge r \wedge w$ (corresponding to W_5) is *more* truth-like than the statement $\neg h \wedge \neg r \wedge \neg w$ (corresponding to W_8). The following, however, can be easily proved: if the actual world is described by means of the logically equivalent statement $h \wedge m \wedge a$, then the statement $\neg h \wedge m \wedge a$ (which is logically equivalent to $\neg h \wedge r \wedge w$) is *less* truth-like than the statement $\neg h \wedge \neg m \wedge \neg a$ (which is logically equivalent to $\neg h \wedge \neg r \wedge \neg w$). One can easily see that the world picked out by $\neg h \wedge m \wedge a$ is W_8, while the world picked out by $\neg h \wedge \neg m \wedge \neg a$ is W_5. So, two logically equivalent formulations receive different degrees of verisimilitude.

In fact, what has been proved is even stronger: under equivalent translation, the verisimilitude of two theories is reversed.[2]

There is, however, something strange with the example above, which, if properly explicated, may point towards an answer to the translation objection. Although it is true that the two formulations, $h \wedge m \wedge a$ and $h \wedge r \wedge w$, are logically equivalent, one can argue that the latter only should be taken seriously as a theory formulation. For only the latter uses essentially 'natural kind' terms, terms which describe natural properties, such as *hot*, *rainy* and *windy*. To be sure, predicates such as 'is Minnesotan' and 'is Arizonan' are defined in terms of 'natural-kind' predicates. But it is precisely this which suggests that whatever else they are taken to be, they should be considered less fundamental than the predicates 'is hot', 'is rainy' and 'is windy', which are defined in terms of some other more fundamental natural properties. The fact is that the predicates 'is Minnesotan' and 'is Arizonan' are parasitic on the predicates 'is hot, 'is rainy' and 'is windy'. So, a theory formulation in terms of 'is Minnesotan' and 'is Arizonan' may be discarded because it is in some extra-logical sense less fundamental (or less natural) than a theory formulation in terms of the predicates 'is hot, 'is rainy' and 'is windy'. If the above line of reasoning is anywhere near sound, then what follows is that judgements of truth-likeness should *not* be purely syntactic. In a way reminiscent of Goodman's 'grue problem', judgements of truth-likeness should take account of the predicates involved, and should be such that only theories formulated in terms of 'natural-kind' predicates should be taken seriously. .

Be that as it may, there is an even more devastating problem with the 'possible worlds' approach. As Aronson (1990) has noted, whenever more traits are added to the description of the world – say as a consequence of scientific discoveries – the verisimilitude of propositions changes. Let us again consider the weather model. Initially, i.e. when there are three basic states, the verisimilitude of h is $Vs(h) = 0.67$. After the addition of a fourth basic state, e.g. cloudy (c), the verisimilitude of h drops to $Vs(h) = 0.625$. When one more state is added, $Vs(h)$ drops further to 0.6. More interestingly, after the addition of a fourth state, the verisimilitude of the false proposition $\neg h$ increases from $Vs(\neg h) = 0.33$ to $Vs(\neg h) = 0.375$; and when a fifth state is added $Vs(\neg h)$, it increases further to 0.4. Generally, the truth-likeness of h, as a function of the number of states, is given by the formula $(n+1)/2n$, and the truth-likeness of $\neg h$ is given by the formula $(n-1)/2n$. Then, as the number n of states increases, the verisimilitude of h gets closer to the verisimilitude of $\neg h$. When n goes to infinity both verisimilitudes tend to 1/2. That is, as the number of basic traits tends to infinity, a false proposition has the same truth-likeness as a true one, and their truth-likeness is 'frozen' to 0.5 no matter what h says and $\neg h$ denies (see Table 11.2).

This dependence of truth-likeness on the number of states is unpleasant. For, unless the newly added state has some connection with the already existing ones, we would expect that the addition of an irrelevant state in the description of the world, e.g. that a butterfly flew in the rain, must not affect the truth-likeness of statements which describe causally independent facts. It is also noteworthy that in the weather model some contingent propositions, i.e. molecular propositions with two conjuncts one of which is negated, e.g. $\neg h \wedge r$, or $\neg r \wedge h$, have precisely the same verisimilitude, i.e. 0.5, independently of the number of states. The only case in which addition of new states results in an increase of truth-likeness is when the propositions contain two negated states.

The foregoing suggests that, despite its ingenuity, the 'possible worlds' approach fails to give a proper explication of truth-likeness. Truth-likeness turns out to possess odd features such as (a non-uniform) dependence on the number of states of the world. True propositions end up having the same verisimilitude as false ones. Some contingent propositions turn out to have a fixed verisimilitude irrespective of the states of the world. And some other

Table 11.2 Changes in truth-likeness with the number of states

Number of states	h	$\neg h$	$\neg h \wedge r$	$\neg r \wedge h$	$h \wedge \neg r \wedge w$	$\neg h \wedge r \wedge \neg w$
$n = 2$	0.75	0.25	0.5	0.5		
$n = 3$	0.67	0.33	0.5	0.5	0.67	0.33
$n = 4$	0.625	0.375	0.5	0.5	0.625	0.375
$n = 5$	0.6	0.4	0.5	0.5	0.6	0.4
	.*	.*				
	.*	.*				
	$(n+1)/2n$	$(n-1)/2n$				

*Signifies indefinite extension of n.

contingent propositions have their truth-likeness increased by merely adding new states in the world.

There is, however, a possible reply to be considered. Niiniluoto has suggested (private communication) that this criticism misses the mark because measures of truth-likeness are 'contextual'. Questions of verisimilitude are relative to a target specified in connection with some information, and hence one would expect that when the information changes (i.e. when the target changes), the degree of truth-likeness of a certain statement might change, too. Suppose, for instance, that you are asked to tell the colour of Professor Niiniluoto's eyes, and that you have a theory h which says (correctly) that they are blue. But now suppose you give the same answer in the context of a question that concerns the colour of his eyes, hair and skin. In this context the answer h is less verisimilar than it was in the context of the previous question, because it gives much less information about the relevant truth.

This is a fair point, although one may be a bit uneasy about judgements of truth-likeness being relative to a context. Be that as it may, the foregoing reply is not totally adequate. For as we have seen, when the information tends to become maximal – when the truth-likeness of a statement – is judged with respect to a cognitive problem which involves a great number of basic states, then on the possible words approach, the verisimilitude of both statement h and its negation tends to 'freeze' at 0.5, irrespective of what h asserts and $\neg h$ denies. So, in a certain sense, the more complete the information becomes, the more difficult it is to discriminate between any statement h and its negation in respect of their verisimilitude. In most realistic situations, one would expect that the number of basic states involved is very large, and hence one would expect that, if one relied on the possible worlds approach, no meaningful comparison between the verisimilitude of a statement and its negation would be forthcoming. So, I conclude that the possible worlds approach fails to offer a cogent formal account of truth-likeness.

The 'type-hierarchies' approach

In a recent book (1994) Aronson, Harré and Way (henceforth AHW) construe scientific theories as type-hierarchies which intend to capture the structural relationships between natural kinds. Generally, a type-hierarchy (more broadly, a semantic network) is a tree-structured graph of nodes joined by links, where nodes represent objects or concepts and links represent the relations between them. One of the most useful ways to characterise type-hierarchies is as having higher nodes standing for (super-)types (e.g. ANIMAL), intermediate nodes standing for sub-types (e.g. DOG) and leaf-nodes standing for tokens/individuals (e.g. Fido). Then links are taken to exemplify 'a-kind-of' or 'an-instance-of' relation between nodes in the hierarchy. This kind of representation is useful because it moves from the less to the more specific (e.g. from type ANIMAL to sub-type DOG) and this move is accompanied with property inheritance (e.g. if animals are living organisms, so are dogs). Practically, this means that type-hierarchies can facilitate knowledge representation and, in particular, inference (e.g. one can infer that since Fido is an instance of the type DOG, it is also an animal, etc.). An example of an animal type-hierarchy is shown in Figure 11.1.

There are lots of interesting issues relating to this type-hierarchical account of scientific theories. But here we are interested only in AHW's characterisation of verisimilitude. Armed with the representation of theories as discourses about type-hierarchies, AHW attempt to give an account of verisimilitude in terms of similarity relations within type-hierarchies. AHW's novelty consists in reversing the problem-situation concerning the characterisation of verisimilitude. Instead of defining verisimilitude in terms of the distance from the whole truth (as the 'possible worlds' approach did), they define truth in terms of verisimilitude. Truth, for AHW, is 'a limiting

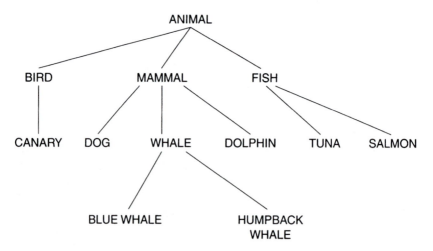

Figure 11.1 Animal type-hierarchy

case of verisimilitude' (1994: 123). The rough idea is that verisimilitude pertains to cases where the type picked out is similar to the actual type, whereas truth pertains to cases of real match between two types. More precisely, two types (of object) are said to be similar when they are represented as sub-types of the same super-type (e.g. WHALE and DOG are both sub-types of the super-type MAMMAL).

Similarity is certainly a notion that admits of degrees, and AHW capture this feature rather nicely by suggesting that the degree of similarity between two types is a function of their relative locations within the type-hierarchy. So, in the example above, DOLPHIN is more similar to WHALE than it is to TUNA. AHW define verisimilitude by means of a distance-function (borrowed from Amos Tversky) such that the distance (degree of similarity) between two types is the weighted difference between (a) the properties that the two types have in common and (b) the properties in respect of which the two types differ. Then the degree of verisimilitude of a truth-claim is calculated by finding the distance of the type picked by this claim from the type of the actual object. For instance, assuming that the actual object is a humpback whale, the verisimilitude of the claim that the object is a dolphin depends on the distance (defined as above) between the type DOLPHIN and the type HUMPBACK WHALE in a type-hierarchy. On this account, a claim C (that a given object is a dolphin) can be more or less verisimilar than another one C* (that it is a haddock), depending on whether C's distance from the actual object (a humpback whale) is smaller or greater than C*'s distance from it. Similarly, truth is presented as a limiting case of verisimilitude to the extent that the type picked out is identical to the type corresponding to the actual object.

This is certainly an innovative attempt to characterise truth-likeness. There is, however, a general problem with the use of similarity to explicate verisimilitude. AHW construe similarity in terms of locations in a type-hierarchy. If a type-hierarchy is fixed, then it seems cogent to say that what is similar is determined by their respective locations in the type-hierarchy. But what determines a type-hierarchy in the first place, if not some prior similarity relation between the types chosen to stratify the hierarchy? If this is so, then it seems rather trivial – and not explanatory – that type-hierarchies determine similarity relations: they are simply constructed on the basis of similarity relations.

Similarity relations are context-dependent. Here, one may need only to note the so-called 'qua problem': two animals may be similar qua aquatic beings, but dissimilar in the ways they feed their young, or in the shapes of their tails. If verisimilitude depends on similarity, then it too, becomes contextual. Different similarity relations will give rise to different type-hierarchies, and hence to different ways to assess the verisimilitude of a certain claim. What type-hierarchy shall we choose in order to determine the verisimilitude of this claim? If verisimilitude depends on locations in type-hierarchies, then the verisimilitude of a given claim will vary from one type-hierarchy to another. So, for instance, the claim that a given object is a dolphin may end up having different verisimilitude depending on, whether the embedding type-hierarchy is that of mammals or that of aquatic animals. And, similarly, the assertion that, say, an object is a dog – given that the actual object is a dolphin – may be more verisimilar in the type-hierarchy of mammals, less verisimilar in the type-hierarchy of animals with tails, but simply false in the type-hierarchy of aquatic animals. Which of all these constitutes the degree of verisimilitude of the assertion? I think that although, strictly speaking, AHW's characterisation avoids the standard objection of language dependence, it is no less contextual than the 'possible words' approach, discussed in the last section. On AHW's theory, claims to verisimilitude can arise only in particular contexts, expressed in terms of certain type-hierarchies, and they can be questioned in other contexts, where different type-hierarchies are chosen.

This 'contextualism' then, creates two important philosophical problems for AHW's approach.

1   What – or who – is going to determine the relevant context in which the truth-likeness of a certain truth-claim will be judged? In other words, what – or who – is going to pick the contextually relevant type-hierarchy? If no objective criteria are offered, then, to say the least, the degree of verisimilitude of a truth-claim becomes conventional, and even ambiguous.

2   Suppose that one replies that we should appeal to pragmatic considerations, e.g. to what currently interests us, in order to pick the appropriate context (type-hierarchy). Suppose, for example, that we try to determine how truth-like is the claim that an object is a dolphin, given that our interest is in aquatic animals. Then, the presently examined reply will be that our interest in aquatic animals *ipso facto* fixes the context in which the truth-likeness of the certain claim will be judged. I think, however, that this appeal to pragmatic factors, or to interests, will not disperse the charge that the claim of truth-likeness may well end up ambiguous. For, even given a set of interests and pragmatic factors, there may well be more than one type-hierarchy relevant to determining the truth-likeness of a claim. For example, suppose that the actual object is a swordfish, that our guess is that it is a dolphin, and that our present interest is in aquatic animals. Still, we may choose to embed our guess in a type-hierarchy of sea-mammals, or in a type-hierarchy of animals with gills, or whatever else. The result will obviously be that, even relative to a specific set of interests, a particular truth-claim could receive very different degrees of verisimilitude.

Contextualism cannot capture a realist understanding of verisimilitude. From a realist point of view, we want to make meaningful assertions of the form: claim C is more verisimilar than C*. Yet it does not make good sense to say that a claim C has such-and-such verisimilitude according to *this* type-hierarchy, but different verisimilitude according to *that* type-hierarchy. Unless there is a way to pick a type-hierarchy as the one according to which the verisimilitude of assertions should be determined, we are left in the dark as to the degree of verisimilitude we should deem the correct one, especially when the degree of verisimilitude varies dramatically from one context to the other. I therefore think that, although this type-hierarchical approach to verisimilitude is promising, it needs to be freed from the context-dependence of hierachical classification. It should be such that it tracks the causal structure of the world. In other words, the least that can be said is that those type-hierarchies are relevant to judgements of verisimilitude which capture objective dependencies among natural kinds. The more natural the type-hierarchy is – the more it respects objective connections and relations among natural properties – the better-founded the verisimilitude judgement made. If, as AHW suggest, 'there is no way of answering the question of what the real ordering of biological types is', and if 'this [ordering] will depend on the purpose for which this type or that type hierarchy is to be put' (1994: 134), I cannot see how the type-hierarchical approach to scientific theories can offer a realist account of verisimilitude, and of truth (if truth is a limiting case of verisimilitude).

Giere on truth-likeness

The failure of formal and quantitative approaches to truth-likeness has led some realist philosophers of science, most notably Ronald Giere, to abandon talk of truth-likeness, and to opt for similarity comparisons between theoretical models (construed as non-linguistic entities) and real systems (Giere 1988: 82–86, 106–110). Giere's view is that to the extent to which the model and the real system are similar, we may say that the model provides a better or worse approximation to the real system. He suggests that the notion of similarity between models and real systems provides the resource for understanding approximation in science and avoids 'the bastard semantic relationship' of approximate truth (ibid.: 106). Giere's approach deserves much more attention than it can be given here. What I try to argue for in this section is that whatever the merits of Giere's approach, it hardly avoids use of some notion of truth-likeness.

Giere subscribes to the so-called semantic view of theories, according to which theories are seen as families of models.[3] For him, models are taken to be abstract entities which satisfy a certain *theoretical definition* (typically, a mathematical equation, or a set of them). How, then, do models (and theories) get linked to (or make claims about) the physical world? Giere suggests that this is effected by means of *theoretical hypotheses*.

Theoretical hypotheses have the form: the physical system X is, or is very close to, M – where M is the abstract entity described by the model. So, theoretical hypotheses provide the link between the model and the world.

As Giere says, they provide a link between 'a theoretical model and that of which it is a model' (1988: 80). Here is an example of a theoretical hypothesis. The position and velocities of the earth and the moon in the earth-moon system (i.e. the physical system X) are very close to those of a two-particle Newtonian system with an inverse-square central force (the abstract entity M described in the *model*). Or, equivalently, the earth and the moon form, to some degree of approximation, a two-particle Newtonian system.

It is by means of such hypotheses that models (which, as such, are abstract structures) get to represent concrete physical systems, and theories acquire empirical content. Theoretical hypotheses make substantive claims about the world. They claim that the behaviour of a given physical system stands in a particular relation to the behaviour of the abstract entity described in the model. Given that the model describes the behaviour of the abstract entity M, and given that this behaviour stands in a particular relation to that of a concrete physical system X, we can come to know (predict, test etc.) the behaviour of X. We can, therefore, acquire some substantive information about the concrete physical system X.

What, however, is the required relation between the model and the physical system? Here the opinions of advocates of the semantic view are divided. Suppe (1977: 223–225; 1979: 324) suggests that the model M should be isomorphic (or homomorphic) to the physical system X, the latter conceived to be an idealised replica of the phenomena. Being an empiricist, van Fraassen (1987a: 111) restricts his attention to a theory's being empirically adequate, and suggests that the required relation is that of embedding: the observable phenomena should be isomorphic to an empirical substructure of the theoretical model. For Giere, the required relation is that of similarity (1988: 81). Giere's theoretical hypotheses state that the behaviour of a concrete physical system is *similar* to the behaviour of the abstract entity described in the model.

However, similarity is a notion that Giere takes to be primitive. To be sure, he suggests that similarity between a model M and a physical system X is always a matter of *degrees* and *respects*, and therefore similarity claims should involve a specification of relevant respects and degrees (1988: 81). But this does not shed much light on the similarity metric which is involved in judging whether X is similar to M.

Be that as it may, what is noteworthy is that theoretical hypotheses do all the representational work that has to be done if theories are to acquire empirical content. In fact, theoretical hypotheses are linguistic entities which have truth-values: they are either true or false, according to whether the physical system X is relevantly similar to the model M. I think this is just a roundabout way of saying that the description of the real system offered by the model is truth-like. To be sure, Giere insists that theoretical hypotheses do not specify relationships between linguistic entities and real objects, but rather specify connections between 'two objects, one abstract and one real' (1988: 82). This being true, the difference is not really important. For models, after all, license linguistic descriptions. Theoretical hypotheses associate these descriptions of abstract systems (normally, given by means of a set of equations) with idealised descriptions of real systems. Then, they state that the two descriptions are similar in certain respects and to a certain degree. Take for instance, the study of the behaviour of the earth–moon system. A theoretical hypothesis says that its behaviour is similar to the behaviour of a two-body system, where the latter is an abstract mathematical entity described by Newton's law of gravitation. The similarity judgement is grounded in several idealisations. Strictly speaking, the moon is not a point-mass, the bodies involved are not perfect spheres, the gravitational force between the earth and the moon is not the only force acting on them, etc. Yet, thanks to suitable idealisations, the influence of the earth on the moon can be adequately studied by being subsumed under the mathematical description of a Newtonian two-body system. It is trivial to conclude that the description of a Newtonian two-body system is approximately true of the earth–moon system and, hence, that it is a truth-like description, where the degree of truth-likeness is a function of the idealisations and approximations involved in the description of the earth–moon system, (i.e. of the real system). Figure 1 'says' just this.

The upshot of all this is that I do not share Giere's misgivings about the notion of truth-likeness. In fact, I think his own approach can legitimise talk of truth-likeness, because it captures the intuitive appeal of this notion: that a theoretical description is truth-like to the extent to which it is roughly right in what it says about what it describes. Perhaps, we can do better than that and offer a more definite qualitative explication of the notion of truth-likeness. I try to do that in the next section.

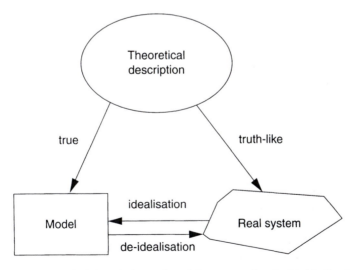

Figure 11.2 Theoretical descriptions of models are associated with idealised descriptions of real systems

An 'intuitive' approach

Truth-likeness is the working notion of truth in science. In our interactions with the world, the exact truth cannot generally be had, especially concerning the unobservable and spatio-temporally remote aspects of the world. A perfect match between theories and the world is almost impossible. This is so for many reasons. The complexity and interconnected character of natural phenomena is such that nature could not be effectively studied and represented in unified and comprehensive theories unless some idealisations and simplifications are made. Scientific theories involve many idealisations, like point-masses and ideal gases, which provide a simplified, yet more easily investigable, representation of the world. The laws which govern natural phenomena are represented by bracketing off several distorting features and conditions, such the air-resistance in the law of free fall. Some laws are deduced from others under specific conditions of approximation, and certain *ceteris paribus* assumptions. Theoretical predictions are tested against experimental results, but almost no experimental result is error-free, and almost no prediction exactly matches the experimental results. Most predictions stand within an ε, however small, from the experimental outcome, which itself has an error-estimate. Demanding the exact truth in science would amount to demanding the exclusion of all approximations, simplifications, idealisations, approximate derivations, sources of error in measurements and calculations. Even were this sort of science possible, it would not be the science with which we are familiar.

However, scientific results, mostly, are self-corrective. Not only do scientists specify the idealisations and approximations involved in theoretical laws and mechanisms, but also they specify, as exactly as possible, the respects and in degrees to which the natural phenomena deviate from their theoretical representations. Take for instance the case where a law is derived from other more fundamental laws, e.g. the derivation of Kepler's first law from Newton's inverse-square law. This derivation is, strictly speaking, false. Actually, from premises which are strictly speaking false, i.e. considering the revolution of Mars around the sun as a two-body problem, a false conclusion is derived – that Mars' orbit is elliptical. But the degree of accuracy of the derivation is specifiable, as are the respects in and degrees to which the conclusion, Mars's orbit is elliptical, deviate from the actual orbit of Mars. This is where the idea of truth-likeness enters science. For both the premises of the derivation (i.e. two-body problem) and its conclusion (Mars's orbit is elliptical) are, in one sense, truth-like. For instance, Kepler's laws are truth-like, because they approximate to a high degree of accuracy the motion of planets. The two-body approach in the derivation of Kepler's first law from the law of universal gravitation is truth-like, because the gravitational effects of the other planets on the motion of Mars are negligible compared to the Sun's gravitational field.

If truth is understood as *fittingness*, that is, if it accepted that a theory (or theoretical description) is true if and only if it fits the world, then truth-likeness should be understood as *approximate fittingness*: a description, statement, law, theory are truth-like if and only if there are respects and degrees to which they fit with the facts. As Thomas Weston has nicely put it: 'A statement will count as approximately true to the degree that it is accurate in whatever it asserts' (1992: 54).

I call the approach I am defending currently 'intuitive' because it stays as closely as possible to our intuitions about truth-likeness. According to these intuitions, a theory is approximately true if the entities of the general kind postulated to play a central causal role in the theory exist, and if the basic mechanisms and laws postulated by the theory approximate those holding in the world, under specific conditions of approximation. The positive argument for the claim that a false description of a law, or entity, can be truth-like, is this: strictly speaking false descriptions may well be cognitively significant; they may fit better or worse with the facts they purport to describe. They may represent their intended domain to a low or high degree of accuracy. The wave theory of light is strictly speaking false. Yet, its description of the interference phenomena is a better approximation to the truth than is the relevant description of the theory of luminous molecules. Similar examples can be generated at will. The point then is that instead of abandoning any talk of truth-likeness, since all truth-like assertions are – strictly speaking – false, we had better try to capture as adequately as possible the conditions under which a representation fits as accurately as possible the relevant facts.

One natural way to spell out the intuitive notion is this:[4]

> A description *D approximately fits* a state *S* (i.e. *D* is approximately true of *S*) if there is another state *S'* such that *S* and *S'* are linked by specific conditions of approximation, and *D fits S'* (*D* is true of *S'*).

So, for instance, a theoretical law is approximately true of the world, if it is strictly true in a world which approximates ours under certain conditions. Take, for example, the law of gases, $PV = RT$. This is approximately true of real gases, since it is true of ideal gases and the behaviour of real gases approximates that of ideal gases under certain conditions.

This is just a skeleton of a theory of truth-likeness. But, it also captures the sound intuitions behind the 'possible worlds' approach as well as behind Giere's views, examined in earlier sections. According to those intuitions, judgements of approximate truth involve some comparison between the actual world (or a description thereof) and the world, or state, described by the theory.[5]

Does the fact that there is no formally adequate understanding of truth-likeness spoil the integrity of this concept and make it implausible as an aim of science? Laudan, for instance, suggests this much (see 1996: 78). If 'truth-likeness' proves to be an elusive notion, then Laudan may be right. But the lack of a formal account is not necessarily a defect. I think we must avoid confusing clarity with formalisation. I am personally sceptical about the prospects of *formalising* the notion of truth-likeness. There is an irreducibly *qualitative* element in the notion of approximation, i.e. the respects in and degrees to which one description may be said to approximate another. But I do not think that the intuitive notion of truth-likeness already operating in science is unclear. Here the comparison with the formal Tarskian understanding of truth is not helpful. The need for formalisation *à la* Tarski arose, at least partly, from the fact that the intuitive notion of truth led to paradoxes, such as the 'Liar paradox'. No similar paradoxes are known *vis-à-vis* the intuitive understanding of approximate truth, or of truth-likeness. Hence, there is no relevant need for a formal introduction of the predicate 'is approximately true', or the predicate 'is truth-like'.

An objection here may be that the intuitive notion of approximate truth is vague.[6] To an extent, this is correct, especially in light of the fact that the notion of approximation is qualitative. Nonetheless, I think that vagueness is not an insoluble problem. In order to overcome vagueness, we do not necessarily need to formally introduce the new predicate 'is truth-like'. Instead, we need to focus on the notion of approximation. This notion can be more precise and accurate, if not as a generic notion which applies in an abstract way to any theory whatsoever, then at least as a discrete notion which applies to particular theories. When it comes to examining particular theoretical descriptions, the respects and degrees of similarity – a notion which is crucial in explicating truth-likeness – can certainly be made more precise and concrete.[7] Insofar as such judgements are meaningful and can be made, the intuitive notion of truth-likeness gets all the clarity it needs.[8]

Another possible objection is that the intuitive notion is not *robust* enough to serve the realist needs. For, the thought may be, it basically relies on the notion of approximation, and this may not be enough to defend the realist's epistemic optimism that current theories are approximately true. I think, however, that this objection is misguided. For it is one thing to explicate the claim that a theory (or a theoretical statement) is approximately true, that is, to explicate what is meant when it is claimed that a certain theory – or theoretical description – is approximately true, but it is quite another to *ground* the judgement that a theoretical description, or a theory, is approximately true. The first is, broadly speaking, an issue in semantics, whereas the second is an epistemological problem. Very little, if anything, of what I have said in this chapter relates explicitly to the second issue. The present aim has been to show that insofar as the notion of approximation is clear, and insofar as the conditions under which a certain description (or state) approximates another are specifiable, to say of a statement D that it is approximately true of state S is to say that it is true of a state S' which approximates S. Whatever else it does, this explication at least legitimises ascriptions of approximate truth when there are specifiable conditions of approximation.[9] When such ascriptions are shown to be legitimate, the issue *still* remains as to whether a certain statement (or theory) can be warrantedly said to be approximately true. The epistemic optimism associated with scientific realism asserts that such ascriptions of approximate truth can be (and are) warranted. The arguments for this optimism are none other than those presented in earlier chapters, especially in Chapter 4. In a nutshell, the warrant for ascribing approximate truth to mature and genuinely successful theories comes from the fact that it is only if they are seen as approximately true that their impressive predictive successes are best explained.

12 Reference of theoretical terms

Why is the demonstration of referential continuity in theory change such a central element in the defence of scientific realism? Realists typically defend a cumulative approach to science: past theories are superseded by newer ones, but the successor theories are more truth-like than their predecessors. As science progresses, scientific theories offer a more refined and truer description of the world, i.e. of the natural kinds (observable and unobservable) which populate it and of their properties and causal powers. The Platonic metaphor of 'cutting the world at its joints' is, to use Boyd's expression (1993), a 'theory-constitutive' metaphor of the realist doctrine. Not only do realists perceive the world as already constituted by natural kinds to which the theoretical descriptions that theories offer ultimately answer, but they claim that the natural-kind taxonomies of newer theories are better approximations to the objective natural-kind structure of the world.

Throughout this book I have tried to motivate and defend the above theses. But there seem to be some genuine difficulties in entertaining the cumulative element of the realist image of science. The only evidence that we might have for such an optimism, the fact that as science has grown there has emerged some stable taxonomy of natural kinds in our world-picture, seems to be undermined by the radical theoretical changes which constitute much of the history of science. Theories of radical meaning and reference variance – associated with Kuhn (1970) and Feyerabend (1958) – suggest (at least on their 'standard' interpretation) that there are not even ways of comparing past taxonomies with those that superseded them. If each theoretical tradition, or 'paradigm', or 'conceptual scheme', creates its own taxonomy, and if there is no way to compare one taxonomy with another, then we had better opt for a different theory-constitutive metaphor, that of saying that each paradigm 'creates its own world', its own primitive taxonomy of natural kinds (cf. Kuhn 1970: 150).[1]

As is well known, such imputations of radical incommensurability have been challenged by the causal theory of reference. This theory offers an argument for realism by showing how it is possible to talk of a theory-independent trans-theoretical taxonomy of natural kinds. Similarly, it shows that there is substantive continuity in theory change, in the sense that the conceptual changes which occur in the transition from one theory to another have been attempts to better characterise the same entities, and to better accommodate the linguistic categories of science to the causal structure of the world. Meaning changes do occur as science grows, but they are, typically, accompanied by referential stability: the new theories, and the new descriptions associated with old terms, in the final analysis, are about the same theory-independent natural kinds, or physical magnitudes. The meaning of 'electricity' may well have changed since the time of Ampère, but more or less everyone since him, and every theory since his, have attempted to describe the same natural kind, viz. *electricity*, or the causal agent whose salient effects include well-known electrical phenomena.

In this final chapter, I hope to achieve two tasks. First, I try to show that the causal theory of reference can be suitably amended to accommodate some of the criticisms that have been levelled against it. But there is a price to pay, viz. that the theory should give way to what David Lewis (1984) has called 'causal descriptivism'. The need for a theory of reference which is, in effect, a hybrid between purely causal theories and purely descriptive theories, has been repeatedly pointed out ever since, I think, Evans (1973) published his seminal paper on the Kripke-style causal–historical theories of reference. What has not yet been achieved, I think, is the development of an adequate theory of reference for theoretical terms. In what follows, I try to advance such a theory based on the following suggestion by Berent Enç (1976: 271): that 'the burden of reference for the [kind-word or theoretical] term will be carried by the kind-constituting properties attributed to the object by the explanatory mechanism developed in the theory . . .'.

My second task is to show how the causal–descriptive theory of reference can adequately deal with referential continuity in conceptual transitions in which theoretical terms are abandoned. This seems to be an independently interesting issue, because the purely causal theories yield the wrong results; and because, as already stressed towards the end of Chapter 5, it is imperative for realists to show that there can still be continuity of reference even when a term is abandoned. The test-case I use is the transition from the term 'luminiferous ether' to the term 'electromagnetic field'.

Causal theories

According to the received descriptive theories of reference, the reference (or denotation) of a referring expression (e.g. a proper name, or a singular term) is specified by a description (normally understood as specifying the *sense* of the referring expression). Each term (or proper name) is associated with either a unique propositional (attributive) description or, in a more sophisticated manner, with a cluster of (probably weighted) descriptions. If the description, or a weighted most of the descriptions, associated with a term t is satisfied by an individual y, then t refers to y, but if nothing satisfies the description, or a weighted most of the descriptions, t does not refer.

The thrust of the descriptive theory is that the relation between a word and its referent is mediated by the sense of the word. So, an expression acquires its reference (if any) via its sense.

As is well known, Saul Kripke (1980) pointed out that a proper name can refer to an individual even if the descriptions associated with the name are false, (or even if the users of the name cannot put together a set of descriptions that are uniquely true of the particular individual). Conversely, an individual may fit a set of descriptions associated with a name, and yet the name might fail to refer to *that* individual (Kripke's Schmidt–Gödel case). So, when it comes to proper names, satisfying a set of descriptions is neither necessary nor sufficient for reference. Briefly put, the main problem with the descriptive theories is that they generally associate too rich a description with a term/name: it is not necessary, sometimes not even true, that the individual referred to satisfies all (even most) of the descriptions associated with the name.[2]

Kripke's own well known alternative is that reference of proper names is fixed by means of a causal–historical chain which links the current use of a term with an 'act of baptism', where a name was picked to dub an individual. Descriptions associated with the name might (all) be false, and yet the users of the name still refer to the individual dubbed, insofar as their use of the name is part of a causal transmission-chain which goes back to the dubbing ceremony. Occasionally, the introducing event can involve *some* description of the individual introduced. In fact, there are cases in which the introduction of an entity, or an individual, is made *only* via a description, e.g. the introduction of the planet Neptune, or of 'Jack the Ripper' (cf. Kripke, 1980: 79–80, 96). But the description is not analytically tied to the term, as traditional descriptive theories would have it. The description just 'fixes the reference by some contingent marks of the object' (ibid.: 106). As a rule, however, the causal theorists insist that what fixes the reference of a term is not the descriptions associated with it, but the causal chain which connects the term with the object named in the dubbing ceremony. So, the thrust of the theory is that the relation between a word and an object is direct – a direct causal link – unmediated by a concept. In particular, the causal theory dispenses with word-sense as a reference-fixing device and suggests that the reference of a word is the entity which 'grounded' the word in the dubbing ceremony in which the word was first introduced. The superiority of causal theories when it comes to proper names is well taken even by some of the most incisive critics of the theory (see Unger 1983).

As Putnam observed, Kripke's (1980) theory of proper names offers a model for a theory of reference of 'natural-kind' terms that feature in folk and scientific theories: the reference of a natural-kind term is fixed during an introducing event, i.e. an event during which the term is attached to a substance, or a kind, and samples of this substance or instances of this kind are present and ground the word. According to Putnam, reference is fixed by 'things which are given existentially' (1983b: 73). In the case of a natural-kind term, e.g. 'water' or 'tiger', this means that one picks out by ostension an object, attaches a name to it, and then asserts that this name applies to all and only those objects which have the same nature as that present in the introductory event. So, 'a term refers (to the object named) if it stands in the right relation (causal continuity in the case of proper names; sameness of 'nature' in the case of kinds terms) to these existentially given things' (Putnam 1983b: 73). When the introductory event is completed, the term is transmitted through a linguistic community. The term is borrowed by other users, this borrowing being reference-preserving, if the users are connected to the introductory event in some causal chain of term-transmission.

Fixing the reference of 'physical magnitude' terms is a variation of the same theme: when confronted with some observable phenomena, it is reasonable to assume that there is a physical magnitude, or entity, which causes them. Then we (or indeed, the first person to notice them) dub this magnitude with a term t and associate this magnitude with the production of these phenomena. This is the event in which the term t is introduced as referring to this magnitude. One will, typically, surround the term with a description – a causal story – for the nature of the posited magnitude and for the properties by virtue of which the magnitude causes its paradigmatic observable effects. This initial description will, most likely, be incomplete, or even misguided. It may even be a wrong description, a totally mistaken account of the nature of this causal agent. But, on the purely causal account, one has nonetheless introduced *existentially* a referent – an entity causally responsible for certain effects to which the term t refers.

There is no doubt that the causal theory is intuitively very appealing. This appeal rests on a well-taken distinction: it is one thing to assert that *there is* an entity to which a term t refers, quite another matter to find out the exact nature of this entity, and hence to specify the correct description to associate with the term t used to refer to this putative entity. The beliefs that the users of the term might have about the referent may initially be incorrect. But these beliefs are prone to change – and to correction – as the users' causal interaction with the entity becomes more elaborate and complete. It is only natural to admit that, as the causal give-and-take with a posited entity advances, the knowledge of its nature advances, too. Yet, the initial positing of an entity causally responsible for certain effects remains invariant under changes in the beliefs about this entity: *what exactly this entity is taken to be* is subject to change, but *that this entity is* is not.

It is easily seen how the causal theory disposes of semantic incommensurability. If, for instance, the referent of the term 'electricity' is fixed 'existentially', if, that is, the beliefs or the descriptions associated with this term do not determine what this term refers to, then all different theories of electricity, refer to, and dispute over, the same 'existentially given' magnitude, viz. *electricity*; or, better, the causal agent of salient electrical effects.

The causal theory lends credence to the claim that even though past scientists had partially or fully incorrect beliefs about the properties of some causal agent, their investigations were continuous with the investigations of subsequent scientists, since their common aim has been to identify the nature of the same causal agent, i.e. of the agent posited to be causally responsible for the production of certain phenomena. Insofar as successor theories afford better descriptions of the same causal agent and its relations with other causal agents, one can conclude that science has improved our understanding of the world. And insofar as successor theories are more truth-like than their predecessors in their descriptions of the nature of these causal agents, one can argue that science has achieved a better approximation to the objective causal structure of the world. What, then, the causal theory makes available is a way in which to compare theories and to claim that the successor theory is more truth-like than its predecessors. For, unless these theories can be seen as aiming to describe the same causal agents – 'elements of physical reality' might be a better term – there is no straightforward way to make realist-style comparative judgements of truth-likeness.

Another neat feature of the causal theory is that it tallies with the realists' appeal to the 'naturalisation' of epistemology and semantics. The determination of the reference (and of the meaning) of a term becomes, by and large, an issue which cannot be solved a priori by means of conceptual analysis, but is amenable to empirical investigation into the features of the world and of the natural kinds which populate it. The way the world is constituted and causally interacts with the language users is an indispensable constraint on the theory and practice of fixing the reference (and meaning) of the language used to talk about the world: the conceptual and linguistic categories we use to talk about the world are tuned to accommodate the causal structure of the world.

All this is good and desirable, as far as it goes. But it does not seem to go very far. When it comes to the nitty-gritty details of the project, the causal theories face some important problems which impair their promise to show how reference-fixing is a causal process. These problems have been discussed extensively in the relevant literature (cf. Berk 1979; Devitt and Sterelny 1987: 72–75; Enç 1976; Evans 1973; Fine 1975; Papineau 1979:161, 165; Unger 1983). In what follows I try to summarise these problems, focusing first on the case of natural kind-terms and then on theoretical terms. Concurrently, the elements of the causal–descriptive account I want to motivate are put together.

Problems with natural-kind terms

According to the causal theories, natural-kind terms get their reference during an introductory event in which some instances of the kind (or a sample of it) are present. In a first approximation, it is correct to say that ostension allows us, in principle, to introduce names for kinds prior to having any knowledge of what makes them into a kind. We do this by appealing to situations in which we believe that such kinds are exemplified (cf. Boyd 1993: 492). But ostension is not enough to fix the reference of a kind-word unambiguously. It will often establish referential connections between a word and more than one kind. At any rate, there is no guarantee that it will not. Besides, ostension brings us in contact with a sample, or an instance, of the kind, and not with its extension as a whole. But the word does not refer only to the sample present. It refers to everything that belongs to its extension. What exactly, then, 'binds together' the sample, or the instances, present at the introductory event *and* the other items that belong to the extension of the term? Ostension cannot possibly do the trick. So, reference-fixing should involve more than ostension. Devitt and Sterelny (1987: 72) suggest that it should involve also a 'structural component': the extension of a kind-term includes all and only those items which have the same *internal structure* as the ostensively given samples. Manifest properties are not robust enough to circumscribe the boundaries of the kind. Causally relevant differences as well as similarities in the behaviour of two items that are grouped together into an 'intuitive kind' (cf. Quine 1969: 40) are typically due to some internal structural differences or similarities. Ice is a kind of water not because of its manifest properties but because of its internal structure. And a liquid which has the appearance of water might well kill you if you drink it, unless it is H_2O.

Once, however, an appeal to the internal structure is made, the burden of reference is borne by some parts of the *theoretical environment* in which the term is embedded. An item is said to belong to the extension of a kind-term because it is relevantly similar to the samples present in the introduction of the term. But the *properties* in virtue of which it is deemed to be relevantly similar to the known samples are those specified in the theoretical description of the internal structure of the samples. In fact, it is these properties which determine that there is a natural kind to which these samples, as well as the item at hand, belong. What, if anything, binds together into a *natural* kind all the samples or items we have encountered, as well as others we have not, is the fact that they all have the same internal structure. But there is no theory-independent way of specifying what constitutes the internal structure of the members of a kind. It is theoretical descriptions of the internal structure which show that the extension of the kind-word is not gerrymandered. If we did not rely on such theoretical descriptions of the internal structure to fix the reference of a kind-word, then we would have no way to argue that the extension of the kind-word is a natural kind. An example will help to drive the point home. Causal theories are certainly right in saying that 'water' refers to the substance with chemical structure H_2O. But this assertion amounts to admitting that the *manifest* properties of the samples we encounter are not sufficiently robust to determine the extension of the kind-term 'water'. Instead, appeal should be made to the unobservable properties of the samples. But to claim that the unobservable structure of the samples is H_2O is to adopt a *theory* about the structure of this substance. Hence, what bears the burden of reference of 'water' is the part of the theoretical environment in which the word is embedded.

Causal theorists may be content with rehearsing their point that, still, what determines reference is not beliefs or theoretical descriptions, but the internal structure, *whatever that is*: our beliefs about, and descriptions of, the internal structure might all be wrong and yet 'water' still refers to *whatever substance* exhibits certain manifest properties of the samples used to introduce the term 'water'. Even so, *some* theoretical descriptions (or beliefs) are neces-sary, for instance that there is a unique substance (a natural kind) which exhibits all these manifest properties, and that it does so because of its (unknown) internal structure. But the issue is more complicated than that. Suppose, for instance, that we discovered that the chemical composition of the samples used to introduce the term 'water' is *not* H_2O. (If you think that this is a science-fiction story, then you may think of phlogiston instead of water.) Then, there are two options available to the causal theory: either that the term 'water' does not refer to *water*, or that it still does.

The move favoured by pure causal theories would surely be to say that 'water' still refers to *whatever* it is that has the manifest properties of the samples which were present at the introduction of the term 'water', even though the real constitution of the samples is not H_2O. This move, however, makes it vivid that the purely causal theory should get its priorities right. For, the causal theory had to put the internal structure of the posited kind *ahead* of the manifest properties of some samples in order to argue that the similarity among these samples is robust enough to warrant positing a natural kind – *water* – to which the term 'water' refers. But when faced with a misidentification of the internal structure of the posited kind, the causal theory has to reverse the order and put the manifest properties ahead of the internal structure in order to argue that samples (or items) which share these properties are nonetheless sufficiently similar to be grouped together as a natural kind with some internal structure or other, even though they do not have the internal structure we thought they did.

These reversals of priority seem, to say the least, ad hoc. For, if the internal structure, as specified by our best theories, is appealed to in order to posit and identify the referent of a natural-kind term, then it should also be put ahead of the manifest properties when it comes to a misidentifica-tion of the referent of a natural-kind term. To think otherwise is to think that manifest properties are robust enough to determine natural kinds, a thought which we saw to be problematic.

I think the problem just discussed leaves the causal theory with a pressing dilemma. If the internal properties are consistently put ahead of manifest properties in positing a kind as natural and in taking it to be the referent of a natural-kind term then, when faced with a misidentification of the internal structure of the referent, the causal theory has either to perform a reversal of the roles of internal and manifest properties in reference fixing, or else it has to concede that the natural-kind term whose referent was misidentified by our current best theoretical descriptions does not refer to anything. Opting for the first horn of the dilemma would be unmotivated and ad hoc, while opting for the second horn would amount to admitting that theoretical descriptions *do* play a central role in reference fixing. The upshot, I think, is that the causal theory should seriously take the role of theoretical descriptions of the internal structure of a posited kind. Positing a natural kind with a certain internal structure should not be a mere place-holder for whatever theoretical description of this 'existentially given' kind will be spewed out by ideal science. Rather, positing a natural kind with a certain internal structure should be tied to a description of its properties – a description, that is, of what this internal structure is – in such a way that if there is no kind which has these properties, then we may have to just admit that a word which was taken to refer to this kind does not, after all, refer.

Given what I have just said, it may be thought that the shortcoming of the purely causal theory lead us directly into the arms of the rival descriptive theories as ways to fix the reference of natural-kind terms. Yet, there *is* another alternative: to try to offer an account which utilises resources from *both* the purely causal and the traditional descriptive theories, without, if possible, falling foul of their shortcomings. One may call such an account, following Lewis's hint (1984), 'causal descriptivist'. Lewis (followed by Kroon 1985; 1987) suggested that reference-fixing descriptions should be couched in causal terms. But I think we can do better than that. While we should accept that reference fixing should involve *some* descriptions, we can also accommodate the main insight of the causal theories, viz. that causation – and not just causal talk – plays an ineliminable role in reference fixing. In order to accommodate this suggestion into the sought-after causal–descriptive theory of reference, a central role will be given to Enç's claim (1976) that the burden of reference is borne by the *kind-constitutive properties* attributed to the posited kind, substance or object. Here is how we might proceed.

Generalising on Enç's ideas, one may say that a kind-term refers to a natural kind by virtue of the fact that the body of information which is typically associated with a kind-term has its *causal origin* in the kind-constitutive properties of the kind. This means that this information has the propositional content it does because the kind has the kind-constitutive properties it does. For instance, to say that the causal origin of the body of information associated with the term 'water' lies in the chemical constitution of water is to say the following: if the liquid which is colourless, odourless, still, thirst-quenching, etc., and whose boiling point is 100° Celsius, its freezing point 0° Celsius etc., were not H_2O it would not have these manifest properties, and the propositional content of the information associated with the term 'water' would be different.[3] As noted above, however, there is no theory-independent way to identify the kind-constitutive properties of a natural kind. Hence, the foregoing explication of what it is for the information associated with a kind-term to have its causal origin in the kind-constitutive properties of the kind should be seen as offering only an *external standard* to assess the correctness of our taxonomies of kinds: a taxonomy is correct if and only if the information it associates with the kinds it posits has its causal origin in the kind-constitutive properties of natural kinds. So, a phlogiston-based taxonomy is wrong because no natural kind has the kind-constitutive properties attributed to phlogiston. And an oxygen-based taxonomy is right – insofar it is right – because its elements correspond to the kind-constitutive properties of chemical kinds.

Since the kind-constitutive properties of a kind (or physical magnitude) are not the kind of thing to which we have theory-independent access, we have to rely on theories and their causal–explanatory descriptions of the entities they posit. There is no other way. Only theories can tell us in virtue of what internal properties or mechanisms, as well as in virtue of what nomological connections, a certain substance possesses the properties and displays the behaviour it does. Similarly, only theories can tell us in virtue of what internal properties an item belongs to *this* rather than *that* kind. And only theories can tell us whether a certain collection of entities, samples or items is a candidate for a natural kind. All this is part of the empirical inquiry, and hence it is subject to change and revision. More importantly, if the theories we rely on are indeed correct, or nearly so, then we succeed in referring to natural kinds; if not, then we fail. So, defending the truthlikeness of our best theories goes hand in hand with defending the claim that, as science grows, it describes more accurately the causal structure of the world.

The kind-constitutive properties are those whose presence in an item makes that item belong to a kind. I will not argue here for the existence of natural kinds. But if there are natural kinds at all, then there are kind-constitutive properties. Members of kinds do not share all of their properties. All samples of water do not have the same size or shape, or the same volume or density. Yet they are all samples of water *insofar* as their molecular structure is H_2O. The kind-constitutive properties are those whose presence makes a set of objects have the same, or sufficiently similar, manifest properties, causal behaviour and causal powers. Water typically quenches thirst and evaporates when, at standard pressure, it reaches its boiling point because, ultimately, it has the molecular structures it does. This is not a matter of logical necessity, but it is a matter of *nomological* necessity. Had the laws of nature been different, water would have different properties. But those laws being what they are, water has the kind-constitutive properties it does. Naturally, identifying the kind-constitutive properties is a matter of empirical inquiry. Equally naturally, the empirical inquiry may show that there are borderline cases, or untypical cases (especially when it comes to biological kinds). But the very possibility of untypical, or borderline, cases requires that there are typical and clear-cut cases of belonging to the extension of a kind. Be that as it may, to say that a kind is natural is to say that, typically, its members have some kind-constitutive properties in common which make them sufficiently similar to each other, and sufficiently dissimilar from members of other kinds.[4]

I have now motivated some central elements of the suggested causal–descriptive theory. Let me simply recapitulate what is what. The theory has a *causal* element because reference is ultimately fixed by the causal origin of the information associated with a term. But it has a *descriptive* element, too. In order to identify the causal origin of the information (i.e. the kind-constitutive properties of the kinds posited) we have to rely on theories, and on their causal–explanatory descriptions. Since there is no theory-independent way to identify the causal origin, what bears the burden of reference is these causal–explanatory descriptions of the kind-constitutive properties. This is not pure descriptivism, however, precisely because the process of reference fixing has an ineliminable causal element: in order for the reference to be successful, the causal–explanatory descriptions of a posit should have their causal origin in the kind-constitutive properties of the posited entity.

Yet more problems with theoretical terms

Before I 'fill in' the contours of the suggested causal–descriptive approach, let me examine in some detail the case of the reference of theoretical terms (or physical magnitude terms) and so lend support to my claim that the failures of the purely causal theories motivate a causal–descriptive account.

As noted earlier, the causal theory suggests that reference is fixed by things which are given purely existentially. Is was agreed also that when it comes to the positing of observable natural kinds, ostension does play some role in fixing the reference of natural-kind terms. But when it comes to the reference of theoretical terms, ostension cannot be of any help at all. When, for instance, Benjamin Franklin introduced the term 'electricity' what he offered was something like this: the phenomena of sparks and lightning-bolts indicate, or suggest, that there is a physical magnitude which causes them – adding, that their cause, which he called electricity, is possibly a substance capable of flow or motion (see Putnam 1975a: 199). The magnitude which 'electricity' was coined to refer to was given not by ostension, but by stating some of its manifest effects and, possibly, an elementary description of its causal powers, i.e. that, whatever else it is, electricity is capable of flow. The term 'electricity' could have been introduced on different occasions. In fact, André Ampère also introduced 'électricité' to account for a set of different effects, viz. currents and electromagnets. His own introduction of the term was based on a different description, say, along the lines of a particulate electric fluid.

What was there in common on all occasions where 'electricity' was introduced? What was there in common between Franklin's 'electricity',

Ampère's 'électricité' and indeed, anybody else's 'electricity'? Putnam's response is that 'that each of [the occurrences of the term 'electricity'] is connected by a certain kind of causal chain to a situation in which a *description* of electricity is given, and generally a *causal* description – that is, one which singles out electricity as *the* physical magnitude *responsible* for certain effects in certain ways' (1975a: 200). Even had all these descriptions of electricity been wrong, according to the causal theory they would still have been *mis*descriptions of electricity, rather than descriptions of nothing at all (ibid.: 201). So, it seems to me that Putnam's response boils down to the following claim: what there is in common in all occurrences of the term 'electricity' in different theories and descriptions is that they all refer to the physical magnitude causally responsible for salient electrical phenomena. This physical magnitude is the referent of the term 'electricity' and guarantees the sameness in reference of the occurrences of this term. It then follows that in the case of the reference of theoretical terms, the 'existentially given thing' is nothing but a *causal agent*, i.e. an agent which is posited to have the causal power to produce certain effects.[5]

A quick worry here might be that there is no guarantee that there is just one causal agent which brings about all these phenomena – electric currents, lightning-bolts, deflections of magnets, etc. This may well be so, but the causal theorist would quickly dismiss this worry by noting that he is not concerned with the epistemological problem of how we can come to assert that all these phenomena are due to electricity. All he is concerned with, he would point out, is to show how all these different tokens of the term 'electricity' can nonetheless refer to the very same entity. On his view, if it happens that electricity is not responsible for, say, lightning-bolts, then Franklin's 'electricity' does not refer to *electricity*, after all. But we have no reason to think that it does not.

A more promising critique is that given that the causal theory reduces referential stability to the bare assertion that a causally efficacious agent operates behind a set of phenomena, continuity and sameness in reference become very easily satisfiable. If the unobservable causal agent behind a set of phenomena is given only existentially, and if no description of its nature is essentially employed in fixing the reference of the terms that purport to refer to it, then the term will *never* fail to refer to something: to *whatever causes* the relevant phenomena – provided of course that these phenomena do have a cause. To put the same critique negatively, on a purely causal account it is not clear what could possibly show that the relevant theoretical term does not refer. If the reference of theoretical terms is fixed purely existentially, then insofar as there *is* a causal agent behind the relevant phenomena, the term is bound to end up referring to it. Hence, there can be no referential failure – even in cases where it is counter-intuitive to expect successful reference. Taken to its letter, the causal theory makes referential success necessary.

Take, for instance, the case of 'phlogiston'. It offers a neat example in which the pure causal theory yields counter-intuitive results. 'Phlogiston' was introduced on many occasions by means of a causal description, i.e. one that singled out phlogiston as the physical magnitude causally involved (given off) in combustion. *Phlogiston*, however, does not exist; hence, it is not causally involved in combustion. Instead, oxygen is. Does this mean, or imply, that phlogiston theorists had been referring to oxygen all along? If we follow the letter of the causal theory and accept that 'phlogiston' was coined to refer purely existentially to whatever is causally involved in combustion, then the conclusion is inescapable – 'phlogiston' refers to oxygen, since the latter is what is causally involved in combustion. This surely is far-fetched. Joseph Priestley and other advocates of the phlogiston theory were causally connected to oxygen – they breathed it and it was causally involved in the experiments they made to investigate combustion. But none of the properties of oxygen were the causal origin of the infor- mation they had associated with phlogiston. And nothing in nature could possibly be the causal origin of such information. What it is correct to say is that 'phlogiston' refers to nothing. But in order to say this, we need to say that there is nothing in nature which possesses the properties that phlo- giston was supposed to possess. That is, we need to say that there is nothing which fits a description which assigns to phlogiston the properties it requires in order to play its intended causal role in combustion. So, once again, we have to rely on theoretical descriptions. More generally, there is no way of demonstrating that a putative causal agent does not exist apart from showing that there is *no* entity possessing the properties attributed to this agent. This procedure involves examining whether the descriptions associated with the term that purports to refer to this agent are satisfied. Referential failure cannot be assessed without appealing to some descriptions, and I contend – by symmetry – the same should be the case for referential success.

Causal descriptivism comes to the rescue once more. If the kind-consti- tutive properties attributed to the referent are not the causal origin of the information associated with the term employed to refer to it, then the term fails to refer. To put it more bluntly, according to causal descriptivism the burden of reference of theoretical terms lies with *some* descriptions which specify the kind-constitutive properties by virtue of which the referent, if it exists, plays its causal role. If there is an entity which answers to this causal description, then the term refers. If there is not, then the term does not refer. On this account, then, the term 'phlogiston' presents no problem: since nothing answers to the kind-constitutive properties attrbuted to phlo- giston, 'phlogiston' is an empty term. As a result, referential continuity between theories is no longer easy to obtain.

Causal descriptivism and theory change

That some descriptions of an entity's sort, as the referent of a term, or of its kind-constitutive properties, are necessary in reference fixing becomes apparent when we want to judge whether two distinct terms nonetheless refer to the same entity. As we saw in Chapter 5, defending the possibility of such descriptions is central to a realist account of science. In order for realists to defend the claim that there is some substantive continuity in revolutionary theory-change, they have to show that not all abandoned theoretical terms are in the same boat as 'phlogiston': some distinct terms in different theories may plausibly be taken to refer to the same entity – even when one of them has been abandoned. If past mature and genuinely successful theories are to be seen as having been truth-like, then it should be the case at least that their central theoretical terms recognisably referred to those entities to which the theoretical terms in their successors also referred (or refer).

Hardin and Rosenberg versus Laudan

On the basis of the causal theory of reference, Hardin and Rosenberg (1982) have argued that it is plausible to think that the term 'luminiferous ether' refers to the *electromagnetic field*. They defend their claim by saying that the luminiferous ether has played the 'causal role we now ascribe to the electromagnetic field' (1982: 613). On their view, if one allows that reference plays a causal role, and given that the ether and the electromagnetic field played the same causal role with respect to optical and electromagnetic phenomena, it is not unreasonable 'for realists to say that "ether" referred to the electromagnetic field all along' (ibid.: 614).

Although I agree with Hardin and Rosenberg's conclusion, I do not think that the best way in which a realist can argue for this conclusion is via this 'sameness-of-causal-role' account of reference. The reason for this is that the 'sameness-of-causal-role' account falls foul of two important objections which Laudan has levelled against it.

The first of Laudan's objections is that Hardin and Rosenberg's account 'proves to be far too *tolerant* for the realist's purposes, since it countenances as genuinely referring all manner of ill-developed theories' (1984b: 160): all (or most) abandoned entities can be said to have played the same causal role in relation to a range of phenomena as does some currently posited entity. For instance, Aristotle's *natural place*, Newton's *gravitational action-at-a-distance* and Einstein's *space–time curvature* can all be said to have played the same causal role *vis-à-vis* gravitational phenomena. So, Laudan argues, on a literal reading of the 'sameness-of-causal-role' account, claims to referential stability become trivial and uninteresting. They are trivial because they are too easily derived. They just amount to the claim that all phenomena have a cause. In the example above, claiming referential continuity amounts to claiming that 'natural place', 'gravitational force' and 'spacetime curvature', have all referred to the *cause of free fall*. And they are uninteresting because, as Laudan notes, they suggest 'no interesting commonality of causal role at the level of explanatory structure' (ibid.).

The second of Laudan's objections against Hardin and Rosenberg is that the 'sameness-of-causal-role' account of reference 'confuses a shared explanatory agenda (i.e. common problems to be solved) with a shared explanatory ontology (i.e. the characteristics of the postulated explanatory entities)' (1984b: 161). According to Laudan a mere similarity in the phenomena to be accounted for does not warrant sameness in the internal structures which cause these phenomena. After all, one may think, it might be the case that the putative internal causes are merely analogous, rather than identical. Laudan goes on to state: 'To make reference parasitic on what is *being explained* rather than on what is *doing the explaining* entails that we can establish what a theory refers to independently of any detailed analysis of what the theory asserts' (ibid.).

I think that both of Laudan's objections are fair. He is right to stress that, unless the sameness of causal role is grounded in the explanatory structure of the posited entities, the alleged commonality of reference is trivial and uninteresting. And he is also right to point out that what the advocates of referential stability in theory-change must show is not just continuity in the phenomena to be explained; however important that is, it is not sufficient for continuity at the level of the entities which are posited to explain these phenomena.

If sameness of causal role is not sufficient for a substantial and interesting explication of sameness of reference, is there anything else for which a realist can hope? Realists should fall back on a causal–descriptive theory of reference. When it comes to judgements of referential stability this means that the relevant theory of reference should show that there can be some substantive continuity at the level of the properties attributed to the putative referents, properties by virtue of which they play their ascribed causal role. Such an account of reference will be able to ground and explain the claim that the posited entities share the same causal role, thereby meeting Laudan's objections. Here is exactly where the idea that the burden of reference is carried by the kind-constitutive properties attributed to the referent of the term comes into play and bears its fruits.

End of drama: how theoretical terms get their reference

In arguing that the reference should be fixed by causal descriptions of the above sort, I have followed Enç's lead (see Enç 1976). What Enç has not adequately dealt with is the following problem: the causal–explanatory structure associated with a newly posited entity may, if it is sufficiently rich, explain by virtue of which mechanisms it is supposed to play its causal role; but there will be no guarantee of referential continuity in theory-change. For the entities posited by successor theories rarely, if ever take up the greater part of the explanatory–causal structure attributed to the abandoned entities. If, on the other hand, the causal–explanatory structure attributed to a newly posited entity is considerably slimmed down, then there is no guarantee that the new descriptions pick out a unique natural kind.

In order to deal with this problem, we may proceed as follows. If we take the line that reference is fixed by means of detailed descriptions associated with a theoretical term, then, typically, it will turn out to be the case that no entity posited by a newer theory will satisfy them. Then, there will be no point in arguing that, from the vantage point of the newer theory, there is a sense in which the advocates of the superseded theory referred to the entity posited by the new theory. Not only, however, were the advocates of both the old theory and the new one dealing with the same phenomena, they were trying to identify the causes behind these phenomena. To this end, they posited certain causal agents to which they attributed several properties which were taken to bring about these agents' effects. The two theories may differ in the full descriptions of the properties they ascribe to the posited causal agents. But there may well be a *substantive overlap* between them. Should this happen, there will be a sense in which there is some referential continuity between the two theories.

The claim here is not merely that some subsequent posit has taken the place of the entity posited by the older theory as the putative cause of a set of phenomena. What is important is that the subsequent posit is invested with some of the *attributes* ascribed to the abandoned putative entity, attributes by virtue of which the abandoned entity was thought to produce its effects. Hence, although there may well be nothing in the world which possesses all the attributes ascribed to an abandoned posit α, there may well be a current posit β to which are ascribed some (sometimes most) of the attributes ascribed to α, and which is also considered to be causally responsible for the same phenomena as α had been taken to produce. Should this situation occur, we may be willing to say that the term intended to refer to the abandoned posit α refers (or, at any rate, *approximately refers*) to the current posit β.

Before I try to make this claim more precise, let me block a quick objection to my outline. Any two putative entities might have some properties in common; hence, finding some overlap in properties would be trivial. But that is no objection to my account so far. For, simply, referential continuity requires not a mere overlap in properties, but a substantive continuity in those properties which explain/ground the causal role attributed the posited entities. That there are such common explanatory properties is far from trivial.

Let me then return to my attempt to explicate the conditions of referential continuity in theory change. The process of positing theoretical entities – and hence the problem of fixing the reference of theoretical terms – is associated with specific problem-situations, in which an entity is posited in order to stand for the cause of some phenomena. In these problem-situations a term is selected to denote the putative entity. When an entity is posited, there is, normally, some account of certain fundamental – kind-constitutive – properties which this entity must possess if it is to play its intended causal role. What these properties are is suggested, typically, by background theoretical knowledge as well as by new experimental knowledge. So, the term which is employed to denote the posited entity is associated with a *core causal description* of the properties by virtue of which it plays its causal role *vis-à-vis* the set of phenomena. Insofar as these kind-constitutive properties comprise the causal origin of the core information associated with the term, then the term can be said to refer to this entity.

The appeal to kind-constitutive properties is essential because it is *these* properties which, ultimately, fix the reference of the term. It is the presence of descriptions of these properties in the core causal description which suggest that there is *at least* one (putative) entity – characterised by these properties – to which the term refers and that there is *at most* one entity to which the term refers. The one and only entity to which the term refers is the entity characterised by the relevant kind-constitutive properties. So, the core causal description associated with the term identifies the referent in such a way that (a) if no entity satisfies it, (i.e. if it is true of no entity), then the term does not refer; and (b) if an entity y does not satisfy the core causal description of an entity x, y and x cannot play the same causal role. So, on this view, we have a readily available account of referential success and failure.

The core causal description need not necessarily, and does not generally, include detailed accounts of the specific constitution of the posited entity; nor of the specific causal mechanisms it activates. For, simply, such detailed information is not, *ab initio*, necessary either for positing an entity or for a general explanation of how the posited entity plays its causal role. This is as it should be. It signifies the open-ended character of scientific concepts and of the scientific inquiry itself. A fuller characterisation of a putative entity can be discovered only by further scientific investigation. Nor is it reasonable to argue that before a full characterisation becomes available the scientists who employ the relevant term do not refer to anything at all. They do refer to the (putative) entity which satisfies the core causal description, and they aim to know more about it. As their causal give-and-take with the world advances, the posited entity is invested with yet more properties which feature in more detailed explanations of the production of its effects. Insofar as these descriptions are mere additions to, and specifications of, the core causal description, there is no change of reference. All that there will be by way of change is an improved understanding of how the posited entity plays its causal role.

What I want to add here is that some of the deletions made do not matter either. That is to say, some parts of the full description associated with a term may be abandoned – or replaced by others – without change of reference, insofar as the core causal description remains intact. This, too, is as it should be. For instance, some detailed descriptions of the structure of the posited entity may have only a tentative or exploratory character: how would it behave, if its constitution was such-and-such?

To sum up: a theoretical term t typically refers by means of a core causal description of a set of kind-constitutive properties, by virtue of which its referent x is supposed to play a given causal role in respect of a certain set of phenomena. Given this, the following conditions are easy to motivate.

1   A term t refers to an entity x if and only if x satisfies the core causal description associated with t.
2   Two terms t' and t denote the same entity if and only if (a) their putative referents play the same causal role with respect to a network of phenomena; and (b) the core causal description of t' takes up the kind-constitutive properties of the core causal description associated with t.

Let me illustrate this abstract account by means of an example. As we saw in Chapter 6 (see pp. 130–132) in the context of the nineteenth-century dynamical wave-theories of light, the postulation of an ethereal medium as the carrier of light-waves was associated with some fundamental, kind-constitutive, properties that this putative entity must possess, if it was to serve its causal role. In particular, the luminiferous ether was posited as a dynamical structure with two important and interconnected sets of properties. The first set of properties were, broadly speaking, kinematical. Given that it was experimentally known that light propagates with finite velocity, its laws of propagation should be medium-based as opposed to being based on an action-at-a-distance.[6] The second set of properties was, broadly speaking, dynamical: the luminiferous ether was the repository of potential and kinetic energy during the light-propagation. The term 'ether' was employed – in fact it was borrowed – in order to denote the entity which, if it existed, should possess the foregoing kind-constitutive properties. The term 'ether' was associated with a core causal description of the properties by virtue of which the ether was supposed to play its intended causal role.[7]

We can now explain why the term 'luminiferous ether' may be seen as referring to the electromagnetic field. It is not just because the electromagnetic field plays the causal role with respect to light-phenomena that the luminiferous ether had been posited to play, as Hardin and Rosenberg's theory would have it, but mainly because the core causal description associated with the term 'electromagnetic field' takes up the core causal description associated with the term 'ether'. Maxwell's postulation of the electromagnetic field was, in essence, associated with the same sets of properties that had been associated with the postulation of the ether, *vis-à-vis*, however, the broader class of electric and magnetic interactions (see Maxwell 1873: 432, 493; also Hesse 1970: 299). So one can conclude that the kind-constitutive properties through and for which the ether was posited were 'carried over' to the conception of the electromagnetic field.[8] In particular, one can conclude that the denotations of the terms 'ether' and 'field' were (broadly speaking) entities which shared some fundamental properties by virtue of which they played the causal role they were ascribed. If this is granted, it is not hard to conclude that 'luminiferous ether' and 'field' referred to the same entity. Then the term 'ether' *is* referential: its referent is no other than the electromagnetic field.[9]

The foregoing account of reference does not fall foul of the objections that Laudan raised against Hardin and Rosenberg. For judgements concerning sameness of reference are not just a matter of ascribing similar causal roles to the putative referents of two terms. To be sure, I also argued that the referents of the terms 'luminiferous ether' and 'electromagnetic field' share the same causal role. But such a commonality of causal role has been grounded on the commonality of fundamental properties – encapsulated in the core causal descriptions associated with the relevant terms. 'Luminiferous ether' and 'electromagnetic field' refer to the same entity precisely because their referents share the same core explanatory structure – as the latter is specified in their respective core descriptions. Similarly, the suggested theory of reference does not infer shared ontology merely from shared explanatory agenda. Rather, the shared ontology is the result of a core of shared theoretical views about what is doing the explaining. For instance, as noted earlier, it is theoretical descriptions of the kind-constitutive properties of the carrier of light-waves that warrant the referential stability in the passage from the luminiferous ether to the electromagnetic field.

As I have pointed out, in order to judge referential success and stability, it is indispensable that the relevant core causal descriptions are specified. But, an objector may ask, how (and when) is the core description to be singled out? There seem to be, at least, three issues here: (a) How is the core description fixed? (b) Who is to fix it? and (c) What should the core description include, and why? Clearly, the whole idea of the specification of a core description involves an element of *rational reconstruction* of the actual problem-situation in which an entity was initially posited, and the reader may worry as to whether this reconstruction is ad hoc.

These issues are serious enough. However, they are not intractable. It is at least in principle possible – and as the ether-to-field example suggests, it is also possible in practice – to locate and partition the descriptions associated with the postulation of an entity and to analyse them in terms of their significance for the causal role ascribed to the putative entity. For instance, some descriptions associated with a term are less fundamental in view of the fact that the posited entity would play its intended causal role even if they were not true. In the luminiferous ether case, less fundamental descriptions include accounts of its possible constitution, e.g. Green's elastic-solid model, McCullagh's rotational elasticity model (see pp. 132–135). What is really needed is:

1 a careful examination of the circumstances under which a specific entity was posited and named;
2 an analysis of the descriptions associated with this entity in view of their importance for the causal role ascribed to the entity; and

3   a careful tracing of the putative entity's history, so that possible changes
in the core description can be spotted.

The point I wish to stress is that this attempt to specify core causal
descriptions is by no means ad hoc. To be sure, the reader may observe
that the attempt to identify a core description is selective, in that not all
descriptions associated with a term are taken to be part of the reference-
fixing core causal description. But this does not entail that the selection of
the kind-constitutive properties which feature in the core description is arbitrary and ad hoc. Nor does it entail the arbitrary dismissal of major descriptive
differences which appear to defeat retention of reference. The selection of
the properties which feature in the core causal description is guided by
considerations concerning the requisite properties of the posited entity if it
is to play its intended causal role in respect of a set of phenomena. It is
certainly constrained by the way in which the scientists who posited this
entity described it. This means that, on my account, not all abandoned theoretical terms refer. Whether or not they do will depend on whether or not
their core causal description is satisfied. For instance, as it is difficult to
understand the use of the term 'ether' in the context of the nineteenth-
century optics without taking into account the core causal description
previously suggested, it is equally difficult to understand the use of the term
'phlogiston' without including in its core causal description the property
that it is released during the process of combustion. The result is that,
although it may be reasonable to argue that the term 'luminiferous ether'
refers, it is not equally reasonable to maintain that the term 'phlogiston'
does. And this is certainly welcome. It is an improvement on the purely
causal theory which would have the term 'phlogiston' refer to oxygen, just
as it is an improvement on the purely descriptive theories which would have
the term 'luminiferous ether' refer to nothing at all. I think it is a major
advantage of the suggested account of reference that it does not render referential stability too easily obtained, while at the same time it does not render
referential stability impossible to get.

The reader may be still worried about what distinguishes between abandoned terms like 'ether', which I claimed to be referential, and abandoned
terms like 'phlogiston' and 'absolute space' which we think are obsolete.
Surely, in my proposal I can claim that if the core description fails, then
the putative entity does not exist. Therefore, I can explain why 'phlogiston'
does not refer. But, it may seem, I cannot explain why terms such as 'ether'
were abandoned, even though, as I argued, their core description was correct.
Perhaps, a philosophical theory of reference need not be concerned with
these, ultimately sociological, issues. But it is worth pointing out that scientific terms like 'ether' do not have denotations only. They have connotations,
too. For instance, even though the models of the elastic solid-like composition of the ether were not part of the core causal description of the term
'luminiferous ether', they can be seen as belonging to the connotations of

the term. Hence, the fact that a term like 'ether' is abandoned may be explained on the ground that it was desirable that the term associated with the carrier of light-waves should avoid the connotations of 'ether'. In any case, what it is worth repeating is that realists do not need to show that *all* abandoned terms refer. As explained in Chapters 5 and 6, they need only to argue for those abandoned terms which were central elements of past mature and genuinely successful theories, where the 'centrality' of a term is a function of how indispensable were the descriptions of the putative referent of the term in the derivation of predictions and in the well-founded explanations of phenomena. This selective attitude towards abandoned terms is enough to show that there is referential continuity on theory change where it matters.

Commenting on an earlier version of the account offered, Niiniluoto (1997: 549) has complained that 'in many real cases' even the core causal descriptions of theoretical terms 'are to some extent mistaken'. By way of example, he notes the case of the HI-virus, where, he argues, the 'initial assumptions of the causal processes' activated by the posited virus 'were simplified'. Note, however, that 'initial assumptions' might not be part of the core causal description associated with the term. The initial assumptions might just be exploratory or speculative. The core causal description becomes available with the development of some definite theoretical hypotheses about the properties that the posited entity should possess in order to play its ascribed causal role. The more supported these hypotheses are by the evidence, the more likely it is that they correctly ground and explain the causal role of the posited entity. So, it is perfectly possible that a theoretical term begins its life as part of some abstract speculations about the causes of a set of phenomena, and subsequently becomes part of a rather firm theory which associates with it a core causal description. Although I cannot judge the case of the term 'HI-virus', mentioned by Niiniluoto, the case I have discussed in some detail, the ether-to-field transition, is precisely a case in which a theoretical term – 'luminiferous ether' – becomes part of a set of developed theories which associate with it a far-from-mistaken core causal description.

If this case is typical, then it offers a positive argument for realism. If, however, it turns out that all or most causal descriptions associated with theoretical terms are typically mistaken, then realism is in trouble. But Niiniluoto's claim needs further argumentation in order to be taken seriously. To say that the core causal description associated with a theoretical term is 'to some extent mistaken' can be trivial, if the description is taken to be very broad – that is, taken to include reference to properties which are not essential for the putative entity to play its causal role in respect of the phenomena for which it was posited. For then it should be relatively easy to find *some* elements of the description which are, by our present lights, mistaken. If, for instance, we take the core causal description of 'luminiferous ether' to include particular models of the constitution of the carrier of light-waves, then, as we have seen, it will be easy to argue that this term does not refer. The issue, then, is to determine the core causal descriptions in such a way that they are neither too broad nor too narrow. If it is *then* shown that they are mistaken, then we have to admit that they are empty. But, to repeat what I said above, showing that requires extra work and further argument.

There is certainly need for a more detailed specification of the suggested account of reference. But if my arguments have made sense, then it seems that there is space for an account of reference which grounds claims of referential stability, not in mere sameness of causal role but in substantive claims about continuity in the explanatory structure of the posited entities. So, on this account of reference, referential stability is far from trivial and uninteresting.[10]

So, hopefully, the last loose end has now been tied. The suggested causal–descriptive theory of reference is what can best support the realist claim that, as science grows, it moves on to more truth-like theories. Not only are competing, or successive, theories rendered comparable in the claims they make about the world, but there is a clear sense in which the process of theory change can be progressive: it better describes the causal structure of the world, and it better accommodates out linguistic categories and concepts to that causal structure.

Notes

Introduction

1 It is implicit in its metaphysical stance that scientific realism is incompatible with much-in-fashion social constructivism (or constructivist anti-realism). Its defence against constructivism, though, is not part of this book and has to await a different project.

2 Putnam, for instance, says: 'Naturally I do not intend to say that positrons are not real' (quoted in Marsonet 1995: 61).

3 A non-epistemic account of truth may be a substantive 'correspondence' theory or a minimal–deflationist one. I defend the thesis that realists can and should go for a substantive 'correspondence' account in Chapter 10.

4 Here I am in good company. The same view is defended by Jarrett Leplin in his recent (1997) book on scientific realism.

1 Empiricism and theoretical discourse

1 I apply the label *semantic instrumentalist* to all those reductive empiricists who believe that theoretical discourse cannot be reduced to observational discourse, and hence that it is just meaningless.

2 Carnap's idea at this time (1928) was that the definiens would ultimately involve only terms and predicates with reference to 'elementary experiences'. However, Carnap soon abandoned this aim and took the class of material (middle-sized) objects as his reductive basis, and their observable properties and relations (size, colour, shape, weight, etc.) as his basic reductive concepts.

3 See Carnap (1937a: 321) for the relevant discussion of Schlick's position.

2 Theories as instruments?

1 Wesley Salmon (1984) discusses this episode in great detail. His line is that Perrin's argument for the existence of atoms can be seen as an instance of the common-cause principle, which, I think, is correct. The debates about the atomic hypothesis in the late nineteenth century have been extensively investigated by the historian Mary Jo Nye (1976).

2 Craig (1956) presented the philosophical significance of his theorem. For further discussion, and a proof of the theorem, see Putnam (1965).

3 This point is explored by Earman 1978 in order to argue that realism is a better methodological strategy than instrumentalism.

4 Here is Hempel's own example: Take a simple theory whose only theoretical terms are 'white phosphorus' ('P') and 'ignition temperature of 30° C' ('T'). The theory has two general principles: 'White phosphorus ignites at a temper-

ature of 30° C', and 'When the ignition temperature is reached, phosphorus bursts into flames'. Let us express these two principles as follows:

(1) $\forall x\, (Px \rightarrow Ix)$;

(2) $\forall x\, (Ix \rightarrow Fx)$.

Suppose now that we know of certain necessary conditions for the presence of white phosphorous, e.g. that white phosphorous has a garlic-like odour ('G'); it is soluble in turpentine ('T'), in vegetable oils ('V') and in ether ('E'); it produces skin burns ('S'). Let us express them as follows:

(3) $\forall x\, (Px \rightarrow Gx)$;

(4) $\forall x\, (Px \rightarrow Tx)$;

(5) $\forall x\, (Px \rightarrow Vx)$;

(6) $\forall x\, (Px \rightarrow Ex)$;

(7) $\forall x\, (Px \rightarrow Sx)$.

Let all these seven sentences represent the total content of the theory T. Clearly, principles (1) and (2) above do not have any observational consequences and hence they cannot be used for the relevant deductive systematisation. However, these principles can be used to establish *inductive connections* between observables. Suppose that a certain object b has been found to have a garlic-like odour, to be soluble in turpentine, in vegetable oils and in ether, and to produce skin burns. Then, one can use sentences (3)–(7) to inductively conclude that b is white phosphorous. One can then use principles (1) and (2) to infer that b will burst into flames if the temperature reaches 30° C. That is, one can derive a certain observational prediction that could not have been derived without the inductive transition from certain observational sentences 'Gb', 'Tb', 'Vb', 'Eb', 'Sb', via sentences (3)–(7), to the theoretical claim that the object under investigation is white phosphorous, i.e. 'Pb'. The same inductive transition could not have been made had one replaced the original theory by Craig (T).

5 A variant of this point was put forward by Putnam 1963, but the main idea had already been suggested by Feigl (1950a).
6 For a more detailed study of Duhem's overall philosophy, one should look at *Synthese* 83, 1990, especially the articles by Brenner, McMullin and Lugg.
7 Duhem was vehemently opposed to atomism and advocated the phenomenological programme of *energetics*. This was a whole theoretical framework for doing science (espoused also by Mach and Ostwald). Duhem described energetics as follows:

> the principles it embodies and from which it derives conclusions do not aspire at all to resolve the bodies we perceive or the motions we resort into imperceptible bodies or hidden motions. Energetics presents no revelations about the nature of matter. Energetics claims to explain nothing. Energetics simply gives general rules of which the laws observed by experimentalists are particular cases.
>
> (1913: 183)

However, energetics was nothing but a promissory note, a hope that at some point scientists would put aside the 'hypothetical mechanisms' and just try to classify empirical laws by means of principles that did not involve reference to atoms, etc.

8 Duhem seems to have taken a *temporal* view of novel predictions: those predictions are novel which predict hitherto unnoticed phenomena. As I argue in Chapter 5, this view of novelty is restrictive. For theories can certainly gain support by providing explanations of known facts and regularities.

9 Lugg (1990) argues that Duhem was a realist. But, as I argue in the text, such a straightforward answer is really difficult to justify.

3 Carnap's neutralism

1 Here I use the description of L_T that Carnap (1958) gives. This description is the same, only more detailed, as that in MCTC.

2 The interested reader should look at Maxwell (1962), Quine (1951) and (1985), and Sellars (1963) for rather conclusive criticisms of Carnap's distinction.

3 Feigl elaborates further on his defence of semantic realism in his splendid 1956 publication.

4 An annotated version of this lecture, with an introduction by me, is now due to appear in *Studies in History and Philosophy of Science*.

5 This defence is given in Carnap (1961). For more on this see Psillos (forthcoming).

6 Take any sentence S which contains no theoretical terms. It can be proved to follow from the Ramsey-sentence if and only if it follows from the original theory. The proof is as follows

$$\vdash \exists u\ \Phi(u,o) \to S \Leftrightarrow \vdash \neg S \to \neg \exists u\ \Phi(u,o) \Leftrightarrow \vdash \neg S \to \forall u\ \neg\Phi(u,o) \Leftrightarrow$$

$$\vdash \forall u(\neg S \to \neg\Phi(u,o)) \Leftrightarrow \vdash \forall u\ \Phi(u,o) \to S \Leftrightarrow \vdash \Phi(t,o) \to S.$$

7 Hempel (1958: 81) follows Braithwaite's account when he says:

> But this means that the Ramsey-sentence associated with an interpreted theory T' avoids reference to hypothetical entities only in letter – replacing Latin constants by Greek variables – rather than in spirit. For it still asserts the existence of certain entities of the kind postulated by T', without guaranteeing any more than T' does that those entities are observable or at least fully characterisable in terms of observables. Hence the Ramsey-sentences provide no satisfactory way of avoiding theoretical concepts.

8 As Feigl (1950: 46–47) brilliantly characterised it, syntactical positivism *is* instrumentalism: it is

> the view that the entities which figure in the laws of theoretical science are nothing but useful formal constructs; the theories themselves being 'nothing but' mathematical models. The upshot then is still: the theoretical constructs are auxiliary devices, they are façons de parler, abbreviatory schemes for the description of the complex relationships between observables.

9 Carnap refers to the example n_p: 'the cardinal number of planets'.

10 Carnap's approach is explained in detail in his lecture course *The Philosophical Foundations of Physics* 1958–1959 (Lecture 14, Carnap Archive, 111–23–01).

11 See also Carnap (1966: 253).

12 A similar view was widely advertised by Ernst Nagel (see e.g. 1960: 151–152).

13 This is in essence how Carnap solves the problem of analyticity for a theoretical language. The Ramsey-sentence of $(^R(TC) \to TC)$ has, obviously, no

empirical content. So, Carnap takes it to be a meaning postulate. For as more detailed discussion of this issue, see Psillos (forthcoming).

14 This is as close as one can get to Creath's characterisation of Carnap as an 'irenic realist' (1985: 18). I am not sure, though, that the terminology is apt. It seems essential not to lose the neutralist element of Carnap's empiricism. At any rate, Creath's perspective is different. He presses the point that Carnap must, after all, be more of a scientific realist than he seems willing to accept. For if observational discourse is ontologically committing, and if there is no sharp dichotomy between observational and theoretical discourse, then – by continuity – theoretical discourse, too, must be ontologically committing. The issue I have tried to raise is that Carnap was willing to accept all this, and yet unwilling to accept that his empiricism commits him to physical unobservable entities.

15 In the case of the set of natural numbers, such a full structure is, essentially, what is called the second-order structure of natural numbers. By letting the second-order variables range over the whole power set of natural numbers, and by *decreeing* that only full models of Peano Arithmetic should be considered, we exclude non-standard models of Peano Arithmetic. That is, we make the Peano axioms characterise the natural numbers, up to isomorphism.

16 As Demopoulos and Friedman (1985) have documented, Russell conceded this point to Newman. In a letter to Newman, Russell observes: 'You make it entirely obvious that my statements to the effect that nothing is known about the physical world except its structure are either trivial or false, and I am somewhat ashamed at not having noticed the point myself.' Russell goes on to say that he had tacitly assumed that the important relation is that of spatio-temporal continuity, or causality, between the world of percepts and the world of unperceived objects. Be that as it may, it should be clear that this is just an admission of defeat. Either there are things about the unobservable world which can be known although they are not purely structural claims, or no substantive knowledge of the unobservable is ever possible.

17 A similar point is made by G.H. Merrill in his (1980) defence of realism against Putnam's model-theoretic argument (cf. Putnam, 1978).

4 In defence of scientific realism

1 The same line of thought has been employed by Reichenbach in defending the existence of unobservable entities (cf. 1938: 114–124, especially note 4).

2 (1981: 617–618; 1984: 59–60; 1989: 8; 1990: 181; 1990a: 360).

3 An example might illustrate this. The classical explanation of the photoelectric phenomenon is right insofar as it accounts for the photoelectric current in terms of the emission of electrons from the metallic surface. But the classical explanation of the emission of electrons – based on the Lorentz force – is not 'good enough' even before it is contrasted with Einstein's explanation. Although it explains why the intensity of the photoelectric current increases with the intensity of the light falling on the metallic surface, it does not explain a salient feature of the phenomena: why the maximum velocity of the emitted electrons is independent of the light-intensity but dependent on the frequency of the electromagnetic radiation. This last fact was explained by Einstein's hypothesis that light is quantised: it is photons – whose energy depends on the frequency of the radiation – that 'knock' electrons out of their atoms.

4 It is worth noting that, given the foregoing analysis, deductive arguments are *not* viciously circular, even though, by being non-content-increasing, they are such that the conclusion is, in some sense, contained *implicitly* in the premises. This idea of 'implicit containment' needs some elucidation. It is meant to show that, given some set of propositions, if one follows some valid rules of inference,

one will be able to derive their logical consequences. These logical consequences are 'contained' in the premises in the sense that the truth of the premises guarantees *their* truth. But, these logical consequences are neither identical with, nor paraphrases of, the premises. Apart from trivial cases (e.g. $p \rightarrow p$), what these logical consequences are is not known prior to the application of the rules. So, it is not the case that in deductive reasoning one proves the truth of whatever one wishes by choosing a suitable set of premises. Deductive arguments have probative force because they do not assume what needs to be proved.

5 This point is pressed and developed by van Cleve (1984).

6 The idea of an inference machine was first used by Braithwaite (see 1953: 291). Paul Churchland (1979: 6, 137ff.) has appealed to a similar idea, when he suggested that belief-forming processes must be seen as operations of epistemic engines.

7 McGee's (1985) counter-example is the following: 'If a Republican wins, then if Reagan does not win, Anderson will; A Republican (Reagan) wins; Therefore, if Reagan does not win, Anderson will.' The premises are all true, but the conclusion is false, McGee says, because if Reagan had failed to win the 1980 US Presidential Election, Carter (the Democrat candidate) would have won. Lycan (1994: 233) produces the following counter-example: 'If you insult me, I'll be polite, but if you insult my wife, I won't be; [The hearer insults both me and my wife]; Contradiction!' The hearer insulted me, but I was not polite.

8 These considerations have been explored by Friedman (see 1988: 157), who largely follows Dummett (1974).

9 Don't rule-circular arguments prove too much? A standard claim (see e.g. Salmon 1965) is that rule-circular arguments could be offered in defence of 'counter-induction', or in defence of the fallacy of affirming the consequent. Counter-induction, for instance, moves from the premiss that 'Most observed As are B' to the conclusion that 'The next A will be not-B'. A 'counter-inductivist' might support this rule by the following rule-circular argument: since most counter-inductions so far have failed, conclude, by counter-induction, that the next counter-induction will succeed. Similarly, the fallacy of affirming the consequent might be defended by the following rule-circular argument: if the fallacy of affirming the consequent is truth-preserving, then $2 + 2 = 4$; $2 + 2 = 4$; therefore, the fallacy of affirming the consequent is truth-preserving. But this objection is too quick. First, there are good reasons to doubt the reliability of counter-induction. Since counter-induction is typically unsuccessful, the rule-circular argument is simply pointless. (In fact, as Max Black 1958 has pointed out, if we reformulate counter-induction so that it has successful instances, then the rule-circular argument becomes incoherent). As for the fallacy of affirming the consequent, and given the meaning of the logical connectives, this cannot *possibly* be truth-preserving (and that is exactly what we should demand of it, since it is supposed to be a deductive rule). Hence, any rule-circular argument in its defence is pointless, too.

10 The theory-ladenness of ordinary inductive inferences about observables has been pointed out by Hempel in his critique of Craig's theorem (see pp. 25–26).

5 Resisting the pessimistic induction

1 For Laudan's argument against realism, see Laudan 1981: 32–33, 36–45; 1984: 91–92; 1984a: 121; 1984b: 157.

2 This point has been repeatedly pressed by Worrall (see e.g. 1982; 1994).

3 The notion of 'novelty' is carefully analysed in Jarrett Leplin's 1997 book on scientific realism. He analyses 'novelty' by reference to two requirements: *independence* and *uniqueness*. The core idea is that a prediction of a phenomenon

O, be it already known or hitherto unforeseen, is novel for a theory *T* if no information about *O* is necessary for the prediction of *O* by *T* and if there is no other theory available which explains why *O* should be expected. My own views on novelty are very much in accordance with Leplin's.

4 A paradigmatic case of such an ad hoc move is the initial modification of Lorentz's theory of light by means of the Lorentz–FitzGerald contraction in order to accommodate the observed null result in the attempts to calculate the motion of the earth relative to the ether. Zahar (1989: 17–19) explains in some detail how exactly information about the null result was used in order to make the contraction hypothesis predict the absence of interference fringes. (Lorentz's subsequent 'molecular forces hypothesis' offered a non-ad hoc accommodation of the Lorentz–FitzGerald contraction, but as Zahar implies, this accommodation was *not* ad hoc precisely because Lorentz's molecular forces hypothesis had excess theoretical content.) Another historically interesting case of ad hoc accommodation is discussed in Psillos (1993).

5 I think, however, that the issue over the comparative *confirmational weights* of use-novel and temporally-novel predictions cannot be solved on purely theoretical grounds. The actual scientific practice, too, must be examined closely. For instance, in actual scientific practice, a non-ad hoc accommodation of a known fact may lend more credence to a theory than a temporally novel prediction that the theory makes, as it seems to be the case with the predictions of the anomalous perihelion of Mercury and the red shift by the general theory of relativity (cf. Earman 1992: 114).

6 John Maynard Keynes, who is well known for dismissing the significance of temporal order in predictions, observed (1921: 338) that there is no 'logical basis' for the claim that a theory may be 'cooked up' to yield the evidence, but he admitted that working scientists who stress the importance of temporal novelty do so on the grounds that the possibility is always there to fiddle with the data in order to make the theory that yields them, and sometimes will be a strong temptation. It is also noteworthy that one of Whewell's motivations for stressing temporal novelty comes from considerations concerning the possible ad hoc accommodation of known facts in a theory. He was worried about the possibility that 'as new circumstances are discovered, we may *adjust* the hypothesis so as to correspond to these also' (1989: 155; emphasis added). The excess confirmational weight of temporally-novel predictions comes, for Whewell, from the fact that such predictions spring naturally from the theory, i.e. 'without adjustments' or without being 'contemplated in its construction' (ibid.).

7 Kitcher and I differ on our positions concerning the theory of the reference of theoretical terms. For a criticism of Kitcher's position, see Psillos (1997).

6 Historical illustrations

1 As Laplace put it: 'The real speed of sound equals the product of the speed according to the Newtonian formula [i.e. $c = \sqrt{(dP/d\rho)}$] by the square root of the ratio of the specific heat of the air subject to the constant pressure of the atmosphere at various temperatures, to its specific heat when its volume remains constant' (1816: 181).

2 Later on, in 1822, Laplace again calculated the velocity of sound, but this time based on the much better specification of γ by Gay-Lussac and Welter (cf. Laplace 1825: 303–304). The result was 337.7 m/sec.

3 I deal with Laplace's account of the advanced caloric theory in my 1993 paper. In this present study of the development of caloric theory, I leave aside Laplace's account of caloric and its interaction with matter, as it was presented in his monumental *Traite de Mechanique Celeste, Livre XII* (1823) and in a series of

articles in the *Connaissance des Tempes* for 1824 and 1825. However, this does not affect the argument of the chapter.

4 The references to Carnot's paper are given in the text by two numbers referring to the relevant pages in the Mendoza and the Fox English translations of Carnot's memoir; where only one page number appears, the Mendoza translation is intended.

5 It is noteworthy that the passage quoted replaced the following statement, favourable to the fundamental hypothesis, which appears in the draft of Carnot's memoir: 'The fundamental law which we proposed to confirm seems to us to have been placed beyond doubt. . . . We will now apply the theoretical ideas expressed above to the examination of different methods proposed up to now for the realisation of the motive power of heat' (Carnot 1824: 46). For other doubts concerning the 'fundamental hypothesis', (see ibid.: 19/76).

6 In Carnot's own words: 'The motive power of heat is independent of the agents employed to realise it; its quantity is fixed solely by the temperatures of the bodies between which is effected, finally, the transfer of the caloric' (1824: 20/76–77).

7 For a similar point see Klein (1976: 216–217, 219).

8 Already in his published paper, and having just utilised the principle of the impossibility of perpetual motion, Carnot stated that perpetual motion would amount to 'an unlimited creation of motive power without *consumption* either of caloric or of any other agent whatever' (1824: 12/69; emphasis added). It is difficult to be sure that this statement is anything more than a slip. But, it can be seen to imply that the law of the impossibility of perpetual motion yields that heat must be consumed during a thermal cycle in which work is produced. So, it can be seen as suggesting that the impossibility of perpetual motion (of the first kind) is at odds with the principle of the conservation of heat, when work is being produced. In fact, this very line of thought is used by Clausius in his own demonstration of Carnot's theorems.

9 Investigating Carnot's manuscripts, E. Mendoza (1959: 389) has suggested that: 'it seems that many of the notes were written at virtually the same time as the *Reflexions*. . . . In fact, by the time he came to correct the proofs (or to write the very final draft if there was one), he had begun to lose confidence in all that he had written. The surprising thing is that he published his book at all.'

10 This localising of evidential relations is, I think, akin to the position put forward by Glymour (1980). The spirit of Glymour's bootstrapping account of confirmation is that empirical evidence may support some theoretical claims made by a theory better than it does others: the evidence reaches the several parts of a theory in a non-uniform way.

11 Elsewhere Clausius stated: '[Carnot's] proof of the necessity of such a relation [i.e. the maximal efficiency of a Carnot cycle] is based on the axiom that it is impossible to create a moving force out of nothing, or in other words, that perpetual motion is impossible'. And, he added:

> Nevertheless I did not think that Carnot's theory, which had found in Clapeyron a very expert analytical expositor, required total rejection; on the contrary, it appeared to me that the theorem established by Carnot, after separating one part and properly formalising the rest, might be brought into accordance with the modern law of equivalence of heat and work, and thus be employed together with it for the deduction of important conclusions.
> (Clausius, 1867: 406–407)

Helmholtz arrived at similar conclusions in 1847. Referring to the general importance of the principle that perpetual motion is impossible, he stated: 'By this proposition [i.e. the impossibility of perpetual motion] Carnot and Clapeyron have deduced theoretically a series of laws, part of which are proved by experiment and part not yet submitted to this test, regarding the latent heats of various natural bodies' (1848: 93).

12 This point of view has been taken by Paul Churchland (1979: 19).

13 In view of this situation, Joseph Larmor stressed

> [t]he division of the problem of the determination of the constitution of a partly concealed dynamical system, such as the aether, into two independent parts. The first part is the determination of some form of energy-function which will explain the recognised dynamical properties of the system, and which may be further tested by its application to the discovery of new properties. The second part is the building up in actuality or in imagination of some mechanical system which will serve as a model or illustration of a medium possessing such an energy function.
>
> (1894: 417)

14 In mechanical terms, it has to exhibit sufficient rigidity as to allow the propagation of light with a certain finite velocity, and also a certain elasticity – or capability of deformation – so as to allow transversal propagation.

15 For a more elaborate account of Green's theory, see R. T. Glazebrook (1885: 159–163) and Kenneth Schaffner (1972: 46–58).

16 It is worth noting that this failure related to the negative analogy between the propagation of disturbances in elastic solids and light-waves. In Green's model, should the incident light be polarised at right angles to the plane of incidence, it is impossible to satisfy all the boundary conditions without assuming that the reflection of light generates longitudinal waves (cf. Whittaker 1951: 140). So one cannot simply suppress this negative analogy in order to create a 'suitable' model.

17 For a brief account of Maxwell's derivation of the equations of the field, see Andrew Bork (1967). Hunt (1991: 122–128 & 245–247) gives a detailed historical account of the derivation of the equations in the symmetrical form known today.

18 For some similar thoughts, see Stein (1970: 280).

19 The semantic view of theories is examined and criticised in Hendry and Psillos (1998).

20 These formal aspects of model construction have been studied in more detail by Michael Redhead (1980). He has suggested that such mathematical models are the source of the very important process of cross-fertilisation in theoretical physics (ibid.: 149).

7 Worrall's structural realism

1 Worrall should be credited for being the first to note that an adequate defence of scientific realism should take the form of something like the *divide et impera* move.

2 In a later article, Stein elaborates on this point and states that the history of science has shown that

> on a certain very deep question Aristotle was entirely wrong, and Plato – at least on one reading, the one I prefer – remarkably right: namely, our science comes closest to understanding 'the real', not in its account of 'substances' and their kinds, but in its account of the 'Forms' which phenomena 'imitate' (for 'Forms' read 'theoretical structures', for 'imitate', 'are represented by'.
>
> (1989: 57)

He has added that it is structural deepening which remains quasi-invariant in theory change, and not entities and their basic properties and relations (ibid.: 58).

3 As I noted in Chapter 2, Duhem, too, can be seen as a kind of structural realist. The Duhemian distinction between the representative and the explanatory parts of a theory may be seen as co-extensive with Worrall's structure versus content distinction.

4 Wasn't Poincaré the archetypical conventionalist? I discuss this issue in detail in my 1995 essay on Poincaré and mechanical explanation. There I show that Poincaré had a rather complicated theory of what constitutes a convention. In particular, he called the most general principles of geometry and Newtonian mechanics 'conventions' in order to account for the fact that they are neither a priori true nor dictated by experience. He stressed, however, that there is always an empirical element in conventions, in that their adoption is being guided – but not dictated – by certain empirical facts. In fact, he had a theory as to how there can be rational choice among conventions, based on what he called 'convenience'. So, conventions are those general principles which are constitutive of a theoretical framework *without* being a priori true and *with* a certain empirical input. Lesser hypotheses, such as Maxwell's laws and the laws of optics, were for Poincaré, genuinely empirical hypotheses. In any case, it seems possible to reconcile the view that he was a conventionalist about the most general theoretical principles with the claim that, insofar as any theoretical facts are knowable, they concern structural relations among otherwise unknowable entities.

5 James Ladyman (1998) makes an attempt to overcome both styles of structural realism and argues for a purely metaphysical version of the doctrine.

6 Zahar (1989) has suggested that for Poincaré 'convenience, and convenience alone, operates like an index of verisimilitude'. He then goes on to claim that for Poincaré convenience is 'a purely syntactical notion based on the mathematical structure of a given proposition, not on any semantic relation between its descriptive terms and some external reality' (1989: 161). For Zahar, Poincaré was a neo-Kantian who subscribed to the thesis that we can 'simulate the physical world, but not to refer to it directly' (ibid.). This is an interesting claim which introduces a possible philosophical motivation for structural realism, but I still think that it needs the support of some argumentation.

7 Comparing Ptolemaic and Copernican astronomy, Poincaré points out that the two theories are kinematically equivalent. Yet, he also observes that Copernican astronomy gives a better dynamical explanation of some phenomena which under the Ptolemaic framework appear coincidental. He then asks: 'Is it by chance ... ?' His answer is that Copernican astronomy provided 'a bond between the ... phenomena' and that '[this bond] is true' (1905: 185).

8 Whittaker has noted that mechanical models of ether were not central in Fresnel's theory of light. For instance, he states:

> Fresnel's investigations can scarcely be called a dynamical theory in the strict sense as the qualities of the medium are not defined. His method was to work backwards from the known properties of light in the hope of arriving at a mechanism to which they could be attributed; he succeeded in accounting for the phenomena in terms of a few simple principles, but was not able to specify an ether which would in turn account for these principles. The 'displacements' of Fresnel could not be a displacement in an elastic solid of the usual type, since its normal component is not continuous across the interface between two media.
>
> (1951: 125)

I think this is generally true. Yet, Whittaker (1951: 19) has also argued that Fresnel used basically geometrical reasoning to arrive at his results, and that he then devised a dynamical scheme to fit them. I think this is wrong. For, as I have shown, Fresnel also utilised *physical principles* in his reasoning, in particular, dynamical principles such as the principle of conservation of energy.

8 Underdetermination undermined

1 Actually, Quine has admitted, 'for my own part I would say that the thesis as I have used it is probably trivial' (quoted in Grunbaum 1962: 132).
2 For more on this subject see Earman (1992: Chapter 6); Clark Glymour (1977, 1980); David Malament (1977); Lawrence Sklar (1974).
3 Recently, Kukla (1993) has argued that there *is* a recipe for constructing empirically equivalent theories. Kukla suggests that if we take any theory T, a theory T' can be constructed such that T' says that T is true of the universe whenever some observation is being made, but that whenever the universe is not observed the universe follows the laws of T^*, where T^* is any theory which is incompatible with T. There should be no doubt that T' tells a consistent story. But insofar as it can be called a 'theory' at all, it is utterly implausible as a rival to T. Taking T' seriously would require believing in an immense number of coincidences. Besides, as Laudan and Leplin 1993 have noted, T' would be totally parasitic on the explanatory and predictive mechanisms of T. The only reason to accept T' as a serious rival to T would be inductive scepticism, viz. the claim that, in spite its possible high confirmation, T is *not proven* to be true by the observations which support it.
4 I do not want to suggest that a realist can never argue that two empirically equivalent theories are merely different linguistic formulations of the same totality of facts. For an interesting discussion of this issue, as well as a specification of the conditions under which two theoretical formulations are equivalent, see de Bouvere (1965); Glymour (1971); Putnam (1983a).
5 The essential Chapter 3 of Laudan's 1996 book was co-authored by Jarrett Leplin.
6 An attentive reader may think that there is a tension between my claim that theories can get indirect support from evidence which they do not entail and my attempt, described in Chapter 5, to characterise those components of a scientific theory which contribute *essentially* to the generation of the theory's predictive success. The objection might be the following. I have presently argued that a piece of evidence E may indirectly support hypothesis H', although it is not entailed by H', because it supports a 'larger' hypothesis H^* which also entails H'. It should be clear, however, that H' has not essentially contributed to the prediction E. How can it nonetheless get support from it? In response to this objection, it should be noted that there is nothing problematic about the admission that some theoretical components get indirect support from the evidence, although they do not essentially contribute to its prediction especially when these theoretical components are other theoretical consequences of an essentially contributing hypothesis. What I certainly disallow is the following situation. Suppose that a hypothesis H is such that it entails another theoretical hypothesis H' which is supported by the prediction E. If H is not essential for the derivation of E, in the sense described in Chapter 5, then it does not get supported by E. Nor do any other consequences of H, call them H'', get any indirect support, either.
7 A similar view has been defended by Giere (1985).
8 Here, I am not claiming that all questions of theoretical truth can be decided. But, remember that the sceptical claim is that *none* can. If my arguments are sound, then this claim is false.

9 Constructive empiricism scrutinised

1 For a similar point see Sober (1993).
2 I think Rosen (1994: 171–174) has identified a real problem with van Fraassen's position. It is the following. It is reasonable to think that van Fraassen is an agnostic about modal facts. (They are no less unobservable than electrons, etc.) But to say of an entity that it *is* observable is to report a modal fact: it is *possible* for us to observe this entity. If someone is an agnostic about modal facts, then they should be agnostic about which entities are observable. (More precisely, the point is that, although if they know that an entity *is* observable, then they can trivially derive the modal fact that it is *possible* to observe it, agnosticism about modal facts deprives them of a *general* characterisation of which entities *are* observable.) If this argument is sound, van Fraassen's position cannot even get off the ground. For it requires that theories should be accepted as empirically adequate, where a theory is empirically adequate if and only if whatever it says about the *observable* entities (and phenomena) is true. Yet, if there is no way to characterise which entities are observable, there is no way to give any content to the belief that a theory is empirically adequate: it is totally unspecified for which entities the theory must be right about.
3 Van Fraassen dissociates his constructive empiricism from both of the following theses:

    (1) All (or most) scientists aim to construct empirically adequate theories, and believe the theories they accept to be empirically adequate.
    (2) (All or most) scientists consciously understand the aim of science to be to produce empirically adequate theories (1994: 181; 187, 188).

4 Chihara and Chihara (1993) give nice relevant examples.
5 Couldn't one just re-state the empirically adequate analogues of T1 and T2 as follows: $\exists\phi(P)$ and $\exists\phi(Q)$? Still, it does not logically follow that $\exists\phi(P\&Q)$. For as Friedman (1983: 245–246) has pointed out, from the facts that a) there is mapping M of the phenomena P into structure ϕ and b) there is mapping M' of phenomena Q into structure ϕ, it does not follow that there is a common mapping M'' that maps phenomena $P\&Q$ into ϕ. So, for instance, 'there is a mapping M that maps the gas phenomena into a molecular structure' and 'there is a mapping M' that maps chemical phenomena into a molecular structure' do not entail that 'there is a mapping M'' that maps the gas phenomena *and* the chemical phenomena into a molecular structure'.
6 The logical structure of abduction, as well as of some attempts towards its computational modelling, is examined in Psillos (forthcoming a). See also McMullin (1992).
7 Gilbert Harman (1996), and Day and Kincaid (1994: 285–287) have already successfully argued against van Fraassen's claim that IBE – conceived as a rule – is incoherent. A recent defence of the coherence of IBE is offered by Douven (1999).
8 For some similar thoughts, see Forrest (1994) and Norton (1993).
9 A similar point is made by Musgrave (1985: 202–203).

10 NOA, cognitive perfection and entity realism

1 Characterising anti-realism, Dummett notes: 'The anti-realist opposes to the [realist] view that statements of the disputed class are to be understood only by reference to the sort of thing which we count as evidence for a statement of that class' (Dummett 1963: 146).
2 I do not intend here to discuss how this view relates to Ramsey's 1927 'redundancy theory' of truth. For further discussion the reader should see Kirkham

(1992: 317–321) and Papineau (1993). It is, however, arguable that, unlike Horwich, Ramsey took it that there is a general theory of why statements of the form '"P" is true if and only if P' are correct. Field (1986) goes so far as to argue that Ramsey offered a 'correspondence theory' of truth, based on the claim that Ramsey had a substantive theory of why statements have the truth-conditions they do.

3 Isn't that too quick? One could, for instance, argue that there is no need to posit substantive truth-makers. Instead, one could proceed as follows. For any theoretical statement 'p', accept in the *meta-language* a statement of the form '"p" is true if and only if p'. The thought may be that this would be enough to fix the literal interpretation of the theoretical language. I beg to differ. For, clearly, the meta-linguistic device will work only if the theoretical object-language is well understood. Otherwise, the meta-linguistic device specifies *no* interpretation. For someone, like a positivist anti-realist, who claims not to understand the theoretical language (that is, who claims that it is not apt for truth and falsity), the meta-linguistic device would be hopeless. Carnap indeed perceived this (see 1939: 62–63).

4 All this does not mean that once an assertion is understood literally one should believe that its truth-maker obtains. Agnostic positions, *à la* van Fraassen, are possible. But it does mean that once the assertion is understood literally the attention is shifted to epistemological questions. The issue then is not whether theoretical assertions have truth-makers, but whether scientific investigation can (or should aim to) lead to warranted beliefs about them.

5 Hence, I think, it is no accident that van Fraassen adopts a 'correspondence theory of truth' alongside his 'literal understanding of theories' (see 1980: 197). It seems to me he just acknowledges that literally understood theoretical discourse requires truth-makers, and he chooses the realist way to characterise the latter.

6 Kitcher (1993: 167–168) offers an excellent defence of truth-as-correspondence based on the success of action.

7 Reiner and Pierson (1995) also note that Hacking's argument for realism relies on an IBE. But they think this renders Hacking's argument as problematic as other abductive arguments for realism. I think that the fact that Hacking's argument is abductive is one of its strengths. In any case, my main point is that, being abductive, Hacking's argument can establish a stronger realist position than Hacking wants to.

8 McMullin has noted that 'it is important to realise that Hacking opposes his experimental realism not to instrumentalism but to idealism' (1987: 61–62).

11 Truth-likeness

1 In his 1982 Preface to *Realism and the Aim of Science*, Popper admits that the idea of verisimilitude 'is not an essential part of [his] theory' (1956 [1982]: xxxvii).

2 Pavel Tichy (1978) has, however, contested the soundness of the above proof.

3 The semantic view of theories, at least in its 'strong version' which identifies theories with families of models, is criticised in Hendry and Psillos (1998).

4 The essence of this suggestion has been defended by Weston (1992: 61). A similar view is also defended by David Lewis (1986: 21–27).

5 Niiniluoto has suggested (personal communication) a variant of this claim: T is approximately true in S if and only if T is close to some T' which is true in S. The advantage of the latter formulation, Niiniluoto suggests, is that it is easier to define closeness or similarity between statements rather than between structures.

6 This is an objection anticipated by Fine (see 1984: 90–91).
7 For a careful study of the several notions of approximation and idealisation employed in science, see Moulines (1976).
8 For a survey of the recent developments in the attempts to capture formally the notion of truth-likeness cf. Niiniluoto (1998).
9 Recently, Peter Smith (1998) has also pointed out that the notion of 'approximate truth' is best analysed on the basis of the notion of 'approximation'. His suggestion is that the claim *that* '*P*' is approximately true is equivalent to the claim *that* approximately *P*. Hence, '*P*' is approximately true if and only if approximately *P* (AP). I think this is essentially correct, although I disagree with Smith's insistence that this account parallels a deflationist account of truth. The schema (AP) above is entailed by a more robust realist account of approximate truth, too.

12 Reference of theoretical terms

1 For a thorough discussion of the Kuhnian metaphor, as well as of the whole issue of Kuhnian incommensurability, see Hoyningen-Huene (1993) (especially 6.3).
2 For a thorough discussion of the description theory, in both of its classical (Frege–Russell) and modern (Wittgenstein–Searle) forms, see Devitt and Sterelny (1987, Chapter 3) and Bach (1987).
3 If being xyz is kind-constitutive of a substance that looks like water on Twin-Earth (see Putnam 1975b), then the Twin-Earthians do not drink *water* after all. One may let one's imagination conceive of the laws of nature allowing two microscopically distinct substances share exactly the same observable properties in common. But such imagination would also conceive of the physical possibility that these differences in the microscopic nature be detectable. Should such a thing happen on earth, we would have to resolve in favour of the view that the extension of 'water' is either H_2O or xyz.
4 I do not intend to offer a diatribe on natural kinds. I defer to Kornblith's (1993, Chapter 3) for the required defence. For some similar suggestions, the reader can see Boyd 1989; 1991; 1993. What Boyd has rightly emphasised is that the idea of natural kinds can be explicated by the concept of 'homeostatic property clusters'. What makes a kind natural is the presence of a homeostatic mechanism which brings about and sustains the co-occurrence of a number of properties.
5 Occasionally, Putnam seems to suggest that 'an approximately correct definite description' is required for successful reference (cf. 1975a; 200).
6 J. S. Mill put this point like this:

> What has most contributed to accredit the hypothesis of a physical medium for the propagation of light, is the certain fact that light *travels*, (which cannot be proved of gravitation), that its communication is not instantaneous, but requires time, and that it is intercepted (which gravitation is not) by intervening objects.
>
> (1872: 501)

7 In order to further substantiate the claim that the aforementioned sets of kinematical and dynamical properties were kind-constitutive, one has to contrast the theoretical research in optics of the 1820s with research in electricity and magnetism. Before Faraday's work on electric and magnetic induction, and especially before Maxwell's theory, electric action was taken to be action-at-a-distance. The laws of its propagation were not medium-based, but instead

modelled either upon a Newtonian type of interaction, (e.g. Coulomb's law) or on pseudo-contiguous actions in terms of electric potentials, (e.g. Poisson's equation). Hence, no medium for the propagation of electric interactions – as a new natural kind – was postulated. For, if action-at-a-distance were the case, then no such medium would be necessary. G. F. FitzGerald summarised this point as follows:

> It is only when you wish to take account of actions that take some time to be transferred from you to the body, it is only then that it is necessary mathematically to introduce symbols expressly referring to a medium. We may gather from this how it was absolutely necessary in the case of the action of light to introduce the notion of something existing between the sun, for instance, and the earth, while it was not necessary, as far as was known, to make a similar assumption in regard to electric action.
>
> (1888: 164)

8 Clearly, the term 'ether' was in use much ealier than the beginning of the nineteenth century. So, I must stress that here I focus only on the need for positing a carrier of light-waves – and the use of the term 'ether' to refer to it – in the context of the nineteenth-century dynamical wave-theories of light.

9 The reader may find this conclusion unwarranted on the grounds that it cannot help us understand the function of the ether as the absolute frame of reference and the developments that led to the advancement of Einstein's special relativity. A full treatment of this worry needs much more space that is now available. But the following is worth mentioning. As is well known, Maxwell's theory – especially in its advanced form as shaped by Lorentz – implied the existence of an absolute frame of reference to which Maxwell's equations hold good. This meant that there was a privileged frame of reference in which the velocity of light was the well-known constant c, independently of the direction of propagation and the local state of motion. According to Lorentz, this privileged frame of reference was supposed to act in connection with an immobile ether. So, one can point out that, in advanced electromagnetic theories, the ether was given yet another set of properties, i.e. those associated with an absolute frame of reference. We may call this set of properties *positional*. What I want to stress here is that it was precisely this positional function of the ether which was irrevocably superseded by the special theory of relativity. On the contrary, both its dynamical and kinematical properties were absorbed by the electromagnetic field.

10 Kitcher (1993) also attempts to devise a theory of reference which is a compromise between causal and descriptive theories. However, his theory is context-sensitive: it allows that different tokens of the same expression-type may systematically purport to refer to different entities in such a way that some tokens may be referential, while others are not. Kitcher applies his theory to Joseph Priestley's 'dephlogisticated air' in order to show that although, *qua* type, this expression fails to refer uniformly, it nonetheless has tokens which refer to *oxygen*. In his attempt to evaluate and solve disputes about referential continuity and progress in scientific theory-change, Kitcher employs the principle of humanity and a notion of the 'correct historical explanation' of the production of each expression-token. In Psillos (1997), where Kitcher's theory is examined in detail, I argue that the application of the principle of humanity does not offer a principled way to show that the historical actors were involved in different modes of reference when they produced different tokens of an expression-type. I also suggest that the principle of humanity, coupled with Kitcher's view that tokens of expression-types may systematically refer to different things, makes conceptual progress too easy and thus uninteresting.

Bibliography

Achinstein, P. (1965) 'The Problem of Theoretical Terms', *American Philosophical Quarterly* 2; repr. in B. Brody (ed.) *Readings in the Philosophy of Science*, (1970), Englewood Cliffs, NJ: Prentice-Hall.

Achinstein, P. (1968) *Concepts of Science: A Philosophical Analysis*, Baltimore, MD: Johns Hopkins University Press.

Arago, F. and Fresnel, A. (1819) 'On the Action of Rays of Polarised Light upon Each Other', *Annales de Chimie et de Physique* 10: 288; translated in F. Crew (ed.) *The Wave Theory of Light: Memoirs by Huygens, Young, and Fresnel*, New York: American Books Company (1902).

Armstrong, D. (1988) 'Discussion: Reply to van Fraassen', *Australasian Journal of Philosophy* 66: 225–229.

Aronson, J. L. (1990) 'Verisimilitude and Type Hierarchies', *Philosophical Topics* 18: 5–28.

Aronson, J. L., Harré, R. and Way, E. (1994) *Realism Rescued*, London: Duckworth.

Bergstrom, L. (1984) 'Underdetermination and Realism', *Erkenntnis* 21: 349–365.

Berk, E. (1979) 'Reference of Theoretical Terms', *Southwest Journal of Philosophy* 10: 139–146.

Bach, K. (1987) *Thought and Reference*, Oxford: Clarendon Press.

Black, J. (1803) *Lectures on the Elements of Chemistry*, ed. J. Robison, Edinburgh: all page references are for the excerpts as they appear in D. Roller 'The Early Development of the Concepts of Temperature and Heat: The Rise and the Decline of the Caloric Theory', in J. B. Conant (ed.) *Harvard Case Histories in Experimental Science*, Cambridge, MA: Harvard University Press (1950).

Black, M. (1958) 'Self-supporting Inductive Arguments', *Journal of Philosophy* 55: 718–725.

Bork, A. (1967) 'Maxwell and the Electromagnetic Wave Equation', *American Journal of Physics* 35: 83–89.

Boyd, R. (1973) 'Realism, Underdetermination and the Causal Theory of Evidence', *Nous* 7: 1–12.

Boyd, R. (1981) 'Scientific Realism and Naturalistic Epistemology', in P. D. Asquith and T. Nickles (eds) *PSA 1980*, Vol. 2, East Lansing, MI: Philosophy of Science Association.

Boyd, R. (1984) 'The Current Status of the Realism Debate', in J. Leplin (ed.) *Scientific Realism*, Berkeley: University of California Press.

Boyd, R. (1984a) 'Lex Orandi est Lex Credenti', in P. M. Churchland and C. A. Hooker (eds) *Images of Science*, Chicago: The University of Chicago Press.

Boyd, R. (1985) 'The Logician's Dilemma: Deductive Logic, Inductive Inference and Logical Empiricism', *Erkenntnis* 22: 197–252.

Boyd, R. (1989) 'What Realism Implies and What it Does Not', *Dialectica* 43: 5–29.

Boyd, R. (1990) 'Realism, Conventionality and "Realism About"', in G. Boolos (ed.) *Meaning and Method: Essays in Honour of Hilary Putnam*, Cambridge: Cambridge University Press.

Boyd, R. (1990a) 'Realism, Approximate Truth and Philosophical Method', in C. W. Savage (ed.) *Scientific Theories*, Minnesota Studies in the Philosophy of Science, Vol. 14, Minneapolis: University of Minnesota Press.

Boyd, R. (1991) 'Realism, Anti-Foundationalism and the Enthusiasm for Natural Kinds', *Philosophical Studies* 61: 125–148.

Boyd, R. (1992) 'Constructivism, Realism and Philosophical Method', in J. Earman (ed.) *Inference, Explanation and Other Frustrations*, Berkeley: University of California Press.

Boyd, R. (1993) 'Metaphor and Theory Change: What Is a 'Metaphor' a Metaphor for?', in A. Ortony (ed.) *Metaphor and Thought*, Cambridge: Cambridge University Press.

Braithwaite, R. B. (1953) *Scientific Explanation*, Cambridge: Cambridge University Press.

Brenner, A. A. (1990) 'Holism a Century Ago: The Elaboration of Duhem's Thesis', *Synthese* 83: 325–335.

Bridgman, P. W. (1927) *The Logic of Modern Physics,* New York: The Macmillan Company.

Carnap, R. (1928) *The Logical Structure of the World*, trans. R. George, Berkeley: University of California Press.

Carnap, R. (1936) 'Testability and Meaning', *Philosophy of Science* 3: 419–471.

Carnap, R. (1937) 'Testability and Meaning – Continued', *Philosophy of Science* 4: 1–40.

Carnap, R. (1937a) *The Logical Syntax of Language*, London: RKP.

Carnap, R. (1939) 'Foundations of Logic and Mathematics', *International Encyclopaedia of Unified Science* 1(3), Chicago: The University of Chicago Press.

Carnap, R. (1945) 'The Two Concepts of Probability', *Philosophy and Phenomenological Research* 5; repr. in H. Feigl and W. Sellars (eds) *Readings in Philosophical Analysis*, New York: Appleton-Century-Crofts (1949).

Carnap, R. (1945/46) 'Remarks on Induction and Truth', *Philosophy and Phenomenological Research* 6: 590–602.

Carnap, R. (1947) *Meaning and Necessity: A Study in Semantic and Modal Logic*, 3rd enlarged edition, Chicago: The University of Chicago Press (1956).

Carnap, R. (1950) 'Empiricism, Semantics and Ontology' *Revue Intérnationale de Philosophie* 4: 20–40; repr. in *Meaning and Necessity: A Study in Semantic and Modal Logic*, Chicago: University of Chicago Press (1956).

Carnap, R. (1956) 'The Methodological Character of Theoretical Concepts', in H. Feigl and M. Scriven (eds) *The Foundations of Science and the Concepts of Psychology and Psychoanalysis*, Minnesota Studies in the Philosophy of Science, Vol. 1, Minneapolis: University of Minnesota Press.

Carnap, R. (1958) 'Beobachtungssprache und Theoretische Sprache', *Dialectica* 12: 236–248; trans. as 'Observation Language and Theoretical Language', in J. Hintikka (ed.) *Rudolf Carnap, Logical Empiricist*, Dordrecht: Reidel (1975).

Carnap, R. (1961) 'On the Use of Hilbert's ε-operator in Scientific Theories', in Y. Bar-Hillel *et al.* (eds) *Essays on the Foundations of Mathematics*, Jerusalem: Magnes Press.

Carnap, R. (1963) 'Replies and Systematic Expositions', in P. Schilpp (ed.) *The Philosophy of Rudolf Carnap*, La Salle: Open Court.

Carnap, R. (1966) *Philosophical Foundations of Physics*, New York: Basic Books.

Carnap, R. (1968) 'Inductive Intuition and Inductive Logic', in I. Lakatos (ed.) *The Problem of Inductive Logic*, Amsterdam: North-Holland Publishing Company.

Carnap, R. (1974) *An Introduction to the Philosophy of Science*, New York: Basic Books.

Carnot, S. (1824) 'Reflections on the Motive Power of Fire', in E. Mendoza (ed.) *Reflections on the Motive Power of Fire by Sadi Carnot and other Papers on the Second Law of Thermodynamics by E. Clapeyron and R. Clausius*, New York: Dover Publications (1960); also in R. Fox (ed. and trans.) *Reflections on the Motive Power of Fire, A Critical Edition with the Surviving Manuscripts*, Manchester: Manchester University Press (1986).

Carnot, S. (1986) 'Notes on Mathematics, Physics and Other Subjects', in R. Fox (ed.) *Reflections on the Motive Power of Fire, A Critical Edition with the Surviving Manuscripts*, Manchester: Manchester University Press (1986).

Cartwright, N. (1983) *How the Laws of Physics Lie*, Oxford: Clarendon Press.

Chihara, C. and Chihara, C. (1993) 'A Biological Objection to Constructive Empiricism', *British Journal for the Philosophy of Science* 44: 653–658.

Churchland, P. M. (1979) *Scientific Realism and the Plasticity of Mind*, Cambridge: Cambridge University Press.

Churchland, P. M. (1985) 'The Ontological Status of Unobservables: In Praise of Superempirical Virtues', in P. M. Churchland and C. A. Hooker (eds) *Images of Science,* Chicago: University of Chicago Press.

Churchland, P. M. and Hooker, C. A. (eds) (1985) *Images of Science,* Chicago: University of Chicago Press.

Clapeyron, É. (1834) 'Memoir on the Motive Power of Heat', in E. Mendoza (ed.) *Reflections on the Motive Power of Fire by Sadi Carnot and other Papers on the Second Law of Thermodynamics by E. Clapeyron and R. Clausius*, New York: Dover Publications (1960).

Clausius, R. (1850) 'On the Motive Power of Heat, and the Laws which can be Deduced from it for the Theory of Heat', in E. Mendoza (ed.) *Reflections on the Motive Power of Fire by Sadi Carnot and other Papers on the Second Law of Thermodynamics by E. Clapeyron and R. Clausius*, New York: Dover Publications (1960).

Clausius, R. (1867) *Die Mechanische Warmetheorie*; all page references for the excerpts are to S. Sambursky (ed.) *Physical Thought from the Presocratics to the Quantum Physicists*, London: Hutchinson (1974).

Craig, W. (1956) 'Replacements of Auxiliary Assumptions', *Philosophical Review* 65: 38–55.

Creath, R. (1985) 'Carnap's Scientific Realism: Irenic or Ironic?' in N. Rescher (ed.) *The Heritage of Logical Positivism*, Lanham: University of America Press.

Day, T. and Kincaid, H. (1994) 'Putting Inference to the Best Explanation in its Place', *Synthese* 98: 271–295.

Davy, H. (1799) 'An Essay on Heat, Light, and the Communication of Light', *The Collected Works of H. Davy*, Vol. 2: 1–86, London: Smith, Elder & Co. Cornhill (1839); repr. New York: Johnson Reprint Corporation (1972).

de Bouvere, K. (1965) 'Synonymous Theories', in L. Henkin *et al.* (eds) *The Theory of Models,* Amsterdam: North-Holland Publishing Company.

Demopoulos, W. and Friedman, M. (1985) 'Critical Notice: Bertrand Russell's *The Analysis of Matter*: Its Historical Context and Contemporary Interest', *Philosophy of Science* 52: 621–639.

Devitt, M. (1984) *Realism and Truth*, 2nd rev. edn, Oxford: Blackwell (1991).

Devitt, M. (1991) 'Aberrations of the Realism Debate', *Philosophical Studies* 61: 43–63.

Devitt, M. and Sterelny, K. (1987) *Language and Reality*, Oxford: Blackwell.

Doppelt, G. (1990) 'The Naturalist Conception of Methodological Standards in Science', *Philosophy of Science* 57: 1–19.

Doran, B. G. (1975), 'Origins and Consolidation of Field Theory in Nineteenth Century Britain: From the Mechanical to the Electromagnetic View of Nature', *Historical Studies in the Physical Sciences*, Vol. 6: 133–260, Princeton, NJ: Princeton University Press.

Douven, I. (1999) 'Inference to the Best Explanation is Coherent', *Philosophy of Science* (Proceedings, PSA 1998).

Duhem, P. (1893) 'Physics and Metaphysics' in R. Ariew and P. Barker (eds) *Pierre Duhem: Essays in the History and Philosophy of Science*, Indianapolis: Hackett (1996).

Duhem, P. (1906) *The Aim and Structure of Physical Theory*, trans. P. Wiener, Princeton, NJ: Princeton University Press (1954).

Duhem, P. (1908) *To Save the Phenomena*, trans. E. Doland and C. Mascher, Chicago: University of Chicago Press (1969).

Duhem, P. (1913) 'Examen logique de la théorie physique', trans. P. Barker and R. Ariew as 'Logical Examination of Physical Theory', *Synthese* 83: 183–188 (1990).

Dummett, M. (1963) 'Realism', in *Truth and Other Enigmas*, London: Duckworth.

Dummett, M. (1974) 'The Justification of Deduction', *British Academy Lecture*, Oxford: Oxford University Press.

Dummett, M. (1982) 'Realism', *Synthese* 52: 55–112.

Earman, J. (1978) 'Fairy Tales versus an Ongoing Story: Ramsey's Neglected Argument for Scientific Realism', *Philosophical Studies* 33: 195–202.

Earman, J. (1992) *Bayes or Bust? A Critical Examination of Bayesian Confirmation Theory,* Cambridge, MA: MIT Press.

Earman, J. (1993) 'Underdetermination, Realism, and Reason', *Midwest Studies in Philosophy* 18: 19–38.

Ellis, B. (1985) 'What Science Aims to Do', in P. M. Churchland and C. A. Hooker (eds) *Images of Science*, Chicago: University of Chicago Press.

Enç, B. (1976) 'Reference of Theoretical Terms', *Noûs* 10: 261–282.

Evans, G. (1973) 'The Causal Theory of Names', *Proceedings of the Aristotelian Society*, 47: 187–208.

Feigl, H. (1943[1949]) 'Logical Empiricism', in D. D. Runes (ed.) *Twentieth Century Philosophy*, New York: Philosophical Library; repr. in H. Feigl and W. Sellars (eds) *Readings in Philosophical Analysis*, New York: Appleton–Century–Crofts, Inc.

Feigl, H. (1950) 'Existential Hypotheses: Realistic versus Phenomenalistic Interpretations', *Philosophy of Science* 17: 35–62.

Feigl, H. (1950a) 'Logical Reconstruction, Realism and Pure Semiotics', *Philosophy of Science* 17: 186–195.

Feigl, H. (1956) 'Some Major Issues and Developments in the Philosophy of Science of Logical Empiricism', in H. Feigl and M. Scriven (eds) *The Foundations of Science and the Concepts of Psychology and Psychoanalysis*, Minnesota Studies in the Philosophy of Science, Vol. 1, Minneapolis: University of Minnesota Press.

Fermi, E. (1936) *Thermodynamics*, New York: Dover Publications.

Feyerabend, P. (1958) 'An Attempt at a Realistic Interpretation of Experience', *Proceedings of the Aristotelian Society* 58: 143; repr. in *Realism, Rationalism and Scientific Method: Philosophical Papers*, Vol. 1, Cambridge: Cambridge University Press.

Feyerabend, P. (1965) 'Problems of Empiricism', in R. Colodny (ed.) *Beyond the Edge of Certainty*, Englewood Cliffs, NJ: Prentice-Hall.

Field, H. (1972) 'Tarski's Theory of Truth', *Journal of Philosophy* 69: 347–375.

Field, H. (1986) 'The Deflationary Conception of Truth', in G. Macdonald and C. Wright (eds) *Fact, Science and Morality*, Oxford: Blackwell.

Field, H. (1992) 'Critical Notice: Paul Horwich's *Truth*', *Philosophy of Science* 59: 321–330.

Fine, A. (1975) 'How to Compare Theories: Reference and Change', *Noûs* 9: 17–32.

Fine, A. (1984) 'The Natural Ontological Attitude' in J. Leplin (ed.) *Scientific Realism*, Berkeley: University of California Press.

Fine, A. (1986) *The Shaky Game*, Chicago: University of Chicago Press.

Fine, A. (1986a) 'Unnatural Attitudes: Realist and Instrumentalist Attachments to Science', *Mind* 95: 149–179.

Fine, A. (1991) 'Piecemeal Realism', *Philosophical Studies* 61: 79–96.

Fine, A. (1996) 'Afterword' in *The Shaky Game*, 2nd edn, Chicago: University of Chicago Press.

FitzGerald, G. F. (1878) 'On the Electromagnetic Theory of the Reflection and Refraction of Light', *Proceedings of the Royal Society* (1879); repr. in FitzGerald (1902).

FitzGerald, G. F. (1880) 'On the Electromagnetic Theory of the Reflection and Refraction of Light', *Philosophical Transactions of the Royal Society* (1878); repr. in FitzGerald (1902).

FitzGerald, G. F. (1902) *The Scientific Papers of the Late G. F. FitzGerald*, ed. J. Larmor, Dublin: Hodges & Figgis.

Forrest, P. (1994) 'Why Most of Us Should Be Scientific Realists: A Reply to van Fraassen', *The Monist* 77: 47–70.

Fresnel, A. (1822) 'Second Mémoire Sur la Double Réfraction', in *Oeuvres Complètes D' Augustin Fresnel*, Vol. 2: 479–596, Paris.

Fresnel, A. (1823) 'Mémoire sur la Loi des Modifications que la Réflexion Imprime a la Lumiére Polarizèe' in *Oeuvres Complètes*, Vol. 1: 767–799, Paris.

Fresnel, A. (1866) 'Considérations Mécaniques sur la polarisation de la lumiére', in *Oeuvres Complètes*, Vol. 1: 629–630, Paris; trans. in Swindell (ed.) *Polarized Light*, Stroudsburg, PA: Dowden, Hutchinson & Ross, Inc. (1975).

Friedman, M. (1974) 'Explanation and Scientific Understanding', *Journal of Philosophy* 71: 5–19.

Friedman, M. (1983) *Foundations of Space–Time Theories*, Chicago: University of Chicago Press.

Friedman, M. (1988) 'Truth and Confirmation', in H. Kornblith (ed.) *Naturalising Epistemology*, Cambridge, MA: MIT Press.

Giere, R. (1985) 'Philosophy of Science Naturalised', *Philosophy of Science* 52: 331–356.

Giere, R. (1988) *Explaining Science: A Cognitive Approach*, Chicago: University of Chicago Press.

Glazebrook, R. T. (1885) 'Report on Optical Theories', *Reports of the British Association*: 157–261.

Glymour, C. (1971) 'Theoretical Realism and Theoretical Equivalence', *Boston Studies in the Philosophy of Science*, Vol. 8, Dordrecht: D. Reidel Publishing Company.

Glymour, C. (1976) 'To Save the Noumena', *Journal of Philosophy* 73: 635–637.

Glymour, C. (1977) 'Indistinguishable Space–Times and the Fundamental Group', in J. S. Earman, C. N. Glymour and J. J. Stachel (eds) *Foundations of Space–Time Theories,* Minnesota Studies in the Philosophy of Science, Vol. 8, Minneapolis: University of Minnesota Press.

Glymour, C. (1980) *Theory and Evidence,* Princeton, NJ: Princeton University Press.

Goldman, A. I. (1986) *Epistemology and Cognition,* Cambridge, MA: Harvard University Press.

Goodman, N. (1946) 'The Problem of Counterfactual Conditionals', *Journal of Philosophy* 44: 113–28 – repr. in his (1954).

Goodman, N. (1954) *Fact, Fiction, and Forecast,* Cambridge, MA: Harvard University Press.

Green, G. (1838) 'On the Laws of the Reflexion and Refraction of Light at the Common Surface of Two Non-Crystallised Media', *Transactions of the Cambridge Philosophical Society*; repr. in Green (1871) pp. 245–269, and Schaffner (1972).

Green, G. (1871), *Mathematical Papers*, ed. N. M. Ferrers, New York: Chelsea Publishing Company.

Grunbaum, A. (1960) 'The Duhemian Argument', *Philosophy of Science* 27: 75–87.

Grunbaum, A. (1962) 'The Falsifiability of Theories: Total or Partial? A Contemporary Evaluation of the Duhem–Quine Thesis', in M. Wartofsky (ed.) *Boston Studies in the Philosophy of Science 1961/1962,* Dordrecht: D. Reidel Publishing Company.

Hacking, I. (1983) *Representing and Intervening*, Cambridge: Cambridge University Press.

Hacking, I. (1984) 'Experimentation and Scientific Realism', in J. Leplin (ed.) *Scientific Realism*, Berkeley: University of California Press.

Hardin, C. and Rosenberg, A. (1982) 'In Defence of Convergent Realism', *Philosophy of Science* 49: 604–615.

Harman, G. (1996) 'Pragmatism and the Reasons for Belief', in C. B. Kulp (ed.) *Realism/Anti-Realism and Epistemology*, New Jersey: Rowan & Littlefield.

Harman, P. M. (1982) *Energy, Force and Matter: The Conceptual Development of Nineteenth-Century Physics*, Cambridge: Cambridge University Press.

Helmholtz, von H. (1848) 'The Conservation of Force', in S. Brush (ed.) *Kinetic Theory*, Vol. 1: *The Nature of Gases and of Heat* Oxford: Pergamon Press (1965).

Hempel, C. (1945) 'Studies in the Logic of Confirmation', *Mind* 54: 1–26.

Hempel, C. (1950) 'A Note on Semantic Realism', *Philosophy of Science* 17: 169–173.

Hempel, C. (1958) 'The Theoretician's Dilemma: A Study in the Logic of Theory Construction', *Concepts, Theories and the Mind-Body Problem*, H. Feigl, M. Scriven and G. Maxwell (eds), Minnesota Studies in the Philosophy of Science, Vol. 2, Minneapolis: University of Minnesota Press.

Hempel, C. (1963) 'Implications of Carnap's Work for the Philosophy of Science', in P. Schilpp (ed.) *The Philosophy of Rudolf Carnap*, La Salle: Open Court.

Hempel, C. (1965) *The Philosophy of Natural Science,* Englewood Cliffs, NJ: Prentice-Hall, Inc.

Hendry, R. F. and Psillos, S. (1998) 'Theories as Complexes of Representational Media', presented at the *Philosophy of Science* Association 1998).

Hesse, M. B. (1953) 'Models in Physics', *British Journal for the Philosophy of Science* 4: 198–214.

Hesse, M. B. (1966) *Models and Analogies in Science*, 2nd printing, Notre Dame: University of Notre Dame Press.

Hesse, M. B. (1970) 'On the Notion of Field: Comment by Mary Hesse', in R. Stuewer (ed.) *Historical and Philosophical Perspectives of Science,* Minnesota Studies in the Philosophy of Science, Vol. 5, Minneapolis: University of Minnesota Press.

Hesse, M. B. (1970a) 'Is there an Independent Observation Language?', in R. Colodny (ed.) *The Nature and Function of Scientific Theories*, Pittsburgh, PA: University of Pittsburgh Press; repr. as 'Theory and Observation', in M. B. Hesse, *Revolutions and Reconstructions on the Philosophy of Science*, Brighton: The Harvester Press (1980).

Hesse, M. B. (1976) 'Truth and Growth of Knowledge', in F. Suppe and P. D. Asquith (eds) *PSA 1976*, Vol. 2, East Lansing, MI: Philosophy of Science Association.

Hooker, C. A. (1968) 'Five Arguments Against Craigian Transcriptionism', *Australasian Journal of Philosophy* 46: 265–276.

Hooker, C. A. (1985) 'Surface Dazzle, Ghostly Depths', in P. M. Churchland and C. A. Hooker (eds) *Images of Science*, Chicago: University of Chicago Press.

Horwich, P. (1982) 'How to Choose Between Empirically Indistinguishable Theories', *Journal of Philosophy* 79: 61–77.

Horwich, P. (1987) *Asymmetries in Time*, Cambridge, MA: MIT Press.

Horwich, P. (1990) *Truth*, Oxford: Blackwell.

Horwich, P. (1991) 'On the Nature and Norms of Theoretical Commitment', *Philosophy of Science* 58: 1–14.

Howson, C. and Urbach, P. (1989) *Scientific Reasoning: The Bayesian Approach,* La Salle: Open Court.

Hoyningen-Huene, P. (1993) *Reconstructing Scientific Revolutions*, Chicago: Chicago University Press.

Hunt, B. (1991) *The Maxwellians,* New York: Cornell University Press.

Jardine, N. (1986) *The Fortunes of Inquiry,* Oxford: Clarendon Press.

Keynes, J. M. (1921) 'A Treatise on Probability', *The Collected Works of J. M. Keynes*, London and Cambridge: Macmillan and Cambridge University Press, Vol. 7.

Kirkham, R. L. (1992) *Theories of Truth: A Critical Introduction*, Cambridge, MA: MIT Press.

Kitcher, P. (1981) 'Explanatory Unification', *Philosophy of Science* 48: 207–231.

Kitcher, P. (1993), *The Advancement of Science*, Oxford: Oxford University Press.

Kitcher, P. (1993a) 'Knowledge, Society and History', *Canadian Philosophical Quarterly* 23: 155–178.

Kitcher, P. (1995) 'Author's Response', *Philosophy and Phenomenological Research* 55.

Klein, M. J. (1972) 'Mechanical Explanation at the End of the 19th Century', *Centaurus* 17: 58–82.

Klein, M. J. (1976) 'Closing the Carnot Cycle', in *Sadi Carnot et L'essor de la thermodynamique,* Paris: Edition du Centre National de la Researche Scientifique.

Kornblith, H. (1993) *Inductive Inference and its Natural Ground,* Cambridge, MA: MIT Press.

Kornblith, H. (1994) 'In Defence of Deductive Inference', *Philosophical Studies* 76: 247–257.

Kripke, S. (1980) *Naming and Necessity,* Oxford: Blackwell.

Kroon, F. (1985) 'Theoretical Terms and the Causal View of Reference', *Australasian Journal of Philosophy* 63: 142–166.

Kroon, F. (1987) 'Causal Descriptivism', *Australasian Journal of Philosophy* 65: 1–17.

Kuhn, T. S. (1970) *The Structure of Scientific Revolutions,* 2nd enlarged edn, Chicago: University of Chicago Press [1962].

Kukla, A. (1993) 'Laudan, Leplin, Empirical Equivalence and Underdetermination', *Analysis* 53: 1–7.

Kukla, A. (1994) 'Scientific Realism, Scientific Practice and the Natural Ontological Attitude' *British Journal for the Philosophy of Science* 45: 955–975.

Kukla, A. (1994a) 'Non-Empirical Theoretical Virtues and the Argument from Underdetermination', *Erkenntnis* 41: 157–170.

Ladyman, J. (1998) 'What is Structural Realism?', *Studies in History and Philosophy of Science* 29: 409–424.

Ladyman, J., Douven, I., Horsten, L., and van Fraassen, B. C. (1997) 'A Defence of van Fraassen's Critique of Abductive Reasoning: Reply to Psillos', *The Philosophical Quarterly* 47: 305–321.

Lakatos, I. (1968) 'Changes in the Problem of Inductive Logic' in I. Lakatos (ed.) *The Problem of Inductive Logic,* Amsterdam: North-Holland Publishing Company.

Lakatos, I. (1970) 'Falsification and the Methodology of Scientific Research Programmes' in I. Lakatos and A. Musgrave (eds) *Criticism and the Growth of Knowledge,* Cambridge: Cambridge University Press.

Laplace, P. S. (1816) 'Sur la Vitesse du Son dans l'air et dans l'eau', *Annales de Chimie et de Physique,* Vol. 3; trans. in R. B. Lindsay (ed.) *Acoustics: Historical and Philosophical Development,* Stroudsburg: Dowden, Hutchinson & Ross, (1972) pp. 180–181.

Laplace, P. S. (1825) 'Sur la Vitesse du Son', *Connaissance des Temps,* repr. in *Oeuvres Complètes de Laplace,* Paris: Gauthier-Villars, Vol. 13: 303–304 (1904).

Laplace, P. S. and Lavoisier, A. (1780) 'Mémoire sur la Chaleur', *Oeuvres Complètes de Laplace,* Paris: Gauthier-Villars, Vol. 10: 149–200 (1904).

Larmor, J. (1893) 'A Dynamical Theory of the Electric and Luminiferous Medium', *Proceedings of the Royal Society* 54: 438–446; repr. in Larmor (1929).

Larmor, J. (1894) 'A Dynamical Theory of the Electric and Luminiferous Medium (Part I)', *Philosophical Transactions of the Royal Society* 185: 719–822; repr. in Larmor (1929).

Larmor, J. (1929) *Mathematical and Physical Papers,* Vol.1, Cambridge: Cambridge University Press.

Laudan, L. (1981) 'A Confutation of Convergent Realism', *Philosophy of Science* 48: 19–49.

Laudan, L. (1984) 'Explaining the Success of Science', in J. Cushing *et al.* (eds) *Science and Reality,* Notre Dame: Notre Dame University Press.

Laudan, L. (1984a) *Science and Values,* Berkeley: University of California Press.

Laudan, L. (1984b) 'Discussion: Realism Without the Real', *Philosophy of Science* 51: 156–162.

Laudan, L. (1990) 'Demystifying Underdetermination', in C. W. Savage (ed.) *Scientific Theories,* Minnesota Studies in the Philosophy of Science, Vol. 14, Minneapolis: University of Minnesota Press.

Laudan, L. (1990a) *Science and Relativism,* Chicago: University of Chicago Press.

Laudan, L. (1996) *Beyond Positivism and Relativism,* Boulder, CO: Westview Press.

Laudan, L. and Leplin, J. (1991) 'Empirical Equivalence and Underdetermination', *Journal of Philosophy* 88: 449–472.

Laudan, L. and Leplin, J. (1993) 'Determination Underdeterred: Reply to Kukla', *Analysis* 53: 8–16.

Lavoisier, A. (1789) *Traite Élémentaire de Chimie,* Paris; trans. R. Kerr, As *Elements of Chemistry* (1790); repr. New York: Dover Publications (1965).

Leplin, J. (1990) 'Renormalising Epistemology', *Philosophy of Science* 57: 20–33.

Leplin, J. (1997) *A Novel Defence of Scientific Realism,* Oxford: Oxford University Press.

Lewis, D. (1970) 'How to Define Theoretical Terms', *Journal of Philosophy* 67: 427–446.

Lewis, D. (1984) 'Putnam's Paradox', *Australasian Journal of Philosophy* 62: 221–236.

Lewis, D. (1986) *On the Plurality of Worlds,* Oxford: Blackwell.

Lilley, S. (1948) 'Attitudes to the Nature of Heat about the Beginning of the Nineteenth Century', *Archives Intérnationales d'Histoire des Sciences* 27: 630–639.

Lipton, P. (1991) *Inference to the Best Explanation,* London: Routledge.

Lipton, P. (1993) 'Is the Best Good Enough?', *Proceedings of the Aristotelian Society* 93: 89–104.

Lugg, A. (1990) 'Pierre Duhem's Conception of Natural Classification', *Synthese* 83: 409–420.

Lycan, W. (1994) 'Conditional Reasoning and Conditional Logic', *Philosophical Studies* 76: 223–245.

Lycan, W. (1994a) 'Reply to Hilary Kornblith', *Philosophical Studies,* 76: 259–261.

Mach, E. (1893) *The Science of Mechanics,* trans. T. J. McCormack, 6th edn, La Salle: Open Court.

Mach, E. (1910) *Popular Scientific Lectures,* Chicago: Open Court.

Malament, D. (1977) 'Observationally Indistinguishable Space–Times' in J. S. Earman, C. N. Glymour and J. J. Stachel (eds) *Foundations of Space–Time Theories,* Minnesota Studies in the Philosophy of Science, Vol. 8, Minneapolis: University of Minnesota Press.

Marsonet, M. (1995) *Science, Reality, and Language,* Albany: State University of New York Press.

Maxwell, G. (1962) 'Theories, Frameworks, and Ontology', *Philosophy of Science* 29: 132–138.

Maxwell, G. (1962a) 'The Ontological Status of Theoretical Entities', *Scientific Explanation, Space and Time,* H. Feigl and G. Maxwell (eds) Minnesota Studies in the Philosophy of Science, Vol. 3, Minneapolis: University of Minnesota Press.

Maxwell, G. (1970) 'Theories, Perception and Structural Realism', in R. Colodny (ed.) *The Nature and Function of Scientific Theories,* Pittsburgh: University of Pittsburgh Press.

Maxwell, G. (1970a) 'Structural Realism and the Meaning of Theoretical Terms', in *Analyses of Theories and Methods of Physics and Psychology*, Minnesota Studies in the Philosophy of Science,Vol. 4, Minneapolis: University of Minnesota Press.

Maxwell, J. C. (1855 [1890]) 'On Faraday's Lines of Force', in *The Scientific Writings of James Clerk Maxwell*, Vol. 1: 155–229.

Maxwell, J. C. (1861–62 [1890]) 'On Physical Lines of Force', in *The Scientific Writings of James Clerk Maxwell*, Vol. 1: 451–513.

Maxwell, J. C. (1864) *A Dynamical Theory of the Electromagnetic Field*, edited with introduction by T. F. Torrance, Edinburgh: Scottish Academic Press (1982).

Maxwell, J. C. (1873) *A Treatise on Electricity and Magnetism*, Vol. 2, 3rd edn, Oxford: Clarendon Press.

Maxwell, J. C. (1890) *The Scientific Papers of James Clerk Maxwell*, ed. W. D. Niven, Vols. 1 and 2: published in one volume by Dover Publications.

Maxwell, J. C. (1890a) 'Ether', in *The Scientific Writings of James Clerk Maxwell*, Vol. 2, New York: Dover.

McCullagh, J. (1839), 'An Essay Towards a Dynamical Theory of Crystalline Reflexion and Refraction', *Transactions of the Royal Irish Academy*; repr. in S. Haughton and J. H. Jellett (eds) *The Collected Works of J. McCullagh*, Dublin: Hodges and Figgis (1880); also in Schaffner (1972).

McGee, V. (1985) 'A Counter-Example to Modus Ponens', *Journal of Philosophy* 82: 462–471.

McMullin, E. (1984) 'A Case for Scientific Realism', in J. Leplin (ed.) *Scientific Realism*, Berkeley: University of California Press.

McMullin, E. (1987) 'Explanatory Success and the Truth of Theory', in N. Rescher (ed.) *Scientific Inquiry in Philosophical Perspective*, Lanham: University Press of America.

McMullin, E. (1990) 'Comment: Duhem's Middle Way', *Synthese* 83: 421–430.

McMullin, E. (1991) 'Comment: Selective Anti-Realism', *Philosophical Studies* 61: 97–108.

McMullin, E. (1992) *The Inference that Makes Science*, Milwaukee: Marquette University Press.

Mendoza, E. (1959) 'Contributions to the Study of Carnot', *Archives Intérnationales d'Histoire des Sciences* 12: 377–396.

Menuge, A. (1995) 'The Scope of Observation', *Philosophical Quarterly* 45: 60–69.

Merrill, G. H. (1980) 'The Model-Theoretic Argument Against Realism', *Philosophy of Science* 47: 69–81.

Mill, J. S. (1872) *A System of Logic, Ratiocinative and Inductive*, 8th edn; repr. in *J. S. Mill: Collected Works*, Vol. 7, ed. J. M. Robinson, Toronto: University of Toronto Press and London: Routledge & Kegan Paul (1974)

Miller, D. (1974) 'Popper's Qualitative Theory of Verisimilitude', *British Journal for the Philosophy of Science* 25: 166–177.

Miller, D. (1976) 'Verisimilitude Redeflated', *British Journal for the Philosophy of Science* 27: 363–380.

Miller, R. (1987) *Fact and Method*, Princeton NJ : Princeton University Press.

Moulines, U. C. (1976) 'Approximate Application of Empirical Theories: A General Explication', *Erkenntnis* 10: 201–227.

Musgrave, A. (1985) 'Realism vs Constructive Empiricism', in P. M. Churchland and C. A. Hooker (eds) *Images of Science*, Chicago: The University of Chicago Press.

Musgrave, A. (1988) 'The Ultimate Argument for Scientific Realism', in R. Nola (ed.) *Relativism and Realism in Sciences*, Dordrecht: Kluwer Academic Press.

Musgrave, A. (1989) 'NOA's Ark – Fine for Realism', *The Philosophical Quarterly* 39: 383–398.

Nagel, E. (1950) 'Science and Semantic Realism', *Philosophy of Science*, 17: 174–181.

Nagel, E. (1960) *The Structure of Science*, 2nd edn, Indianapolis: Hackett (1979).

Newman, M. H. A. (1928) 'Mr. Russell's "Causal Theory of Perception"', *Mind* 37: 137–148.

Newton-Smith, W. H. (1978) 'The Underdetermination of Theory by Data', *Proceedings of the Aristotelian Society* 52 (supplement): 71–91.

Newton-Smith, W. H. (1981) *The Rationality of Science*, London: RKP.

Newton-Smith, W. H. (1987) 'Realism and Inference to the Best Explanation', *Fundamenta Scientiae* 7: 305–316.

Newton-Smith, W. H. (1989) 'Modest Realism', in A. Fine and J. Leplin (eds) *PSA 1988*, Vol. 2, East Lansing, MI: Philosophy of Science Association.

Newton-Smith, W. H. (1989a) 'The Truth in Realism', *Dialectica* 43: 31–45.

Niiniluoto, I. (1987) *Truthlikeness*, Dordrecht: Reidel Publishing Company.

Niiniluoto, I. (1997) 'Reference Invariance and Truthlikeness', *Philosophy of Science* 64: 546–554.

Niiniluoto, I. (1998) 'Verisimilitude: The Third Period', *British Journal for the Philosophy of Science* 49: 1–29.

Norton, J. (1993) 'The Determination of Theories by Evidence: The Case for Quantum Discontinuity 1900–1915', *Synthese* 97: 1–31.

Nye, M. J. (1976) 'The Nineteenth-Century Atomic Debates and the Dilemma of an "Indifferent Hypothesis"', *Studies in History and Philosophy of Science* 7: 245–268.

Oddie, G. (1986) *Likeness to Truth,* Dordrecht: Reidel Publishing Company.

Papineau, D. (1979) *Theory and Meaning*, Oxford: Clarendon Press.

Papineau, D. (1993) *Philosophical Naturalism*, Oxford: Blackwell.

Parrini, P. (1994) 'With Carnap, Beyond Carnap: Metaphysics, Science, and the Realism/Instrumentalism Controversy', in W. Salmon and G. Wolters (eds) *Logic, Language and the Structure of Scientific Theories*, Pittsburgh: University of Pittsburgh Press.

Perrin, J. (1913) *Les atomes*, Paris, Alcan.

Planck, M. (1909) 'The Unity of the Physical World-Picture'; repr. in S. Toulmin (ed.) *Physical Reality*, Harper Torchbooks (1970).

Poincaré, H. (1900) 'Les Relations Entre la Physique Expérimentale et la Physique Mathématique', *Rapports Présentés au Congrés International de Physique de 1900*, Paris, pp. 1–29; (repr. in *La Science et L'Hypothèse*, chapters 9 and 10).

Poincaré, H. (1902) *La Science et L'Hypothèse*, repr. Paris: Flammarion (1968).

Poincaré, H. (1905) *La Valeur de la Science*, repr. Paris: Flammarion (1970).

Poincaré, H. (1913[1963]) *Mathematics and Science: Last Essays*, New York: Dover.

Poisson, S. D. (1823) 'Sur la Chaleur des Gaz et des Vapeurs', *Annales des Chimie et de Physique*, 23; trans. J. Herapath, 'On the Caloric of Gases and Vapours', *Philosophical Magazine* 62: 328–338 (1923).

Popper, K. (1956/1982) *Realism and the Aim of Science: From the Postscript to the Logic of Scientific Discovery,* ed. W. W. Bartley III, London: Hutchinson.

Popper, K. (1959) *The Logic of Scientific Discovery*, London: Hutchinson.

Popper, K. (1963) *Conjectures and Refutations*, 3rd rev. edn, London: RKP (1969).

Popper, K. (1972) *Objective Knowledge*; repr. with corrections, Oxford: Clarendon Press (1973).

Psillos, S. (1993) 'Laplace and the Caloric Theory of Heat: A Case of ad hoc Modifications', paper presented at the 19th International Congress of the History of Science, Zaragoza, Spain, August.

Psillos, S. (1995) 'Poincaré's Conception of Mechanical Explanation', in Jean-Louis Greffe, Gerhard Heinzmann and Kuno Lorenz (eds) *Henri Poincaré: Science and Philosophy*, Berlin: Academie Verlag and Paris: Albert Blanchard.

Psillos, S. (1997) 'Kitcher on Reference', *International Studies in the Philosophy of Science* 11: 259–272.

Psillos, S. (forthcoming) 'An Introduction to Carnap's "Theoretical Concepts in Science" (together with the hitherto unpublished lecture by Carnap: "Theoretical Concepts in Science")', *Studies in History and Philosophy of Science*.

Psillos, S. (forthcoming a) 'Abduction: Between Conceptual Richness and Computational Complexity', in A. K. Kakas and P. Flach (eds) *Abduction and Induction: Essays in Their Relation and Integration*, Dordrecht: Kluwer Publishing Company.

Putnam, H. (1962) 'What Theories Are Not', *Philosophical Papers*, Vol. 1: *Mathematics, Matter and Method*, Cambridge: Cambridge University Press (1975).

Putnam, H. (1963) '"Degree of Confirmation" and Inductive Logic', in P. Schilpp (ed.) *The Philosophy of Rudolf Carnap*, La Salle, IL: Open Court; repr. in *Philosophical Papers*, Vol. 1: *Mathematics, Matter and Method*, Cambridge: Cambridge University Press (1975).

Putnam, H. (1965) 'Craig's Theorem', *Philosophical Papers*, Vol. 1: *Mathematics, Matter and Method*, Cambridge: Cambridge University Press (1975).

Putnam, H. (1975) *Philosophical Papers*, Vol. 1: *Mathematics, Matter and Method*, Cambridge: Cambridge University Press.

Putnam, H. (1975a) 'Explanation and Reference', *Philosophical Papers*, Vol. 2: *Mind, Language and Reality*, Cambridge: Cambridge University Press.

Putnam, H. (1975b) 'The Meaning of "Meaning"', in *Philosophical Papers*, Vol. 2: *Mind, Language and Reality*, Cambridge: Cambridge University Press.

Putnam, H. (1978) *Meaning and the Moral Sciences*, Routledge & Kegan Paul.

Putnam, H. (1983) *Philosophical Papers*, Vol. 3: *Realism and Reason*, Cambridge: Cambridge University Press.

Putnam, H. (1983a) 'Equivalence', *Philosophical Papers*, Vol. 3: *Realism and Reason*, Cambridge: Cambridge University Press.

Putnam, H. (1983b) 'Reference and Truth', *Philosophical Papers*, Vol. 3: *Realism and Reason*, Cambridge: Cambridge University Press.

Putnam, H. (1985) 'A Comparison of Something With Something Else', *New Literary History* 17: 61–79.

Quine, W. V. (1951) 'Carnap's Views on Ontology', repr. in *The Ways of Paradox and Other Essays*, Cambridge, MA: Harvard University Press (1966).

Quine, W. V. (1969) 'Natural Kinds', *Ontological Relativity and Other Essays*, Cambridge, MA: Harvard University Press.

Quine, W. V. (1975) 'On Empirically Equivalent Systems of the World', *Erkenntnis* 9: 313–328.

Quine, W. V. (1985) 'Carnap's Positivistic Travail', *Fundamenta Scientiae* 5: 325–333.

Ramsey, F. P. (1926) 'Truth and Probability' repr. in D. H. Mellor (ed.) *Foundations: Essays in Philosophy, Logic, Mathematics and Economics*, London: RKP (1978).

Ramsey, F. P. (1927) 'Facts and Propositions', repr. in D. H. Mellor (ed.) *Foundations: Essays in Philosophy, Logic, Mathematics and Economics,* London: RKP (1978).

Ramsey, F. P. (1929) 'Theories', repr. in D. H. Mellor (ed.) *Foundations: Essays in Philosophy, Logic, Mathematics and Economics*, London: RKP (1978).

Redhead, M. (1980) 'Models in Physics', *British Journal for the Philosophy of Science* 45: 145–163.

Reichenbach, H. (1938) *Experience and Prediction*, Chicago: University of Chicago Press.

Reichenbach, H. (1958) *The Philosophy of Space and Time,* New York: Dover Publications.

Reiner, R. and Pierson, R. (1995) 'Hacking's Experimental Realism: An Untenable Middle Ground', *Philosophy of Science* 62: 60–69.

Rosen, G. (1994) 'What is Constructive Empiricism?', *Philosophical Studies* 74: 143–178.

Rosenberg, A. (1990) 'Normative Naturalism and the Role of Philosophy', *Philosophy of Science* 57: 34–43.

Russell, B. (1927) *The Analysis of Matter*, London: RKP.

Salmon, W. (1965) 'The Concept of Inductive Evidence', *American Philosophical Quarterly* 2: 265–280.

Salmon, W. (1970) 'Bayes's Theorem and the History of Science', in R. Stuewer (ed.) *Historical and Philosophical Perspectives of Science*, Minnesota Studies in the Philosophy of Science, Vol. 5, Minneapolis: University of Minnesota Press.

Salmon, W. (1984) *Scientific Explanation and the Causal Structure of the World*, Princeton, NJ: Princeton University Press.

Salmon, W. (1985) 'Empiricism: The Key Question', in N. Rescher (ed.) *The Heritage of Logical Positivism*, Lanham: University Press of America.

Salmon, W. (1990) 'Rationality and Objectivity in Science, or Tom Kuhn Meets Tom Bayes', in C. W. Savage (ed.) *Scientific Theories*, Minnesota Studies in the Philosophy of Science, Vol. 14, Minneapolis: University of Minnesota Press.

Salmon, W. (1994) 'Carnap, Hempel and Reichenbach on Scientific Realism', in W. Salmon and G. Wolters (eds) *Logic, Language and the Structure of Scientific Theories*, Pittsburgh, PA: University of Pittsburgh Press.

Salmon, W. (1994a) 'Comment: Carnap on Realism', in W. Salmon and G. Wolters (eds) *Logic, Language and the Structure of Scientific Theories*, Pittsburgh, PA: University of Pittsburgh Press.

Schaffner, K. (1972) *Nineteenth Century Ether Theories*, Oxford: Pergamon Press.

Scheffler, I. (1963) *The Anatomy of Inquiry*, New York: Alfred A. Knopf.

Sellars, W. (1963) 'Empiricism and Abstract Entities', in P. Schilpp (ed.) *The Philosophy of Rudolf Carnap*, La Salle, IL: Open Court.

Sklar, L. (1974) *Space, Time and Spacetime*, Berkeley: University of California Press.

Sklar, L. (1985) *Philosophy and Spacetime Physics,* Berkeley: University of California Press.

Smart, J. J. C. (1963) *Philosophy and Scientific Realism*, London: RKP.

Smart, J. J. C. (1979) 'Difficulties for Realism in the Philosophy of Science', in L. J. Cohen *et al.* (eds) *Logic, Methodology and the Philosophy of Science VI*, Amsterdam: North-Holland Publishing Company.

Smith, P. (1998) '"Approximate Truth" and Dynamical Theories', *British Journal for the Philosophy of Science* 49: 253–277.

Sober, E. (1993) 'Epistemology for Empiricists', *Midwest Studies in Philosophy* 18: 39–61.

Stein, H. (1970) 'On the Notion of Field in Newton, Maxwell and Beyond', in R. Stuewer (ed.) *Historical and Philosophical Perspectives of Science*, Minnesota Studies in the Philosophy of Science, Vol. 5, Minneapolis: University of Minnesota Press.

Stein, H. (1982) '"Subtler Forms of Matter" in the Period Following Maxwell', in G. N. Cantor and M. J. S. Hodge (eds) *Conceptions of Ether*, Cambridge: Cambridge University Press.

Stein, H. (1987) 'After the Baltimore Lectures: Some Philosophical Reflections on Subsequent Development of Physics', in R. Kargon and P. Achinstein (eds) *Kelvin's Baltimore Lectures and Modern Theoretical Physics*, Cambridge, MA: Cambridge University Press.

Stein, H. (1989) 'Yes, but. ... Some Skeptical Remarks on Realism and Anti-realism' , *Dialectica* 43: 47–65.

Stich, S. (1991) 'Do True Believers Exist?', *Proceedings of the Aristotelian Society,* Vol. 65 (supplement): 229–244.

Stokes, G. G. (1848) 'On the Constitution of Luminiferous Ether', *Philosophical Magazine* 32; repr. in *Mathematical and Physical Papers of G. G. Stokes*, Cambridge: Cambridge University Press, Vol. 2: 8–13.

Stokes, G. G. (1849) 'On the Dynamical Theory of Diffraction', *Transactions of the Cambridge Philosophical Society* 9; repr. in *Mathematical and Physical Papers of G. G. Stokes*, Cambridge: Cambridge University Press, Vol. 2: 243–328.

Stokes, G. G. (1862) 'Report on Double Refraction', *Reports of the British Association* 253–282 – repr. in *Mathematical and Physical Papers of G.G. Stokes*, Cambridge: Cambridge University Press, Vol. 4.

Suppe, F. (1977) 'The Search for Philosophic Understanding of Scientific Theories', in F. Suppe (ed.) *The Structure of Scientific Theories*, 2nd edn, Urbana: University of Illinois Press.

Suppe, F. (1979) 'Theory Structure', in P. D. Asquith and H. E. Kybourg (eds) *Current Research in Philosophy of Science*, East Lansing, MI: Philosophy of Science Association.

Thomson, B. (Count Rumfort) (1798) 'An Inquiry Concerning the Source of the Heat which is Excited by Friction', *Philosophical Transactions of the Royal Society* 88: 80–102; repr. in S. C. Brown (ed.) *Men of Physics, Benjamin Thomson – Count Rumford*, Oxford: Pergamon Press (1967).

Thomson, B. (Count Rumfort) (1799) 'An Inquiry Concerning the Weight Ascribed to Heat', *Philosophical Transactions of the Royal Society* 89: 179–194; repr. in S. C. Brown *Men of Physics, Benjamin Thomson – Count Rumford* (1967), Oxford: Pergamon Press.

Tichy, P. (1974) 'On Popper's Definition of Verisimilitude', *British Journal for the Philosophy of Science* 25: 155–160.

Tichy, P. (1978) 'Verisimilitude Revisited', *Synthese* 38: 175–196.

Unger, P. (1983) 'The Causal Theory of Reference', *Philosophical Studies* 43: 1–45.

van Cleve, J. (1984) 'Reliability, Justification, and the Problem of Induction', *Midwest Studies in Philosophy* 9: 555–567.

van Fraassen, B. C. (1975) 'Platonism's Pyrrhic Victory' in A. R. Anderson *et al.* (eds) *The Logical Enterprise*, New Haven, CT, and London: Yale University Press.

van Fraassen, B. C. (1980) *The Scientific Image,* Oxford: Clarendon Press.

van Fraassen, B. C. (1983) 'Theory Confirmation: Tension and Conflict', *Seventh International Wittgenstein Symposium*, Vienna: Hoedler–Pichler–Tempsky.

van Fraassen, B. C. (1983a) 'Glymour on Evidence and Explanation', *Testing Scientific Theories*, J. Earman (ed.) Minnesota Studies in the Philosophy of Science Vol. 10, Minneapolis: University of Minnesota Press.

van Fraassen, B. C. (1985) 'Empiricism in Philosophy of Science', in P. M. Churchland and C. A. Hooker (eds) *Images of Science*, Chicago: University of Chicago Press.

van Fraassen, B. C. (1987) 'Armstrong on Laws and Probabilities', *Australasian Journal of Philosophy* 65: 243–260.

van Fraassen, B.C. (1987a) 'The Semantic Approach to Scientific Theories', in N. Nersessian (ed.) *The Process of Science*, Dordrecht: Martinus Nijhoff Publishers.

van Fraassen, B. C. (1989) *Laws and Symmetry*, Oxford: Clarendon Press.

van Fraassen, B. (1994) 'Gideon Rosen on Constructive Empiricism', *Philosophical Studies* 74: 179–192.

van Fraassen, B., Ladyman, J., Douven, I. and Horsten, L. (1997) 'A Defence of van Fraassen's Critique of Abductive Reasoning: Reply to Psillos', *The Philosophical Quarterly* 47: 305–321.

Weston, T. (1992) 'Approximate Truth and Scientific Realism', *Philosophy of Science* 59: 53–74.

Whewell, W. (1989) *Theory of Scientific Method*, ed. and introduced by R. Butts, Indianapolis: Hackett.

Whittaker, E. (1951[1910]) *A History of the Theories of Aether and Electricity*, rev. enlarged edn, London: Thomas Nelson & Sons Ltd.

Williams, M. (1986) 'Do We (Epistemologists) Need a Theory of Truth?', *Philosophical Topics* 14: 223–242.

Worrall, J. (1985) 'Scientific Discovery and Theory-Confirmation', in J. Pitt (ed.) *Change and Progress in Modern Science*, Dordrecht: D. Reidel Publishing Company.

Worrall, J. (1982) 'Scientific Realism and Scientific Change', *The Philosophical Quarterly* 32.

Worrall, J. (1988) 'Review Article: The Value of Fixed Methodology', *British Journal for the Philosophy of Science* 39: 263–275.

Worrall, J. (1989) 'Structural Realism: The Best of Both Worlds?', *Dialectica* 43: 99–124.

Worrall, J. (1989a) 'Fix it and Be Damned: A Reply to Laudan', *British Journal for the Philosophy of Science* 40: 376–388.

Worrall, J. (1989b) 'Why Both Popper and Watkins Fail to Solve the Problem of Induction', in F. D'Agostino and I. C. Jarvie (eds) *Freedom and Rationality: Essays in Honour of John Watkins,* Dordrecht: Kluwer Publishing Company.

Worrall, J. (1989c) 'Fresnel, Poisson and the White Spot: The Role of Successful Predictions in the Acceptance of Scientific Theories', in G. Gooding *et al.* (eds) *The Uses of Experiment*, Cambridge: Cambridge University Press.

Worrall, J. (1990) 'Scientific Realism and the Luminiferous Ether: Resisting the "Pessimistic Meta-Induction"', unpublished manuscript.

Worrall, J. (1990a) 'Scientific Revolutions and Scientific Rationality: The Case of the "Elderly Holdout"' in C. W. Savage (ed.) *Scientific Theories*, Minnesota Studies in the Philosophy of Science, Vol. 14, Minneapolis: University of Minnesota Press.

Worrall, J. (1994), 'How to Remain (Reasonably) Optimistic: Scientific Realism and the "Luminiferous Ether"', in D. Hull, M. Forbes and R. M. Burian (eds) *PSA 1994*, Vol.1, East Lansing, MI: Philosophy of Science Association.

Wright, C. (1992) *Truth and Objectivity*, Cambridge, MA: Harvard University Press.

Zahar, E. (1973) 'Why Did Einstein's Programme Supersede Lorentz's', *British Journal for the Philosophy of Science* 24: 95–123 and 223–262.

Zahar, E. (1989) *Einstein's Revolution*, La Salle, IL: Open Court.

Zahar, E. (1996) 'Poincaré's Structural Realism and his Logic of Discovery', in Jean-Louis Greffe, Gerhard Heinzmann and Kuno Lorenz (eds) *Henri Poincaré: Science and Philosophy*, Berlin: Academie Verlag and Paris: Albert Blanchard.

Index

Printed in the United Kingdom by
Lightning Source UK Ltd., Milton Keynes
136718UK00003B/93/A